Kundalini Rising

My Journey To Spiritual Mastery and beyond

SOPHIA MOON

BALBOA.
PRESS
A DIVISION OF HAY HOUSE

Copyright © 2019 Sophia Moon.

All rights reserved. No part of this book may be used or reproduced by any means, graphic, electronic, or mechanical, including photocopying, recording, taping or by any information storage retrieval system without the written permission of the author except in the case of brief quotations embodied in critical articles and reviews.

This book is a work of non-fiction. Unless otherwise noted, the author and the publisher make no explicit guarantees as to the accuracy of the information contained in this book and in some cases, names of people and places have been altered to protect their privacy.

Balboa Press books may be ordered through booksellers or by contacting:

Balboa Press
A Division of Hay House
1663 Liberty Drive
Bloomington, IN 47403
www.balboapress.com
1 (877) 407-4847

Because of the dynamic nature of the Internet, any web addresses or links contained in this book may have changed since publication and may no longer be valid. The views expressed in this work are solely those of the author and do not necessarily reflect the views of the publisher, and the publisher hereby disclaims any responsibility for them.

The author of this book does not dispense medical advice or prescribe the use of any technique as a form of treatment for physical, emotional, or medical problems without the advice of a physician, either directly or indirectly. The intent of the author is only to offer information of a general nature to help you in your quest for emotional and spiritual well-being. In the event you use any of the information in this book for yourself, which is your constitutional right, the author and the publisher assume no responsibility for your actions.

Any people depicted in stock imagery provided by Getty Images are models, and such images are being used for illustrative purposes only.
Certain stock imagery © Getty Images.

Scripture quotations from The New Testament for Everyone are copyright © Nicholas Thomas Wright 2011.

Print information available on the last page.

ISBN: 978-1-9822-2674-9 (sc)
ISBN: 978-1-9822-2675-6 (e)

Balboa Press rev. date: 11/21/2019

My wish for you, dear reader, is that you experience the joy that comes from communing with the God inside of you. You are multi-million times valuable. Thank you for blessing the world with your holy divinity.

CONTENTS

Chapter One 1
Chapter Two 29
Chapter Three 59
Chapter Four 85
Chapter Five 115
Chapter Six 141
Chapter Seven 167
Chapter Eight 193
Chapter Nine 221
Chapter Ten 245
Chapter Eleven 271
Chapter Twelve 299
Chapter Thirteen 321
Chapter Fourteen 347
Chapter Fifteen 361
Chapter Sixteen 385

CHAPTER ONE

The highest revelation is that God is in every man.
Ralph Waldo Emerson (1803-1882)

This universe is a tree eternally existing, its root aloft its branches spread below. The pure root of the tree is Brahman, the immortal, in whom the three worlds have their being, whom none can transcend, who is verily the Self.
Katha Upanishad

"Ask and it will be given to you; seek and you will find; knock and the door will be opened to you. For everyone who asks, receives; and the one who seeks, finds; and to the one who knocks, the door will be opened." Matthew 7:7-8

"For to everyone who has, more will be given and he will grow rich; but from the one who has not, even what he has will be taken away." Matthew 25:29

Don't rob the world of your talent.

I trembled as I closed the curtain. Veering toward a nervous breakdown, I crouched down on the floor like a hunted rabbit. No one knew where I was. Other than my panicked breathing, my expensive hotel room near Disneyland was silent, like a tomb. Just two days ago, I'd arrived, after driving across the country to receive my Doctoral degree in Hypnotherapy. Because of my empty wallet, I had had to skip the twenty dollar banquet. I wished they had made it free as I listened to my stomach grumble with hunger. However, I was too proud to beg and too ashamed to tell anyone I was disabled. In a year I would turn forty five and I wanted to acquire the sophistication of the successful Hypnotherapists I had mingled with.

Many labels had been given to me by psychiatrists, including catatonic and schizophrenic. Now that I was a Doctor of Hypnotherapy, surely I could shed that old limitation, I bravely thought. And, luckily, humans had advanced beyond their primitive treatment plans that drugged people and locked them up. Yet, often, I felt that there was something wrong with me. Someone had said that they thought I had post-traumatic stress disorder about thirteen years ago. I had kept on going, working at my monkey, minimum wage jobs and feeling lonely in my empty, sterile room at night. My government disability check left me with lots of month at the end of my money, and social events cost money so I knew very few people.

While at the Hypnosis convention, I'd taken a captivating seminar on past life regression. In fact, I had even volunteered to be demonstrated on. I used to hide in silence, but the hypnosis sessions I had done had assisted me in speaking up and being seen. I loved the attention as I sat on the stage. The president of the university led me through a hypnotic process in which he assisted me in releasing pent up anger. Anger and fear had kept me stuck in a rut for a long time. It was tearing my life apart and ruining my opportunities to be close to my family and others.

I didn't know why I considered moving or what exactly I wanted. My life was better than many others, though not perfect. My father was no longer the cruel, physically abusive alcoholic who had terrified me in my childhood. He gave me financial support and called me "sweetie" affectionately, which tied together my loose ends and gave me solid, steady grounding and the joy of being loved. Since I had grown up and been kicked around by life, I had developed compassion for him.

With great courage, he had moved from his warm Southern town to the snow covered, 40 degrees below zero days of Alberta, Canada. Studying for his Ph.D. in Internal Medicine and riding the bus and subway to his medical research lab five days a week had been no piece of cake. The times when he was at home, I had longed for his love but had had to accept that studying was more important to him than listening to me was. After hearing him say, "Shut up" many times, I began to speak in a whisper and tiptoe around. My heart would shatter when he looked right through me as though I wasn't there. Hearing my mother cry for hours, I had decided he must be the meanest man in the world.

When my grammar school friends came to our house to visit, he would embarrass me, stumbling around drunk and slurring words that made no sense. The strappings he gave me with his leather belt terrified me. I dreaded going home after I visited with my close school friend who lived several long blocks away. Staying in her extra twin bed as often as I could kept me safe.

He had a kind side and I knew he was suffering. One day, I sat next to him in the movie theater in Canada, on an excruciatingly cold day. He cried agonized tears as the Yankees burned the southerners down in Gone with the Wind. He was fragile and shy, with his Diabetes to cope with, his limited money and foreign accent which people laughed at.

"People ask me if I'm from Texas and I tell them I'm from the south. They look at me like I'm from the back woods where ignorant people walk around barefooted and everyone has hook worm."

One freezing, snow covered morning, I thought he had died. I gasped in horror as he lay stone still on the floor.

"Call an ambulance", my mother had cried hysterically to my older brother.

A few days later, when he came home from the hospital, I had hugged him with tremendous love and increased gratitude. When I heard my mother say he had been in a Diabetic coma, I prayed that it would never happen again. He was like God to me because he went to work every day, through the freezing snow, to help people who had his illness. Every night, before I went to sleep, I prayed that he would discover the cure for diabetes.

The thought that I had lived many times before was fascinating, and I pondered over what various experiences I may have had in past lives. I would like to explore them more and find out what fears and what talents I had brought with me. However, past life regressions were too expensive for me. Still, I was curious about the pioneering therapy methods that people on the West coast were using. It was nothing like the old, stifling, ineffective psychiatric approach, which locked people away and kept them drowsy with drugs.

A psychic had told me I should move from the East to the West, because the city I lived in would never be my home. Racing down the foreign expressway, I thought about the sophisticated, successful doctors I had met at the convention. I had felt awkward and had troubling thoughts about them laughing at me, if I told them I worked for seven dollars an hour washing dishes and putting frosting on cookies. The sound of trucks groaned through my mind as the foul smell of carbon monoxide disgusted me. I realized the West was an endless sprawl of strip malls and traffic. I hated its crowded freeways, high prices, and sterile, manicured lawns that stretched toward looming skyscrapers.

Yet, like a zombie, I searched for a room to rent, as though a spell had been cast on me by the psychic. To keep my sanity, I began going to the Divine Light center every day. Back in the East, I had gone to the Divine Light center regularly. Sitting in the beautiful, peaceful temple, surrounded by kind people calmed me. Only one woman knew I was planning to move to their busy, Western city.

I recognized friendly faces from across the room. I had seen them in Japan when I traveled there, on the generous gift of my Divine Light leaders. My room in Tokyo had been luxurious and the food plentiful and served by polite, hospitable people. They had transported us in a bus over lush, green gorges up into a mountainous area. We had celebrated the opening of a gorgeous, new temple. In this sacred space, they would teach people about the spirit world and perform healings on them.

I came back to the moment. Someone gave me a healing, sweeping my aura with their hands and removing any spirits who might be floating in my aura and causing me disturbances, out of revenge for some mistreatment I had given them in a past life.

The Japanese people wished me a good evening, with much warmth, when I told them goodbye later on. Fear stiffened me as I drove to my hotel room, my heart heavy with loneliness. Through the dark night, I turned over with anxiety, sometimes opening my eyes and staring hopelessly at the ceiling. My nightly bill was eating me alive and I needed a shoulder to cry on.

In the morning, I found an ad for a room in a rental booklet I had found in the hotel lobby. I called the number and talked to a friendly woman. She agreed to let me take a look.

I got lost. Fear ravaged me, tearing me to pieces as I drove along the hectic freeway. Just when a loud, passing truck shook me to the bones, my cell phone rang. It was the friendly woman who had spoken with me on the phone.

"I have no idea where I am," I choked out in a timid voice. "I'm so lost." With gentle patience, she directed me along the treacherous freeway back to my hotel room near Disneyland.

It took me a day to recover from my nightmare on the highway, but I was determined to meet and thank the landlady who had helped me. I struck out again and eventually found her house, though only after a long, confusing search. She was just as kind in person as she was over the phone.

Sadly, though I wanted to rent from her, I realized I couldn't afford the rent on my disability check. She gave me a kind smile and wished me the best as I told her goodbye. Her warmth came to my memory often, whenever I felt too paralyzed with fear to breathe.

I visited the Divine Light Center every day, desperate for some relief from my anxieties and fears. Calm energy filled me as smiling people performed their healing method, invented by the Japanese, which cleared away malevolent spirits who might be lingering in someone's energy fields. A Japanese man once used the example of murder to explain it. If a person stabbed someone in a past life, that victim may hover in their aura and cause the assailant difficulties in their present life.

I wanted to understand spirituality but I had trouble trusting the myriad New Age methods that were taught at workshops I saw advertised often. I couldn't help but be suspicious of them, especially when they charged high fees. This Japanese group charged me nothing and their sincerity gave me a good feeling, like I was cared for.

One sunny day, I rode with three of my spiritual sisters to a healing fair.

Their friendly, appreciative words warmed my heart and, together, we gave divine light to curious receivers.

During a break, I mentioned to one of the participants that I was considering moving to her town. One of my fellow light workers—a middle aged, heavy set, brunette woman, with a degree in business, had offered to rent me a room.

However, I felt frightened in this strange place. It moved at a frightening, frantic pace and had mind-pulverizing traffic and astronomical prices. A shudder went down my spine as I came to an embarrassing realization: I had been duped by the psychic. If I had been meant to live here, surely I would have felt it by now. When I told the woman, who had offered to rent me a room, I wasn't sure if I wanted to move she took it personally and berated me.

I turned to the Japanese spiritual leaders in dismay. A pretty, kind woman noticed my fragility and compassionately suggested that I drive back across the country and settle back down in my hometown where things were familiar. She handed me a list of shelters where I could spend the night. Then, she said she would pray for my safe travel as she handed me a map.

I knew they were right. Shaking their hands, I thanked them and said goodbye. My money would soon be spent and I prayed that I could stretch it enough to cover the gas for my three thousand mile trip.

My motor roared and I drove down the street, stiffening with tension as I entered the crowded freeway. After a while, I took the exit on my map. Watching drug addicts talk to themselves as they staggered along the streets of the concrete jungle, seeking crimes to feed their needs, I held my breath with anxiety. Following my map, I kept going until I finally recognized the street name and saw a YMCA in the distance.

Pulling into the parking lot, I picked up a paper bag with some pajamas and a toothbrush in it. Then, I locked my car, walked into the shelter and checked in at the front desk. I was grateful for the uncomfortable cot, and the hospitable volunteers who fed me pancakes for breakfast after my sleepless night.

Starting my car, I wondered who was thinking about me. Merging onto the freeway, I drove with my shoulders reaching up to my ears. The sounds of trucks hurt my eardrums and the stench of carbon monoxide disgusted me. Sharp sciatica pains ran from my buttock down to my knee and my shoulders and neck ached.

After a grueling day of driving for twelve hours, I pulled into a Motel Six. Taking a New Age paper out of a box, I walked to the front desk and a pretty clerk checked me in.

The hot shower water massaged my shoulders as I lathered my hair and breathed deeply. The humming of wheels on pavement and roaring of trucks still raged through me and I felt like I could be knocked off balance any second. Rubbing my skin with the bleached, cheap towel I began to feel alive again. Looking into my wide eyes in the mirror, I felt lost in space.

I needed some good advice. Pulling on my nightgown, I prayed to God. Longing to feel a touch on the shoulders or hear a kind voice, I pulled back the covers and leaned against some pillows. When I opened the New Age magazine, my eyes landed on an advertisement for a world renowned psychic. My hand trembled as I called his number. Listening in fascination, I let him read me.

"It's almost like Madison is not your home", he said, part of the way through, and I relaxed like a lonely dog who is getting rubbed right where he itches by a kind stranger. I was amazed. He had never even seen me. How could he know my true feelings? He went on to talk about the physical abuse my father had given me. I had gone out of my body when it happened and I still went out of my body when I felt threatened. He suggested Yoga or some other activity to help me stay in my body.

Then, he told me he did not want to scare me, but there were two spirits who got into my head sometimes. When I thought I was talking to myself, it was really them talking to me. I had a very open crown chakra, which caused this to happen, he explained. My father, he said, had this to a much greater extent.

When the beatings had happened, when I was a child, it had been a demon acting through him, he explained. I was relieved to know that my true father did not want to hurt me. He had been out of control, over his head in deep waters and sabotaged by an evil spirit.

At the end of the reading, he suggested that I move to Northern California, saying that it is calmer and easier than Southern California.

For the next three days, I drove down noisy, overwhelming expressways from six a.m. until six p.m. By the time I got to my parents' house in Madison, I was a nervous wreck. I wanted to live with them, but I didn't ask if I could. I feared I already knew the answer: no. They would not want me there. They had been irritated when I had lived in their garage and used their refrigerator. My mother had complained that I left rotten vegetables in it.

However, this time they enjoyed my presence, though we did not sit and talk much. They even praised my talent as I painted a watercolor still life in the kitchen. My thirsty, dried up heart softened because of their sweet attention, but I only stayed for three days, like the psychic had predicted. I wondered if I was only following his forecast.

Maybe my parents would let me live there permanently if I explained to them that I had post-traumatic stress disorder, I thought hopefully. However, I could not gather my courage and ask for their help.

I called my old voice teacher, and she said her landlord had a room available in the same house where she lived. My mother filled my arms with flowers as she told me goodbye. "I love you", she said, looking at me with her devoted Leo eyes. If anyone had the strength of a lion it was her. My father's cruel treatment had caused her immense sorrow. She had dealt with it courageously, healing her heart by painting and creating beauty, often staying up all night.

Moving into the creepy house, I missed being near shops and malls. It was far, far away, in suburban sterility. Longing for anything and anyone familiar, I looked through magazine advertisements for places to go meet people.

My disability check ran out so fast that I felt grateful when a publisher hired me to edit books that his customers sent him. I drove long hours to work for minimum wage for him, drowning in my isolation. The feeling that I needed to run kept nagging at me. Some big change was needed--that was all I was sure of. No matter where I was, this feeling of insecurity and unhappiness stayed with me. If the psychic was right and moving would ultimately make me happy, then I would do that. It would spare everyone from the downer that my miserable expression and sad lamentations gave them. At the ripe old age of forty five, I ought to have some control over my life and some success. However, I felt on the edge, even though I tried to do things that successful people did. They got rewarded with money and respect regularly, whereas that happened to me only very rarely.

Three months later, I finally made the agonizing decision to drive to California again. This time, I told myself I would drive up the coast from

Southern California and would make my new home out of wherever I ended up. That turned out to be a vast, desolate mountain top.

I sat at the end of a dirt road, holding my breath in terror as I watched the sun go down. If I hadn't purchased a cell phone back in Madison, it might have been the end of me. With trembling hands, I dialed a number on a brochure of emergency contacts.

A woman, with a soft, gentle voice, came through the phone. She gave me directions to a women's homeless shelter in Glendale. Once there, I reclined on the top bunk of my bed and enjoyed the still, quiet comfort. After resting, I ate spaghetti, salad, and bread and talked with the other women. They looked bedraggled and stressed but normal. One of them invited me to go to church with her the next day.

The day was radiant with bright sun. At the Cosmic Consciousness Church, we stood around a table laden with delicious cakes, cookies, pies, quiches, sandwiches, vegetable dishes and more. Enjoying connecting with others, we listened to lively, informed people who regularly volunteered their time and energy to create a better world.

A frail, skinny man with a wisp of grey hair and big eyes, which widened with friendliness behind his spectacles, introduced himself.

"Hi, I'm Gene", he said, extending his hand. I shook it and smiled, feeling charmed by the sweetness of this dear man. His hands moved with excitement as he talked about fun activities he participated in. He made us laugh.

"We have great projects going on here, helping the needy and cleaning the environment. You are always welcome here. This Thursday we are having our open mic night. I'm going to recite my poetry and others will play instruments or sing."

As we left, I wished him a good day.

Later on, I sat on the top bunk of the bed and talked with my church companion, who was laying on the bottom. The aroma of spaghetti and garlic bread lifted the atmosphere from the depressing odor of damp, dirty socks and used bed sheets. Touched by her easy going friendliness, I sat at the table with her and ate.

The next day, I searched for a job. I liked the small town atmosphere of Glendale's streets which were laid out in clearly numbered grids and dotted with quaint shops and restaurants. There were no overbearing skyscrapers to make me feel small and insignificant. In fact, none of the buildings were higher than two stories. It felt like Mister Roger's neighborhood. I applied in drug stores, grocery stores, book stores. Everyone I spoke with was friendly.

I went to the E.S.P. Academy, in downtown Glendale, late in the afternoon. As a woman with light, blond hair, sparkly eyes and a round, gentle face gave me a healing, I asked her how it worked. She moved her hands around, about a foot from my body, saying she was clearing the energy. Then, she explained that a healing spirit plugged into her hands and worked through them. I felt skeptical. How could she even know a spirit was near her? What if they just wanted my money?

Going on interviews was daunting and, when I finally got hired at a camera shop, I rejoiced. However, when I discovered that the commute was awful, I wished I was unemployed. I had to drive a long way across a bridge over the bay every day to get to work. A week of the rapidly moving, heavy traffic took a toll on my nerves and I felt myself falling apart at the seams. I remembered someone telling me, fifteen years ago, that I had Post Traumatic Stress Disorder. They must have been right because fear of being in an accident caused my whole body to tense up.

My anxiety level got too high to handle when I got kicked out of the homeless shelter for arriving late one night. Talking with someone at the E.S.P. Academy, I had felt mesmerized and had lost track of the time. The curfew was six p.m. and, looking back, I realized that I had been warned at the Orientation meeting, when I first arrived.

In desperation, I called Gene, the sweet, ninety-three-year-old man I had met at the Cosmic Consciousness church, when I went there with the woman who slept on the bottom of my bunk bed. He offered me his sofa for the night and, as I sat talking with him, in his high rise apartment, I could tell he genuinely cared for me.

The next morning, he asked me to stay in touch. With a sincere smile, he said he would be glad to help me any way he could.

I began to drive home to Madison and, soon, became bothered by a stabbing pain in my buttock that radiated down my hamstring muscle. My shoulders burned with pain as I sped down the crowded expressways. Dismal, droning sounds came from cars and the calamitous clattering of overpowering trucks frightened me. Skylines of cities rose like stoic soldiers in the distance as I got to know America. The ten or twelve hours of driving

I did each day exhausted me. Occasionally, I would stop in a Mom and Pop restaurant and drink some tea while I observed the local people.

I arrived at my aunt's house, in Glendale, depressed and falling apart, like a flat tire with no treads left. Her eyebrows knitted together with concern when she first saw me.

"You look hungry". The sound of her voice relaxed me. Following her to her car, I listened to her talk as she drove to the Farmer's Market, my favorite place to shop. Good memories of my father buying me groceries there ran through my mind.

We browsed through the market. She bought me a fabulous salad. Talking cheerfully, she drove us home and we sat down at her round kitchen table by the window.

"You don't want to grow old out there. It is very expensive and difficult to live there and you'll be all alone. If you were twenty and had a good job, maybe it would work. But you're not getting any younger and it is not healthy to put yourself through all that stress."

She rested her chin on her hands with serious conviction. Her concern relaxed me as I looked into her dark eyes with gratitude. Chewing on crunchy, delicious carrots, artichokes, zucchini, squash and other delightful things, I felt at home.

My aunt let me sleep on a sofa bed in her downstairs basement room. Sleep eluded me, as I remembered how I had wanted to jump on the train that ran behind our house and run away when I was seven years old. Hearing my mother cry, I had thought my father must be the meanest man in the world.

Later, I knew he was--when he had beat me with his leather belt, because I refused to eat blueberries, on our vacation at Cape Cod--which would have been heavenly, otherwise.

Desperately wanting my family members to love me, I had cringed with tension and been afraid to speak most of my childhood. My older sister screamed to the neighborhood children that I was "torturing" her. My older brother gave me a gift and then took it back. I felt invisible when my father looked right through me and worthless when my mother screamed accusingly at me.

Since I couldn't get them to love me, I must be irritating and obnoxious I had come to believe, feeling shattered and worthless. Wrestling with memories of my childhood, I fidgeted nervously, staring at the ceiling. Finally, I fell into a deep sleep.

Still feeling as though I was rolling over asphalt, being blown into shakes by massive trucks, I stared at the ceiling in a daze the next morning. From my basement room, I could hear my father's voice upstairs. He was telling my aunt about how he had gone out there and rescued me when I was in my twenties. Getting him to worry and talk about me was the only way I could get his attention.

It reminded me of the time he and my mother had talked about me with their friend, a psychiatrist. The psychiatrist, a serious man with a judgmental gaze, had decided to commit me into a mental institution when I was seventeen. For a year, I had been given drugs every day, and therapy sessions with a psychiatrist three times a week. Like a shrinking person, I felt myself collapsing into that powerless child again.

My mind replayed the time when he had found me, in my twenties, forlorn and bedraggled in a homeless shelter. He had had to rescue me because I was unable to support myself and function normally. Though I didn't know the name for it back then, I had Post Traumatic Stress Disorder. In order to survive, I had needed treatment in a series of halfway houses in Santa Rita, on the West coast.

I missed my old roommate in Madison, even though I had been horribly allergic to her three cats. She had seemed stunned, when the Japanese leaders came to the apartment to talk with me about my move out to the West. It had been so sudden, and I realized I had given away a good situation. She had often given me nice gifts, sudden surprises that filled me with joy. Pointing out my abilities, she had compassionately built my confidence. We were like sisters who brought out the best in one another. With delight, I listened to her play guitar and sing songs she wrote. A new enthusiasm and love for life revitalized me when I sang harmonies with her.

Calling her on my cell phone, I remembered the fun and peace of living with her and wished I had not brought chaos into my life by listening to a psychic. Her voice relaxed me.

"How are you? I've been sending you prayers. When are you coming back?"

I hesitated, afraid to tell her my thoughts about driving West again.

"I'm not sure. Is my bed still there?"

"No. I had to get rid of it so I could rent the room to someone else. I gave it to someone at work", she replied nonchalantly as though it was nothing.

It was everything to me. I had not had such a comfortable bed in ages and I had finally gotten deep sleep on it. Loneliness and fear tightened me like a coil.

Though hesitant, I walked up the stairs and into the kitchen. He gave me a disgruntled look, as though he was angry with me for being a troublemaker. I hated him telling me, "Do this, do that!" as he had done all my life. Still, I smiled and tried to relax.

"It's really good to see you, Dad," I told him. I listened to him chat with my aunt for a while. Then, he asked me where I was going to go to live.

"I'll move back in with my old roommate. She said she wants me back. She gave away my mattress though."

He chatted with my aunt for a while. When she suggested that I better get my car checked, he offered to pay for it, as he always did. Despite all my apprehension about my father, he had mellowed through the years and I could rely on him when I needed something.

We all drove to the mechanic. Following my father and my uncle, I drove my old, yellow Honda I had bought for a thousand dollars. My father and uncle enjoyed having conversations on the phone and I felt glad that they had one another. The clutch was so hard to press that pain throbbed in my hip. I had had to shift frequently during my drives across the country and, driving fifty hours in four days twice had been damaging to my body. The car was dented and the paint was peeling off. There were rips in the seats and in the ceiling.

Once we had all parked and left our vehicles, the pair of them stood side by side with their arms folded. They had scowling, disapproving looks on their faces. Fire crackled on my father's breath as he threatened that he would not pay for my car repairs if I didn't discard my plan to move to the West. My uncle nodded in agreement. Hanging my head toward the ground, I shriveled inside, like a child being bullied.

"Where are you going to move?" my father asked in a scolding tone.

I told him I was going to settle in with my old roommate and get a job.

"I paid eight hundred dollars for that mattress and she gave it away. If you move back in with her, I will not give you another penny!" he yelled.

I shrunk with shame and fear as I followed him into the mechanic's office, staying silent.

"That car could have blown up in the middle of the expressway. It is time to buy a new car", the mechanic said.

I didn't have the money to buy one. My government check just barely let me make ends meet each month. My total dependence on my father made me feel inadequate. I changed the subject, fidgeting nervously.

We left my car with the mechanic and I climbed into the back seat. Listening to my father chat with my uncle, I wondered what they said when they criticized me. The lush, home town trees I loved sent me fresh oxygen and I breathed in deeply, observing the passing scenes.

Sitting at the kitchen table with my aunt, I looked through a newspaper advertising apartments for rent. My father took me to see a few. They were all located far away from anything or anyone familiar. I knew I wouldn't like living in any of them.

He had too much control over me and I didn't like having to swallow my anger when he berated me.

I called my old roommate, Cindy, and she said I could move back in with her. Driving to her place, I wondered if I should go to Al Anon meetings like she did. She had many friends, went on dates and talked with people with an ease and open joviality that I wanted to have. Something about me frightened friends and men away, it seemed.

Carrying my few possessions up the stairs, I looked forward to reuniting with her. Putting my things down, I knocked on the door. With exuberant joy she welcomed me and threw her arms around me appreciatively.

After we caught up with each other, I walked into my old room. Then, longing for connection, I called my father.

"You're on your own kiddo," he told me in a curt, foreboding tone, after I told him I had moved in with my old roommate. An intense feeling of doom overcame me as I visualized becoming a mad, homeless woman. I needed him to pay my rent, as he had done for years. Without that assistance, I didn't know what my future might hold.

In desperation, I searched a New Age paper. When I saw an advertisement for a psychic fair, I wrote it on my calendar. The day arrived quickly.

While at the fair, I got a reading with a psychic. Her eyes conveyed deep concern for me as she warned me that it was very expensive out West.

I spent a lovely evening at her apartment eating a delicious dinner and talking. Like me, she had spent time in a mental institution. Unlike me, she was proud of it. I admired her intelligence and creativity.

One day, I attended a psychic fair where she gave me a tea leaf reading. She saw me flying on some malfunctioning motorcycle sputtering black exhaust, my hair blowing behind me.

"Please don't go. Don't abuse yourself like this. You're barely making it here, and it is very expensive out there," she pleaded. I loved listening to her English accent, and her concern was touching.

I went to her workshop at a local Community Center. She had everyone draw pictures as Art Therapy. I left myself out of my drawing.

"Put yourself in the picture more", she suggested lovingly.

"She's planning to move. She's going to drive herself in a twenty year old car. All the way to bloody California. That's three thousand miles." She looked at the group of students and they looked at me with protective, shocked eyes.

Her Mother Mary, compassionate side enveloped me in a warm glow of serenity when I spent another night eating dinner with her in her small apartment.

One night, she asked me to go out to a bar with her and the risk taking, wild side of her came out. As we sipped our rum and cokes, she talked about various people she had recently met. Flirting with the young, slender but muscular bartender, she captured his attention. His face reddened with passion as she talked seductively. She suddenly lifted her skirt saying, "Want to see my tattoo?" Lifting the bottom of her underwear, she revealed a red rose. He looked like a cartoon character as his dark eyes grew as large as saucers. Sitting back down, she heaved her breasts in her low cut dress and, in a sultry voice, asked him to come home with her.

Worrying about her, I hoped she would be safe and secure.

I appreciated that she cared about what became of me. The thought of uprooting myself and moving to a land of strangers frightened me. She stayed very busy and we did not talk on the phone much, though I wanted to.

When I heard that a famous psychic was coming to town to do a seminar, I wrote it on my calendar with excitement. My curiosity bubbled passionately inside me.

The day of the psychic seminar arrived. I paid my entry fee, went into the large room, and sat in a chair near the front. Since I was in grammar school, I had been interested in ESP. My brother had given me cards with symbols on them to practice ESP when I was in High School.

Like a fairy, the psychic moved gracefully through the rows of eager people. Dressed in a long, flowing, lavender and green sparkling dress, that flattered her perfect figure, she looked gorgeous. Her heart shaped face had a peaches and cream complexion and her dark eyes shone, like gems, accentuating its beauty. Her crown of glory was her shiny, long, blond hair. Listening intently, I felt intrigued as she gave people messages from their deceased relatives and friends. Holding my hand up, I patiently waited for her to notice me. When she looked at me, finally, it took my breath away.

"Should I move out West?" I asked, in an unsteady voice.

"Oh, yes. You need to learn faith."

I told her my worries about money. She touched my solar plexus gently and told me that I had an instant teller machine right there. Excitement rolled through me as I imagined myself being paid large sums of money.

My decision was made. Three psychics now had said I would be better off somewhere else. Soon, I would move far, far away and be a stranger to everyone. My guts knotted, and I held my breath, staring into the void with wide eyes. I needed a huge dose of courage. Fear gripped me like a cruel dragon with steel claws.

I worked as a cashier and lived on refried beans and taco shells I bought at a store closing sale. Punching cash register keys and bagging groceries, I dreamed about how my life would be when I reached my new, utopian home: the land over the rainbow. Stuffing twenty dollar bills into a fanny pack my younger sister had given me, I planned to carry it around my waist, hidden by my shirt, so no one would ever know about it.

I was counting the days and counting my money. My time in Madison was almost gone forever. My father had cut me off and my mother seemed angry with me. Sometimes, when I rang the doorbell she did not let me in to visit. I longed to go back in time to when she was sweet and loving. One evening, I cried for an hour, looking at a photograph of us sitting together by a swimming pool when I was young.

Four years ago, I had injured my shoulder lifting heavy coffee urns at a bakery where I worked fifty hours a week. With my mid-life crisis in a fiery flair, I had scrambled madly to accomplish my goals before I became too "over the hill". Working like a dog to pay to record my poetic, spiritual songs, I had felt deeply hurt when my father had denounced my labor of love. He had said that I was foolishly letting myself get ripped off by the producer in Nashville who I paid to record my album. However, I had loved music since I was a child and had won an award for the first song I ever wrote. Part of me wanted to yell angrily at my father but I was too afraid.

The pain in my shoulder drained me of all energy and love of life. I needed help breaking out of my depression. So, I started attending a class at a Baptist church down the street. Old ladies with wrinkled, sagging skin and grey hair sat around and read the Bible. I worried about aging as they discussed their aches and pains. I was approaching forty-five and it seemed to me that I had missed a lot in life: marriage, children, and career.

Much to my delight, an old high school friend started going to the class. She was happily married and employed at a lucrative, classy job. I hoped my envy didn't show, as I tried to rebuild the closeness we had enjoyed as teenagers. I had fond memories of going to the mountains with her and her parents.

One day, I got a call from my cousin, Carol. My father had fallen and broken his hip. I rushed to the hospital. Post-surgery, he seemed so sweet and fragile that I held my breath with emotion, wanting to rock him like a baby. I gave him a watercolor painting I had done.

When he finally got to return home, he cheered up greatly because it was the place he loved most. I visited him and brought him things from the store. One day, I was sitting next to him as he reclined on his hospital bed in the dining room. I sat in silence, wishing I was good at telling jokes so I could get him to laugh and cheer him up.

"Make yourself useful", he used to say, and I longed to be a contribution.

My mother walked in and sat down beside him, not greeting me and looking disgruntled by my presence. Suddenly, she attacked me out of the blue.

"Get out of my house! Get out of my house!" she yelled, as she pounded on my chair with her fists. Her rage flared with such heat that I knew she wanted to hit me. Luckily, she still had enough sanity to restrain herself. I worried about her.

Next Sunday, I told my Sunday school teacher about the attack. I explained that I needed to get some car repair money from my father but I was afraid of seeing my mother. She asked me if it would help if she went with me to their house to visit. I gratefully replied that it would. We made a plan to meet at the church. My Sunday school teacher would drive me to Mom's house.

Feeling like I'd come in from a hail storm, I soaked in the kindness of my Sunday school teacher as I met her a few days later. She talked calmly and kindly as she drove through the tree shaded streets which glistened with rain drops.

Soon, we arrived at my house and she drove up the long driveway. I called my mother on my cell phone when we got to the side door. Several times in the past, she had ignored the ringing bell of the front door or yelled out of a window that she was too busy to visit. My shoulders rose with fear.

"Hi, Mom," I said, my voice trembling.

"Who do you have with you this time?" she barked.

"My Sunday school teacher," I replied meekly.

"Tell her you love her," my Sunday school teacher whispered.

"I love you, Mom. I just want to see how you're doing."

My mother opened the side door begrudgingly and walked away without greeting me. My Sunday school teacher followed me into the dining room where my father was lying on his hospital bed, his hip hurting. He greeted me and instructed me to talk to my mother.

"She's come here to visit with you. She's concerned about you. I can talk with her mother while the two of you catch up." It had been ages since I had felt so understood.

I enjoyed connecting with my father. My mother could call and talk with me. I needed time with him. He expressed his gratitude for my visit and wrote me a check to pay for my car repairs. Tears filled my eyes as I walked out, feeling guilty I could not do more to ease his pain. Sadness over the distance between my mother and I dripped through me, stealing my energy.

My Sunday school teacher invited me over for lunch with her and her husband. Her motherly protectiveness felt like a lullaby, as we talked over bacon, lettuce and tomato sandwiches.

Part of me did not want to leave my home town, which I had moved to when I was eleven and which I loved in many ways. I cried when I told her and her husband I was moving.

It was hard to sleep as I anticipated my journey. Like an angry, rebellious child, I was going to run away and leave my parents wondering where I was. I worried that they wouldn't even miss me.

It was still dark the next morning, when I tiptoed across the wooden floor to leave. Cindy gave me a beautiful, pink candle with the Mother Mary on the front. She hugged me warmly and wished me the best. I would miss her laughter, encouragement and lovely gifts. Memories of us singing beautiful harmonies together and playing our guitars made me smile.

I drove around the corner to a casual diner with black booths and white Formica tables. The walls were decorated with brightly colored posters and fold art. A friendly waitress smiled warmly and called me "dear". As I ate warm grits with butter, a torrent of rain began to pummel the cars and buildings outside. I clung desperately to the southern hospitality which assured me that all was well in the world. My heart somersaulted as I paid my bill and told my waitress goodbye, clinging to her sensitive energy.

Gulping with fear, I unlocked my car and sat down. Red and green lights and honking horns agitated me as I drove and, soon, I merged onto the bleak, dangerous freeway, which stretched forever. A soul shattering loneliness overtook me. The rain pummeled my car furiously, and I felt like a leaf caught in a tornado's destructive vortex.

Every night, after ten hours of driving, I pulled into a hotel and got a room. I tossed and turned in the cold, strange beds, and my mind ran wild with worry.

My body ached and my head swam when I finally arrived in Glendale. For the third time now, I had driven almost three thousand miles. It had been so frightening and tiring that I doubted I could handle it again.

My ninety-three-year-old friend, Gene, who I had met at the Cosmic Consciousness church during my investigatory trip a year earlier, welcomed me with happy warmth, making me feel like his daughter.

He lived in a tall, concrete, high rise building on the tenth floor. His apartment had one room with a sofa, dining table, T.V. on a stand and an office area, with a large, wall sized window. There was a separate bedroom. I slept on his large, brown sofa, covered with a blanket and some sheets he loaned me.

We had good conversations when I wasn't out searching for a room to rent. Sleeping on his sofa was more comfortable than I expected. Some nights, we went out and danced at a club, which was a few blocks down the street. He showed me a picture of his ex-wife who was a beautiful blonde. His two children lived in town and visited him sometimes. He beamed with pride whenever he talked about his son's success as a graphic designer and his daughter's success as a psychologist.

"I want you to meet my friend, Mary. Sometimes I think she has lost her mind but she's a dear friend. She forgets things a lot. She just sits and watches T.V. all day. I keep telling her she needs to get out and walk with me and she won't do it. I encourage her to do some crossword puzzles every day. I keep saying, 'Mary, if you don't use it you'll lose it!' but she won't do them and she won't budge from her sofa."

"That's too bad. I hope she'll start following your example," I looked at him, studying his aged face and hands and hoping I would be as caring and upbeat as he was when I got to be his age. He told me to help myself to anything I wanted to eat. I ate mixed nuts and fruits, and listened to him talk.

"I'm Jewish, and I grew up in an orphanage. My father was a crazy drunk, and he abandoned my mother and my brother and I. Our mother couldn't take care of us, so she gave us to the orphanage. It was hard, but I learned a lot from the experience. You'll love living in Glendale. Everyone looks out for each other at the Cosmic Consciousness Church. If you'd like to go to the open mic with me, there's one coming up on Friday. I'm going to read my poetry, and you can play your guitar and sing."

I looked and looked for a room to rent during the day. I applied for a job in a preschool where a woman told me I needed twelve Early Childhood Education credits to be a teaching assistant. That sounded better than the other jobs I had done, like scooping ice cream, cleaning houses and cashiering. A friendly, blonde woman, who knew Gene, told me I could take my classes for free at the community college.

The next morning, I drove a long way to the campus. A perky, pretty, Mexican clerk got me enrolled into Early Childhood Education.

I also enrolled in a class at the E.S.P. Academy, which I could walk to from Gene's apartment. The healing I had received there a year ago, when I stayed at the homeless shelter, had relaxed me more deeply than anything I had ever experienced.

In a blink of an eye, the day for my first class arrived.

"People learn more when they're having fun," my beautiful, African American teacher at the E.S.P. Academy said. Her name was Erica and her tall elegance, colorful clothes and peaceful voice were appealing. She had a great sense of humor and a relaxed teaching style. I listened with fascination while she talked.

"There is no such thing as 'selfish' in the psychic world. This study is about learning how to get what you want. You are the creator of your reality, and you can learn to manifest exactly what you want. Today we're going to practice doing mock-ups. It is a simple process, but don't underestimate its power. To make a mock-up, you close your eyes and visualize what you want. Put it in a balloon made of your two favorite colors. Then ground it by imagining roots connecting it to the center of the earth. Then, imagine cutting the string. Watch it fly up into the sky, release it and trust that it will manifest. I've gotten what I want over and over by doing this simple process." Her tall, slender body and her dark, large eyes gave her the look of an African Goddess. Speaking with clarity, she conveyed her teachings with love.

There was an incredibly uplifting energy in the E.S.P. Academy. It reminded me of the enchanted school in "Harry Potter". I started attending their church services and listening, in intrigued fascination, as people talked about their healing masters, bending spoons, healing the blind, and manifesting huge sums of money, soulmates and other desires. Like a thirsty sponge, I listened, self-conscious because I'd rarely created what I wanted. They encouraged me to pamper myself. I followed their advice and started giving myself lavender bubble baths and little gifts.

Walking back to Gene's, I contemplated. He was watching T.V. when I came in. When he greeted me with a smile and asked me to sit down, I told him I needed to use the phone. With grandfatherly supportiveness, he pointed to where it was.

Tiptoeing into the bedroom, I called the psychic who had originally advised that I move. I told him I was staying, temporarily, with a friend and looking for a place to live.

"I thought you had made a friend. I see things really starting to open up for you now that you've moved to Glendale." His intelligent voice captivated me.

"Yeah. I really like it here. I'm taking a class at the E.S.P. Academy."

"Oh, I can't put into words how great that is. I know you've had a lot of classes and it doesn't seem like much to you but, as time goes on, you'll realize how valuable it is. Are you studying with Erica? The tall, black girl?"

"Yeah. She's a great teacher." My enthusiasm lifted my voice tone.

"That's great. You're doing well and you—as a spirit—are pretty happy, in spite of the circumstances. It's sort of like there's a tornado going on inside of you, and you're all stirred up, but it's a good sort of chaos. You're going through a rebirth, and I think you know that. I see that you've been thinking, 'Oh, my God. What have I done? I'm going to end up in the Salvation Army dumpster,' and all sorts of silly thoughts. I see you've even been thinking that you could sell your car and take a bus back East," he laughed, his happy voice chasing the cobwebs of worry from me.

He had my undivided attention until he ended the call.

Walking out of the bedroom, I looked forward to talking with Gene. He looked at me with grandfatherly love.

"Help yourself to anything in the refrigerator, world traveler", he said, showing me the plates. I scooped some rice and vegetables out of his Tupperware. Then, he showed me how to heat it in his microwave. As we sat at his table, he asked me how my home hunting was going. I told him I had interviewed at a place in Danville with an Asian-American woman.

A week later, the Asian-American woman called me and said I could move in. Affection sparkled in Gene's eyes as I told him good bye and thanked him for his hospitality.

"Come and visit me. I want to go out dancing. And I want you to meet my daughter and my son." He hugged me sweetly and the frailty in his old body reminded me of the frailty I had felt in Dad. Dad's voice echoed through my mind, "Aging is not for sissies."

Driving to the apartment, where my new Asian American landlord lived, I felt frightened by the creepy looking people walking along the streets. I walked up the stairs to my new home. There was a comfortable bed in my new room and I settled in, hanging my old clothes and pushing my few boxes of books into the closet.

A few days later, when I drove through traffic to my first class in Early Childhood Education, at the local community college, panicked feelings rushed through me. Memorizing and academics had been challenging for me and I wasn't sure I could handle it.

The big, crowded classroom overwhelmed me. An overweight, black woman sat next to me. She smiled a wide, white smile and introduced herself, then shook my hand warmly. Her name was Connie. She was like the sun shining into my life. When I offered her a ride to school, she accepted.

Eagerly anticipating her friendly greeting, I picked Connie up every morning to go to class. She lived in a bad section of Danville, where gang members walked the streets, scaring people with their scowls and fighting over drug dealing territory. Her playful joking about her suffering kept me sane.

"Our landlord is threatening to evict us because we're behind on our mortgage. God, the way people grab money here—right and left—is crazy. It's all about money here. People are so wrapped up in their own worlds, they don't care. My husband and I both work very hard and pay our bills, but someone is always demanding more and more money from us. We're trying to sell our old car because we can't pay for it, but the people who sold it to us won't let us out of the contract. We've got to finish paying for it even though it won't run, and we never drive it. They could let us out of the contract, but they're greedy. It makes me sick that people are so selfish. The lady in the cafeteria at my church gave me some cooking oil the other day. Maybe I can polish the car with it and get it really shiny and pretty and say, 'Look how great this looks. You can have it back.' I'd be happy as a lark to be free of that payment." She laughed and I laughed, grateful to release my tension.

"I hope you can get free of that. You're such a kind person. My roommate is really unfriendly toward me. I'm glad to have you as a friend," I confided.

"Yeah. That's how people are here. They're cold. I wouldn't be here if I didn't have my husband."

I drove up the hill to the college and parked. People were sitting quietly at their desks and looking over their textbooks when we walked in. The professor talked about childhood development, and I imagined myself going through the various stages—growing from a thumb-sized embryo to the huge, complicated organism I was now. I loved the magical freshness of children and knew teaching preschool would be more rewarding than telemarketing, stuffing envelopes, carrying heavy trays as a banquet server, or the many other menial jobs I had done. I had a college degree, after all, and my grandmother had always told me I would be a good teacher.

I kept my nose to the grindstone and studied every night, highlighting lines in my text book with a yellow highlighter. Much to my surprise, I made A's on my tests and papers. I was finally the straight-A student my father had always wanted me to be. I wanted to call him and tell him, but I was afraid he would yell at me for rebelling against his rules and moving to Glendale.

The Asian American woman seemed relieved that I was quiet and conservative. However, she would not answer me when I greeted her in the morning. Her rudeness stunned and unraveled me. A dark depression dragged me into a deep well.

I couldn't have survived without Connie, who kept me laughing and got me in touch with my inner child. She reminded me of Irma, the African American maid who had taken care of me from the time I was born until I was three years old. Irma, my soft powerhouse full of love, had saved my life while my mother juggled car-pooling my older brother and sister to school, singing in the local opera company, and taking care of a house and husband. I spent long, lonely times in my crib but, when Irma lavished me with love, holding me close to her ample bosom, I beamed with happiness. She made me believe I was special, lovable, and deserving. Though she was treated like a nobody, she made me a somebody.

When I was a toddling three-year-old, my whole family had moved from the sunny south to the great, frozen tundra of Canada. I missed her, and the thought of never seeing her again broke me like a branch on an ice-devastated tree. I shivered in the paralyzing cold of Canada, longing to be held close to the bosom of my irreplaceable Irma.

When we rode the ferry boat to Center Island, I would stop and stare with longing at a statue of a black woman in a coin-operated, fortune teller box. Mom would cup my face lovingly and say, "She thinks that's Irma behind the glass."

Now Connie was my Irma, keeping me sane as the cruelty of the world pummeled me, and my mid-life crisis shook me to the bones. The weeks quickly turned to months. Exams would be coming soon and we both had much reading and studying to do. The teacher gave interesting lectures and I listened with concentration, determined to learn and make good grades.

The next class was fascinating and it ended too soon, and the sound of closing textbooks and chattering students filled the air. Connie smiled at me and I followed her out of the classroom and down the hall.

"I want to show you The Gold Place. It's a great restaurant that looks out over the ocean. They have great food and desserts. I'll take you there," Connie said. As we walked out into the parking lot, she touched my shoulder. We arrived at my car and climbed inside. With protective patience, she directed me through the strange streets. Soon, we arrived.

Sitting in the old fashioned restaurant, I enjoyed her sweet smile and watched seagulls flying overhead in the radiant gold and pink sky. The menu was full of colorful pictures that made my mouth water.

"It's my treat. Get anything you want!" I looked at the colorful pictures of food in the big menu.

"I come from a big family," Connie explained. "I have three sisters and four brothers. We grew up poor. My mother used to staple cardboard together to make us shoes. Sometimes, kids at school would laugh at us."

She thanked the waitress as she put a glass of water on the table. Looking over the menu, she pondered slowly. After a few minutes, she ordered a cheeseburger. I thought a few minutes more and then ordered a grilled cheese sandwich and soup. The waitress smiled and took our menus.

Connie smiled and her eyes sparkled as she rested her chin on her fist. Then, she clasped her hands on the table in front of her, exuding emotion.

"My mother had a very hard time. She found out that my father was running around on her, and she was crushed. She just kept going, doing everything she could to support us children. She worked at two or three jobs so we could have what we needed. I hated to see her struggle like that. I grew up in Mississippi. I moved out here because there's no work there. I'm really close with my mom and we talk every day."

Grieved envy moved through me. I remembered how my mother had pounded her fists on my chair and ordered me out of her house.

"You've got a lot of courage to move out here all by yourself. I had to have my husband to move out here with me."

"I was scared to death speeding down that endless freeway. I kept worrying the car might break down. I'd drive ten hours straight and then stop in a hotel. Even though I was exhausted, it was hard to sleep."

"Boy, you're brave. You're a great person too. No one else has offered to give me a ride to classes." Her pure, loving praise and light filled, sensitive eyes nourished me.

I looked out toward the ocean and saw a sliver of blue water shining under an intense sun. Thoughts of my father lying in his bed with his hip and heart hurting sent pangs of guilt through me. I shouldn't be making him worry about me. Reflecting seriously, I reeled dizzily, in numb disbelief over the fact that I was three thousand miles away from home.

Connie laughed as she watched a waitress precariously balancing her huge tray on her arm. Then, she pointed at an old lady shuffling down the street.

"She looks like she's about to fall over, hobbling along on that cane. The wind could blow her over any minute. Look. That little boy on his skateboard wants to speed up behind her and surprise her. He might knock her over."

I laughed a half laugh and realized I was holding my breath. My shoulders were raised with fear.

"It's getting close to Halloween. I wonder what my two little girls are going to dress up as. I want to get them out of public school because the gangs are selling crack and kidnapping young children. I'm saving all of my money so I can send them to a private school. They're really sweet, smart girls. The public schools these days are horrible. It's not peaceful like it was when you and I were in high school."

"Yeah. We were all well behaved in high school. I always wanted children but maybe it's best that I didn't have any. I never could find Mister Right."

"We've got to find you a husband. I'd like you to come to my church sometime. I sing in the choir. You'll have to come to our concert."

CHAPTER TWO

In seemingly empty space there is one Link, one Life eternal, which unites everything in the universe--animate and inanimate--one wave of Life flowing through everything.
Paramahansa Yogananda

The kingdom of heaven is like a treasure buried in a field, which a person finds and hides again, and out of joy goes and sells all that he has and buys that field. Again, the kingdom of heaven is like a merchant searching for fine pearls. When he finds a pearl of great price, he goes and sells all that he has and buys it." Matthew 13:44-46

Know your purpose.

Not wounded by weapons, not burned by fire,
Not dried by the wind, not wetted by water; Such is the Atman.
Not dried, not wetted, not burned, not wounded.
Innermost element, everywhere, always,
Being of beings, changeless, eternal, for ever and ever.
Bhagavad-Gita

A few weeks later, I listened to her belt out a song like a Broadway star. Her resonant voice sent electrical vibrations through the air. Afterwards, I went to a party with her and her fellow choir singers. Stretching beyond my shyness, I chatted with people, feeling stimulated by the buzz of conversation all around me. I went to the snack table, and enjoyed delicious vegetables, fruits, artichoke dip, crackers, cheeses, and nuts. Then, I wove my way through the web of conversations and strangers to find Connie.

"You were fantastic," I congratulated her, feeling comforted by her presence. Her blue flowered dress dove down at the bosom and the ruffles around the hem looked soft and appealing. Her femininity shone, as her pearl necklace and earrings reflected the light. Her large, dark and compassionate eyes gave her a spiritual vibration. With enthusiasm, she raised her arms heavenward in a gesture of celebration. Then, I relaxed into the sensation of peace as she held me close in a hug. Introducing me to several of her friends, she then began chattering vivaciously. Drinking in the pleasant vibrations, I realized that church people have a special loving manner.

Reluctantly, I left the party a couple of hours later. Not able to find Connie in the crowd to say goodbye, I anticipated, eagerly, the time when I would be with her again.

Soon, I got a job telemarketing for the Glendale Theatre. I did the best I could, in spite of pinching pains in my neck and stabbing pains in my buttock and left leg. The parking places had two hour limits, so I would have to move my car every two hours to stay in compliance. In spite of my efforts, I often got expensive tickets. The parking police reminded me of the "blue meanies" from my Beatles days as they gobbled up my scant grocery money.

Before or after work, I walked to the E.S.P. Academy and got free healings from friendly, interesting people who had graduated from the clairvoyant program. As they moved their hands around my aura, they cleansed away negative energy. It sent me into a state of relaxed euphoria, and I felt pleasant sensations, like I was being massaged all over.

I studied for long hours, alone in my room. The weekend crawled by in somber stillness. When I received a letter from my younger sister, I cried, overcome with longing to be with her.

My roommate did not respond when I greeted her in the kitchen Monday morning. Feeling lonely and overwhelmed, frightened beyond repair, I drove to Connie's.

She walked down her stairs to my car and squeezed herself in.

"How are you?" Her big, soulful eyes radiated love.

"I'm okay. I'm glad I got all my reading done last night, and I finished my paper", I replied, overjoyed to be with her.

"Congratulations! I bet you'll get an A in the class. Boy, I tell you, I want some money. My back has been hurting and I'm going to have to go see a chiropractor. I'm gonna tell him I've been eating a lot of beans and to be careful where he touches me. He might get something he doesn't like. Those beans turn me into a gas bag!" she laughed, her big body shaking. Her sweatshirt and blue jeans were clean and fresh smelling and her ebony hair shone, as though it had been brushed thoroughly.

I half laughed with her, remembering times when I could enjoy a real, full belly laugh. It seemed like forever ago. After driving in silence for a while, I told her I had written my brother, who lived in the area, and that he had not written back. I was deeply hurt that he was avoiding me.

"Well, just send him love, and I'm sure he'll come around and call you. Why don't you call him up and tell him you love him? I know he loves you. He just might feel like he needs to be free from the family. I'm sure he'll be glad to see you if you invite him over." Like a protective mother, she exuded sympathy.

"I've lost my temper with him a few times. I think he's written me off permanently." I sighed hopelessly.

"Oh, I'm sure he forgives you. He knows he's been mean to you too. Don't worry. God will help you. I think you're a great person. You can call me to talk any time."

When we arrived at the college, people bustled through the halls, with notebooks under their arms and pens in their pockets. The large, white room shone with fluorescent lights and a myriad conversations buzzed through the air, as we sat down in our wooden chairs.

Soon, a slender woman with a healthy tan, dark eyes and neatly bobbed, light brown hair began the class. As she lectured about Early Childhood development, I had memories of the stages of my own childhood. Many brilliant psychologists had theorized about children and I listened to their ideas with great interest.

On our five minute break, I jotted down a quick letter to my brother, reminiscing about the closeness we had enjoyed as children, and the light and love he had given me.

At the end of the school day, I drove Connie to her home in Danville. Ignoring the tough looking gang members walking the streets. She climbed the stairs and disappeared into her home. On the way home, I mailed my letter to my brother.

The following Sunday, I picked Connie up because she had invited me to church. She chattered cheerfully as we flew like angels, past the angry street children who were being lured into gangs. Hoping I could rescue children with my love, when I began teaching, I felt the desperation and misery in the world.

Parking my car, I watched Connie clutch her big Bible and open the door. Following her into the church, I remembered my rebellious childhood days of playing hooky from Sunday school with my brother and two sisters.

Mustering phony reverence, I walked with her into the Sunday school class and sat down in the hard, wooden desk. People began to read passages from the Bible. They gave me neither hope nor answers with their boring, incomprehensible words. Stabbing pains pinched my sciatic nerve and burned down my hamstring and into my knee. My injured shoulders hurt too, especially the right one that I had injured, working overtime, to make money to record my music. What was the use of ambition? It only made me miserable when I pursued goals.

The E.S.P. Academy, on the other hand, glowed with life. The air crackled with mystery and miracles. Happy people told jokes and laughed. They welcomed me with smiles and hugs. People brought their dogs and cats to get healings. The interesting sermons translated Bible passages into practical messages that I could understand and apply to my life.

The city of Danville exuded an energy of desperation and unspeakable violence as I drove Connie home, after we attended the church service. When I told Connie I wanted to move back to the East coast, she suggested that I ask a minister to pray for me.

Disoriented, confused feelings unraveled me as I went through the week, making shy attempts to connect with people or studying alone in my room. Connie was my life preserver in a surging sea.

The next time I attended church with her, she pointed me in the direction of a blondish, grey haired woman wearing a purple sash. Gentle compassion flowed from her as she took my hand and showed me how to kneel down on the red velvet knee rest. She prayed out loud for me, under the beautiful stained glass windows of the chapel, as Jesus smiled down on me.

"God will give you the answer, and you will make the right decision." She looked into my eyes as though I was a priceless, precious being. I didn't want to let go of her hand as she finished.

The next week, I told Connie I couldn't go to Sunday school with her. Instead, I went to the E.S.P. Academy to listen to a speech given by the wife of the former director. A powerful sense of awe rolled through me as I sat in the congregation, surrounded by psychics. They talked and laughed vivaciously as I breathed in a pleasing aroma of incense. Suddenly, they became silent, as she stepped behind the podium.

She was a tall, slender woman with brown hair that curved around her face a few inches above her shoulders. Though in her sixties, she looked good. I admired her ability to say what she wanted to say. Looking over the congregation with encouragement and tough love, she reminded us that Jesus once said, "All these things I do ye shall do and greater."

"The idea that psychic power is the work of the Devil is ignorance. We are claiming our own gifts and becoming gods in our own universes. This is the only church you'll ever go to that teaches you how to manifest what you want."

I felt liberated. I didn't have to repent, make confessions, or take vows of poverty and chastity. I just had to dedicate myself to making myself happy. It was a fresh, new beginning compared to church services in which I would sit on hard pews, solemnly saying I was a sinner and singing dirge like hymns.

After the service, I stood listening to the various psychics, shyly inserting a comment here and there. Their high vibrations filled me with aliveness and I didn't want to go home when I left.

The silence of my room deadened me and jealousy floated like poison in my blood, as I listened to my housemates talk and laugh. My body hurt and my mind burned with worry as I stared at the ceiling, unable to fall asleep.

Looking forward to being with my co-workers, I drove to work on

Monday. Walking around the farmer's market, after work, I observed people who had plenty of money and happy marriages, growing green with envy.

After a few months of working and a coaching session from the boss's wife, I was fired. I walked out of the building, staring down at the ground in shame. I realized I couldn't survive without my father's help. Reliving him calling me "a hopeless case", I internally abused myself for being a failure.

The E.S.P. Academy was always peaceful and welcoming, so I went to receive a healing. The crimson cushioned chairs were arranged in a circle and one wall was completely covered in windows that revealed cars passing and people walking. There was another large area, on the other side, where classes and banquets were held. Laughter tickled my ears as the fragrance of incense relaxed me.

Meditating in the sunny room, I enjoyed the pleasurable waves of peace that rolled through me as a chubby woman, with naturally, curly, blonde hair, moved her hands around my aura. She suggested that I join the choir and I responded that I would love to.

With great excitement, I arrived at church, at the E.S.P. Academy, early the next Sunday, to practice with the choir members. Everyone was cheerful, laughing and joking. A slender, blonde woman who was about my age smiled gently at me. I listened with pleasure as she played unique, lovely tunes on the piano. When I asked her where they came from, she replied that graduates of the E.S.P. Program had written them.

Soon, the room began to fill up with psychics, and the service began. We sang a song that one of the graduates of the E.S.P. program had written.

"In my bubble, I can be anything I want to be. I can be an acrobat. I can be a purple cat. La, la, la, la, la, la, la, la." We turned around as we sang our refrain. I felt at home with these lively, magical people.

They encouraged me to go through the E.S.P. Program. However, tuition cost eight thousand and five hundred dollars. That was more than I got from the government to live on for an entire year. I didn't want to admit I was on disability because I felt too ashamed.

No one knew I lived on a government check and I longed for a best friend, someone who knew me fully and accepted me. The psychics, who had graduated from the program, seemed so happy.

"You've got to create your miracle," one of the graduates chided me.

I could barely pay for the E.S.P. class I was taking and was even behind on my utility payments. Tossing through the night, and waking up soaking in sweat was unraveling me more and more. One night, I had a nightmare about being evicted by my cold land lord.

At the community college, one day, I looked at the bulletin board. My hopes rose when I saw an ad on a bulletin board for free rent in exchange for helping a sick man in Danville named "Ray". The advertisement also mentioned he needed help caring for and walking his five dogs.

When I went for my interview, I was impressed by his intelligence and friendliness. He was an emergency medical doctor. The cast on his leg was big and bulky and, when I asked him about it, he said his broken ankle was taking a long time to heal because he had diabetes. His five dogs sat near him, and on his lap, as he talked. Luckily, none of them made me sneeze. I was surprised because my high school dog had given me severe allergies. Hopefully, that was a problem of my past.

I moved into the downstairs of his house very suddenly, which upset my landlord.

The first night I was there, tension tied me into knots. I climbed into my bed, and sat in a fetal position, looking around the tiny room which had a twin bed, a puny closet, about ten by fifteen feet floor space and a large, grimy window which looked out over a long skyline with towering skyscrapers peeking through the trees. I knew Ray about as well as I knew the man in the moon and wondered if I was safe. As the sleepless hours stretched by, I comforted myself by thinking about my kind Indian friend who I had met in Madison. Her name was Hansa and she had moved to nearby Santa Rita a year and a half before I did. Her Eastern Indian light, brown skin, dark hair, dark eyes and heart shaped face, combined with her tall, slender body made her beautiful. She was even more beautiful inside, and she radiated a peaceful, compassionate love.

I called her the very next day.

"I've been busy taking healing classes and working at the bank. I'm busy building a side business too. Every now and then I do a healing on someone for no charge. It will grow through word of mouth and, eventually, I'll start charging." Her friendly voice soothed me like healing balm.

"That's great. My place got too expensive to rent so I moved to a place where I'm taking care of five dogs in exchange for a room."

"You can save money. You are really doing well getting yourself established here", she said, relaxing me with her kind voice.

"Thank you. I'm going to school too, learning about Early Childhood Education so I can work in a pre-school. I like being with children."

Her friendly voice washed away much of my anxiety. When she asked me to come visit her, I sighed with relief, looking forward to feeling human, instead of like a lonely leper.

As soon as I was able, I took the train to Santa Rita. The doors whooshed open, and I began walking up and down the hills at a brisk pace. I watched streetcars roll by and people from various nationalities saunter along. At the top of an unbelievably steep hill, I recognized a magnificent, European looking church that Hansa had told me to turn left at. Fog floating in the sky looked mystical, as it cooled the city.

As I turned left, I looked down the deeply sloping street. Unusual shops lined the sidewalk, and I stopped in one to look around. A thin, brunette woman watched me from behind a counter as I surveyed beautiful clothes and gifts. I reminisced about the first time I'd met Hansa.

We'd become friends several years ago, after meeting at a training in Madison. In our class, we were taught how to do deep breathing sessions to release ourselves from the limiting decisions we had made during our own birth experiences. For example, if someone had been pulled quickly from the birth canal, they might form the belief that people always hurried them.

Back when we both lived in Madison, Hansa had invited me to spend a lovely afternoon in her house watching a movie about Gandhi. While I was there, she performed a free, deep breathing session for me. Afterwards, I felt lighter and more trusting of others.

When I arrived at Hansa's door step, my fear melted. Memories of sitting on her comfortable sofa, watching the movie Gandhi, flashed through my mind. Her soothing voice, kind smile and happy laughter moved, like a healing tonic, through my blood. She welcomed me with a hug and I sat down on her emerald green sofa. There was a living area, kitchen and one bedroom. I sunk down wearily and watched the sun radiate through a stained glass ornament hanging in the nearby window. We talked about various things and, when I asked her how much she paid for her apartment, she said it was twelve hundred a month. I gasped in despair. That was twice the amount of money my monthly disability check provided.

She told me she would like to do a healing on me. With gratitude, I told her I was suffering from anxiety as well as back, hip, and shoulder pain. She led me into a state of relaxation by instructing me to feel my feet touching the floor, feel the air on my skin, feel the breath moving in and out of my lungs, and to feel the weight of my body pressing into the sofa.

"Now concentrate on the areas in your body that feel good. Feel all the good feelings there and experience them fully. Expand and magnify this good feeling. Now, briefly dip into the areas where your pain is, just feel it for two seconds. Then, move your focus back to the areas that feel good, feeling the good feelings completely. You are peeling away layers, like peeling an onion."

By the end of the session all of my pain was gone. A surge of optimism came over me as I savored the treasure of feeling good. Remembering the pleasures of being pain free and energetic when I was a child, I felt renewed.

She served me a cup of tea and some cookies. I mentioned my immense frustration at being unable to operate the old computer someone had given me. She showed me how to work her more modern computer.

At the end of the day, she dropped me off at the train station. I didn't want to say goodbye. We embraced and agreed we would stay in touch. I already couldn't wait to see her again.

She smiled and waved goodbye as I closed the car door. I walked down the long stairs that led to the train, and passed a newspaper box with a disturbing headline. Reading about a gang and how they'd murdered someone again, I held my breath. Attempting to calm myself, I listened to her voice in my mind.

The ride back to Ray's was long. Once I was home, I sat and talked with my new employer-landlord. He told me he had grown up in the area and elaborated on his work as a doctor in the Emergency department. The cast on his leg looked heavy. I sympathized with him when he told me his injury was taking a long time to heal because of his diabetes.

One day, he said he used to be like me and think he was not worth anything. I felt deeply touched by his insight into my inner psyche.

Sometimes, I helped him rummage through his tool shed for hours as he searched for things he needed. At other times, I rode in his truck with him and his five dogs as he ran errands. My arms could barely surround the huge bags of dog food I carried into his house, while I wobbled under the weight, my shoulders hurting.

One of the dogs was named after an Indian princess. He was a black and white, large dog. Another dog, about the same size, had white fur and a sweet face. He looked like he had some Husky blood. Another one was named Feather----he was a small, white dog with a long, swishy tail. One other was called Peanut and he was cute, brown and small. The other one was a caramel/golden, smiling Golden Retriever. He had rescued them from the pound. Their grateful faces glowed with contentment when their care taker held them close to him, on his big sofa.

One day, as I washed and folded his laundry, panicked feelings overcame me, and I felt like a leaf being blown away by the wind. I wanted to go home, to live with my parents. However, memories of my mother ordering me to leave, as she hit my chair angrily, shattered my dream.

Looking forward to being with Hansa, I kept coping with the pain the five dogs, tugging me on their leashes, caused. Maybe I should walk them one at a time. Too frightened to discuss it with my employer, I swept the problem under the rug.

Hansa had said she was going to take me to a Buddhist temple. Talking on the phone with her briefly, I set the time and day to meet and wrote it in my calendar happily.

Finally, the day arrived and I rode the train under the bay, feeling fascinated by the fact that I was moving under the ocean in a tube. Wondering how much the train would shake if there was an earthquake, I looked around fearfully. People listened to music through their headphones, read books, and jabbered to themselves.

Soon, I was on the other side of the bay. I squeezed my way off of the train, through the crowd, and up the stairs. It was a bright, beautiful day outside and my heaviness left me when I saw Hansa waving at me from her car. Her soft voice lifted my spirits as she drove me through the colorful, lively streets. Watching pedestrians, I critiqued their clothes and hairstyles. Hansa turned into a lot and parked her car. Following her, I walked beside her, listening to her talk cheerfully.

The temple had multi-colored, marble walls and floors and domed, Roman ceilings. The altar was decorated with gold embellishments, flowers, bowls of fruit and incense holders. Gorgeous paintings and sculptures of

Buddhist Gods and Goddesses delighted my eyes. Hansa and I took a seat on a crimson cushion on a wooden pew. My eyes feasted on the gorgeous colors and I breathed in the fragrance, imagining I was in a garden, as my spirit soared. Contemplating the power of God's love and grace, I watched incense curl over the golden, glowing altar. The priest looked holy in his saffron robe. Buddhist monks and nuns sat behind him, and everyone in the room chanted together. Soon, the room was vibrating with divine, ecstatic energy.

After the celestial, enrapturing ceremony, I floated out the door. Hansa pointed to a basket of fruit and told me to take as much as I wanted. It was my gift from the compassionate Buddhist community. Relaxing in the passenger seat, as Hansa drove, I looked out over the vibrant, mystical city with the ocean shining on the horizon.

When we arrived at Hansa's apartment, I sat at her round kitchen table. She suggested that we go to her favorite cafe.

After a brisk walk, we entered an unusually decorated place filled with chattering people. Their voices buzzed loudly. We reflected on how much more interesting Santa Rita was than Madison, celebrating that I had moved. She complimented me on my independence, congratulated me for finding a free rent situation and encouraged me to build a savings account. Good feelings flowed through me as she praised me for all that I was doing—studying to work with children, taking classes, and making friends. Soon, she predicted, I would find a nice boyfriend.

As I finished eating a delectable plate of collards, broccoli, green beans and sweet potato, I observed the lively people. A smiling, pretty waitress with Italian, dark, curly hair took my money and wished us a good day.

Walking quickly, we enjoyed the sun. After a while, we entered her dark parking area and climbed into her car.

Loneliness grabbed me, like a dark phantom, the moment she dropped me off at the train station. Luckily, I could drive to school with Connie in two days. The train and bus ride was noisy but interesting. I observed all sorts of characters: beggars, psychotics, old people, fidgeting children and teenagers decked out in the latest hip style.

Once back in my quiet, basement bedroom, I collapsed onto the bed and stared at the ceiling, wondering how my parents and sister were doing back in the sunny South. I hoped they were missing me. I hoped they often wondered why I had left. Those thoughts tumbled to self-analysis. When I

Kundalini Rising

compared my life to the lives of people with successful marriages, careers and children I blushed. Forty-five years old was a very old age to be a runaway from one's parents.

The next day, I tried to be a responsible adult. Driving his big van full of five dogs to the park was difficult. I'd never driven such a big vehicle. Arriving at the park, I parked and got out.

Pulling the back door open, I` attempted to hold the five dogs so I could put leashes on each of them, but they bounded out, almost knocking me over, and began running around, overflowing with endless energy.

Suddenly, a police officer, wearing an immaculate suit and a threatening, shining badge looked at me with stern judgement.

"I will have to write you a ticket. All these dogs are supposed to be on leashes", he informed me with confident, authoritarian command.

Stammering out an apology, I took the ticket from him. Looking at the fine, which was a hundred and twenty five dollars, I gulped with fear. Now, I couldn't go to the grocery store. Driving the big van of yapping dogs home, I wondered how I was going to survive in this strange new land.

Watching the sun rise over the trees the next morning, I felt fragile and invisible. Old college boyfriends flitted through my mind and I wished I had married one, wondering who would have been the best husband. Fumbling nervously, I pulled on a torn T-shirt and some old, stained pants. Walking up the stairs, my affections rose as I saw Ray sitting on the sofa, brushing his dogs' hair. He looked at me and smiled. Then, he asked me to help him find some things in his storage shack.

It was piled high with machines, tools, and every sort of gizmo under the sun. After that, I cleaned the kitchen counters, loaded the dishwasher, swept and mopped the floor. Then, I vacuumed. When I sat down to rest, Ray walked in and sat down. I dreaded telling him my troubles but I did anyways.

"I got a hundred and twenty five dollar ticket at the park yesterday when I was walking the dogs." A warm redness came to my cheeks.

"Don't you remember? I told you specifically several times to not walk the dogs without a leash. I told you that they would ticket you. You should have listened to me."

"Sorry. I forgot. I understand what you're saying. It's just a lot of money for me."

"Well, it's a lot of money for me too. I'm not going to pay it. You can go to court and appeal it. They might let you off if you explain to them that you didn't know the rules." His authoritarian manner intimidated me.

I shrunk fearfully and walked in listless despair to my room. Staring out of the window, looking at the looming glass and steel buildings, where people operated computers, I ruminated about all of my failures. People sometimes told me that it was like I was not all there.

Since I couldn't hold a job, I ought to be painting full time like my mother had encouraged me to do. I remembered her driving me to drawing classes when I was in high school. I'd always been talented but I couldn't afford to buy art supplies and I never got inspired. I looked through my photo album of pictures of parents and siblings and friends. Then, I thumbed through books that I had kept with me through many moves. The Rubayat of Omar Khayyam, that my parents had given me, when they visited me in the mental hospital when I was seventeen, gave me a feeling of connection with God. Sheet music had stayed with me through many moves, reminding me to practice guitar and piano and inspiring me to write songs. A book of color reproductions of Van Gogh's paintings soothed me with its mystical, uplifting beauty.

My mother had joked about how the nurse on the locked ward had come, clanging the big keys that she carried around her waist, to let her and my father in to see me. Playing the Grand Piano on the ward had saved me, when the hopelessness of my schizophrenia diagnosis spun me into despair.

My poor abused mother. I would never forget my father driving the rented car, the day I was committed. With shattering cruelty, he yelled at her as she sat next to him. Tension gripped me as I put my hands on her shoulders and massaged them, hoping to comfort her. Knowing I could not protect her from him, I prayed for someone to save her. Suddenly, he spat on her.

We arrived at the huge, gothic mental institution. My father parked and locked the car. Walking through the glass and steel doors, I worried about what was going to become of me. A blond, pretty nurse in a crisp, white uniform greeted us and had my parents fill out information on a sheet of paper on a clipboard. She told me she would take me to my ward, after the three of us had a talk with my psychiatrist.

Feeling foggy and confused, I walked down the maze like hallways until we reached the psychiatrist's office. Knocking on his door, the nurse gave me a kind wink. A male voice told us to come in.

We sat down and looked at a short man, with dark hair, sitting behind a desk. He greeted us and asked how our travels had been, looking at us with dark, penetrating eyes from behind his dark glasses. He seemed pleasant, yet I felt myself closing, like a clam retreating into a shell. Reassuring me that I had come to a good place, he asked me how I was feeling.

About ten minutes passed as chit chat was exchanged between him and my parents. Then, the nurse said she would take me to my ward. Hugging my parents good bye, I felt numb.

Arriving on the ward, I sat down at a table underneath a large, gold framed mirror. A nurse brought me lunch on a plastic tray. Eating in silence, a feeling of alienation came over me. Finishing the bland meal, I stood up and looked around. An official looking door which was cut in half and had a top part which looked like it would swing open caught my attention.

I wandered despondently down the hall and sat on a sofa. A depressed looking woman was crocheting. The pretty blond nurse handed me two strange blue pills and a tiny paper cup of water. Swallowing them obediently, I wondered what they would do for me and why I needed them. After a few minutes, my eyelids began to droop and my head to bow down. Soon, I fell asleep, sitting up on the sofa.

When I woke up it was dinner time. An orderly unlocked a door, at the end of the long hall, and let me out with a group of other patients. Silently, I walked with them to the dining hall. Taking a tray off of a stack, I slid it down the steel counter, observing green beans, corn, broccoli, baked potatoes, chicken, roast beef and more. Tired looking workers, with hair nets on their heads, filled my plate.

Following the people I now lived with, I sat down at a round table. No one spoke as we ate, and I wondered what was wrong with them and what was wrong with me. Numb disbelief that I was in a mental institution silenced me like a shot of anesthesia. When the dark haired woman, who had been crocheting on the ward, spoke to me, I felt like a prisoner who had just been set free.

My psychiatrist began doing therapy with me three times a week. He often asked me how I felt. He said that my father didn't care.

Sitting on the sofa on the locked ward, a night when I was in eighth grade came back to haunt me. It had been a quiet evening and I had been reading a book in my room. Suddenly, a scream sliced through the silence.

"Help! He knows how to kick me in the kidneys so it kills me", my mother had screamed.

In a panic, I had run into her bedroom and saw her lying on the floor on her back, in an icy blue nightgown. My father towered above her, about to kick her with his hard shoe. I had hurried to the phone and called the police.

"My father is trying to kill my mother", I cried, in a shaky, terrified voice.

The police had come. He had told him everything was fine, so he had left without questioning him.

I had felt overjoyed that my mother's life was saved. However, I had felt hurt when, sometimes, through the years, she blamed me for calling the police.

I told my psychiatrist that my mother had been kind to me. He replied that she had been nasty, at times, too. Wondering how he knew, I remained silent. Most of the time, he had to make great effort to get me to talk.

My parents began to visit me every two weeks. Sometimes it was nice and calm, and other times the high drama was too hard to handle.

One emotionally overwhelming visit, my parents had made to the mental institution, flashed through my mind, as I sat on the small bed in my new room, 3,000 miles away from home. I had wanted to save my mother as she cried, on the verge of a breakdown.

"He's been threatening to blow his head off with a pistol."

Her anguished face, with tears rolling down it, filled me with empathy. However, I was not David with a slingshot and I could not kill the Giant with one shot. I would have if I could have. It would have saved us from miserable nights of escaping in her car, hurrying in a panic to get in, so he wouldn't disconnect the wires so she couldn't drive.

She would drive my two sisters and me under the glowing stars for hours, waiting for him to come out of his drunken rage. Sometimes, we would buy vanilla ice cream cones dipped in chocolate and sit in the car enjoying some sweetness, which we could not get from our father.

Praying that my doctor would help her, I had given her a long hug.

I came back to the present. Now that I was forty five, going through my midlife crisis, I attempted to make sense of my life. I picked up an old

Kundalini Rising

photo album and looked at pictures of myself at eighteen, smiling at my male friends at the halfway house, where I went after I was discharged from the mental institution. I longed for that simple, innocent time when men took me out on dates.

Staring at a drawing pad, I felt afraid to make a mark on it so it remained blank. Inspiration never came to me anymore. I despaired that my imagination must have withered and died long ago.

"Always remember you're special because you're an artist", my mother's voice said softly in my mind. I flashed back to a beautiful spring day in high school when she drove me to my class at the Art College. Dreaming of sitting with her on the sunny back porch at home relaxed me and, after a while, I fell into a deep sleep in the silence of my basement room.

My new landlord sat on the sofa cuddling with his dogs, when I walked into the living room the next morning. Greeting him in a friendly tone, I listened to him express his frustration over not being able to find his credit card. Eager to please him, I began looking through the stacks and stacks of newspapers and magazines that filled the house.

Soon, I found it. It was as though a magnet had drawn me to the pile it was in and I thought, with astonishment, that I had become psychic. As I handed it to him, he thanked me over and over, bursting with great gratitude.

I got dressed and headed to the Danville Police Department. The sterile atmosphere numbed me, as I sat on a hard, wooden pew for a long time. Finally, the judge turned his attention to my case. I explained that I was deeply sorry, but that I had not known the rules.

"That's no excuse. Signs are posted there as plain as day. You'll have to pay the fine in full."

God, the people in this land had no mercy. I rummaged through my bag for a pen and wrote a check, which left me with barely enough money to get half a tank of gas. Dreading eating plain oatmeal for the rest of the month, I handed my check to a clerk who looked through me as though icicles were growing in her heart. Turning to leave on wobbling legs, I walked down the bleak corridor, into the elevator, and out the entrance into the cold air.

Grey fog shrouded the bleak buildings. I could not find my car in the maze-like parking lot and wandered around lost for what seemed like forever. Someone told me I could get a security officer to drive me around, but I kept wandering. Eventually, I found it on my own. I paid the huge parking fee and drove out of the lot, gritting my teeth in anger.

The weekend ended, and it was time to return to Early Childhood classes at Community College with Connie. When I picked her up, she was glad to see me and willing to listen to my troubles.

"He's making you pay the fine for his dogs?" My glum depression was heavy and Connie did her best to get me to lighten up.

"Yeah. The authorities say that it is a crime to walk dogs in the park. Anyone who is so evil that they let their dog walk in the park deserves a big fine." I laughed and laughed, enjoying the wonderful release.

"That's how it is here. People grab your money every day and blame it all on you. I wouldn't be here without my husband. It's a tough place, but you're going to be all right. Stick with me, and I'll always be there for you."

After class, I went to Connie's flat. I sat at her dining room table and flipped through my Early Childhood textbooks. The pain in my shoulders had become so severe that I had neglected the dogs for days because I was afraid of making the injuries worse.

"Bring Sophia something to eat," she instructed her adorable, little daughter.

I poured over my class notes and then, suddenly, felt her magical child standing near me. My eyes grew wide with delight as she handed me a big plate of waffles, strawberries, and ice cream. She smiled at me sweetly. Connie knew how to nourish my soul and sweet tooth.

I wanted to call my father and tell him I was finally the straight-A student he had always wanted me to be. Unfortunately, I was too afraid that, if I called, he would yell at me for defying him and moving. My tendency to rebel against authority figures certainly caused upheavals in my life.

After a delightful visit, I hugged Connie goodbye. With tense fear, I drove though the dangerous, gang infested Danville streets. Relaxing feelings moved through me when I arrived home and patted the friendly, smiling dogs who wagged their tails gratefully.

Days and weeks of walking the dogs soon turned to a couple of months. My shoulders burned with pain as the five dogs charged full speed ahead, dragging me behind them. One day, a panicked feeling took me over and I retreated into my bedroom, after I removed the dog's leashes and gave them fresh water. A dizzy confusion spun me around as negative, scattered thoughts raced in my mind. Then, a deep depression conquered me and I sunk to the bottom of a dark hole, as though a lead weight was attached to me. Death beckoned me like a friend and the invitation was rather pleasing. With a relieved sigh, I felt the world disappear.

My muscles felt like lead as I struggled lethargically, forcing myself out of bed the next morning. As I walked up the stairs, I felt as invisible as a wave in the ocean. I could die and no one would know I was gone. Walking to the cabinet to take out my oatmeal, I turned around suddenly, as Ray stormed in, glaring at me in anger.

"You haven't walked the dogs in three days. You're living here doing nothing basically, and I'm giving you a twelve hundred dollar a month apartment."

"I need some new leashes. The ones I'm using are rubbing blisters on my hands. I injured my shoulders. They hurt when the dogs pull me."

"No. I don't like you demanding that I buy something for you. That's an expense that I don't want to have." He reminded me of my father.

"Okay then. I'll just find another place to live!" I responded defiantly, my ancient rage at men boiling in my blood.

"You better find one fast because I want you out of here in three days," he demanded, raising his voice and looking at me like I was a criminal. Guilt ran through me as I realized I should have told him, at the very beginning, I was incapable of doing the job because of my injured shoulders.

I walked down the stairs into my bedroom on trembling legs. I'd picked up a newspaper earlier and I began reading it. Holding my breath, I read about a woman who had been homeless for three years. Fear squeezed the life out of me, as I imagined myself sleeping under bridges, in doorways and on park benches.

I found a list of numbers I had gotten from a rental service and called one after another, setting appointments to interview with land lords. Driving around the city was daunting. During my interviews, I tensely stated that I lived on a disability check. Most people stiffened as though I had a contagious disease. With as much politeness as they could muster, they told me they needed someone who could work full-time.

On my third and last day, I had an interview with a woman who lived in the Glendale Hills. As I drove there, I felt drenched in lush greenery, renewed by fresh oxygen. Veering around curve after curve, admiring the gorgeous trees, flowers, and mansions of the elite, my jaw dropped. They were a huge contrast to the ugly, impoverished neighborhoods I had looked in. As I turned onto the side street where my interview was to be held, the aqua blue ocean sparkled through magnificent, evergreen trees. A precious deer suddenly stepped onto the sidewalk, and I put on the brake. He stood like a statue, gazing at me with innocent, gentle eyes. Then, he began nibbling on some pink flowers. My mind became serene and still as I enjoyed the moment.

However, it did not last for long and my monkey mind began jabbering, torturing me again.

"You used to say you wanted to be a millionaire," my father's belittling voice echoed in my mind.

I still wanted to be a millionaire, I thought, as I drank in the luxurious surroundings which were lush with elegant fir, cedar and pine trees that majestically shaded the green, clean lawns. All around were pristine palaces with shiny, elegant, leaded and stained glass windows, revealing expensive furnishings, tapestries, paintings and treasures from around the world. I was captivated. Daffodils, crocuses and various, brightly colored flowers, which only bloomed out West, dazzled me with their beauty.

Julie, the woman who interviewed me, was friendly and relaxed. She didn't request a long list of references, inquire about what I did for a living, or scrutinize me the way other landlords had. As she showed me around the house, I admired the beautiful furniture, big windows, and high ceilings. A black, upright piano stood in the corner, waiting to be played. I remembered my joyful nights of playing the piano by candlelight in my parents' living room.

"The man who lives next door is a concert pianist!" Julie said with cheer. "You can hear him practicing sometimes." When I was a child taking piano lessons, I had decided that was what I wanted to be when I grew up. However, I had not played a piano for years, as I frittered away my energy cashiering, delivering cookies, washing dishes and other stifling jobs.

The fancy kitchen was equipped with every type of invention one could imagine. There were garlic presses, pastry mixers, an oxygenated water machine, and gadgets for doing everything a chef could ever want to do. The tile counters were colorful and they sparkled in the golden, cascading sunlight that poured in through the clear windows.

We walked upstairs and she showed me my room. I liked the white walls and white carpet, and the windows which looked over a garden. There was a closet with plenty of room and a bathroom just ten feet down the hall.

"You seem like a nice, honest person. I want you to move in. The rent is five hundred a month." That would leave me twenty five dollars a week to pay for everything else. Julie's blue eyes glowed with sensitivity and her strong muscles and intelligent manner conveyed that she must do very well at her job as a Paramedic.

"Thank you very much. I'm allergic to the five dogs that I live with, and I've been sneezing non-stop. This place is so much better."

I wondered if my allergy to animals was psycho somatic. My father used to say that every disease was psychosomatic.

One summer, while he traveled with my mother in Europe and we children stayed with our grandmother down south, someone had hung my beloved cat. I can't even remember who told me the circumstances of her demise. However, I remember that I was shattered and that I had needed a shoulder to cry on, which no one had given me. I loved her immensely, and she had gifted me with five adorable kittens, who brought delight to everyone. My parents had rescued her and brought her to me at Camp Happy Time, where I spent the summer, swimming, canoeing, horse-back riding and doing skits with fun children.

The trauma of losing my cat, who I loved deeply, must have caused my body to react so I would never get close to an animal again. I longed to recapture the wonder and excitement of childhood. To laugh and play again. To be innocent and unaware of the cruelty in humans.

A couple of days later, she drove to my place in her truck. Her gay girlfriend, Laura, sat in the front seat with her. They greeted me courteously and asked what they could do to help.

I led them downstairs to my room and showed them my few belongings. Swiftly, they began their task of carrying my arm chair up the stairs, out of the house, and to the truck. I had bought it for twenty dollars at St. Vincent De Paul, and it was perfect for sitting and meditating.

"This is the big, heavy chair she didn't want to trouble us with" Julie laughed good-naturedly. I followed them, with my arms filled with clothes. Then, I watched with amazement as Julie hoisted it up into the back of the truck, as though it was weightless.

Her girlfriend touched me on the shoulder amiably. A feeling of belonging surged through me as we carried my few boxes of books out of the house. Ray looked angry. Smug pride simmered inside me because I'd found a much better place to live. I told him good bye, feeling like a rebellious teenager with her stern father.

Living with women would relax me. As I settled into my all white, silent room, I heard the Cat Steven's song "Into White" playing in my head. Things were getting better and better every day. I must have mastered some skills from my class at the E.S.P. Academy about manifesting what I want. I was now taking my second class there, learning how to run my energy.

Every morning, I sat in my chair for an hour—as my teacher at the E.S.P. Academy instructed—and imagined cosmic energy coming in through the crown of my head and earth energy coming up through my feet. I imagined them blending together in the area below my navel and circulating throughout my body. Then, I imagined all my worries dropping down a grounding chord into the center of the earth.

My government disability check was not much money, and I needed to find a part-time job to supplement it. I applied to an agency which placed substitutes in various schools and daycare centers.

The day for my interview arrived. A fat, wrinkled woman looked at me with critical, cold eyes. Her scrutiny made me nervous, and I looked down at my clothes, hoping they didn't have any spots on them. I answered her questions, doing my best to seem confident. When she asked me what experience I had, I told her I had been a nanny, cared for children in a YMCA, and taught children painting. Then, I told her that I was studying Early Childhood Education.

She asked for my I.D.s, transcript and application. Then, she informed me that I would have to get fingerprinted so a criminal background check could be done.

The next day, I went to a sterile high rise office building and waited in line. I paid an obese woman twenty five dollars and she handed me a form to fill out. As she pressed my fingers into an ink pad and onto a piece of white paper, I became lost in thought. Like a sinner making confessions to a priest, I thought of the times I had wanted to hit or kick someone. Children were so innocent and loving though. Acting out anger on one of them would be cruel.

Kundalini Rising

The agency hired me and I started going out on substituting jobs. Some of them required driving an hour and a half across hot, barren land. I would invariably get lost, so I began giving myself plenty of extra traveling time. At daycare centers, I rocked little infants in their cribs. In grammar schools, I helped children do assignments. They were charming, adorable, and sweet. Watching them race around the playground, I longed for their energy.

I had injured both of my shoulders and the left one had become frozen. It would get stuck, as though it were sealed with super glue, whenever I attempted to raise my arm. It made things like washing my hair extremely challenging. I wished I had not tried to save my right injured shoulder by shifting my car gears with my left arm. It had been awful advice an acquaintance had given when I complained about pain.

Four years ago, I should have quit my job in the bakery where I carried heavy coffee urns that damaged my right shoulder. All I had gotten was an album of my original music that I could not sell and that no one was interested in.

Depression drowned me as I drove, three times a week, to a crowded public clinic for treatment. I crawled down the freeway like a snail, in horrendous rush hour traffic.

My housemates were great, but the extent of our contact was "Hello" and "Goodbye." I longed for a best friend, someone who looked forward to being with me. I tried hard to join in conversations at the E.S.P. Academy after the Sunday services, but no one knew me, and I rarely was heard. I felt awkward and shy as I listened to them laughing and talking about their fun experiences together.

Then, as if God had heard my prayer, Nancy appeared in my life. She was slender with long, dark hair, and dark eyes--like a Hawaiian islander. Her laugh was effervescent and her smile healed me. She worked in a medical research lab and was studying to earn a Ph.D. She sang beautifully, painted, played guitar, piano, and violin, and took ballet lessons.

She invited me into her room. We laughed exuberantly as we played cards. Her happy voice vibrated through all the cells in my body, enlivening me. Taking me with her to fun activities, she breathed new life into me.

We learned the tango, the waltz, the rhumba, and swing dancing at the university's dance nights. As we jumped, swayed and twirled my spirit soared. Handsome men from all nationalities swirled me like a feather around the dance floor. Ecstatic exhilaration bubbled through my body like a fountain of eternal youth.

Afterwards, we went to Denny's with several of her friends.

When Nancy heard me play my guitar, later on, at our mansion in the hills, she suggested we do a duo. As I improvised harmonies to her melodies, our voices blended like they were made for each other, filling the room with pleasing, angelic notes. We learned several folk songs and began to perform them at a local open mic night. Before the open mic, we took Irish dance lessons. I skipped and hopped like a carefree leprechaun with the smiling dancers. Everybody radiated surprising warmth, like hippies in the Summer of Love I had read about.

One day, I rode the train into Santa Rita and applied to teach a weight loss hypnosis class at the Mind Growth Depot. An Oriental woman, with long, shiny hair and stunning eyes, greeted me kindly and gave me an application. As I sat at a table, filling it out, I didn't expect them to hire me.

However, they did. My humble decades of scooping ice cream, cleaning houses, and canvasing door-to-door for peanuts were over. Teachers received great respect. I could practically hear my grandmother's voice in my head. I drifted off into a daydream.

"You would be a good teacher!" she would tell me when she came to visit. She had loved and understood me. When no one else could ease my pain over being afraid of my father, she could.

"He didn't say goodbye, hello, go to hell, kiss my ass", she would say when she observed his behavior with me. My feelings were important to her. It lit a candle of worthiness in my dark pit of low self-esteem.

I was too mortified to ever tell anyone about my dark fantasies of going into my father's bedroom and murdering him with a kitchen knife. Wanting to be a good warrior, I imagined the peace that my mother and siblings would have when he was no longer there, frightening and hurting us.

Sometimes, he would speed down the highway and frighten us all. At other times, he would not stop the car to let us use the bathroom. Every day, he looked through me as though I didn't exist. When we went to the lake, he demanded that I bail out the boat. Feeling too frightened to say "no", I had struggled to remove the water from a half filled boat with a paper cup. Often, he would threaten, with a mean look, and say that I would "be in hot water" if I did not bring home straight As. My knees would go weak and wobble so much that I would almost fall down.

When I called him a bastard for getting drunk and hurting my mother, he had struck me hard across the face. Walking around school in the ninth grade, with a black eye, a profound isolation had enveloped me as people looked at me with uncomfortable shock. Longing for someone to hold my hand and comfort me, I went through the motions of doing my assignments, feeling devastated. A couple of my peers asked me how my eye had gotten hurt and I replied that I had bumped into a door knob. My parents never acknowledged or apologized for my ugly, bruised face. I felt like an odd ball.

When I spent time with my grandmother, however, I relaxed and life became beautiful again. Sometimes, I would sit on the piano bench beside her and listen to her play old popular tunes by ear.

"Nothing could be finer than to be in Carolina in the morning" would pour through the living room on a sunny Saturday morning and I would feel as happy as a lark. Through the day, I would sing the tune to myself.

Also, she would show me how to do the Charleston dance, which filled me with playful happiness. She had earned a degree in music in college and had been a flapper in the roaring twenties. While she raised my mother and her son, she had worked as the church organist and in a doctor's office. She would sleep in the extra bed which was next to mine in my room. I loved having her all to myself.

Coming back to the present moment, I took a deep breath and looked at my application. With deep concentration, I completed it and handed it to the woman, who thanked me graciously. She told me someone would notify me in two weeks to tell me if I had been hired.

Walking through the city streets, I hoped that I would do well. Improving peoples' lives gave me a feeling of worth and connection. Even when I was a child, I had wanted to save people from cigarettes. When I stayed with my grandmother, I used to walk around the room and put out her guests' cigarettes.

I boarded the train in Santa Rita and rode back to Glendale.

My two housemates were pruning the bushes when I arrived in the hills, after a long walk from the train station. Climbing the stairs, I felt glad to be home. I organized my room and, as I reviewed my calendar for the week, I felt my grandmother's spirit encouraging me.

Sitting in my comfortable meditation chair, I visualized satisfied people who had lost weight thanking me, feeling my confidence rise. Then, I read an interesting book about metaphysics until late. Drifting off into a peaceful sleep, I enjoyed the relaxing vibrations emanating from the magnetic mattress my land lord had loaned me.

In two weeks, I received a letter stating that they had accepted me at the Mind Growth Depot.

When my first day as a teacher arrived, excitement lit a fire inside me. The Mind Growth Depot was happy to have my expertise and a new confidence surged through me. Tiptoeing out of my room and down the stairs, I left the house early in the morning. With hopeful and curious thoughts, I walked down through the hills, past the University campus and to the train station. Observing people on the train, I wrote in my diary.

Soon, it arrived in Santa Rita and the doors made a loud whooshing sound. Passengers crowded through them and I walked out into the clamor and chaos of people hurrying and vehicles roaring down the busy streets. As I walked through the city, I remembered various stores and streets that I had seen when I lived there in my twenties.

When I arrived at the Mind Growth Depot, I was led into a room where a friendly woman had me read and sign a form. After I finished, she led me into a huge room filled with rows of chairs.

I stood at the podium and reviewed my notes. People began walking in and sitting in the neatly arranged rows of seats. After everyone was seated, a woman closed the doors and left. Then, I explained how hypnosis worked and reassured everyone that they could lose weight. Instructing them to relax and make themselves comfortable in their chairs, I began the hypnosis session.

It went well, and I booked private sessions with two attendees. I also arranged a barter with a pleasant woman in her fifties, named Kay, who said she would teach me ballroom dancing if I would hypnotize her to lose weight.

For years, I had wanted to hypnotize a room of people but had been frustrated because every place I inquired at expected a huge rental payment from me. I had gritted my teeth in anger and had wanted to yell that they couldn't squeeze blood out of a turnip.

However, the past was dead and gone. Success was mine at last. My clients would be impressed by my mansion and think I was successful. I would keep getting regular clients, and I could tell my father I didn't need his help. He had always resented giving it and had angrily told me, "It's *my* money." Fine. He could keep his stinking money.

Going to Kay's weekly ballroom dance classes was fun. We formed four couples and, as we waltzed around the big room, I felt like I could fly. Now and then, I glanced at myself in the huge, mirrored wall.

At my second class, Kay beamed with happiness when she told me that her clothes were looser. When she invited me to go to the pier, I happily accepted. Watching sea lions lounging on the rocks, I enjoyed the sounds they made.

Happy, laughing children rode a carousel when we walked into the shopping area. Others tugged on their Mom's skirts as we walked through the shops that were filled with intriguing things. Kay pointed out clothes that were the best color for me. Her easygoing sense of humor and gentle, encouraging ways were a fresh breeze of happiness, which lightened my load.

The days turned into weeks and months and then it was almost Thanksgiving. My landlord, Julie, invited me to share a Thanksgiving feast with her mother, her, and her partner, Laura.

I didn't call my parents, and they did not call me. A great sadness and longing to be close to them filled my heart. Guilt flowed through me as I visualized my weakened, hurting father recovering from his hip surgery.

While I was apartment hunting, a woman, named Jane, had invited me to do a candlelit, world peace meditation with her. I liked thinking about her kind eyes, so I called her. Her friendly voice soothed my worried mind and I felt my heart open. We made plans for me to visit her in a few days.

When I arrived, I looked around the neighborhood with apprehension. A dangerous looking man walked past me, and I walked faster, my heart racing, anxious to disappear into her house. When I reached her doorstep, I knocked frantically.

The front door creaked open and she smiled and welcomed me in. I sat in a padded chair as she sat on her sofa. Telling her I had found a nice place to live in Glendale, I relaxed. She was the flower child I had always wanted to have befriend me; someone who would watch over me like a big sister.

"You'll never go hungry in Glendale. It's a great place to live."

Her tubby body was motherly looking and her brown eyes shone in her round, caring face. Light brown hair fell a few inches below her shoulders. The small, one story house was cozy, with bookshelves, a small fireplace and a round table. She lit candles around the room and serenity graced the silence, like the dusk vibrated with the silent flapping of angels' wings. White candles glittered on her mantel, bookshelf, coffee table, and dining table. We meditated in the candlelight for an hour.

Afterwards, we talked about E.S.P., tea leaf reading and other interesting things.

While I drove home, the James Taylor song, "You've Got a Friend" played through my mind.

I started applying for jobs in preschools. My fear rolled away, like a retreating tide, when I got hired by a slender, blonde, blue eyed teacher who owned a Montessori school. The ten minute, downhill drive to the school was fun, like a roller coaster, and I loved looking at the tall, lovely clock tower looming over the University campus. It shone beautifully in the early morning sun. Affection rose in me as I anticipated being with the children.

Sitting and reading stories or watching the children play opened my heart. They looked angelic as they played with blocks, slid down slides, rode tricycles, threw balls, or climbed the jungle gym. I remembered being a child myself as I watched them build castles in the sand. Helping them tie their shoes and washing their small, soft hands before lunch gave me a feeling of importance and belonging.

My second quarter in early childhood classes was better than the first. My teacher was young, lively, and dedicated. She praised me for my good work. Her love for children shone in her eyes as she talked about how they learn sensory motor skills and hand-eye coordination when they play with blocks and puzzles. Standing, looking strong, with her slender body and wise face, she showed us how to make straw sculptures, sand bowls and other things for children to play with.

"We, as teachers, have the future of the world in our hands," she said, emphasizing her serious message by making eye contact.

She congratulated me sincerely when I told her I was working at a Montessori school. With enthusiasm, I told her it was my most rewarding job ever and the children loved me.

As light and lovely as my fresh, new start was, darkness swallowed me at times. Severe panic overcame me whenever I received my telephone and utility bills. I would pay them, and it would completely empty my bank account.

Then, in a daze, I would drive to the supermarket. Taking food off of the shelves, I stared at it, frozen with fear. Putting it back and shuffling out of the store in embarrassment, I felt like a loser.

When I got home, I looked at my credit card statement and gasped in horror. I owed $2,500 and had no idea what source I could pull that huge amount of money out of. With each month, the amount I owed was increasing. Staring at the wall, feeling helpless and hopeless, I wrung my hands tensely.

CHAPTER THREE

"All these things I do, ye shall do and greater."
Jesus Christ

"You have heard that it was said, 'An eye for an eye and a tooth for a tooth.' But I say to you, offer no resistance to one who is evil. When someone strikes you on your right cheek, turn the other one to him as well." Matthew 5:38-39

"You have heard that it was said, 'You shall love your neighbor and hate your enemy.' But I say to you, love your enemies, and pray for those who persecute you, that you may be children of your heavenly Father, for he makes his sun rise on the bad and the good, and causes rain to fall on the just and the unjust. For if you love those who love you, what recompense will you have? Do not the tax collectors do the same? And if you greet your brothers only, what is unusual about that? Do not the pagans do the same? Matthew 5:44-47

It is difficult not to fight back. However, it is more rewarding to love those who cannot love us back.

At the end of the way, the master finds freedom from desire and sorrow---freedom without bounds. Those who awaken never rest in one place; like swans, they rise and leave the lake. On the air they rise and fly an invisible course, gathering nothing, storing nothing. Their food is knowledge....they have seen how to break free.

Dhammapada: Sayings of the Buddha

I would have to find another job and get myself out of credit card debt, as soon as possible. Soon, I found one at Tot's Treehouse. Unfortunately, it would only last for two months. I loved the children, even when they behaved like maniacs. It bothered me when an assistant teacher told me to put a blanket over the children's heads to keep them from acting up at nap time.

I told my early childhood teacher at the community college. She suggested that I ignore that bad advice and trust myself. My inner guidance told me to give the children the gentleness I had wanted when I was a child.

Now, I had three part time jobs. The days were busy as I went to school, to work, drove to the public health clinic to get my injured shoulders treated, and took classes at the E.S.P. Academy. Very quickly, the days were weeks and then months.

The next assignment the agency sent me to turned out to be very far away—about fifty miles. I arrived an hour late at a crowded nursery for pre-school children. That afternoon, I got a call from an angry, critical woman who told me I had been fired.

Yearning for release from my depression, I went to the E.S.P. Academy and received a healing whenever I could. As a dark haired, chubby woman who wore an orange head band cleaned my aura, one day, she talked with me.

"Be sure to pamper yourself every day. It doesn't have to cost much. You are getting much lighter. Your aura is glowing bright pink and blue. I'm cleansing off your parents' energy. You don't need all that disaffirmation in your space."

Her bright eyes twinkled with joy as she invited me to the church service. I thanked her, then told her goodbye and began my drive home. As I wound around curve after curve to my mansion in the hills, I contemplated my goals. I wanted to be a psychic, but the words of the director of the E.S.P. Academy rang through me like a death toll.

"It's like water off a duck's back for the twenty something year olds who come here but--at your age. It would be hard."

Parking my car, I sighed with weariness. Then, I climbed the stairs and unlocked the door, panting for breath. The aches in my muscles made me feel old. I called Connie and left a message on her answering machine. Then,

I brushed my hair and tidied up my room, wondering how I would survive now that I was in the Wild West. I might have to learn how to steal food.

Thoughts of Mom and Dad and my hometown flashed through my mind. After sitting so much, I needed to move, so I walked down the sloping hills of the flower-filled neighborhood and headed toward the rose garden, reviewing my life with its patterns and mistakes. Some sadistic gargoyle, which lurked inside me, had kept me from success all my life. My peers were married, with children and vacation homes and money.

The fragrance of roses intoxicated me as I sat and admired every color and shape in existence. Then, I watched the sun set over the breathtakingly beautiful bay. Misty, indigo mountains loomed on the foggy horizon. A white sailboat drifted, its mast gleaming. A red, fiery sun sent colors across the water.

When I returned to my white, silent room I called Connie. Her peppy voice on the phone brought me back to life. A few days later, she came over and got my computer plugged in and working.

"Wow. You are living in a mansion. How did you find such a great place?"

"God is taking care of me. I want to treat you to lunch."

I drove through downtown Glendale and she directed me to her favorite Thai restaurant. We laughed and talked as we ate an exceptionally delicious meal. A slender, beautiful, Asian waitress talked in a sing song tone as she served us.

As I drove Connie home, we rode past a funeral home.

"That's where my bill collectors want to take me," Connie laughed. She kept me entertained with her funny comments and, when I pulled up to the curb in front of her house, she looked at me with affection.

"Would you like to come in?"

I replied that I would, and I followed her up the long stairs. She told me to make myself comfortable on the sofa. We had both been hired by the same childcare agency.

"That agency has been giving me the run around!" Connie exclaimed. "They expect me to arrive right on time to places that are halfway across the world. God, the places they've sent me are way out in no man's land. It takes me half the day to get to some of them because I take the bus. I have to walk around and ask people if they know where it is. I'm getting sick of them. They ought to be paying me ten times what they are because of all the hassle. I'm really trying but they threatened to fire me yesterday."

"Well, they *did* fire me. I arrived late at a nursery. I couldn't help it. It was very far away and hard to find and I drove forever, all while having a panic attack. I'm glad they fired me."

"Yeah. They can go jump in the lake. I've taken enough crap from them. All the pain isn't worth the peanuts pay," Connie said, disgruntled. We laughed and talked until I felt really good and relaxed.

With reluctance, I told Connie farewell. As I drove home, hearing her welcoming voice in my head, it swept the cobwebs of sorrow and fear from my gut.

That evening, I felt particularly envious of Julia, my landlord and Laura, her partner. They spoke to one another with such affection as they chopped colorful, fresh produce for their dinner. Spinach, kale, broccoli, carrots, mushrooms, onions, garlic, zucchini--it looked life filled and delicious.

I kept a big pot of stew I made out of expired vegetables, which I bought at a big discount, in the downstairs freezer. Walking down the stairs despondently to get it, I gritted my teeth with anger. Glendale was only the land of milk and honey for people who could afford the milk and honey. I took the pot out of the freezer, brought it up the stairs and dropped it angrily onto the stove.

"That looks like southern food," Laura said, wrinkling her nose with disgust. She ladled their delicious dinner onto plates and carried them into the living room.

The days passed, under the Glendale sun, like an evening in front of a fire with nothing to drink. The sun radiated with an intensity I had never seen. It was strange that it never rained. I missed the drenching downpours that I used to enjoy back East--the thunder, lightning, and drama used to thrill me. They would cleanse the air and make everything glisten with fresh vitality.

I called Jane, who had invited me to her candlelight meditation. When I told her I'd like to see her, she drove half an hour to visit me. She was impressed that I had found such a beautiful place so quickly. When I told her I played the piano, she asked me to play. After listening for a few minutes, she asked me if I would teach her granddaughter.

Every Sunday evening, I drove a half-hour to teach piano to her eight-year-old granddaughter, Emily. She progressed quickly and played her beginner songs with enthusiasm. I loved the way her innocent blue eyes sparkled with happiness, when I praised her.

Her mother was addicted to drugs and had left her with her father and his "weird" girlfriend. Emily went to a public school where gang members, drug dealers, and child abductors lurked around, hiding their evil intents by offering children candy. Every day, I learned about some new evil which was being done by the devils of Kali Yuga (the current age of decadence my Indian spiritual group had taught me about).

After the lesson, Jane always treated me to a delicious, home-cooked, Chinese dinner. After my belly was full, I would relax and listen with wonder as she taught me how to read tea leaves. I was amazed, as she pointed out tiny shapes and talked about what they meant.

I stayed busy between appointments at the public clinic, substitute jobs, community college, and the E.S.P. Academy. Sometimes, I went to have a free meal at a church. I liked the kind way that the welcoming servers treated me.

Luckily, I found a job taking care of a man who was paralyzed and confined to a wheel chair. Five times a week, I went to his small apartment and sat with him. I read to him or helped him raise his fork to his mouth. If he asked me to clean or organize I did that also. Seeing how confined he was, I counted my blessings, thanking God for my fully functioning body and mind.

The weeks passed quickly while I absorbed experiences in my new frontier. It was like a different country. Lesbians walked by arm in arm, and gay men walked nonchalantly, holding hands. Several times a week, I walked through the doors of the E.S.P. Academy, eager to absorb the peace and get attention from the friendly psychic healers.

One day, I noticed a poster on the wall about a channeling session that was coming up soon. Suddenly, the concerned gaze of an overweight lesbian with long, dark hair brought me out of my despair.

"You want to know that you're doing things right. You are. You're also worrying about money. You can get into the channeling session for a discount," she reassured me.

"Oh, bless you. I've been worrying about money."

I paid a friendly person and then read a book until the channeling program began.

A pretty, brunette graduate of the E.S.P. advanced program sat in a padded chair. About fifty people sat in rows of seats, waiting with anticipation. My palms sweated as the Director of the E.S.P. Academy introduced her and explained that a spirit from a higher realm was going to speak to us, through her. If anyone had dropped a pin everyone would have heard it. The channeling began.

"Greetings, earthlings. I am delighted to have this time with you. Mother Father God is proud of the progress you are making as you heal your inner wounds and learn to love yourself. As you love yourself more you are beginning to love others more and to share compassion with all. This is sending waves of energy around the planet, shifting the mass consciousness into a higher frequency. I am very proud of you. Know that I am always with you, protecting and guiding you so that you create happiness for the entire universe. Remember that the only person you can change is yourself. As you feel and express joy more this will help others who are sorrowful and depressed to raise themselves to a joyful state. People are going through many transformations and, your earth will also soon be going through many upheavals and changes. Earthquakes, tornados, tsunamis will begin happening all around the world."

A magical high vibration lifted my mood as I listened, mesmerized by the spirit. When the program was over, I wanted to stay and talk to the psychics. However, I couldn't get a word in and felt shy.

Walking out the door, down the stairs and to my car, I bubbled over with wonder. Pondering the message from the benevolent spirit, I drove up into the hills.

The next day, I couldn't wait to go back to the E.S.P. Academy and I needed some exercise. So I walked through the flowering, lush hills down to downtown Glendale. Brimming with curiosity, I walked under the Roman arch through the copper sculpted doors. Watching the psychics move their hands around people's auras, in sweeping movements, I wondered how it worked. A woman with shoulder-length, brown hair finished clearing someone's aura nearby.

Then, she looked at me and her eyes glowed with empathy, as she invited me to receive a free healing.

Sophia Moon

I moved in front of her, sat on a padded, crimson chair and drifted into a lovely dreamland of roses and butterflies. Rippling, tingling sensations relaxed my mind and body as she swept my aura. After about ten minutes, I vibrated all over like I had received a massage.

Walking home, I passed several beggars who asked for money. Then, a strange man started talking with me and I told him I was new in town.

We went to have lunch together the next day. He told me about his serious struggle with poverty and how he wanted to return to Denmark, his home, but could not get the money for a plane ticket and moving expenses. He suggested that we deliver pizzas together since we were both looking for work. I bought him lunch out of sympathy.

One evening, I went to a single's event at the Glendale Marina. A guy I met there liked my shapely figure, which I had showed off in a tight, blue satin pantsuit, and started taking me out to restaurants. It dismayed him when, on our second date, I felt too shy to kiss him on the lips. He was friendly, handsome, muscular and well-dressed. I admired his intelligence as he talked about receiving a scholarship to study for his under-graduate and graduate degrees.

However, as I looked at him, I would have flashes of him losing his temper and pushing or hitting me. I tried to be light and charming when we spent time together, walking through a park or sitting in a restaurant, but fear gripped me. It made me tight-lipped and tense.

A month later, I told him I wanted to stop getting together. Christmas was approaching fast and I wanted to be with people who I felt safe with.

"You are a depressing fool. Haven't I been nice to you? Haven't I taken you to nice places? I hope you have a lousy holiday!" My inner being shook as he loudly hung up on me.

I consulted with my favorite healing teacher at the E.S.P. Academy. She showed special warmth toward me and called me "Queen Sophia." I didn't feel like a Queen however. I just felt like a paranoid basket case who was incapable of relating to men.

"Do you see the humor in the situation?" Her blue eyes shone with sensitive caring as I admired her thick, wavy, blonde hair.

"Yeah, I guess so. I'm still shook up and hurt though." Close relationships were very important to me.

"You're not broken you know. Run your energy every day. You can create anything you want. You have the power within. You're doing really well in class. You will meet your healing master in the next class. I've asked him to give you clarity. You're doing very well, and you are intelligent, beautiful and powerful. You just need to believe that,"

I loved being taught by her and, at her next class, I had the opportunity to practice the aura healing she had taught. I moved my hands around a young man's aura. While I worked to cleanse it, I saw a vision of him working hard. I told him what I saw and he told me my intuition was correct.

The next morning, I embarked on the dreaded drive to my chiropractor's office. When my doctor asked how I was doing, I clung to every word, drinking in his look of concern. He treated my frozen shoulder with a bright pink laser which broke down the adhesions that kept it from moving.

The next class I went to, at the E.S.P. Academy, was wonderful. My friendly teacher taught me how to allow a healing master to plug into the palms of my hands and work through me. Feeling the spiritual energy concentrate in my palms and flow into people, when I placed my hands on their auras, I felt important, like a contribution.

My teacher suggested that I start doing healings at psychic fairs. With great excitement, I said that I would love to.

The day of the fair arrived, and people came to be healed by me. I had never felt so important. With curious faces, they looked at me and sat down in a chair. Telling my healing master to plug into my palms, I began sweeping their auras, feeling for warm and cool places and places that seemed disturbed by negative thought forms. Insecurity filled me. However, I relaxed when their grateful faces assured me that I was doing it correctly. They all thanked me after their sessions, and self-confidence flowed through me.

The psychics at the E.S.P. Academy believed that people learn better when they are laughing and having fun. I went to events whenever I heard about them. We would sing the Hokey Pokey and turn ourselves around or play Duck Goose, chasing one another like happy children. Imagining I was a child again, I recalled the days when my younger sister was the light of my life. I remembered how she would call me to join her in playing Hide and Seek with the boys next door.

I volunteered to work in the kitchen just so I could spend more time with the psychics and soak up their playful, magical vibrations. Their loving words and lighthearted laughter lifted my spirits as I washed pans, cleaned counters and swept the floor.

The psychic who managed my kitchen work gave me a reading and told me I had been a healer in a past life. Then, she cleansed my aura. Feeling myself becoming lighter and freer, I experienced the sensation of rising like a balloon. After a while, the massaging movements, which combed my energy field, stopped. Slowly and reluctantly, I opened my eyes. Smiling, she thanked me for my hard work in the kitchen. I thanked her for the reading and told her goodbye.

Ambling admiringly around the lush University campus, I pondered that I contained quite a cast of characters from God only knew how many past lives. Gorgeous marble buildings invited me in with their artistic, carved entrances with Roman arches. Entering the quiet, large hall of one, I walked past the computer lab and felt the studious vibrations of students as they worked on assignments. Walking outside, I felt refreshed by the magnificent cedar, fur and oak trees. I admired the dramatically tall tower with its huge, ornate clock and bell on the top.

Whenever I drove from the hills down to the Montessori School, I admired the campus clock tower and how it seemed to almost glow. Its presence was a comforting reliability. Its consistent, hourly chimes spoke to me. It urged me to make the most of each moment because they were numbered.

On this day, memories of the simplicity and fun of my first two years of college filled me with nostalgic longing. Climbing steep hills on my way home, I felt strain in my leg muscles and remembered my college coach telling me I needed to exercise every day. I wished I had taken her good advice. My breathing became labored as I struggled, like a mountain goat, passing cafés full of students busily typing on computers, those machines that befuddled me. Feeling as though I had stepped into a Jetson's cartoon and was way behind the times, I stopped now and then to catch my breath. After about a half an hour, I finally reached my home, my leg muscles burning.

The next day, I relived times with caring people and decided I needed to be with them. Remembering the sweetness they had given me, I drove to Santa Rita to visit my old, Indian spiritual family. When I had meditated with them over twenty years ago, their center had been a tiny flat.

When I arrived, I was surprised to see it was a huge, Victorian mansion.

It looked like a photo from House Beautiful, with its stained glass windows, ornate woodwork, gorgeous colors and charming, sculpted turrets. Walking into the grand entry hall, I remembered touching moments with my spiritual brothers and sisters.

A woman I had never met introduced herself and asked what my name was. I asked if I could do some service to prepare for the upcoming meditation program. Following her along an oriental carpet under a glistening chandelier, I listened as she showed me how to dry glasses and fill them with water.

After about fifteen minutes, she told me that my spiritual brother, Mark, would read the Murli to me. The Murli, the words of God, was also called the magic flute that transforms the world.

At first, he did not remember me. I felt slighted. That's what my silence got me. Forgotten by other people too.

He led me into an opulently furnished room and I relaxed onto a red, plush chair. Flashing back in time in my mind, I relived sitting across from him on the train, twenty years ago, as it swayed and clattered down the tracks from New Delhi toward Mount Abu in Rajasthan, India. We would be staying in Madhuban (which meant forest of honey) for two and a half weeks. Dumbfounded with awe over journeying to meet God, I had said few words to him, yet had felt immensely grateful for his gentle company.

Now that I was forty-five--older and wiser--I sat and listened to him read me the words of God--the words we had been fortunate enough to hear sitting in front of the medium in India. A warm glow of love massaged my heart and cooled the fire of worry from my head. In the forest of honey, Madhuban, on Mount Abu, God had told me to remember that his helping hand was always on my head. I relaxed into the chair and savored the encouraging words of God.

When the Murli was over, we sat in silent meditation for a few minutes. Finally, I opened my eyes and breathed in deeply, looking into my long lost brother's eyes.

"Now I remember you." Happy recognition shone in his sweet eyes.

A delightful wave of serenity rolled through me as he led me into a room where the meditation program was about to begin. I sat down on a chair and looked at the platform where an Indian sister, in a white sari, sat.

She was the sister who had said that I was mentally disturbed over twenty years ago. Traveling back in time, I pondered about the Christmas trip I had taken to the New Mexico meditation center. A Yogi, named Bill, who I had met in Madison had taken me there and introduced me to Dr. Sanja and Peter, who both taught meditation. Bill told them that I had been to India once and would like to go back.

Dr. Sanja said, "They are saying you cannot return to Madhuban. A sister in Santa Rita gossiped about you and said 'She is mentally ill. We don't have people like her'."

"Anyone can go to Madhuban", Peter chimed in.

"You are my sister and I will fight for you", Dr. Sanja had said, her fiery eyes glowing with loyalty.

She had traveled with me during my second trip to Madhuban and roomed with me. When I got a fever of 104 degrees, she had taken excellent care of me.

Coming back to the present, I listened to a peaceful spoken meditation and, soon, I floated in a golden bubble of God's love.

After a twenty minute meditation, everyone began to talk and move around. We were served a delicious, vegetarian lunch. I ate gratefully, knowing I was much healthier than I might have otherwise been, because they had taught me to become vegetarian in my twenties. People of all different races and professions talked. Restless children scampered around the room.

After a while, the program officially began. It opened with a talk by a Yogi, who wore a white sari. She discussed the experiences she had been through in Madhuban and the ways her life had improved as a result of daily meditation. Her humble sincerity touched me.

After the program, another brother from twenty years ago recognized me and introduced himself.

"Baba was very protective of you. He told everyone to not let you walk into town alone. He has such great love for you," he said, looking lovingly into my eyes. He was strikingly handsome and I wondered how he remained celibate in spite of probable advances from love-struck females. I was blessed to have him as my spiritual brother.

As I drove home, I looked forward to seeing them again and wondered when the opportunity would come.

It came fast. Two weeks later, the two female head yogis from the

Kundalini Rising

Spiritual University in India, who traveled the world teaching meditation, came to give a program in the public park.

I remembered them on my train ride into Santa Rita. Their welcoming love and generosity had saved my life. With affection, I thought about the special souls, from around the world, who I had met in Madhuban.

The park was filled with towering, graceful trees and gorgeous, brightly colored flowers. Walking into the outdoor Greek Theater, I admired the classical statues of Gods and Goddesses.

Two heavy set, older Indian women, wearing white saris, sat on the stage. The trance medium, who channeled God, sat between them. Ambling through the crowd, my spirits rose when I noticed a familiar face. My old teacher from two decades ago, Lisa, greeted me with great enthusiasm. She had taught me spiritual knowledge at the Santa Rita center, when I was in my twenties. As she gave me a hug, serenity soothed me like a soft sand dune.

She told me she lived in Oregon now and taught meditation. Great peace exuded from her and, as I filled myself, my shoulders dropped. Then, a memory of the psychotic, frightened state of mind I had been in when I met her in my twenties flashed across my memory and shook me inside.

At once, I realized I was not present. I took in a deep breath and focused on the moment, the way she had taught me to. Becoming centered and grounded, I listened gratefully as she talked about the college town she lived in and how she enjoyed teaching meditation.

I also saw Dr. Sanja, the kind, Indian Raja Yoga teacher who had protected me from the gossiper, called me her sister, and taken care of me on my second visit to India. Walking up to her smiling, I hoped she would remember me after more than twenty years. She did.

Affection flowed through me as I remembered how, long ago, she had taught me to pop mustard seeds in oil, and then add grated carrots. Learning how to bake bread had also been great fun, and she and Peter--the other meditation teacher--had complimented me on how delicious my bread was. I'd hummed to myself, enjoying my peaceful cocoon of love, as I stayed in their meditation center for over a month.

Someone told me that Peter, the yogi who had taught with Dr. Sanja in the New Mexico center, now attended the Santa Rita center. I remembered his ability to make me laugh with fondness. Helping him with various projects around the New Mexico center had been fun. I had felt safe and loved, like he was a devoted big brother. The nights were carefree and festive as we enjoyed his delicious, grilled vegetables at our divine family gatherings in the backyard.

Coming back to the present moment, I waved good bye to my friend and sat down. A strong, handsome man, dressed in a white Indian outfit, announced that the program was going to begin.

With concentration, I listened to the white clad Yogi on the stage, as she channeled a message from God. With great love, God encouraged everyone to create a new world of peace and happiness. If everyone would love one another as he loved us, the world would change. He congratulated us for the progress we were making.

When the program was over, I wanted to cling to my spiritual family. However, I waved reluctant good byes and walked to the bus, which I rode to the train, which I rode to downtown Glendale.

Hiking up into the hills, where the millionaires planned their European vacations, I worried. My financial situation was rapidly going downhill. No one was scheduling hypnotherapy sessions with me. My credit card had a balance of $2,500 which was growing larger with each month that passed without me making a payment. Paying my rent and then scraping through the month, eating expired vegetables was depressing me. Substituting in pre-schools was not paying me enough to dig myself out of debt.

So, I started riding the trains around and applying for full time work. Soon, I was hired at a Vitamin Villa in Danville.

A big, burly black man stared at me, sending quivering through my bones, as I walked up the long stairs from the train and headed to work early one Monday morning. A thin man with glasses, beady eyes and curly, brown hair showed me how to run the cash register. As he instructed me on how to count out the money, at the start and end of the day, and balance the ledger, I marveled over how quickly and seamlessly he worked. Listening intently, I decided it was best to stay quiet about my total lack of computer experience.

Sometimes, in the afternoons, he would have me carry a huge amount of cash to the bank, which was on the other side of the shopping center. As I walked through the crowd, past drug dealers, large, muscular gang members, killers and rapists, I kept my jacket tightly closed, so the pack of thousands of dollars around my waist did not show.

One day, when an icy isolation dampened my spirits, a customer stood in front of me, burning with anger.

"These pills did not help me lose weight and I want a refund now", a large, burly black man growled.

My knees went weak underneath me and I noticed my hand trembling as I took his refund form from him. Reading it over, I felt ambivalent. It stated that customers who were not satisfied were entitled to full refunds. There must be some limits though. I told him that I was sorry but I could not give him a refund.

The next day, men who looked like gang members descended on me like vultures who could smell fear in my blood. Their angry glares, threatening voices and strong, clenching fists demanded action.

One after another, I gave cash to them, fearing for my life. Their eyes exuded such hate that I knew they could pull off a grisly murder, like the ones I saw reported on the front pages of the newspapers, without a drop of remorse.

This continued for weeks, until the manager called me aside to talk. He said that the store was losing money so, from now on, he wanted me to take inventory and put products on the shelves. Standing on a ladder, carefully stocking shelves with Vitamins, I dug myself out of my credit card debt grave day by day.

Unfortunately, my anxiety made me forgetful and I began arriving late at my ballroom dancing class. It disrupted the flow of class and, after several times, Kay told me I would have to stop coming. I was shattered.

I missed my dance classes as I immersed myself in work, even working overtime. When I finally got my credit card paid off, I celebrated by walking around the rose garden. Then, I pampered myself like the psychics had taught me to do. Soaking in a warm, lavender bath, I relished the joy and freedom of being debt free.

The next day, I put in my two weeks' notice. Then, I called various preschools, asking for substitute work.

One day, the director of the E.S.P. Academy finally arranged for me to go to her center in the north, to talk with her about enrolling in the two-year program. I knew I did not have the money to go through it. However, I wanted to talk with her.

Traffic clamored around me in a clatter of discordant, agitating sounds.

I could feel my shoulders rise toward my ears while I drove, though I tried to stay at peace. Watching the mountains in the background growing larger, I longed for life to be simple.

After wearing a sore spot into my tail bone for an hour, I finally arrived at my charming, serene destination. The town was full of historical buildings and statues, and it had an ornate, old fashioned clock tower that loomed above the quaint, main square.

When I parked my car, I breathed a sigh of relief, happy that there was no "Tow Away" sign. I walked quickly, with extra energy. Observing the flowers and trees, I smiled at attractive people walking cute dogs. In no time, I found the center, without much trouble, and pulled open the pale blue door.

A slender, brunette lady, the wife of the deceased E.S.P. Academy's founder, greeted me. I followed her to her office.

"It's a miracle you got here with all of the medical programming you've had. You need to get stronger with your tools that you've learned in the classes you've taken. You'll drop out after two months if you start The E.S.P. Program. Come with me."

I followed her out into a large, colorfully decorated room. She looked toward three charming women.

"I want the three of you to do a healing on her and remove all the psychiatric drugs from her body." Like an angel, she touched my shoulder, wished me the best and departed.

They greeted me with sincere kindness. Then, they began beaming their mysterious, magical energy into me by holding their open palms toward me. I drifted into blissful reverie, feeling lulled, lifted and cleansed. Floating in otherworldly peace, I lost track of the time.

After my healing, I thanked them, enjoying their empathetic eyes which looked directly into my soul.

As I drove down the freeway, I boiled with resentment that no one had ever told me about the damage those psychiatric drugs caused. Many different drugs had been subscribed to me by psychiatrists and they had been far from "miracle drugs". They had made me gain weight, fall asleep, lose my ability to be logical or to concentrate. My emotions had been numbed by them and they had probably damaged my internal organs. Yet, I never had had a shoulder to cry on or any real information about them. The lectures my father had given me had convinced me that I was broken. Who was he to insist that I needed them? And how could the psychiatrists be such callous drug pushers. The medical system, which I had trusted, was beginning to show its dark side.

Sighing with relief, when I arrived on my street, I parked in front of my home, walked up the stairs and let myself in. Laying and relaxing on my mattress with magnets on the floor, I felt grateful to my landlord for letting me use it. Opening a letter from the Mind Growth Depot, I read a note which guaranteed me a free class at the Mind Growth Depot in Santa Rita. It was a gift I had received for having presented my weight loss with hypnosis program there.

The next morning, I enrolled over the phone. Tarot card reading was the class I chose. Riding the train to a bookstore, I imagined what the teacher would be like. I bought myself a modern, unique set of Tarot cards and practiced with them every day.

When the evening for my first Tarot class arrived, I bubbled over with excitement. The Tarot teacher was clear, knowledgeable and amazingly intuitive. Her large, blue eyes and wavy strawberry blonde hair made her attractive, though she was probably in her sixties.

One night, after class, I got a reading with her. Wringing my hands anxiously, I told her I had moved from far away and wasn't sure if I should stay.

"I don't think you are meant to stay here forever. I think you came here to learn a lesson. I suggest that you get into therapy." Her sensitive voice and concerned eyes calmed me.

I told her goodbye and said I looked forward to seeing her at the next class. Luckily, I slept better that night.

As I woke the next morning, I felt excited about the new things I was learning. After calling a few numbers, I found a nearby therapist, named Amy, who had an office in downtown Glendale. I booked a session with her.

The day of my appointment arrived and I followed her into her office. She was blind, yet very present--a totally engaged, attentive listener. Her eyes glowed with empathy as I told her about my mother ordering me out of the house and my father's withdrawal of financial support.

"My father used to pay my rent. He has always resented it though. He yelled at me and cut me off before I moved out here. And I can't relax with my mother. She's cold and critical. I moved here because a psychic told me to. I don't know if I should stay, though. It's so expensive."

"Forget about the psychic and listen to what your inner psychic has to say. I think you need to pay your own rent. I don't want you getting yelled at by your parents. Isn't the cost of living lower back in the south? Don't you have friends and relatives back there?"

"Yeah, but I know those psychics have real powers."

"What does your inner psychic say?"

I had no reply for her. I could not trust myself.

Prosperous, happy looking couples walked hand in hand along the streets as I walked home, feeling anxious. When I asked my tea leaf-reading friend, Jane, what she thought, she said that I would never find the peace I was seeking if I went back East. So, I decided to hang in there, like a brave pioneer.

However, when the student chiropractor, who treated my frozen shoulder at my next appointment, told me he was leaving Glendale and going home I envied him.

To my dismay, I stopped getting calls offering substitute teaching jobs. I found myself out of money way before the end of the month, and unable to pay my telephone bill or buy food. I tossed and turned every night and couldn't get any real sleep. Sometimes I woke up soaking in my own sweat.

"The light's on, retard," my housemate snarled, when I knocked on the bathroom door, one morning. She never returned my friendly greetings. I couldn't imagine what she could be angry at me for or why she wanted to hurt me.

I called my old therapist from twenty years ago. He suggested I find the number for the Resources Center. I found it and, later on, I dialed it hopefully. A man set up an appointment with a job counselor for me.

A few days later, I met my job counselor, Linda. My self-respect rose as she praised me for getting paid so well to be a substitute teaching assistant. She sympathized when I told her how I panicked whenever I got a bill.

After my appointment, I walked around the neighborhood. I noticed a Hare Krishna Temple with a bright red door. A drunk man dressed in stained, torn, stinking rags leered at me as I walked up to the door and pulled it open.

Suddenly, I saw Jyoti. Looking like a loving earth mother, she was serving food to people. Hope rolled through me like a soft summer wave as I picked up a plate. Broccoli, carrots, rice, chapattis and beans exuded a healthy aroma. My stomach hummed in anticipation and, as I ate, I felt healthy nutrients being absorbed into my cells. Vitality bubbled inside me as my body became strengthened by the nutritious food. I admired the light, airy temple, with its high ceilings with sculpted moldings. Staring in awe at exquisite frescoes of Krishna dancing, with powerful detachment and peace, on a bed of cobras, or dancing with gopis in a meadow of wildflowers, I knew that I had found a place of love.

One early morning, I watched the humble devotees dress the cloth deity dolls that sparkled on the altar. Something made them more open-hearted and peaceful than other people. I contemplated this, wondering if their daily rituals did something to their brain chemistry.

Spending hours there, I felt charmed by their childlike rituals. Lord Juggernaut was sick in bed. A sweet devotee took me to a back room, where a wooden doll of him recuperated in bed. I watched her offer him food and drinks. It was like Mr. Roger's neighborhood.

Later that day, Jyoti invited me to walk home with her. The evening glowed under a full moon. She listened to me with interest as we sat in her tiny, dilapidated shack. It used to be a garage. She complained that ants and mice got in because it didn't have a proper floor platform. There was no bath tub and her shower was a makeshift bit of a hose.

As cramped and ugly as it was, life became an oasis of peace and love when I sat with her. She asked me to play my guitar and sing for her, then listened attentively. My confidence rose and I felt rich, holding twenty dollars in my hand, when she purchased both of my CDs.

Some days, we rode the bus to the beach and walked through the cresting waves, enjoying them massaging our feet. Other days, I rode her extra bicycle. I flew behind her as we pedaled through the streets of Glendale. When I told her the washing machine had stopped working in the house I rented, she took me to a laundromat downtown.

I began visiting her at least once a week. Sometimes, we went to the rose garden and walked around talking, enjoying the gorgeous colors and pleasing fragrance. My shoulders dropped and my tense muscles loosened.

"I don't want them being mean to you," she said, after I told her about my housemate's rude behavior.

I felt elated when she invited me to the Hare Krishna feasts at her next door neighbor, Bindu's, apartment.

The night of celebration arrived and happy vibrations lifted me as I arrived at Bindu's apartment. Sincere love poured from the mouths and eyes of the friendly devotees who welcomed me. Several big pots simmered on the stove as I walked into the kitchen, where Bindu hurried to serve the vegetarian feast. When I asked what I could do, she had me ladle food onto the plates.

It was a welcome change from my awful tasting diet of expired vegetables. The cardamom, turmeric and cumin spiced dishes filled my nose with a pleasing aroma. My mouth watered and my stomach growled.

A sweet, eccentric woman named Madhu gave me special attention. She was in her sixties and she had a wrinkled face and brown eyes with sagging eyelids. Her wavy, brown hair, which almost reached her shoulders, was mousy with areas of grey. She wore clunky shoes and mismatched, wrinkled, long skirts and tops.

Everyone began to eat. Sitting down on the sofa next to Madhu, I soaked in her motherly vibrations. She asked me how I was doing and listened with rapt attention.

"You're a very sweet girl, and Krishna is taking care of you. He will do anything to make you happy. When I lived in Hawaii, I was poor and wearing old clothes. I told him I wanted a pretty new blouse, and he sent me ten beautiful, new blouses. They appeared in the trees on the land I was camping on. Krishna loves me. He gives me everything I ask for. Ask him for what you want."

"I want more money and more friends", I replied.

"Krishna is a rascal. He plays games with me. He likes to keep me on my toes by sending me signs and messages. He asked me to start a temple in Santa Rita, so I'm starting one in my house there. You'll have to come and see it. Krishna told me he wanted colorful walls, so I got three devotees to paint it. It has three different colors in the room where the altar is. It has been a heck of a lot of work, and I've been yelling, 'Krishna this is too much!'"

"He just laughs at me and tells me to keep trying. It's hard handling the guys. They say they're going to do something and then don't show up. One of them has been screwing his girlfriend in his bedroom. It's a crazy house."

She was colorful, entertaining, and fun. I laughed, relaxing into the celebration, as devotees began singing "Hare Krishna". Surya, Jyoti's husband, played the harmonium, and two devotees played drums. Incense swirled through the room, as the vibrations lifted heavenward.

After about an hour, I helped Bindu wash and dry dishes. Her complimentary words gave me a feeling of worth. Being a contribution was fun.

When Madhu asked me to give her a ride to the train station, I dreaded leaving the fun. Driving her to the train station, I listened to her chatter. When I stopped the car at the curb, I told her I thought I better head back East. She said that there were many boring people back there and reassured me that I had real friends where I was. Holding my hand, she invited me to come have lunch with her in a few days.

Returning to my substituting work in pre-schools, paying all my money to my credit card, driving through traffic to get my frozen shoulder worked on and sitting alone studying, I slipped into solemn gloom.

Then, one foggy, drizzly day, I took flight like a bird released from a cage. Observing unique characters of all nationalities, I rode the train into Santa Rita to visit with Madhu.

Madhu greeted me with welcoming affection at her house. Touring around, I was impressed with the work she had done to create an altar for Krishna in the living room.

Pedestrians passed us and traffic roared noisily as we walked quickly down the streets. We ordered delicious pizza in a colorful, unusually decorated restaurant. As we talked, her look of protective devotion sent warm waves through me.

"I'm asking Krishna to help me every day. He always does. I'm telling him my troubles, and he just keeps sending me blessings. He wants me to be happy. He will do anything for us. Ask him to help you and he will. You're a very sweet girl, and I want you to be happy."

"That's amazing", I replied, hiding my judgement that she was just a crazy person babbling. Then, I thought about the parable of having the faith of a mustard seed. There must be a reason why I was in Glendale, learning faith from a woman who was able to manifest blouses. More and more, in each moment, I began to trust her good intentions. I didn't trust Krishna though. He looked like a thug, stole butter, danced with women all night and had thousands of lovers.

However, his devotees kept me well fed. I would have starved without them. Every Sunday night, I went to their feast at the temple, and every Wednesday night, I ate with effervescent devotees in Bindu's cozy apartment.

The next Sunday night, I felt grateful for Madhu's company as I observed the hundred or so strangers at the banquet in the Krishna temple. The air vibrated so intensely with the myriad conversations that I felt like I was falling apart.

An Iranian-looking man asked me if I was married. I hesitated to respond and instead nervously stared at the floor.

"She doesn't need a man," Madhu reproached him, staring sternly into his eyes. "She is smart enough to go it alone. She doesn't need to cow tow to a man. She is her own person. Women have been subservient to men for ages and, now, Krishna is giving us back our power and dignity. So don't tell her she needs a man. Men these days are no good. They don't even take care of the children. My daughter was left high and dry with five children to raise by herself!"

I continued to stare at the floor, as the room seemed to sway and the myriad voices turned to buzzing, like a mad swarm of locusts. My head swam, as I contemplated the strangeness of this land I had moved to.

My taste buds celebrated as I ate two big plates full of curried vegetables, samosas, rice and bread. For desert, I enjoyed a honey-dipped, soft pastry. Madhu said something funny and I laughed. Watching the orange clad devotees serve food from big buckets to characters of every size, shape and color who sat on the floor, I felt like I was in a zoo. Some of them were even eating with their hands. Emily Post would be shocked.

The noise faded as we walked outside and down the street to my car. Madhu looked at me like a mother hen protecting her chick. As I drove her to the train station, she talked about what a special person I was and how she wanted me to be happy. She knew a few psychics in Santa Rita that she would like to introduce me to she said, pressing five dollars into my hand.

"Everything is going to be all right. Krishna is looking after you. Promise me you won't worry, okay? I'll see you at the feast next week. I want you to get confident so you speak what's on your mind. Don't end up like Jyoti. She's all scrunched up. Surya has criticized her for so long that she's afraid to say anything. You can barely hear her when she talks. You have a lot of important things to say and I want you to feel proud about speaking out.

There are a lot of mean people in this world and I want you to be strong so none of them can hurt you. Don't get beaten down like Jyoti. You heard how I spoke out tonight. That's how I make it through this cruel world, and you have the right to express yourself too. Promise me you'll take care of yourself and be good to yourself."

She cupped my face in her hands and looked at me with love. Then, she climbed out of my car, walked slowly down the stairs and disappeared into the subway tunnel.

The next day, I felt an overwhelming urge to get in my car and drive back East. I visited Jyoti and asked her what she thought I should do.

"Well, I've never felt at home here. People are cold and they only think about money. I think you should go where you will be the happiest. Only you know the answer. I wouldn't take the advice of any psychic too seriously. They aren't always right. I will miss you if you go but I want you to be happy."

I told my landlord I wanted to leave, then changed my mind over and over. Each new day ravaged me with fear. Sometimes, I went for two weeks with no cash. Worry fragmented me and I felt like a flimsy boat being tossed by the wind and the sea.

There were wonderful things about this place though--Going dancing and singing in my duo with Nancy at the Irish Pub, my wonderful therapist, the Mind Growth Depot, ballroom dancing classes with friendly Kay, walking by the ocean, getting healings and playing Duck Goose or doing the Hokey Pokey with the friendly, magical psychics.

Once in a blue moon, I splurged and ate dinner in a fabulous restaurant. Observing people around me, I would write in my diary.

Pacing back and forth in my room in the hills, I worried that I was going to be forgotten by everyone. If they raised the rent on me, I would become a street person. Maybe I better head back East, where my aunt would give me a sofa to sleep on, until I found an apartment.

The lovely neighborhood I lived in reminded me of my parents' neighborhood. A woman next door grew gorgeous flowers like my mother did. One beautiful day as I was walking home, tired from work, she handed me a big bouquet. Breathing in her love gratefully, I returned her friendly smile and thanked her.

My attachment to Glendale and its loving, enlightened people was growing day by day. Yet, a voice inside me continued to nag me, telling me to return to the East. With kind, gentle patience, my land lord tolerated me telling her I was leaving, and then changing my mind once a month or more.

Then, one day, I told her I wanted to move and it was the straw that broke the camel's back.

"You've changed your mind twenty times now. You're a nice person but I'm not renting a room because I need a friend. I need someone who will stay. I can't live with this uncertainty," my landlord told me.

Her decision was final. I sat in the silence of my room and stared at the wall, immobilized by thoughts of sleeping in my car. Feeling desperate beyond words, I called Jane.

"I've been evicted. I have no place to stay. I'm going to have to sleep in my car. I'm terrified. Can you let me stay in your extra room?" I pleaded with despair.

"All right. Come on over. We can do a work exchange. My house needs a thorough, deep cleaning. Pack up your things and come over." I had already been out West for over a year. It had flown by.

Though I was grateful for the shelter, the room I slept in was ugly and dusty. The mattress had wires that poked me and the grime streaked windows were drafty. Noisy sirens wailed through the night and splintered my sleep.

Day after day, I scrubbed ancient layers of dirt off of her walls, blinds, floors and furniture, sneezing because of the dust. My injured shoulders throbbed and my knees hurt from pressing on the hard floor. By the end of the day my fingers burned with pain.

I took a break one day and walked around the neighborhood. The neighbor who lived across the street stood on his tiny lawn raking some leaves. I walked toward him, shyly. His body was skinny and his face, framed by thinning, dark hair, was worn with age and drawn with worry. Yet, his manner was gentle and he greeted me courteously.

"How do you like living here?" I asked.

"It's okay. I just have to have good security. Some men came and loaded up all my belongings in a big truck one day. They took my refrigerator, my T.V., my stereo, my furniture. They never got caught, and I didn't have insurance, so I had to buy all new things." He looked like he was in his late sixties. His thinning, dark hair, lined face, sad eyes and frailty touched me.

"That's awful." His vulnerability cracked open my heart as I told him good bye.

As I walked home I cringed in fear, looking around the bleak, barren, impoverished neighborhood with its grimy, sterile sidewalks and scraggly, sparse greenery. Terror ravaged me as I despondently shuffled up the stairs and into the front door of my new abode. My employer/roommate and I talked for a while.

"The house looks great. You're doing an excellent job. Emily is coming for her piano lesson tonight. She's looking forward to it. She really loves you, and she loves your CDs. She keeps talking about them."

CHAPTER FOUR

*"Simplicity, patience, compassion.
These three are your greatest treasures.
Simple in actions and thoughts,
you return to the source of being.
Patient with both friends and enemies,
you accord with the way things are.
Compassionate toward yourself,
you reconcile all beings in the world."*

"The journey of a thousand miles begins with a single step."

*"Knowing others is intelligence;
knowing yourself is true wisdom.
Mastering others is strength;
mastering yourself is true power."*

"Stop thinking, and end your problems."

"A good traveler has no fixed plans and is not intent on arriving."

All quotes by Lao Tzu, Tao Te Ching—Taoism

"The yearning for our lost perfection, the urge to do and be that which is the noblest, the most beautiful of which we are capable, is the creative impulse of every high achievement. We strive for perfection here because we long to be restored to our oneness with God."

Paramahansa Yogananda

At her lesson that night, Emily bubbled over with endearing enthusiasm. Looking into her innocent, blue eyes, I remembered being on fire when I was eight years old, like her. I had wanted to be a prima ballerina and a concert pianist.

"You sound like a professional singer on your CDs", she said, wide eyed with admiration. Standing tall with confidence, I realized, for the first time, that I was a contribution to someone's life.

The next day, my session with my chiropractor made me feel human again.

"Don't clean all day. You'll get depressed if that's all you do". Her nurturing energy lifted me like a balloon of motherly love.

"I'm already depressed. I don't like it here. I wish I hadn't moved here," I lamented.

"Yeah. Glendale is tough. My car has been broken into three times since I moved here. I don't want to live here either. When I finish school, I'll probably set up a practice in Colorado."

"I think I'm going to leave Glendale and go back home." My voice droned with depression.

"Well, Glendale will always be here…festering in its poison."

She told me she was from Canada and I exclaimed that I was too. Memories of my grammar school days in Alberta, Canada came back to me. I had been an energetic, creative, hopeful child. Burning with passion and purpose, I had worked diligently in my ballet classes, dreaming of the day the handsome male dancers would lift me in the air as I performed on stage.

Now, I had a career as a scullery maid in a ghetto full of crazy, gun firing criminals. My tight, aching muscles were constantly coiled with fear, and I was drowning in depression. I couldn't accept what I had become.

My friend, Nancy, gave me an escape from the drudgery and boredom. She always offered me something delicious to eat when I visited her at her various apartments. We both moved around like nomads.

I would meet her at Glendale University for dances. My worries dissolved as I danced the rhumba, the tango and the waltz. Men who were twenty years younger than me led me around the floor, spinning me until I felt like taffy, going with the flow, moving with grace and effortlessness.

One night, she took me out to a free dance. I watched in amazement as people made up their own dance steps. They danced by themselves, reveling in creative inspiration. Tall and short, young and old, black and white, rich and poor----all danced around a large room with wild abandon. They did pirouettes, leaps, jumps, stretches, and whirls. I danced around and pretended I was the prima ballerina I had intended to become when I was a child.

When I returned to the ghetto, anxiety crept through me like bony fingers slowly choking me to death. Sleeping hardly at all, racked by worries, I breathed in dust every miserable night.

In the morning, I needed sleep yet I buzzed with energy. My housemate stayed in her room, with the door closed. Too afraid to go out and walk briskly around the neighborhood, I did some jumping jacks.

At eleven a.m. I gave adorable Emily her piano lesson. She did very well and I complimented her, enjoying the joy in her eager eyes. The time flew too fast and I did not want to leave her at the end of every lesson. Hugging her, I enjoyed feeling her angelic arms around me, her tiny fingers pressing my flesh gratefully.

That evening, Jane cooked a Chinese dinner for me and taught me how to read tea leaves. Feeling amazed by the details she saw in the patterns the leaves made, I relaxed into the fun and friendship, feeling lucky to be inside. Jane told me that a bullet had flown by, a couple of inches from her head, when she walked down the street one day.

My mind raced with worries as I tried to fall asleep. The horrifying headlines, which I saw regularly in mailboxes, were unraveling me.

The next morning, I desperately needed a therapy session. I drove for half an hour into Glendale and parked about eight blocks from my therapist's office. I prayed the parking police would not put a boot on my car. It would cost me sixty dollars if they did. Some parking tickets were a hundred and fifty dollars.

I ran down the streets of Glendale, past madmen, beggars, students, and rich people. I needed Amy, my therapist, to perform a miracle and raise me from the dead.

I slumped down into my chair in front of Amy like a carcass. I'd endured another sleepless night after reading about the murder of a woman. A man

Kundalini Rising

had pulled a fence post out of the ground and bludgeoned her to death with it.

I wrung my hands, and my words came out slowly. There was a monotone, dead tonality to my voice as I lamented that I was a worthless failure with nothing but a bag of shame to shoulder. People were sick of paying my bills and no one wanted me.

Amy said I was depressed with a look of concern that moved me. She strongly suggested that I get some anti-depressant medication and handed me a brochure about a place that would supply me with it.

Gritting my teeth with anger over those poisonous drugs, and the damage they had done to me, I got lost on my way to the clinic. Then, after waiting a long time to get a couple of bottles, I decided to not take them.

Driving down the expressway, I longed for life to be simple and sweet. Arriving in the ghetto, I cringed with fear when a cop pulled me over and gave me an expensive ticket. He scolded me, saying I had been going eight miles an hour over the speed limit.

The eighty dollar ticket he handed me made me want to scream. Now, my credit card would gobble up more money because I could not afford to make a payment. My muscles tensed with steel like rigidity.

Soon, I parked and hurried into the house. As I walked in, Jane greeted me but I didn't feel like talking.

Retreating into my room, I tried to read but could not concentrate. After laying there lifelessly for a while, I fell asleep. Nightmares shattered my sleep, ransacking me and robbing me of every drop of peace.

The next morning, I felt frightened and alone in the world. Longing for connection with people, I drove nervously to the Hare Krishna Temple.

Finally, I arrived, and I pulled open the red door in desperation. Calm came over me as a kind devotee served me some vegetables and rice. I ate in peace, sitting at a small table and observing people. Light lifted me, as Jyoti walked in, like an angel of mercy. Her emerald green earrings shone and her spring green sari flattered her slender body. I watched her stand behind the table of food and serve people.

After a while, she asked me to walk home with her. Fluffy clouds floated playfully in the robin's egg blue sky. When I asked Jyoti the names of brightly colored wild flowers I had not seen in the East, she knew them and told me. As we arrived at her shack, Bunny, Bindu's white cat greeted us.

We made sweets for Krishna. I was touched by her humility as I watched her mix confectioner's sugar and butter in a huge bowl which covered her tiny counter. She had the cheapest, makeshift kitchen I had ever seen. Her oven was two slabs of wood with a couple of cheap Bunsen burners on top and her sink was so tiny the dishes just barely fit into it. Yet, she prepared coconut carob balls for Krishna with more love and devotion than any Betty Crocker housewife in a twenty thousand dollar kitchen.

I helped her roll the mixture into round balls, basking in her affection, feeling secure under her wing. She told me to think good thoughts so the sweets would get filled with pure vibrations. I stopped myself when I wanted to gripe about my aching shoulders.

We finished making the sweets and covered them with tin foil. Then, Jyoti held them and we both climbed into my car. Talking with light enjoyment, we headed to the Krishna temple. Jyoti waited in the car as I walked up to the temple and pulled open the red door.

Priya, who lived in the temple, smiled sweetly as I handed them to her.

"Thank you. Krishna is blessing you. It makes him happy that you and Jyoti made these with your own hands." The rest of the evening was lovely and peaceful as I sat with Jyoti talking. Fear gripped me as I left her and drove back to my ghetto home.

I began finishing my cleaning early and driving to Glendale to spend time with Jyoti. We sauntered serenely through the rose garden, browsed at shops or sat in her tiny hovel talking.

The whole top part of Jyoti's hair had turned grey and it looked ugly compared to the honey blonde hair that cascaded beautifully to her waist. I dreaded growing old. She was eight years older than me. She had studied painting at the Philadelphia Art College but said that she didn't have the space or energy to paint and draw like she used to.

She told me about the adventures she had experienced with her husband. They used to travel around the country doing puppet shows. They carved the marionettes themselves out of wood, made the costumes, wrote the stories, and did the voices and movements of the puppets. Children loved them.

"We used to be famous", she said with sad nostalgia.

Pulling a folder off of a dusty shelf, she opened it and showed it to me. An article had been written about them in a local, Rockford paper. I read it with fascination, admiring her young, beautiful face in the photo. Imagining them whittling their puppets out of wood, I admired them for being brave, talented entrepreneurs.

"There was a lot of support for the arts in Rockford. I miss that. Everything is based on money here." Disappointment sat like a sad vulture on her shoulder as her voice broke with longing. We talked until late.

Then, drowning in dread, I drove a half an hour back to my scullery maid gig. My dusty room swallowed me like a black tomb and I worried and itched through the night.

A deep depression held me in its demonic grip, and I could barely muster the energy to get out of bed the next morning. My hands and fingers ached from scrubbing and my sciatica sent painful spasms from my buttock, down my leg, and into my knee. Stabbing tendonitis and bursitis pains burnt in my shoulders, elbows and wrists.

I needed to get a real job. However, every listing I read required computer skills. I had tried practicing on the computer someone gave me, but I couldn't understand their strange language. So, I cleaned and dusted and polished with noxious furniture polish. Soaking and squeezing sponges over and over, and shaking Clorox onto filthy bathroom and kitchen surfaces, my hands became red and dry. The horrible smell was so assaulting, I felt like I could faint.

A few days later, Jyoti and I went to the temple and trimmed the hedges around the Hare Krishna greenhouse. Then, we went inside and watered the Tulsi plants. With tender appreciation of their mystical, healing powers, we talked to them as they drank in the sunlight pouring through the expansive, transparent roof. Suddenly, we were suspended in time. The moment seemed eternal, drenched in some force of divinity that carried us beyond the mundane world of sorrow. A shower of benevolent, unconditional love washed over us and work became play as we breathed in fresh oxygen. We laughed and sang old show tunes until we began to feel hungry.

It had been two hours, we discovered, with amazement, when we walked into the temple and looked at the clock on the wall.

A religious organization had never felt so much like home. I followed Jyoti to the kitchen. We served ourselves some vegetables and rice and sat down in the temple room. Cardamom, cumin and turmeric pleased my palette as I ate the healthy, blessed meal.

Across the room from us was a disheveled woman in tattered clothes. She was sitting in a chair babbling with a vacant expression. My muscles tensed as I observed this desperate being, barely surviving, living like a feral animal. The harshness of life had knocked every bit of spirit from her. Misery seeped from her. Feeling her wretchedness, I pondered that there was no happiness in this world.

I did not want to leave Jyoti but, remembering my responsibilities, I told her I had to go. She hugged me and said that she would ride the train to visit me.

With dread, I drove down the treacherous highway. When I arrived in the threatening neighborhood, I parked my car and hurried inside. Gloom defeated me as I sprawled listlessly in my bed, staring at the ceiling.

The next day, I scrubbed the bath tub and walls and wiped ten years of dust from tables and chairs. Working alone, I missed the serene solace of talking with Jyoti.

Weeks turned into months as I toiled. The boredom, grime and isolation deflated me and I moved lifelessly through the endless, painful hours.

Then, one day, Jane approached me with a grave look on her face.

"My daughter has started using drugs again. She's driving around in an insane delirium, hallucinating and talking to herself. I'm constantly worried that she might kill herself in a traffic accident. I'm going to have to bring Emily to live here. You will have to move out."

"I don't have anywhere to go." I reeled in dizzy terror.

"Here is a list of homeless shelters." She handed me a piece of paper and, as I stared at it, my heart raced.

I drove to Glendale in a frantic state. Parking in the only place I could find, I worried until my brain burned. A parking ticket would eat up my grocery money for the month.

Connie had told me that moving was good for depression, so I started sprinting past the fancy restaurants and shops. I had two and a half hours to kill before my therapy appointment. When I noticed a bookstore, I walked inside and began to browse. Leafing through various books, I marveled over the authors' elegant writing styles.

After a while, I was bored. I wanted to bust out and jump over a fence or climb a hill or something--anything that would wake me up and release me from my morbid prison of tension.

Putting the book in the wrong place, I quickly left the store. Walking at a brisk pace, I dodged the pedestrians who walked toward me. When I turned onto an empty street, I started sprinting, feeling invigorated. Memories of running around the track in college came back to me, and I longed for my youth, with its endless energy. After sprinting past a few buildings, I had to slow down to a walk.

I decided to go to the E.S.P. Academy. When I arrived, some children were doing arts and crafts with a psychic. Laughter peeled through the air and the fragrance of peppermint was pleasant. I sat down and, after a few minutes of silent meditation, I looked up. A dear woman, with brown, shoulder-length hair and brown eyes set in a heart shaped face, looked at me sweetly. She asked me if I would like a healing and I said I would.

She began moving her hands around my aura, sweeping away any cobwebs of negative thought. The sensation of being massaged moved through me.

After a glance toward my watch, I realized I must hurry to my therapy appointment. My thoughts scattered as I walked very quickly for ten blocks. Slowing down, I took in a deep breath. Then, staring at the ground like a zombie, I walked into my therapist's office. Slumping down in the chair, I told her my troubles in a monotone voice.

"Jane is not very nice. She could let you sleep on the sofa. She owes you at least thirty days' notice. You have been fulfilling your end of the agreement with her." I thirstily drank in her understanding.

"Yeah. I'm really hurt. I thought she was my friend."

"She is not being a friend. She's being very mean to you."

I walked to Jyoti's shack after my appointment. In numb disbelief, I told her I was homeless. She told me I could sleep on her floor. The concrete pushed into my back, irritating my already painful sciatica. Praying for deep sleep, I stared at the ceiling, feeling like a worthless failure.

The next morning, she gave me some oatmeal with banana pieces. She listened with sympathy as I told her I didn't want to face my landlord.

Forcing myself, I wished her a good day and walked to my car. Barbaric, angry, obscene music blared from cars as I sped down the hellish freeway.

Once I got back to the ghetto apartment, I creeped around sheepishly. Unable to sleep, I held my breath with fear and worried through the night.

The next morning, Jane confronted me in the kitchen. Her eyes were hard with contempt and she placed her hands on her hips with authoritarian toughness.

"This is not your home anymore."

I packed all of my belongings into my car and, then, told her farewell. None of her original friendliness remained, as she responded coldly, ready to get rid of me. Lovely, sweet memories of reading tea leaves flitted in my mind as I held back tears.

A mesmerizing, confusing mirage swam in my head as I drove in a fog, tortured by thoughts of being attacked by a drive by shooter. Soon, I arrived at my one safe sanctuary, the Krishna house. Jyoti's squalid shack was utterly claustrophobic and I wanted to stand on my parents' porch and look out at the vast expanse of rolling hills of the Golf Course.

However, I relaxed as she welcomed me. Serenity washed me, making me new and young again. She gave me rice and broccoli with almonds—after she offered it to Krishna on her altar.

"Krishna is looking after you. He knows that living in this world is difficult. We chant so that we can purify ourselves. When we become pure enough, we can live in the heavenly abode. We won't have to incarnate again and again on this planet and struggle with the misery of this world."

She gave me some rudraksha beads, seeds of trees in India, for counting the number of chants I did. Then she taught me the chant she did every day to elevate her soul. She explained that it erased her bad karma and caused her to evolve spiritually. Doubt sat in my sour soul and I stubbornly resisted.

When she suggested we go for a walk, I followed her gratefully out onto the sidewalk. I could barely hear her as she chanted Hare Krishna Hare Krishna Krishna Krishna Hare Hare. The words had no meaning for me so I remained silent. Absorbing the oxygen from the lush trees, I enjoyed her peaceful energy. Sun shone on the gorgeous, colorful flowers and I thought about the poet who said that nature laughs in flowers. It had been ages since I had laughed a real laugh.

That night, she gave me a blanket and pillow and showed me a little space where I could sleep. Her cold floor was hard and unforgiving. My back and shoulders ached.

The next day, Jyoti set up a table where I could paint. Then, she gave me a banana for breakfast. I looked through the window into the lush backyard and painted, enjoying Jyoti's compliment about my talent. Dipping my paintbrush into the bright colors and pulling them across the white page, I dreamily watched shapes form out of the pooling watercolors. It washed my worries away.

I remembered how my mother had set up paper and paints for me and showed me how to use complimentary colors. Her talent for painting water colors was remarkable. She had called me "special" because I was talented too. Grieving over the distance between us, both geographical and emotional, I longed for emotional closeness. I had called her on Mother's Day months and months ago, and she had not returned my call.

If only I had been warm toward her and shared my art, she would have felt close to me, I thought. However, she frightened me. She seemed to think I was the lowest of the low and she called me cruel, stupid, crazy, and pitiful. I felt worthless when she put me down.

Jyoti showed me the dolls she was creating. I sat on a metal chair, ducking underneath a closet worth of clothes hanging on a rope behind me. Feeling like a sardine in a can, I wondered how she tolerated the cramped room. We talked about our childhood experiences growing up with an alcoholic, our art classes and our trials with men. As she told me about her feelings and challenges, I felt as though I was listening to myself.

When I told her my mother had encouraged me to paint and draw, she showed me some charcoal drawings she had done. Her talent was remarkable and I told her so. Her face lit up as she talked about going to a prestigious art school when she was young.

It was getting close to lunch time. Looking like a bird balancing on a twig, she inched her way around her tiny, makeshift kitchen. The aroma of vegetables and rice filled the air and incense moved in fragrant spirals through the room, as I watched her make her offering to Krishna. He peered joyfully out of a gold frame, his divine face glowing as he played his magical flute. A celestial sound of clear, chiming bells rang through my ears, lightening my energy field. Then, with love, she gave me green beans with almonds, brown rice, broccoli and bitter melon.

In the afternoon, I decided to go to the E.S.P. Academy because they were having an event. I knew it would be full of laughter and fun. People smiled and greeted me when I arrived. I talked with a couple of people. My favorite teacher, the one who called me "Queen Sophia", greeted me with a hug. When I told her I wanted a reading, she pointed to a graduate of the clairvoyant program who I had never spoken with.

We made eye contact. He motioned me over to a chair and I sat down.

"I want to talk with my mother. She is very angry with me though and I haven't talked with her in a year and a half, since I moved here. Do you see our relationship improving?"

He tuned into my energy and started laughing. It was not a laughing matter to me, but I had gotten used to this response. All of the psychics laughed a lot.

"No. She is just not ready to forgive. She is angry about having mocked up your father and she has low self-affinity."

He was a handsome man and I felt jealous when he mentioned his wife, after we talked for a few minutes. Grief fell like cold rain through me as I slumped despondently and walked away. Feeling lost in a dark world of my own, I distantly observed others laughing and talking lightly. My somber face must be very unappealing to them, I thought, as I hung around the center for a while.

I attended a class at the E.S.P. Academy a few days later. The president gave a demonstration of how to see interfering entities who hang out in peoples' energy fields. He had me stand next to him. Then, he pointed out the earthbound spirits in a woman's energy field. Though I could not see them, I watched with fascination as he sent light to them, swept them up with his hands and guided them back to the divine light, the source they came from.

He let me guide the next earthbound spirit up into the light. With curiosity, I moved my hands, letting my healing master plug into my palms. Though I could not see the spirit, I felt a consciousness. I cupped my hands lovingly around the dear spirit and swept it up into the light, where it would be healed by the unconditional love of God.

As I walked back to Jyoti's, I missed my mother. I longed to be close to her like I had been years ago. There was deep love under the surface anger she expressed. I wanted to learn to understand and love her. I didn't know how hard it was for her to age, how much her body ached, or her nerves suffered overload because of her intensely difficult challenge of living with my father, the violent tyrant. I hadn't given her the love she needed, and had been distant and cold. No wonder she had exploded and ordered me out of her house.

My two siblings treated her with cruelty and I had not been there for her, to soothe her hurt feelings. She must have gone insane, after years of living without love. A tear rolled down my cheek.

I walked, past beggars and people playing guitars and saxophones, to the Krishna house. Knocking on Jyoti's door, I remembered my intention to build a new life and family. Her face lit up when she saw me, and she invited me in, appreciatively.

She pulled out some more old drawings she had done when she studied at the Philadelphia Art College. They were dark, charcoal portraits of people with tense expressions. Their eyes were widened as though they were inhabited by the demons that had tortured her. She had suffered a traumatic upbringing at the hands of her alcoholic, raging father, just like I had. Many stories told about Krishna destroying demons. I wished he had destroyed the demons in both of our fathers, before they hurt us when we were children.

We walked around the neighborhood and, then, came back to her shack and talked. That evening, after she offered it to Krishna, Jyoti handed me a plate of vegetables and rice. I imagined my mother's eyes were looking through Jyoti's.

The next day, I called my cousin, Carol. She told me that I would have to get subsidized housing. So, later that afternoon, I rode the bus to the subsidized housing office. Rows of chairs lined the sterile, glass and steel housing office. After a long wait, my number was called. A black woman, working behind the glass window, handed me some papers.

With laborious concentration, I wrote my name, address, telephone number, disability and income into the tiny boxes. Then, I shoved it the information through the hole in the glass. She said that thousands of destitute people were waiting for their homes, and they would all have to be served first, which would take three to four years.

That Saturday night, I met a friendly guy at a Vegetarian Society meeting. He asked me if I would like to date someone who was on a low income. When I replied "Yes," he said that he would give my phone number to him.

A week later, he called me. His name was Dan and, though he had never met me, he invited me to go to a party. His voice sounded respectful and intellectual.

He picked me up at Jyoti's place. He was slender and tall, with light brown hair and eyes and a sensitive, clear complexioned face. Smiling with sweet sincerity, he introduced himself. Jyoti smiled at him.

As he drove me to the party, he talked about his friends who believed in UFOs. Astonishing stories thrilled me as we went up and down roller coaster hills. I thought a woman in her mid-forties, like me, was considered unappealing by men. However, suddenly, I felt desirable. My ego enlarged as I imagined being a femme fatale who had men making me offers of luxurious, love filled marriages.

He parked on the curb and, then, came around and opened my door for me. Following him up some stairs, I admired his good manners.

The brightly colored, Victorian flat wailed with loud music and a cacophony of chatter. There was a lavish banquet spread over a big table and my mouth watered. I loaded a plate until it was heaped high with goodies. Following Dan, I walked into the kitchen where a lively man showed me several containers full of drinks, then filled my cup. The apple juice tantalized my taste buds. I felt fortunate that I had no desire for booze.

Dan introduced me to his friends. They were artists and intellectuals who sojourned to other dimensions in meditation. Some even claimed to have personally seen aliens. Their vibrant, intelligent conversation and laughter lifted my spirits and I wanted to stay all night.

Dan talked about how he composed and recorded music and played with a band. We listened to a tape of his music as he drove me home.

Wishing him a good night, I enjoyed his gentlemanly clasp of my hand. Opening the car door, I stepped onto the sidewalk in front of the Hare Krishna house. Then I walked to the gate and unlatched it. Knocking quietly on Jyoti's door, I listened for her, like a teenager looking forward to seeing her mother. The door creaked open and she greeted me with a smile, then asked me how my date had been.

With excitement, I told her about the fascinating people I had met, enjoying her undivided attention. When a long yawn made my eyes water, and drowsiness crept through my body, I told her I needed to go to sleep. Warmth washed my worries away as she hugged me. I covered myself with her blanket, rolled up my blue jeans to make a pillow and fell asleep on the floor.

Morning came and I felt disoriented and overwhelmed as I lay on my back like a beached whale. Yawning and stretching, I worried about my low checking account balance and the huge amount I owed my credit card.

Jyoti told me Krishna was protecting me and gave me some mango slices and water for breakfast. After we chatted for a while, I got dressed, grabbed my purse, and walked across the path to Bindu's. Waiting for her phone to be free, I read a book about herbal remedies.

Hope for my finances filled me as I called an elderly care agency. A stern sounding woman asked me questions for a while. I tensely answered, hiding the fact that I was on a fixed income.

She hired me. Her approval washed through me like champagne, splashing effervescence through me.

The following week, I started a daily routine of driving long distances to do elderly care.

A black fog of depression smothered my spirit as I went through the motions like a zombie--cleaning homes, driving the elderly to appointments, or emptying poop out of a foul smelling bag that hung out of the abdomen of a woman who had had digestive surgery.

Each day passed in a monotonous, somber tone. Deep insecurity dampened me as I did my duties, feeling drained of all life. I remembered the days of being silly and laughing, or going into hysterics as a friend tickled me. Because I had lost my ability to feel good, I couldn't even write a song or draw any more. I missed the carefree exuberance of the children.

Halloween came and excitement brought sparkle to my eyes because I had a date with Dan. Happy emotions lifted me as Jyoti painted my face. With a cute giggle, she placed a witch's hat on my head. Handing me a mirror, she admired her handiwork. As I studied my mysterious demeanor, she lit some incense and put it on her altar. Then, she rang a celestial sounding bell. As the fragrance floated into my nostrils, I imagined I was in one of the flower gardens my mother had taken me to when I was a child.

Soon, he arrived. He was dressed in blue jeans and a well-made blue and yellow print shirt. Birds chirped cheerfully as he greeted me. Then, he and Jyoti exchanged pleasant words. He said he enjoyed the aroma of the incense.

Following him to his car, I told him that Halloween had been my favorite day when I was in grammar school. Seeing outlandish characters roaming the streets and coming home with a pillow case full of candy had been thrilling. The chocolate bars, candy apples and caramel popcorn balls had been out of this world.

With sensitive enthusiasm, he talked about his friends as he drove to the party.

Once there, he and his friends talked about politics, metaphysics, and extraterrestrials with great knowledge and sophistication. I listened with shy curiosity until the barrage of rising voices became overwhelming.

I slipped away quietly and took solace in the overflowing banquet bar. As I munched on scrumptious treats, I searched my brain, or what was left of it, for something I knew that I could add to the conversation. Suddenly, my confidence was shaken by a memory of my mother.

"You don't know much, and that's a fact," she would say when I was in high school.

Remembering the tools that I had learned at the E.S.P. Academy, I imagined my insecurity dropping down my grounding chord into the center of the earth. Refusing to let it spoil my fun, I walked back to the group. Listening, in silent curiosity, I observed faces, styles and jewelry, feeling awed by peoples' incredible stories of their encounters with ETs.

Dan talked with light enthusiasm about his music composing and his band, as he drove me home to Jyoti. He played a tape that they had created and the pleasing tones moved me.

Contemplating that I was a failure in my romantic life as well as my professional life, I wondered what was wrong with me as I tried to sleep on the hard floor.

The next day, I walked to the E.S.P. Academy and got a healing from a woman with big, dark eyes and dark hair in a bun. She wore a colorful, butterfly necklace. When she sensed negative thoughts and emotions in my aura, she encouraged me to walk by the ocean and imagine the waves carrying my worries away. As her hands cleaned my energy field, I rose like a helium balloon, feeling lighter and lighter.

After a while, I thanked her and wished her a good evening. Walking toward the door, I saw a poster on the wall, announcing a class called "Why Am I Still Single?" It was based on a book I had read and liked called "The Rules".

When the evening for the class arrived, I ambled past pedestrians on the busy downtown streets, observing their faces and eccentric clothes. Arriving at the E.S.P. Academy, I bounded up the stairs. Fresh energy enlivened me, as I pulled open the door. The room scintillated with the light of healing spirits. Silence felt soft, like velvet, as I sat in a crimson cushioned seat, looking around at my class mates.

A woman, with curly, blonde hair and light blue eyes accented with kohl, introduced herself. Her sixties style, low cut peasant dress was colorful and pretty. Then, she asked how many attendees had read The Rules. I raised my hand.

She began discussing "The Rules", which described how to behave in ways so that men would marry you, instead of taking you for granted. No one had ever taught me how to handle men and I resented it.

"You're spending too much time with him," she commented, when I told her about the man I was dating.

I always said "Yes" when Dan asked me to go somewhere because I was complimented that he liked me and I enjoyed hiking and the other fun things that we did together. For the first time in my life, I was dating a real gentleman, going on more than one or two dates. I enjoyed getting to know him as a platonic friend. Though his financial situation was not much better than my own, he paid for everything. With a sincere desire to help me, he made copies of my CDs for me.

He took me hiking in breathtakingly beautiful areas. Tall Eucalyptus and Cedar trees reached their gnarled, friendly arms out to us as we walked briskly, enjoying breathing pure, fresh air and hearing the ecstatic trills of singing birds. Bright, colorful flowers painted our paths. The sky was vivid blue and radiant, with a dazzling sun which moved between fluffy, flowing clouds. With vulnerable sensitivity, he told me he shared his flat with a difficult landlord. Unfortunately, the West was too expensive to afford one's own place.

Soon, it was October, and a local church gave me an opportunity to exhibit photographs and paintings at a benefit to raise money for homeless people. Jyoti donated a design she had created. The mood was light as a cello player and flute player performed beautiful music. Jyoti looked happy to be out. With charm and enthusiasm, she talked with people.

Dan came for a short time. I imagined I was a sought after beauty, wishing I could be young and beautiful again and practice "The Rules" on many men. He sweetly complimented me on my paintings and photographs.

Introducing him to Jyoti, I smiled at her and touched her shoulder. He greeted her in a friendly way and she responded warmly. Pointing at her design, I told him she had created it and beamed proudly at her. He gazed at the mystical design, looking like he was contemplating.

We walked over to the snack table and munched on vegetables, fruits and cookies. Grateful that I had no desire for alcohol, I avoided the wine. Intent on being Vegan, I passed by the cheese. After a while, I stepped back from the people pooling around the snack table.

Dan came and stood by me. Looking fragile and sounding serious and sad, he told me that he had bone cancer and might die.

"I'm sorry." I replied, looking into his grieving eyes. Wishing I could say more, I felt grateful for the bitter sweet treasure of his company. Soon, he would dissolve into nothingness.

Jyoti's floor felt cold that night as embarrassment over my lifestyle filled me with the desire to hide from the world. I slept on her floor for about two weeks.

Then, she had to go out of town to visit her sick mother. Surya, her husband, did not feel comfortable staying there with me alone. She suggested that I sleep in the attic next door. Bindu, her next door neighbor, would take care of me she said.

When she left, I felt like I had lost my mother. Bindu showed me how to climb up the ladder in the ceiling into the attic. Piles of clutter lined every square inch of the dusty place. Books, boxes, clothes, skis, tennis rackets, and furniture stood in my way. I stumbled over it all until I arrived at a dusty mat by a window. Rolling into a fetal ball, I looked up at the huge pipes running the length of the ceiling. They were covered with silver wrapping and a fleece-like stuffing poked out of them at various places. An odor of sweat, dust and moldy rags assaulted my nose.

I tried to read a book but, soon, I was wheezing from asthma. Angrily pushing on the window, I mustered all my might but it wouldn't budge. Sneezing from the dust, a silent scream of anguish rose inside me. I couldn't bear the junk heap any longer. So, I climbed precariously down the ladder.

Walking around downtown Glendale, like a lost soul, I yearned for connection with someone. Looking at my calendar, I realized I had an hour before my therapy appointment started. I stopped by the E.S.P. Academy.

A teacher invited me to sit in front of her and receive a healing.

Tranquility flowed through me as she moved her hands around my aura. Time stood still as I floated in bliss. The liquid luster in her brown eyes healed me with its empathy.

Too soon, the session was done. I thanked her sincerely and wished her a great day. Looking at my watch, I realized I needed to hurry to my therapy appointment. Running down the sunny streets, observing eccentric characters curiously, I wondered if they were struggling like I was.

My therapist gave me a look of sincere concern as I walked into her office. I plopped down into the large, blue arm chair and slumped listlessly like a Raggedy Ann doll.

"I want you to start going to the Seaside Sanitarium day program. Sleeping on the floor has taken a toll on you. You'll get good counseling there, and it will give you some structure. You need someplace to feel safe and talk with people." Her furrowed brow and wide, motherly eyes reached me. However, I had been in the looney bin too many times.

Stubbornly, I resisted. Already, I had been in four hospitals and had been drugged into a stupor. It looked like spirituality had more to offer me than psychotherapy. How could I still be the same dysfunctional person I was, after the countless psychotherapy sessions I had gone through since I was seventeen?

I told my therapist I did not need to go there. In denial, I assumed I had the strength to keep living like a bum. However, I clung desperately to her, as her caring eyes breathed life into me.

After I left her, I plummeted into unbearable depression. Two weeks without Jyoti seemed like eternity.

My therapist saw me the day Jyoti came home. Her compassionate voice calmed me and I felt grateful for her totally attentive listening, as I talked about how much Jyoti cared for me.

After my session, I walked to her shack. I knocked three times and she let me in. Throwing her arms around me, she welcomed me. I sat in the metal chair under the ugly rope with clothes hanging on it.

Ringing her altar bell, she looked with devotion at Krishna in his gold frame. Her knee length hair swayed as she leaned down and lit an incense stick. The intoxicating fragrance swirled and curled through the air.

She stepped over to her refrigerator, knelt down, and took out a loaf of bread and some butter. A bird trilled as she spread butter on two pieces of bread. Her long earrings dangled prettily as she pushed the bread into the toaster oven. It made a clunking sound. Her soft voice calmed me as she talked about her time with her mother. The buttery bread tasted rich and the aroma lifted my mood.

Yawning and stretching, she told me she needed a nap. She reclined on her mat on the floor. I read her Bhagavad Gita while she slept.

After a couple of hours, she rose, looking energized.

"Would you like to take a bike ride?" Her voice rose with anticipation.

With delight, I told her I would. As I peddled her extra bicycle behind her, my hair flew in the breeze and a childlike joy lifted my spirits to the clouds.

When Friday arrived, we drove for about an hour to visit another Krishna devotee, called Ghandari. She greeted us with an open heart, looking so overjoyed to see me that I wondered why, when she barely knew me. We walked through her simple home and out onto her deck. I looked over a valley of tall trees with blue mountains on the horizon.

With gracious generosity, she served us tea and cookies at her round kitchen table. Her eyes conveyed extreme thirst for community as she said she wished she lived near us and could attend our temple. She was as devoted to Krishna as Jyoti was.

I immediately got along with her husband. He believed that space creatures were actively visiting Earth. Gripping my chair in astonishment, I listened to him talk about his experience watching an ET walk out of a space ship.

Ghandari had a petite, thin figure, an oval shaped, sensitive face and straight, light brown hair. With genuine caring, she asked me how I was doing. We talked for a while.

Then, the three of us took a trip to a five and dime store. Walking around, I had fun looking at toys, plastic flowers, household necessities, and bags of snacks--everything under the sun.

Her humility touched me when, later on, she served her husband greasy fried chicken which, I had heard from Jyoti, she could not stand to look at or smell.

Then, with a loving smile, she served us vegetable curry and samosas at a royally set table with fine plates and silverware and cloth napkins. The delicious Indian spices, in the home cooked meal, sent pleasure through my cells. A desert of soft pastries soaked in honey satisfied my sweet tooth.

At the end of our idyllic day, I dreaded driving back to the sin-filled city with its cruelty, violence and chaos. My guts turned over with angst as I waved goodbye.

Jyoti looked lovingly at me as I drove down the freeway. She talked happily about what a wonderful day it had been. I was touched by her efforts to act carefree, yet I could tell there was something bothering her. Finally, she got the courage to tell me that her husband criticized and yelled at her. She had left him for a year and he had refused to answer her letters. With resignation, she had decided to come back. She said that he wouldn't ever hit her because men in Glendale would get arrested if they hit a woman.

When we arrived at her shack, she invited me in. As she cooked broccoli, rice and carrots, she talked about Krishna and how much love he gives to anyone who asks. The fragrance of cumin and turmeric scented the air as I watched her offer the food to Krishna. I watched her light some incense. Inhaling the heavenly aroma, I relaxed. Meditating in silence, we gave gratitude to Krishna.

We laughed and talked, while eating the delicious food, and I relished the safe, secure feeling until late that night. Then, like the Hunchback of Notre Dame, I climbed up my ladder into my cell. Rolling into a fetal position on the thin, torn mat I felt a painful stab in my hip. My mind raced with worries the entire night.

The next morning, I walked five blocks to a place I had seen advertised. Looking at the cost on a sign, I realized I didn't have enough money to move in. Without Jyoti, I was sunk--no better than a smelly beggar sleeping on a park bench.

Walking back to her place, I felt embarrassed. Her welcoming smile was full of the approval I craved, and it eased my depression when she asked me to sit with her under the oak tree in the back yard. The day passed quickly as I sat and listened or sat in silence, feeling too overwhelmed to do anything else. Hearing about how difficult it had been for her to grow up with her raging, alcoholic father, I felt like her sister.

"When you grow up without a close, secure bond with your father, you are like a lost person, always looking for approval", she said. I agreed with her, and told her how lost I had always felt.

Later, when she asked me to watch a funny movie with her and Surya, I looked forward to forgetting my worries.

When Surya got home from teaching a child how to play the harmonium, he put a movie into the VCR, saying he had seen it before but wanted to see it again because it was so funny. Their laughter rang through the room as the characters on the screen did their crazy antics, but I couldn't laugh a real belly laugh.

When the movie ended, I thanked them for their hospitality and stepped out into the darkness. Watching my steps carefully, I walked into the yard. Standing beside the ancient, magnificent oak tree, I gazed up into the twinkling stars, feeling mesmerized by their beauty and the unlimited nature of the universe.

Then, I walked back to my attic home. Even though I was exhausted, I was unable to sleep because the dust irritated my eyes and my mat smelled awful. Big wads of insulating material hung from the aluminum pipes on the ceiling and I thought about all the toxins they must contain. I cleared my throat, longing for fresh, clean air to breathe, wishing I could open the window.

In the morning, I went downstairs and tried to energize myself enough to call rental advertisements. I had to wait for Bindu's phone to be available, which was rarely. After waiting about an hour, I called the number of an ad in the rental section of the newspaper.

A kind, responsible-sounding woman talked with me. I told her that I received a government disability check and braced myself for her rejection. Much to my surprise, she asked me to come interview at 6 p.m. the next evening.

In the afternoon, I walked through the streets of Glendale with Jyoti, listening to her chant. She encouraged me to chant along with her, saying it would destroy my negative karma.

The next day I laughed, like a child, with Bindu and a friend she had known for years. After an hour passed in light, playful fun, I told them I must leave and go to an interview.

My muscles tensed with fear as I walked through the busy streets. Soon, I recognized the street corner I was looking for. A muscular man, tattooed man charged by in a tornado of angry energy. I whiffed the pungent smell of marijuana coming from a door across the street. Pulling open the black, steel door, I winced at the hostile graffiti on the walls and crept up the dirty stairs, gripping the railing with trepidation.

A nice looking woman with shoulder-length, light brown hair and pretty dark eyes greeted me. I sat down at the kitchen table of her modest, but immaculate one story flat.

"I don't mind renting to people who are on disability, because I know they have regular income. I work for the city transportation system, and I leave for work at five in the morning. I get home around three o'clock. You'll have plenty of privacy, and this is a good, safe area. You can knock on my door if you ever want to talk."

"I appreciate that. I'm still getting my bearings, even though I've lived here for almost two years."

"I leave for my job at five in the morning and I get home at four in the afternoon so you will rarely see me. My job is demanding and I rest when I get home. I have a twenty five year old son. He has problems and he started using drugs. He left home because of my husband's violent behavior. My husband drank too much and went into rages. He tried to kill me."

A rush of horror went through me. How did she function so well, going to work every day like she did? How did she manage to relate to me with such politeness and stability? At a loss for words, I bowed my head in sympathy for a few moments.

"I'm sorry you went through that. And it must be hard working and being a mother."

"Being a mother is a thankless job. I'm just glad I get paid and I can have my peace and quiet."

"It's terrible what alcohol does to people. It turns them into monsters. My father used to drink too much when I was growing up."

"Yeah. Many people are out of control and they damage others", she said. We talked a while longer and, then, she told me she needed to finish something she was working on.

I told her goodbye and she wished me the best.

The next day, I went to Bindu's apartment. She had given me a key and asked me to keep her altar decorated with fresh flowers every day and assist her in preparing for the weekly feast. Carrying flowers I had bought at the local market, I unlocked the door. Looking around the small room, I admired the photograph on the wall of the sacred cows in India, whom

Bindu supported. She had asked me to vacuum and I noticed the vacuum in the corner, leaning up against the wall. Just as I leaned down to plug it in, a loud cry of agony came from Bunny.

His cries became more frequent and desperate, as I searched the living room and kitchen for a telephone book. Finally, I found one and flipped through it with trembling hands. When I saw a listing for a veterinarian on nearby Pine Avenue, I wrote down the address and phone number.

Luckily, I saw a cat carrier when I looked into Bindu's room. Opening the door, I carried it toward Bunny, and put him inside. His wails became more desperate.

Carrying him to my car, I prayed for the animal angels to protect and revive him. As I drove through the streets, he continued to cry. Luckily, I arrived on Pine Avenue soon. Scanning the businesses, suspense and fear for his sweet life overcame me. He could die any minute and poor Bindu would be shattered to lose the love of her life. She often told me how much love Bunny gave her.

Hope filled me as I saw the Veterinarian sign. Pulling to the curb and parking, I breathed a deep sigh of relief. Bunny cried as I lifted him out of the car and carried him into the veterinarian.

A woman checked me in and took Bunny back to the Emergency room. Then, I called Bindu on my cell phone. She was distraught and so concerned about poor Bunny that she arrived very quickly. A worker led her back to the Emergency room and she spoke about him with the veterinarian.

After taking some medication for a few days, Bunny was his old, happy self again. Bindu was overjoyed. Every time she saw me, she praised me for saving his life. Being a hero felt wonderful.

Days sped by like flashes of lightning and Thanksgiving arrived. I moved my few belongings into my new flat.

Amy was glad to see me at my next therapy session. I told her I had seen her walking with her seeing-eye dog. Then, I proudly told her that I had found an apartment.

"Well, congratulations. You have really been working hard, and you owe yourself a pat on the back. I think it will help you to start going to the Seaside Sanitarium day program. There are very fine counselors there who will talk with you and help you stabilize. And some medicine would really help you. I hope you will change your mind and start taking some."

"I don't want to take it because it is artificial and it gets stuck in the cells of the body. I'd rather take Saint John's Wort because it is natural."

"Well, Prozac is the same thing as Saint John's Wort. It is just more concentrated so it works faster and better." Though she was blind, she looked into my eyes with genuine caring.

"Okay. I'll think about it." Stubbornly, I changed the subject.

I told her I enjoyed being with Dan, the man I was spending time with. However, I worried that he might feel resentful that I wasn't giving him sex.

"You can decide if you want to be friends or if you want to be more. You have the power to communicate that, and you do not owe him sex or romance. You can tell him that you just want to be friends. He is getting something out of the friendship too," Amy explained in a caring tone.

Dan and I continued to go to art shows and UFO meetings that his friends had. After we had been dating for about two months, I told him he talked too much. With an utter lack of diplomacy, I had tried to meet my need to be listened to.

I didn't hear from him for a week. So I called him, which was totally against "The Rules". He was angry and he asked me why I was calling him, in an offended voice. Then, he told me how unappreciative and insensitive I had been. I realized that I needed to learn some social skills. Unable to bear my isolation any more, I walked down the street and enrolled in the Seaside Sanitarium Day Program.

The counselors were good listeners. When my doctor, who did not listen to me, wrote prescriptions for Lithium and Celexa, I started taking them obediently. However, I worried as a fellow patient told me a horror story. His kidneys had stopped working because he took too much Lithium.

The counselors told me to not make any major decisions when I told them I couldn't decide whether or not to go back to East.

"You're here now. Why not just stay here since you're here?" a kind, African-American woman said.

I enjoyed Art Therapy and Dance Therapy. In Dance Therapy, I walked around with the other patients, acting like a tiger, a bird, a frog, and so on, and feeling like a child again. Maybe I was being reborn like the psychic had once said. I'd discovered a new frontier which was unlike any place I'd ever imagined. I was letting go of the old, and bringing in the new. I heard the psychic's voice in my head:

"You're going to be shedding lots of old snake skins of the old Sophia."

However, in truth, I was going nowhere--just flapping around like a bird in a booby hatch.

Fortunately, I received fantastic food at the day program. Every morning, I sprung out of bed looking forward to vegetables, salad, soup, soft, baked potatoes with butter and sour cream, fruits, cakes and pies and ice cream.

"You're getting calmer and more relaxed every day," the sweet, blonde counselor told me. The attention and approval I received was grounding and stabilizing.

I couldn't sleep that night on my uncomfortable futon from Goodwill. So, I decided to change my negative thoughts to positive. Thoughts of the kind Rastafarian guy who had carried it up the stairs for me filled me with love and good feelings. I had told him I would pay him twenty dollars for helping me lug it up the long staircase into my room. Then, I had realized I didn't have twenty dollars.

After his hard work, he had not even asked for his payment. Instead, he had gently wished me the best of everything, then turned and walked away peacefully. There were good, giving men.

When I got out of the Seaside Sanitarium at three p.m. every day, I walked to Jyoti's. In that safe atmosphere, I was able to paint with a flowing confidence. I did a few paintings I liked one afternoon.

Walking home, I noticed a charming art shop on the main street of Glendale. Pulling open the door, I admired the unusual paintings. Talking with me in a friendly manner, the gallery owner showed me around.

The next day, I brought her my paintings. The thrill of success lifted me to the clouds, when she said she would display them. Spending the evening with Jyoti and Surya, I let go of my depression as we watched funny movies and laughed.

Never wanting to leave, I would force myself to go. Then, I would speed walk the entire way, clutching the pepper spray Jyoti had given me for dear life.

One evening, I froze in silent hysteria as a muscular, black man, who looked like a gang member, glared at me. Trembling pathetically, I pulled open the metal burglar door and ran up the stairs. As soon as I reached my room, I locked the door, slumped down onto the uncomfortable futon and stared into space, feeling myself unraveling inside. My mind felt scattered in a million different directions. I held my breath. Trying to get some sleep, I tossed and turned through the night.

Around six a.m., the raucous sound of huge trucks, barreling by outside, rattled through my brain and shook me to the core. The radio played a pop song when my alarm went off. "Should I Stay or Should I Go?" the singer repeated. The lyrics pounded through my brain, rattling my nerves. I raked my hands through my hair and shuffled to my cloth, dime store closet to find something to wear. Pulling on my nicest outfit, I looked forward to getting to the Seaside Sanitarium.

I walked through the bathroom and out into the hallway. In a depressed limbo, I baby stepped my way timidly down the stairs. Shuddering, as I walked out of the wrought iron door and onto the street, with my legs weakening underneath me, I feared I would lose my balance. Moving quickly, holding my breath, I hurried past beggars and tough, muscular men. The door was never locked. Any crazy criminal could walk straight up the stairs into my room. I imagined soaking in the big, claw-footed tub some evening when, suddenly, a man, who was out of his mind on drugs, thundered in and raped me savagely and then stabbed me to death.

Cars rumbled by, athletes jogged by and successful looking people walked dogs. Plugging my nose as I smelled car exhaust, I quickened my pace, eager to step into safety. Walking quickly into the building, I ran up the stairs. I needed an aerobics workout.

The friendly greetings of counselors and patients relaxed me and I enjoyed another good day at the Seaside Sanitarium. Drawing and pasting magazine pictures on paper, I expressed my fears and hopes. At group therapy, I talked about my nightmares about getting attacked by gang members who were high on drugs.

The next day, I noticed a Salvation Army across the street, I walked in and asked them what services they offered. A kind woman told me they gave out food boxes every Thursday. It would save me a lot of money.

Then, I walked around in a confused fog trying to find my car. While I wandered up and down the streets, a man noticed me and asked if I was okay.

"I've lost my car. I can't find it anywhere," I told him. I felt overwhelmed with confusion.

"You'll find it!" His eyes beamed caring concern.

After wandering for about half an hour, I did finally find it. I wanted to yell in rage when I saw a thirty-five dollar ticket on it.

Immense relief came over me when I reached the Seaside Sanitarium. The group therapy calmed me as the counselors and patients listened respectfully and responded with compassion to my worries. Feeling their pain, I observed their individual faces and behaviors. They all seemed like they had been hit with something like a freight train. Now, like me, they tiptoed through life, doing their best to avoid trauma and to please people. Just making it through the day was all we could expect of ourselves.

Laughing and talking with my fellow loonies, as I ate a delicious lunch, I became lighter. When it was over, I went to art therapy. Cutting pictures from magazines and making collages, I felt my pain leaving me as I expressed it on paper. At the end of the day, I didn't want to leave.

Walking down the flower bordered sidewalks, I looked forward to the friendliness of the devotees. Soon, I opened the red door of the Krishna temple. Priya stood there, looking angelic in her white sari. Feeling desperately afraid of what was becoming of me, yearning to have a normal life, I confided in her. I asked her if going back East would help me to get my feet back on the ground.

She invited me to sit with her in the room she slept in. A bunk bed stood against a windowed wall. After scanning the tiny room curiously, I watched her sit down on the bottom bunk. The Bhagavad Gita and other spiritual books filled a dark, wooden book case. Her blue eyes calmed me as we talked. I told her about my many drives across the country, and my activities at the E.S.P. Academy, and at the Seaside Sanitarium. Relaxing into the comfort of her kind voice, I let go of my fears. She told me she was going to have a talk with Krishna about my problems.

After an hour or so, she said she needed to do chores and prepare for her trip to visit her mother. I left reluctantly.

It seemed like forever as I struggled through ten lonely days without her.

Finally, my luck changed and I felt Krishna blessing me as I sat in my ghetto listening to traffic roar by. It was Saturday and I was free. I decided to walk to the Hare Krishna Temple and talk with Priya. She smiled, like an angel of love, when I walked in.

"Krishna told me you belong back East. I told him your problem.

Don't worry. He is the master psychic. You don't need to listen to any other psychics." She squeezed my hand reassuringly.

I got into the serving line. Several devotees filled my plate with rice, vegetables and beans, smiling sweetly. Sitting down at a table, I looked around for Priya. Breathing in love, I savored the moment as she sat across from me. Looking into my eyes, she sent healing balm through my cells.

"Krishna sent you here, and he will get you home. He thinks you're special and he knows you will be happier there."

The Indian spices were delicious. Priya's serene face massaged my heart, as we sat together, saying few words but basking in the joy of companionship. Like Glenda, the good witch, she filled me with good feelings. This place of love had stolen my heart.

CHAPTER FIVE

"Let your 'Yes' mean 'Yes' and your 'No' mean 'No.'" Matthew 5:37

"By your words you will be acquitted, and by your words you will be condemned." Matthew 12:37

When in doubt about what to say, say words of love.

"When you go beyond the consciousness of this world, knowing that you are not the body or the mind, and yet aware as never before that you exist--that divine consciousness is what you are. You are That in which is rooted everything in the universe."
Paramahansa Yogananda

He who sees all beings in the Self, and the Self in all beings, hates none. To the illumined soul, the Self is all. For him who sees everywhere oneness, how can there be delusion or grief?
Isha Upanishad

The next Monday morning, I hurried down the street toward the Seaside Sanitarium, eating a Cliff Bar I had bought at Walgreens. Observing smartly dressed, business people, I rode the elevator up to the psychiatric ward. The counselors looked at me with concern as I walked in and sat down in the circle of neurotic patients.

They talked about various problems they were having. One woman fidgeted nervously, as her face twitched in strange ways. Another woman stared blankly ahead as though some unspeakable trauma had knocked the life out of her.

"How are you doing today, Sophia?" the counselor leading the group asked.

"I'm glad to be here. I'm still feeling frightened and having trouble sleeping and I'm thinking about driving back east."

"Don't make any major decisions. You need to take one day at a time and be gentle with yourself. You've made a lot of progress since you've been here. You are much more relaxed and centered than you were when you came in. Give yourself some credit for the progress you're making." Her blue eyes shone with compassion.

I soaked up the soothing company until group therapy ended. Then, I rode the elevator down to the cafeteria. Today they were serving delicious soup, salad, chicken and roast beef. A feeling of wellness came over me as I munched with delight, talking with several kind-hearted patients.

Later on, in dance therapy, we pranced, jumped, spun and swayed with abandon. Moving my body made me feel alive and more grounded. When one of the patients asked if I was going to go back East, I stared blankly, saying nothing.

"I don't think so," the dance therapist said, speaking for me.

I remembered the psychic talking about how I would shed my old snake skins and transform. Determination strengthened my resolve. It was not like me to cop out and run like a weakling. I was a strong, independent Aries.

The rest of my week at the Seaside Sanitarium went well, as I feasted on the attention from counselors and patients, ate like a queen and expressed myself in art and dance therapy.

That Sunday, I took a bath in the big, claw-footed bath tub. The hot water relaxed my muscles. They'd been tensely coiled all night because I had suffered through a nightmare about a gang breaking in to rape and murder me.

Just as I was lathering my body and head with shampoo, my body jumped defensively.

Bang, bang, bang. A loud knocking on the door sent a wave of terror through me.

"I've got to use the bathroom," a threatening, deep, male voice said.

"I'll be out in five minutes", I blurted, desperately, pulling myself over the high edge of the tub. Stepping over to the towel rack I pulled a towel off of it.

"If you're not out of there in five *seconds*, I'm gonna come in and throw you out!"

I clutched my towel around me and ran into my room, then shut the door and locked it behind me. Sitting on the edge of my futon trembling, I wiped my nose with my hand, as it ran like Niagara Falls. Feeling like I might faint, I stood up and put on the wooly, purple bath robe and socks that my cousin had sent me, when I told her I had no heater. Holding my arms around myself for comfort, I felt trapped.

Depression weighed me down so heavily, I wanted to die. With trembling hands, I pulled some clothes out of my closet and got dressed. Then, I turned the door knob but it wouldn't budge. I was locked inside my own room. Frantically, I picked up my cell phone and dialed 911.

Soon, an officer arrived, looking official in his immaculate uniform and sparkling badge. Like a wandering dog, I ravenously consumed the look of concern on his face.

"This is not a good situation. Do you have to walk through this bathroom to get into your room? How many people do you share the bathroom with?"

"My landlord and the guy in the room next to mine. A guy I've never met threatened that he was going to come in and throw me out if I didn't hurry."

"This is not safe. If there was a fire you wouldn't be able to get out."

"Yeah. I don't feel comfortable here. I'm afraid of men."

"Are you on benefits?"

"Yes." I blushed and looked down, burning with shame.

"I hate to say this, but you're doing this to yourself. It's like saying I'm

Kundalini Rising

afraid of trains, and then laying down on some train tracks. I wouldn't live here if I were you."

He said he hoped my situation would improve soon. I thanked him and watched him walk down the stairs.

The next morning my landlord talked with me with an urgent look on her face.

"Don't ever tell the police that I live here or that my son stays here. They are trying to find him because they caught him with just a small amount of marijuana. They put a note on my door, and they're trying to get me to call them, but I won't talk to them. They have no right to hassle me or my son."

"Okay." I couldn't wait for Monday morning to arrive as I sat on my bed twiddling my thumbs, worrying or staring into space.

When it finally came, I hurried down the raucously rumbling street, past beggars and murderers, to the Seaside Sanitarium.

The welcoming words of patients and counselors brought me back to life as I sat down in the group. When my time to talk came, words tumbled, in a disjointed way, out of my mouth.

"I can't sleep. I'm so frightened all the time. Then, in the morning, I'm too depressed to get out of the bed."

"I think you should sue that landlord," the gentle, brown haired man who had gotten kidney damage from his Lithium said.

"She's expecting you to live with no lock on the door. You have drunks and gang members outside. Her son threatens you, and you get locked inside your room. You have to walk through a bathroom to get into your room. You can sue her."

My fellow patients agreed with him and they offered me their sympathy.

The rest of the day was calming and fun. We did art therapy, and I ate from a fabulous salad bar that had soup, vegetables, meat, Jell-O, ice cream, cake, and pie.

After the day program, I walked past beggars, sidewalk preachers, people selling incense, sitting on blankets and musicians performing. When I arrived at Jyoti's shack, I saw an orange clad Krishna devotee pacing around, going from the entry path to the back yard. Sitting under the shade of the magnificent oak tree, I listened to his eloquent monologue.

"Where is the happiness? No one is happy. Look around. *No one* is happy. We've got to return to Godhead. We've got to get back to the peaceful, loving world that Krishna created for us. We've got to chant non-stop and get ourselves out of this Kali Yuga. This is hell. Only the blessings of Krishna will save us. Let Krishna into your heart. He loves you. He's with you always."

I got up and walked to Jyoti's door. She welcomed me in and I sat and talked with her and Surya. I felt depressed when Surya said that "Hell on Earth" was supposed to last for another two thousand years.

Later, we all watched a funny movie together. Then, I slept on the floor next to the painting table Jyoti had set up for me.

Jyoti gave me granola and fruit the next morning. I wondered where I would be without her love. We talked about chanting, being vegetarian and being spiritual. When I told her my Indian group had told me I had to be celibate the rest of my life, she responded that Hare Krishnas are allowed to marry and that that Indian group was very strict. She was glad when I told her they had convinced me to be vegetarian.

After a while, I told her I would like to visit with Bindu. I stepped across the narrow walkway and knocked on Bindu's door. She welcomed me in and we sat and talked for a while.

"I'm proud of you for finding a place. I know the attic was hard to stay in. I don't think you're crazy like your family told you. I don't even think you need SSI. My cousin gets that but she talks like a retard. She's not smart and talented like you. I think you'll return to Godhead after this life. You'll progress spiritually faster if you chant." Her sincere wish for my wellbeing resonated in her voice, yet I resisted.

I didn't like her trying to convert me, so I changed the subject. We talked about the joys of being vegetarian. She told me about her family back in New Jersey and her old boyfriend. He had hurt her by covering his walls with photographs of beautiful Playboy models and ignoring her. We both expressed our disappointment with the men we had dated.

She showed me a hilarious, male doll that talked. He was called "Mr. Wonderful" and he said things like, "Let me take you shoe shopping!" and "How can I help you?' and on and on. We broke into uproarious laughter as we listened to him, and the afternoon glowed with the magical spirit of care free play. It reminded me of days with my grammar school friends.

After a while, I told Bindu goodbye. Her adorable white cat, Bunny, rubbed himself against me as I opened the door.

Walking home, I prayed to be safe. A drunk man leered at me as I walked

Kundalini Rising

to my unlocked, iron gate. Climbing up the dirty, depressing stairway, my whole body strained as it fought with fatigue. My silence gloomily mocked me as I gripped the railing, dreading another night of loneliness. It was cold.

Plopping down onto my bed, I wanted to die. My spirit had been broken and I wanted to go to the dimension of peace that the Krishnas talked about. Shivering, I pulled the bed cover around me. I had found a heater on the curb when I was walking with Jyoti and I hoped it wasn't defective. If it caught on fire, I could be consumed by flames in no time because I wouldn't be able to escape if anyone had locked the bathroom door.

Too frightened to plug it in, I pushed it into the corner. Shivering, as I rummaged through the clothes in my plastic closet, I found the purple robe my cousin had sent me and put it on.

Shadows from passing cars flitted through me, reminding me that life was passing me by. Imagining my cousin was hugging me, I held my arms tightly around myself. Pulling the covers over me and laying back in my bed, I held my knees to my chest and rocked myself back and forth, wishing I was a peaceful fetus in a warm womb.

Morning came with a loud, overwhelming roaring of trucks. Listlessly, I looked through my clothes in the ugly, portable, plastic closet and got dressed. Ugliness seemed to be infusing itself into every large pore of my face as I gazed into the mirror horrified. I longed to be a sexy lady married to a well off man.

A truck lumbered down the street and almost blew me over with its force. Ducking, on trembling legs, into Walgreens, I wandered up and down the aisles in a lost daze and observed the various items. I could buy anything and everything under the sun here. Remembering my father's wise advice about saving, I thanked him for teaching me to spend little. Pulling a Cliff Bar from a shelf, I longed for a break from eating the same breakfast every day.

The cashier rang up my Cliff Bar, and I looked at my receipt. Fortunately, I was getting extra money from the government because I had no kitchen. Yet, still, I checked my balance obsessively at an ATM machine in downtown Glendale because parking tickets were gobbling up my bank balance.

I walked around the neighborhood trying to find my car. There were so many white Toyotas, it seemed like I would never find it. When I did, I groaned when I saw yet another thirty-five dollar ticket under my wiper blade.

I dreaded standing in line at City Hall to give them my food money. Already, I had been through this ordeal twice. This cruel, greedy city was determined to starve me to death. It would be one less backward, ignorant, southern immigrant that the Vegans would have to be bothered with. Why didn't they just become cannibals and cook me? Then they could eat me, covered with some delicious sauce made of herbs and fruits. I ran through the streets of downtown Glendale in a tornado of rage.

My panicked breathing steadied when I arrived at the Seaside Sanitarium. The welcoming words of the counselors and friendly smiles of patients felt like pure water after journeying through a desert. Relieved, I sat down for group therapy.

"Remember, no major decisions. You need to take one day at a time. Be gentle with yourself," the pretty, blonde counselor with sweet eyes said.

After lunch, my doctor called me in for an appointment. His serious face behind his heavy eyeglasses intimidated me. He began to speak in a strong, commanding tone, with an authoritative look in his eyes.

"You are going to have to start taking medication, or you're going to have to leave the program."

"I don't like taking it. I've done all right without it for over twenty years."

"Well, you need medication in order to stabilize, and you need to accept our help. If you won't cooperate, you're just wasting our time and your time." His voice was stern.

"Okay. I'll take it," I agreed humbly.

As soon as the day program ended, I speed-walked through downtown Glendale to the courthouse. I wanted to rant and rave and tear the room to pieces as I stood in line with the other beleaguered people. The corrupt, power hungry, money mongers in the heartless establishment were ruining the lives of innocent, hard-working people. Why didn't they pick on the rich people? They never gave parking tickets to the millionaires who lived in the hills.

After about a half an hour of standing in line, I finally got to speak to a clerk. She told me what I owed. My heart galloped frantically as I wrote out a check for three hundred and fifty dollars. One Cliff Bar was all I could afford for the next three weeks.

The next morning, I drove the long distance to the public chiropractic clinic to get my frozen shoulder cared for, feeling like a corpse.

I arrived at the clinic and parked. After waiting for half an hour, the young student who was treating me called me into his office. I told him I was going to the Seaside Sanitarium and taking medication.

"What? You're taking Celexa and Lithium? That stuff is poison. If you're depressed, it's not because you don't have enough Celexa in your system. How long have you been taking it?" His brows furrowed with horrified compassion.

"Two weeks."

"Luckily, that's not long enough for it to start doing damage to your body. If you stop taking it now you'll be all right."

"Okay. I'll stop taking it and I'll lie to my doctor."

My mind bounced back and forth like a ping pong ball. Maybe I was a fool. After all, those MDs were well trained, and they knew a lot about brain chemistry and the neurotransmitters that affected mood. I heard my father's voice in my head.

"You should be grateful that doctors invented medicine that stabilizes you." He was a world renowned medical doctor, an expert in his field.

Yet, I knew in my gut how lousy their miracle drugs had always made me feel. The explanation that I had heard about how synthetic drugs formed toxic build up within the cells and hardened them made sense to me.

"Don't go to a chiropractor," my father had warned me. "Chiropractors are quacks."

As I drove home, I made up my mind. The chiropractor was right, and the medical doctor was wrong.

After an hour and a half, I finally arrived. I parked my car, tense with worry that I might get yet another thirty-five dollar parking ticket. Not able to find a place that didn't have a two-hour limit sign near it, I parked anyways. Hurrying through the dark streets, I glanced around nervously.

Arriving at my hovel, I trembled with fear as I looked around for gang members. I squeezed the railing as I walked up to my room. The ugly graffiti reminded me of all the violence in the world.

My dismal, barren room vibrated with a grim essence of ghosts and sadness. Desperately pining for a soft touch, I pulled the sheets and blankets around me. Hugging myself, I tried to fall asleep. Then, throughout the black night, like a pendulum, I swung back and forth between deep sleep and awakening from a frightening dream.

I was awoken by the sound of my phone ringing. My spirits rose when I heard the sweet voice of my ballroom dance teacher, Kay, who I had not seen in a long time. There had been a painful hole in my life since I lost her fun class and her friendly, welcoming ways.

"I've got a free ticket for you to go to a self-growth seminar. You can bring a friend of yours for free. The seminar works on your subconscious beliefs and reprograms you so you can get what you really want."

"Wow. I need that." I didn't tell her I was attending the Seaside Sanitarium.

"Great. If you can drive us all down there, I'll give you and your friend a ticket and we can split the cost of the hotel room. We'll have a great time."

Jyoti lit up like a lantern when I invited her. We both needed a big dose of self-empowerment. People had belittled us and we needed to break free of our lack of self-confidence.

The morning of our trip arrived. Feeling lighthearted, we made peanut butter and jelly sandwiches and packed them in a bag with fruit and nuts. Jyoti filled a milk bottle up with water. We both took a bag with a few clothes—just the bare essentials.

Jyoti looked at me protectively as I drove us across the long bridge over the ocean and into Santa Rita, feeling like a time traveler. It was like a trip back to the past: my naive twenties. Trolley cars rumbled along, clanging bells. The old, familiar feelings of suspense descended upon me as I drove up an unbelievably steep hill to Kay's flat, praying I wouldn't roll backwards. What a city. It was enchanted in some ineffable way.

Honking the horn, I watched the door of her flat and, soon, her cheery face popped out, encircled with a red scarf. Kay greeted me with light hearted excitement, as she sat down in the passenger seat next to me. She had said she hoped Jyoti would not try to convert her. I had reassured her that she wouldn't.

The ride took about three hours. The mood was peaceful and light as we chatted. I spoke mainly with Kay. Jyoti sat silently in the back seat.

When we arrived at the hotel, I was delighted by the opulence and beauty. I imagined I was a millionaire as I stretched out on the comfortable, well-padded bed covered with expensive linens and many fluffy, soft pillows. Admiring the gold framed mirror and the colorful paintings, I imagined calling room service and ordering food and drink whenever I had the inclination. Then, I luxuriated in a long, relaxing bubble bath.

With excitement, we ate some food we had brought with us the next morning. Then, we rode the elevator down and walked to the seminar room.

The leader of the seminar was handsome, enthusiastic and warm, and he spoke persuasively. As he talked us through hypnotic processes, designed to allow us to leave our baggage behind and open up to new possibilities for our lives, desires bubbled within me. They multiplied as I wrote them in a hardbound journal the instructor gave me.

"What do YOU want? Forget about what your mother or your teacher or your friend wants. YOU are number one and only YOU can make yourself happy! You CAN have what you want." He gesticulated with passion and his voice was full of conviction and encouragement.

I wanted to stop moving around like a nomad, running myself ragged and wasting my precious energy. I wanted love, laughter, joy, touch, creativity, energy, passion, and aliveness. I wanted to accomplish great things and feel good about myself. Most of all, I wanted to never have to pay rent again.

Jyoti sat next to me, and I glanced at her wants list. There was only one item listed: "To serve Krishna." I worried that she thought the seminar was too materialistic.

The teacher did a hypnosis session. When that was over, we formed groups and expressed what we wanted more of and less of.

When the seminar ended for the day, I walked with Kay and Jyoti to the hotel room, pondering about what I wanted. One thing I wanted was to become a good Tarot card reader. Kay and I sat together on the bed, and I gave her a Tarot reading.

"I want a lover," she said, looking wistful. I empathized with her, thinking about how nice it would be to have money and love and affection for the rest of my life. The cards had positive messages for her, though they did not promise a lover, and she smiled as I explained them to her. We talked and laughed until midnight.

Then, I fell into the bed. Jyoti slept on the floor, even though I repeatedly asked her to share the heavenly, queen sized bed with me. It was the least she could do for herself after sleeping on her thin mat on the cold, hard floor for eternity. She didn't love herself enough. I pondered about how sad it was that people limited themselves and let religious rules stifle them. She lived like a refugee because the Hare Krishnas were supposed to be detached from the material world.

When I woke up, Kay was dressed and cheerful, excited about the day. Jyoti pulled on her long dress. Then, we pulled bananas, bread and peanut butter out of our bag and ate it for breakfast.

Enthusiasm flowed through me as we walked into the seminar room. Soon, the tall, dark, handsome leader walked onto the stage.

"Hang out with millionaires if you want to be rich. You can have everything you want."

I dreamed about what my ideal day would be like. It would include ultimate freedom: the joy of never worrying about being evicted. As the hypnotist spoke with passion, faces glowed with hope.

"Don't focus on what you're moving away from. Focus on what you want to move toward. The past is gone, and you can't change it. Release it, and focus on the present moment. That is where your power is. You create your reality by the thoughts you think. Think about what you want as though you have it now."

At the end of the seminar, everyone broke a board in half with the side of their hand to prove that they could do anything if they believed they could. When I broke my board in half, a feeling of omnipotence filled me.

Kay and I talked with happiness as we walked back to the hotel room. Jyoti shyly spoke now and then. Diving into my soft pillows sent me into serenity and I enjoyed a catnap. Then, I relaxed in a bubble bath, imagining having all my dreams come true.

Kay and I propped ourselves up on the big, fluffy pillows and talked about the day. After a while, I started yawning.

Sleeping deeply for more than eight hours, it was as though I was floating on a peaceful cloud.

As I climbed out of bed, the next morning, I breathed in life with new optimism. We went downstairs and ate breakfast at a sumptuous buffet filled with eggs, sausage, bacon, pancakes, waffles and fruit toppings. My sweet tooth hummed with pleasure as I enjoyed buttery, maple syrup soaked waffles with fruit.

With pleasantly full stomachs, we rode the elevator up to the room. Then, we dragged our suitcases down the hall, descended in the elevator and checked out with a friendly front desk clerk. Admiring the marble floors, expansive, light filled area, beautiful paintings and lovely, classical statues, I breathed in lightness and joy. The seminar had given me hope. I thanked Kay for giving me a big dose of fun and laughter----the best medicine.

The seriousness of city life frightened me as I drove us back to routines, traffic, bills and pollution. Settling back into my room, I fell asleep quickly.

When I went back to the Seaside Sanitarium, the next day, everyone was glad to see me. I relaxed and felt grateful for the friendly, familiar, supportive people.

A couple of days later, Jyoti asked me to drive her to a doctor's appointment. During the drive, she asked me how I was feeling and thanked me for giving her the seminar.

I left her at the entrance of a huge building and went to run some errands. Parking on a crowded street, I bought some toothpaste in a drug store. Then, I wove my way through the pedestrians to a supermarket and bought some groceries. As I drove back to pick up Jyoti, I wondered why she had gone to the doctor. She mostly avoided them because she believed in natural healing with herbs.

When I saw her I worried. Her face looked drawn as she stood in front of the large, brick building. Waving for her to come to my car, I watched her walk toward me.

"It's cancer", she said, climbing into the car. Her eyes were wide with sorrow. Driving home, I said things now and then, worrying that they only made her feel worse.

Birds chirped cheerfully as I walked to the Hare Krishna Temple the next morning. Priya was dressed in her long, white sari. She looked like a saint from centuries ago as she smiled at me. Her grey hair revealed itself at the edges of her head cover, and her light, blue eyes welcomed me as she touched me lightly on my shoulder.

Looking up in wonder at the painting of Krishna dancing with the Gopis, I followed her to her room. She sat down on the bottom bunk bed and I sat on a wooden chair with a cushion, facing her.

"Jyoti has cancer." My voice stuck in my throat as grief clenched it tightly.

"Oh, no. Really? She won't live much longer. You really are good for her. Be sure to spend time with her. She really loves you. Krishna brought the two of you together. You are both artists, and that's why you get along so well together."

Comforting, relaxing waves rolled through me as I listened to her tell stories about Krishna's powers. She listened with compassion as I talked to her about my drives across the country.

Wanting to stay longer in the soothing softness of her company, I reluctantly told her I must be going. Aching with grief, I walked, staring down at the concrete, noticing a flower growing out of it sometimes. Jyoti's love had been the healing balm that had caused me to grow.

When I arrived at the Hare Krishna house, Bunny ran toward me and lovingly licked my ankle. Surya let me in when I knocked on the door. Jyoti laid listlessly on her back, staring hopelessly into space. A devotee had given her a cute stuffed puppy that she clutched anxiously. Sitting next to her bed, I asked her how she felt. She said that the doctors could not help her and that she did not have any money for surgery or chemotherapy. Anguish raged through me as I racked my brains for some solution. Though I felt it was my duty to take her to the doctor, I remained silent. Maybe it was better to let her make her own choice. I read to her from her favorite book and felt glad that it calmed her.

Late in the evening, I walked home, remembering all the care she had given me. I worried about becoming homeless and hopelessly insane.

The next day, I returned to the Temple, got some curried vegetables and rice from the serving line and talked with Priya while I ate. After a while, I felt well fed and relaxed and I threw my plate into the garbage can. She said she would like to go see where I was living.

We walked briskly down the sunny sidewalk. Trucks roared by with a force that felt strong enough to blow us off the road. Priya's sari fluttered in the breeze, as her fragile body moved quickly. As I led her up the bleak, dusty stairwell to my room, she talked about how Krishna was blessing Jyoti and how she was an eternal being.

"Krishna will get you back home. He is always helping you. Don't worry." Her sweet face brought joy into the gloomy, sterile room with its scuffed wooden floor, peeling, dirty paint and smudged, cracked windows. Loud rumbling, clattering sounds came from the street below as we sat and talked for a few minutes.

Then, she gave me a sweet hug and said she had to go. I watched her walk down the sunny sidewalk, her white sari fluttering behind her.

The next morning, I ran past tough gang members and successful, well off people. Cancer was spreading its treacherous, merciless web and would soon kill my best friend. Tears ran down my cheeks as I entered the concrete building and rode the elevator to the Seaside Sanitarium.

The Art therapist smiled at me as I sat down at the table gratefully. Making a collage, I expressed my anger and frustrations on paper. After a while, the art therapist asked me to talk about it. The compassion in her eyes healed me as she listened with undivided attention.

Lunch was delicious. I listened to the man who had been damaged by Lithium. A woman with auburn hair spoke with me also, expressing compassion because she had seen the drunks on the corner where I lived.

Later, at group therapy, I told the counselors how depressed I was. Lying in bed every morning, I could barely muster the strength to move. My mind was scattered and just doing ordinary things felt more and more impossible.

Jyoti became weaker and skinnier every day. However, the seminar had lit a spark within her. She began selling her handmade dolls in an expensive shop a few blocks away. As we walked to the shop together, I felt proud of her. All skin and bones, she looked like a prisoner at a Nazi death camp. Like a brave warrior, she crossed the street, dodging around aggressive drivers, who gunned their motors. Pedestrians, with rings through their noses and safety pins through their eyebrows, took big, intimidating strides past us. Loud, obnoxious rap music pummeled our ears.

I didn't want to live in Glendale after she was gone. Clinging to her kindness, I spent the rest of the day with her, walking and chanting and sitting in the yard. Later on, we watched a funny movie with Surya. When I felt too afraid to walk home, Jyoti said I could sleep on the floor.

When I heard that an alternative health fair was going on in Santa Rita, I drove there, praying with all my might to find a cure. Ambling through the corridors full of booths, where vendors demonstrated miraculous, new age healing methods, my curiosity ran wild. A woman with long hair and a beautiful dress told me about her miracle paste that had healed cancer. I paid a hundred and twenty five dollars for a jar of it.

With happy anticipation, I drove to Jyoti's shack. Hope bubbled, like magical brew, inside me as I instructed her to take two tablespoons per day.

Later in the week, I felt like an extravagant fool, when she told me she was not taking it.

The next day, my doctor at the Seaside Sanitarium told me that insurance would not pay for me to stay any longer. He gave me the name and phone number of a therapist.

I enjoyed art therapy and lunch. The warm encouragement of the counselors during group therapy touched me. The patients looked vulnerable as I listened to them with appreciation, clinging to their gentle ways.

With great sadness, I told everyone good bye, thanking them for their support. Walking to Jyoti's, I stopped and called my new therapist on my cell phone. She set an appointment for me.

A few days later, I walked six blocks from my corner flat to her office. Shaking my hand, she smiled and then told me her name was Jiang Lee. She was Chinese, and had dark hair which was pulled back in a ponytail. Her slender body moved gracefully, like a bird. She was the most extraordinary listener I had ever talked to. Keeping her heartfelt attention on me every split second, she soon earned my full trust.

"Your diagnosis is depression." Looking at me with totally attentive, caring eyes, she calmed my racing mind.

When I asked her what she thought about drugs, I discovered that she was not deluded by the promises of "Miracle Drugs". She commented that some people who took them remained depressed and that I was not required to take them. I felt in control again, like the master of my own ship.

She called me a remarkable person, and my confidence barometer rose every time I saw her. Sympathizing with my longings to go home, she encouraged me to trust my gut feelings instead of the advice the psychic had given me.

When I went to the Krishna Temple next, a pretty devotee enthusiastically said that the Ratha Yatra Festival was being planned. Feelings of belonging relaxed me as a sweet, auburn haired woman showed me how to push a needle through the base of flowers and string them together. As I began stringing them together, in pretty patterns, for the chariots in the parade, I told several devotees, who were working near me, that Jyoti had cancer.

"Take good care of her," a gorgeous, brunette devotee said, furrowing her brow with concern. "You mean a lot to her. She's going to die."

Her name was Radha she told me. She joined me in the creation of flower garlands. We worked and worked for several hours.

Then, Priya came to me and knelt down beside me. Handing me a plate of Prasad (God blessed food), she asked me to give it to Jyoti.

After a while, Radha suggested we go. I followed her to her car. She said kind words about Jyoti as she drove. We arrived and parked on the curb. When we knocked on the door, there was no answer. Walking inside, we noticed that Surya was gone.

Jyoti looked as though she was breathing her last few breaths as she lay on her bed, not moving a muscle. Her skin was chalk white and her bones protruded from her shrinking skin. As I offered her the Prasad she said she did not want to eat.

The day of the Hare Krishna Ratha Yatra festival arrived. Excitement and celebration electrified the air, as I rode with the devotees in a big, black limousine to Santa Rita.

Soon, we arrived and the driver parked the car behind a long row of cars. Following the procession of colorful devotees, dressed in striking saris and formal Indian pants, I enjoyed belonging to a team of peace makers. Radha looked beautiful, with her sari flattering her slender figure. Her dark eyes shone with compassion as she smiled at me. Absorbing the sisterly love, I chatted with devotees and listened to her talk with others. We talked about how much Jyoti meant to us as I enjoyed the trees and flowers.

Shining, gold chariots, covered with the flower garlands I had made, rolled along. Bindu sat up high on one of them, waving and throwing flowers, while Surya pulled it by ropes with some big muscled devotees. A tall, blond devotee blew a conch shell. Sounds of people singing and chanting Hare Krishna vibrated through the air. People stopped their jogging or skate boarding and looked at the opulent, colorful celebration with awe. Watching the smiling, sparkling devotees dancing, I was transported beyond, to a world of bliss and love.

I rode back to the temple with the devotees at the end of the day. Surveying the passing scenery from the big, black limousine, I felt happy to be with spiritual people.

Priya greeted me warmly and gave me a plate of Prasad—"God-filled food"—to take to Jyoti. I carried it through the streets, thinking about all of the special times Jyoti had given me.

I turned into the Hare Krishna compound. Knocking on the door, I absorbed the homey vibrations and looked at the huge oak tree in the back yard. Bindu's white cat, Bunny, greeted me on the sidewalk and affectionately rubbed against my shin.

"Come on in" Surya said. Jyoti lay on her mat on the floor looking exhausted as I walked in. I handed her the plate of Prasad.

After eating just a few bites, she said she could not eat any more. She said she wanted to sit outside under the trees. Assisting her to stand up, I felt shocked by her weakness. Slowly, we walked out to the back yard.

We sat in the sun for a while and she told me about an Indian man who taught seminars on sun gazing. Many people had cured themselves of serious diseases with it she said, as though she was hoping it would cure her.

When I mentioned that I might go back East, she said for me to do what I wanted. The thought of watching her die was unbearable. I wanted to remember her as full of life, riding her bicycle, making dolls, rolling up sweets for Krishna, serving Prasad to people in the temple, trimming the Tulsi plants and singing old show tunes.

Glendale would never be my home. Jyoti didn't like it, and I didn't like it either. She would soon be flying on wings of freedom to Vikuntha, the heavenly planet.

Searching for security and attention, I went to the E.S.P. Academy. A woman with reddish brown hair, which fell past her waist, talked with me. Her name was Lillian.

I enjoyed her friendly vibrancy. A few days later, I rode with her to a gathering of people who sang and played guitars together. They were lively, fun, interesting and loving people. A very obese man paid special attention to me, and I felt myself blush as he asked me for a date. I told him I was not interested.

A distinguished-looking man, named Rob, introduced himself to me and told me that he taught writing classes. His brown eyes conveyed intelligence. With a frustrated sigh, he confided that tax time was driving him crazy. Bravely suggesting that we could help each other, I told him I did hypnotherapy for overcoming procrastination. He agreed to exchange guitar lessons for hypnotherapy.

He treated me to a meal at a Chinese restaurant. His tall body was well toned and his brown eyes exuded wisdom. He shared personal things about his brother, who had been sexually abused.

I accepted when he invited me to his place. We sat in candlelight and talked. He gave me almonds and fruit and told me about his house he was renovating in Napa Valley. After a while, he began playing Bach tunes on

Kundalini Rising

his guitar, laying back on his sofa, propped up by pillows. Uplifting waves of intoxicating music carried me away to a place with no time, where I danced like pure energy.

The next time we met, I hypnotized him. People rarely asked for my service and it increased my confidence. I dreamed about how wonderful life would be with a stable, successful, gentle man like him.

A week passed and I returned for my guitar lesson.

"I got my taxes done", he said happily. Beaming with confidence, I sat in a comfortable arm chair, enjoying his roomy, elegant home. My budget would never allow me to rent such a nice place.

He began to teach me a series of exercises and scales to practice on my guitar. After six lessons with him, I felt more confident with my guitar playing and more relaxed with him.

When he invited me to go with him to his vacation place, I quickly agreed.

He took me to stay in his cottage in Napa Valley for two days. It was a lovely place with a stream in the back yard. We sat and listened to the babbling water flow, eating lunch at a rod iron table. Later, I listened to Handel and Haydn while he went to a local school and taught the children music.

Madhu called me on my cell phone, worried out of her mind.

"You don't know this man! You should not be staying with him! You're going to end up dead someday. You don't know anything about him! Is he behaving okay?" Her voice emoted strongly, with fearful concern, and it comforted my inner child.

"Yeah. I'm fine. I'll be back soon. He is being very respectful. It is beautiful here."

"Well, let me know whenever you get together with some man you don't know. I worry about you. You're too trusting. I don't want you getting hurt. There are a lot of crazy men out there, and you've got to be careful. Tell him you have a very conservative aunt who is worried about you being alone with him."

I thanked her for her concern, and told her I had to go. Maybe I was foolish, but I was enjoying the attention.

When my friend returned from his music teaching gig, he sautéed some vegetables he had gotten at a farmer's market. They were huge, colorful and juicy. As I ate the delicious meal, I listened to him talk about his plans to build a recording studio. It was costing him huge amounts of money he said, resting his forehead in his hands as though he was overwhelmed.

He looked up and his face became flooded with emotion as tears welled up in his eyes.

"I lost my father about a year ago. He was a very loving father." Feeling honored that he trusted me enough to be vulnerable, I sent him love. He sobbed a little, and I wanted to hold him but I didn't.

As he drove me back to the city, I hoped that Jyoti was getting help from a good doctor. As soon as I got home, I walked to her place. Surya told me she had been admitted to the hospital for surgery. I drove us both to the hospital, clinging to the memories of fun I had had with her.

She looked stiff and white, like a plaster mannequin, as an orderly wheeled her down the fluorescent, sterile hall. Surya and I sat beside her hospital bed. Soon, her sister and a couple of her friends arrived with some brightly colored balloons. She blew into a hand held device to build her lung strength.

After a few days, I drove her home from the hospital. Her sister wanted to try soaking her in a bath of herbal solutions.

Searching around nurseries and home supply stores, we finally found a plastic tub she could soak in, the first luxury she had given herself in probably twenty years. Her makeshift shower stall, with its single rubber tube, was inadequate and austere. She deserved better.

Later, she told me she enjoyed soaking in the warm water. I felt relieved that I'd been able to contribute a little bit.

The urge to go home overcame me and I put my one month notice in, changed my mind, and then put my notice in again. My landlord called me mentally disturbed. Then she said I could not change my mind again.

Overwhelmed with confusion and fear, I went to the E.S.P. Academy. As I sat in a healing circle one day, I started talking to my new friend, Lillian who I had had fun with at the music jam. Desperately, I blurted out my problem.

When she offered me shelter in exchange for cleaning her home, I gratefully accepted. Krishna must have saved me from the ordeal of sleeping on a park bench. After talking with her for a while, I told her goodbye.

When I arrived at home, I felt overjoyed as I opened a letter from my father. Inside, was a check for two hundred dollars. Tears of emotion filled my eyes.

I went from place to place trying to cash the check and none of them would do it. Calling Rob, I relaxed, remembering his sweet companionship. When I explained my frustration to him, he drove me to his credit union and got it cashed for me.

He dropped me in front of my apartment and wished me the best. Men made life so much easier.

Walking up the grungy stairs, I felt lost at sea once again--drifting, aimless, merely surviving each day. Throwing my worthless junk into bags, I sneezed from the dust that rose from the floors.

Drunks leered at me and people honked horns as I pulled my car around and parked it in front of my apartment. As quickly as I could, I ran down the stairs with boxes full of junk and pushed them into my car.

Speeding away, insecurity came over me as I drove into the hills, wondering if I could keep my sanity, living so far away from the protection and love of Jyoti. Soon, I arrived at my new, temporary home.

My new friend, Lillian sounded business like as she assigned me my duties.

Scrubbing her filthy stove and oven was daunting and disgusting. It was caked with tough, black grime that took great amounts of elbow grease to budge. Scrubbing again and again, loading sponges and rags with dirt, I winced as my tendonitis flared up, sending stabbing, and burning pains through me.

Later on, we took a walk around her neighborhood and through a lovely park. When we got home, she gave me some salad to eat, and we talked. She told me she had gotten a Master's degree in religion and had been a Sufi.

After a couple of nights, I left at five a.m. and started driving across the country again, still not sure if I was doing the right thing. Two years had flown by since I had defied my father and moved west.

The expressway went on and on forever, like a never ending loop of nothingness. Like a psychotic hamster or the people in Alice in Wonderland, I moved and moved without getting anywhere.

After four days of exhausting, grueling, perilous driving, I drove up my old driveway and walked in to greet my parents. My mother gave me the cold shoulder. My father seemed glad to see me, but said that a huge tree had fallen on their roof, so I couldn't stay with them. There must be room for me I thought, wondering if he was just going along with my mother's desire to reject me to keep the peace.

I took my sorrows to the Krishna temple.

"They don't sound like very loving parents if they won't let you stay with them." The innocent devotee's understanding touched me deeply.

"Yeah. They can be tough. My father said he was going to cut me out of his will if I moved to Glendale, but I did it anyway." I envisioned living the rest of my life in poverty.

"I was cut out of my father's will because he didn't want me being a Hare Krishna. You can stay here if you want to." His sensitive, dark eyes were like those of an angel.

I went to visit my aunt. She let me stay in her bedroom downstairs. She treated me to a delicious salad from the Farmer's Market and, as she listened to me, her sympathy softened my rough edges.

After a few nights, I moved into my cousin's bedroom upstairs. It was clutter free, clean and quiet. Two big windows with shutters were on one wall. A wooden dresser was on the other wall and a bedside table with a good lamp allowed me to read, propped up on the big, supportive pillows.

Good memories of him treating me to rock concerts rolled through me. We had gone to the best of the best----Yes, The Rolling Stones, The Who, Santana, Leon Russell. His innocent, loving nature made him delightful company. We got up and danced and whooped and hollered, having fun like two children.

One day, my uncle stormed in and began berating me. His face was contorted with anger.

"You are the most selfish person I know. Your parents do a lot for you, and you don't do anything nice for them. You come here just expecting everyone to cater to you like no one else matters. This is my house, and I don't like you just inviting yourself over like you own the place!"

"You're an asshole!" I barked back, triggered by his criticism. It reminded me of my mother's.

"What did you just say to me? You have a foul mouth. I'm going to tell your parents what you said to me. It shows what an awful person you are. You don't respect anyone, not even your own parents after all that they have done for you."

"Ted, apologize to Sophia. She hasn't done anything wrong!" my aunt jumped in.

The next day, she drove me to a cheap hotel.

"You can stay here and think about what you want to do. Your father said he would pay the hotel, and you can look for an apartment." She touched me on the shoulder and looked into my eyes with loving concern. Then, she drove away.

I sat on the bleached bed in the sterile, depressing hotel room, and thought and thought and thought. Looking at the psychic's picture in the local New Age journal, I cursed her.

Yet still, I felt dependent on her and her power. My inner voice nagged me to call her and ask if my life would turn out all right if I stayed in my hometown. Shelling out another hundred dollars to her would mean a month of eating nothing but rice though. I lamented over my ship wreck of a life.

I called Anne, a sweet Krishna devotee who I saw at the feasts in Glendale. Many mornings, I had talked with her while she ironed the clothes that the statues of Deities wore. She had invited me to her apartment and introduced me to her adorable son. Pouring my heart out to her, I felt her compassion soothing me.

"They're treating you like a burden. You deserve better than that. We all love you out here. We are your true family. Don't let them make you feel worthless. You're a great person."

After ending the long distance call, I took out my Tarot cards and shuffled them, searching them frantically for the answer. I laid out a spread for moving back to Glendale. The Wheel of Fortune appeared, then the Star, and the Empress. A tidal wave of emotion moved through me as I stared. The cards were telling me to move back to Glendale.

Then, I shuffled and laid out a spread for staying in Madison. The Hangman appeared. I held my breath. The psychic must have been right. The signs were all around me--my parents not letting me stay with them and my uncle criticizing me.

Yet, I missed my Dad and wanted to comfort him. His broken hip must be causing him excruciating pain. Hearing the clock ticking forebodingly, I drove to his house with urgency and began climbing the staircase to his bedroom.

"Don't go up there! Don't go up there!" my mother sternly demanded, looking with anger at me. I continued walking up the stairs, trembling.

My father looked fragile. I watched him give himself a shot of insulin in his leg, as he had done every morning since he was thirty. Wanting to hold him in my arms with love, I talked with him a little bit. Then, I asked him if I could bring him something from the store. He said I could pick up some tomatoes and bread.

Happy for a chance to please him I drove to the store. As I put the things into the refrigerator, I felt frightened by my mother's cold look. Leaving in a hurry, I longed to sit and talk with them on the lovely porch.

When I got back to the hotel, I called Eliot, a sweet minister's son who had been friendly and encouraged me to go to Al Anon meetings. With great compassion, he had understood my struggle growing up with alcoholism.

The next time I went to my parents' home, I asked Elliot to go with me. I brought my father a white chrysanthemum to cheer him up.

"Give me a hug," my father said, as I placed it on the table. I did as he asked, feeling how frail he had become. He needed me.

"Oh, what is she up to now?" my mother asked, looking chagrined, barely making eye contact with me out of the corner of her eye, then reading a book.

Dad ignored her and proceeded to talk with Elliot. I could tell he was pleased when Elliot told him he attended his church. As they talked about the minister and various other things, I pondered that Dad always felt more comfortable talking to a man than talking to me.

I wished Elliott could spend the day with me but he had things to do. Later on, sitting in my hotel room, I worried about my belongings in my car getting stolen. Dying of loneliness, I called Madhu on my cell phone in despair.

"People back there are idiots. They won't even let you stay in their house. That's awful of them to stick you away in a hotel. If they really cared about you, they would have you in their house. The psychic was right. You don't belong there. When are you coming back here?"

"I'm too tired to drive all that long way again. I'm hurting, but at least my aunt is being nice to me. She invited me to go watch the Reagan funeral on T.V."

"That shows how stupid they are that they would even watch that.

Kundalini Rising

They are backward and stuck in their ways. They don't have the spiritual knowledge that you have, and they will never be able to understand you. You have a lot of people who love you here."

"I don't know what to do."

"Get in your car and start driving *now*. You're wasting away there. It is not the place for you. The psychic told you, and he was right!" Her loud voice shook me.

"I've got to go," I said, and quickly hung up.

I collapsed onto the bed and stared at the ceiling. Sinking into a whirlpool of frenetic worrying, I became tight and rigid like a corpse. Throughout the entire black, desolate night, my mind raced, jumping here and there like a Mexican jumping bean.

In the morning, I was as numb as a potato. I thought about Elliot. He had encouraged me, like a big brother. I would call him after I went for a swim in the hotel pool.

My time at the pool wasn't as peaceful as I had hoped. Several people were swearing at each other and I wondered if they were using drugs. I envisioned them breaking into my car and stealing all my belongings. Pounding the water furiously, I swum laps. After swimming about twenty, I felt tired.

Climbing out of the pool, I watched water drip down my legs. I wrapped a towel around myself and put on my tennis shoes. Walking back to my room, I prayed to feel happy again. I locked the door and then fell down onto the bed.

Summers, when I was young, had been wonderful and I wanted to go back in time. I remembered laying on the chaise lounge at the country club or walking along the beach on family vacations. My father would run on the beach, flying a kite, feeling ecstatic that he had escaped the demanding, hectic work routine at the huge, chaotic hospital for poor people.

My aunt had called him and told him she'd deposited me in the hotel. He was paying my weekly fee to stay there. Feeling grateful for his generosity, I still felt confused. I had to pretend with him that I was searching for a local apartment because he insisted I must live in Madison. However, the psychic's voice still haunted me....."Madison is not the place for you."

He would worry himself to death if he knew I was being convinced by Madhu to get back on the road. I felt horribly guilty. I wished I wasn't such a hopeless case, giving my power away to these strange Hare Krishnas who couldn't even keep a hundred dollars in the bank. Madhu didn't know what was best for me. She was just an eccentric old lady.

I returned to the pool. Swimming with every bit of energy I could muster, I pounded the water furiously. I was getting close to fifty. I'd done my best to start a new life in Glendale, but I felt like an invisible ghost hanging somewhere in the stratosphere, with no real home anywhere on Earth. Moving had not made me happier, only more confused.

After I'd exhausted myself swimming, I lay on a lounge chair by the pool and imagined I was young again. I would do my life completely differently if I could get my youth back. Bitterness brewed in my veins when I thought about all that I had missed in life.

Walking back to my room, the smell of asphalt, carbon monoxide and trash made me long for a home cooked meal, at a table with fresh flowers on it, in my childhood home. Or in a home with a husband. The caustic sound of arguing scraped my eardrums as I pushed myself up the two flights of concrete stairs, feeling weary.

In desperation, I called Elliot. His voice brought me back from the edge of insanity, as he suggested we go to Al-Anon.

Smiling from his car, he lifted my mood. Mark, who had grown up down the street from me, was sitting beside him and his face brightened with delight to see me. Mark had listened to me with sensitivity and had given me a job, moving things from his storage unit. I had felt as happy as a lark when he told me that I was beautiful, even though I did not have romantic feelings toward him. He took it well and did not feel a need to hurt me out of a wounded male ego.

"You could be a model," he had said, his eyes bulging with puppy love.

I remembered confiding in him after I returned from my spiritual trip to India twenty-one years ago. The spiritual leaders had convinced me to take a lifetime vow of celibacy, I told him.

"Those vices have been going on for thousands of years," he had told me, back then. "They don't know everything, and you don't have to let them control you. My sister would not be celibate. You might meet the right person and get married! Those people are making those rules for you but *God* isn't." Mark had said. I could relax into his humble gentleness like I could with no one else.

CHAPTER SIX

...*The Supreme Self, having projected the three worlds and set forth guardians to protect them, thought on those guardians,... "If without me, speech can be uttered, breath can be breathed, eyes can be seen, or ears can hear, what then am I? Let me enter these guardians."*

Whereupon the Self opened the door of bliss in the center of each guardian's skull and entered them.

When the Self is unknown, all three states of soul---waking, dreaming and dreamless sleep---are but a dream. In each of these three states the Self dwells. The Self dwells in the eye while we are in the wakeful state, in the mind while we dream, and in the lotus of the heart while we sleep...but if an individual soul awakens from his three-fold dream state of wakefulness, of dreaming, and of dreamless sleep, that souls sees none other than the supreme omniscient and omnipresent Reality.

Aitareya Upanishad

"*The after effects of Kriya bring with them the utmost peace and bliss. The joy that comes with Kriya is greater than the joys of all pleasurable physical sensations put together.*"

Paramahansa Yogananda

I came back into the present moment and tuned into the Al Anon meeting. I listened to a slender, brunette woman talk about her experience with her alcoholic father. After she finished, I began to share. Kind, attentive faces listened to me with touched expressions as I told about my alcoholic father's harsh ways. I talked about how his violence had hurt my mother and all of his children.

Elliott, Mark and I went to The Waffle House after the Al Anon meeting. Their company soothed me as I empathized with the pain they had experienced through relating to an alcoholic. Wanting to settle in somewhere and give up my restless quest for home, I clung to the caring in their eyes.

When Elliott dropped me at the hotel, I sunk into a dark, cold well and drowned in loneliness. As I tried to write in my journal, concentration slipped away. Drowsiness came over me and, soon, I put on my pajamas and crawled under the bed sheets.

In the middle of the night, I woke up with fear raging through me. I had had a horrifying nightmare about being chased by a murderer.

Ringing came from the telephone on my bedside table, waking me. My father told me to meet him in the lobby of the hotel. Watching him write out a check to the clerk, I swung back and forth like a seesaw, unable to decide where to live.

"I need to know that you're staying here," my father said sternly.

"I am. Thank you for paying for me. I want to come visit with you and Mom at the house."

"We can't visit today. The workmen are fixing the hole in the roof where the tree fell."

He had aged dramatically since I moved two years ago. Feeling guilty for making him worry over me, I walked to my hotel room.

I opened my box of Tarot cards and shuffled them. I asked them what would happen if I moved back to Glendale. The Wheel of Fortune appeared again. It must be a sign from my higher power, I thought. However, sadness seeped through me whenever I thought about leaving my father. He was weakening by the day.

I wanted to move back under his roof, and to be his child again. I longed to sleep in my old bed and have my mother bring me warm oatmeal with raisins, butter and brown sugar and a little milk.

I called Madhu on the phone.

"Madison is not the place for you, like the psychic said. Your parents won't let you stay with them. They've stuck you in a hotel room. I've been talking with Krishna about you, and he told me that you need to come back here."

"I'm scared. I wasn't happy in Glendale either. Maybe the psychic wasn't right." I bit my lip in fear.

"Just get in your car and drive!" she yelled. She was as controlling as my father.

The road had turned my body into a weary bag of aching bones and my mind into a ping pong game. I could not handle the grueling drive again.

I called Elliot. My outlook brightened when he said he'd like to come over and visit me.

We sat in the sun by the pool, and he said that he thought I had blossomed as a result of spending the last two years out West. I gave him a healing, moving my hands around his aura. After a few minutes, he looked much more relaxed.

The next day, Elliot and Mark arrived in his car. I was flooded with happy, home town memories as Elliot drove past places where I had spent time with friends and family. Soon, we arrived at the Al-Anon meeting. I poured out my distress to the room full of sympathetic faces.

"I'm trapped in a hotel room after driving three thousand miles. I want to be close to my father, but he won't let me stay in his house. I went there briefly, and my mother would not speak to me. A psychic says I belong out West, but I want to be here because I'm seeing my father weaken, and I'm afraid he's going to die. I want to make our relationship closer. I've always rebelled against him, but he's really the only supporter I have. I'm scared because he said he'll never give me another penny if I move out West, and I can't support myself. I'm disabled. I want to move into his house and be his child again." Tears started running down my face.

"Just take one day at a time. You're going to be alright. Love yourself, and know that your higher power loves you and will lead you to the right decision," a kind woman told me afterwards. She gently touched my shoulder and, then, gave me a long, strong hug.

Mark, Elliot, and I sat in the Waffle House and talked after the meeting. I ate hash browns smothered in ketchup and listened, feeling like they were replacement brothers. I missed my older brother, who had disappeared from my life. He had stopped visiting my parents, sister and I years ago.

Mark's eyes were red and a little hooded from smoking marijuana. His dark, wavy hair hung in a messy clump around his head. He worked with his older brother managing tenants in the various houses his parents owned. His family lived a few houses down from my parents' house. They had attended our Christmas parties when I was in high school.

Elliot was overweight and had thinning hair. He was a few years older than me. His father was a minister who had been very strict with him. His wife was bedridden with arthritis much of the time. He had amazing patience and gave her a lot of love and affection.

"We had the disadvantage of a Methodist upbringing and alcoholism in our families. I became the black sheep. You know, those Methodists put makeup on to cover up their shit. Our parents treated us like crap, and then smiled at church and acted like they were perfect parents. They never apologized or listened to us to find out what our needs were." I relaxed into the understanding in his voice, taking a long, satisfying breath.

"Yeah. I was always afraid of my father."

Guilt flowed through me for judging him. He was a good, fragile man. The psychic who urged me to move west, had told me that a demon had abused me, through my father. I could not blame him for my failures any more. The fault did not lie with him. He had been under the control of a mysterious, malevolent force no one could see. He needed my compassion, not my blame. It was high time for me to grow up and stop holding a grudge.

"Well, he scares me. You know, the way our parents abused us was never a reflection on us. You're a great person. You're traveling the world and learning new things, and you sing and write songs. I want to film you singing some time. We can start our own children's show with my puppets. I'm great at doing voices for them," Elliot said.

"Okay," I replied.

"I think it's horrible the way they've treated you. They should be glad to have you in their house," Mark said sympathetically.

Elliot dropped me off at the hotel. I couldn't stand the silence so I drove to Mark's house, which was just five houses down from my childhood home.

Welcoming me with a warm hug, he showed me around his house. The oppression of our childhoods folded over us like a smothering, dark blanket. Mark and I had suffered here in the lap of luxury, on the fanciest street in town. Our so-called "privileged upbringings" had not been as happy as they seemed.

I told him I felt tired and he gave me a blanket and place to recline on his sofa in the dusty, wood-floored living room. I'd made a mistake coming back. I worried that another experience of being given the cold treatment by my mother would send me into permanent insanity. Wandering around in a dream, I was growing smaller, shrinking into the timid, obedient person who was afraid to speak.

A loud, strong sneeze blew out of me and I woke up suddenly.

Mark walked in and sat beside me.

"I think you're a great person, and I would do anything for you. You're kind, you're giving, and you're a good listener. Not many people really care like you do. I'll be there for you no matter what, so feel free to talk to me any time. We've been through a lot of pain with our families but, now, you and Elliot and I can help each other. Those people at Al-Anon are great and you can always talk with one of them."

I thought about walking a few houses down to my parents' house. Sadness paralyzed me though, as I remembered all the times I had knocked on the door and they had not answered.

After talking with Mark for a while, I told him good night and drove back to the hotel in a depressed fog. I sat on my bed in a stupor staring at the photo of the psychic. Longing for sleep, I suffered as my mind raced all night.

When I told Elliot I couldn't stand the hotel any longer, he told me that a friend of his was renting a room in her house. Depression weighed me down as I called her number and set up an appointment with her. Driving through winding, mislabeled streets, I got very lost.

It took me about an hour, but I finally found it. Breathing deeply and pinching myself to bring myself to life, I parked my car and walked up some stairs to the front door. She greeted me cheerfully and showed me the room. It was an ugly, dirty, concrete basement room with asbestos-covered pipes hanging from the ceilings. The summer sun seared me and, like a sizzling hamburger, I sat on a dusty, lumpy bed, lethargically looking around the dismal, depressing cubicle as sweat trickled down my body.

She smiled as I handed her five hundred dollars. Then, I took my worthless stuff out of my car. As I sat on the old, tattered, uncomfortable bed, I wondered what to do with my days. Trying to write in my journal was futile because I couldn't concentrate.

I got on my cell phone and called Jyoti and Madhu but my phone kept disconnecting so I could not talk to them. Loneliness consumed me as I wandered through the woods, unable to decide whether or not I should stay in Madison.

One day, I walked outside and sat on the tree trunk stoop. Suddenly, Dad came driving down the driveway. Rolling down his window, he called to me.

"I had trouble finding this place. I'm glad I finally did. I'll get you into the apartments where you used to live," he said in a shaky voice. He was probably suffering from hypoglycemia. He handed me some twenty dollar bills.

I refused to take them. Yet, grief overcame me as I watched him drive away. I wanted to run after him, to hold him close and tell him I loved him. They were words I had never said.

Out of desperation, I called Madhu.

"Come back here. You're wasting your time there. Your father is controlling you, and your mother won't speak to you. No one wants you there. You can't go home again-- like the famous book says. You have a lot of people who love you here. We all miss you. You need to leave early tomorrow morning."

"Oh, I'm so tired. The heat here has zapped all of my energy." Fanning myself with a newspaper, I felt sweat trickle down my face.

"Krishna is taking care of you, and you're going to be fine. Call me from the road, and I'll see you when you get back. You're a very sweet girl, and I want you to be happy." She sounded motherly.

My cell phone suddenly cut off, like it had been doing repeatedly since I'd moved into the wooded, hilly place. I walked down the hill and around the driveway, observing the garage apartment that my bohemian landlord rented to people. She was probably at her dance class. She taught children to dance in the studio at her home.

On Saturday, I watched a performance she did with the children. The music, costumes, and stories were beautiful. The children looked adorable as they twirled and leaped on a stage in her backyard. After the performance, people explored her woods, gazing in awe at a mystical pond made of mirrors. Beautiful, sparkling crystals hung from the trees.

Nervous exhaustion had all but incapacitated me. I could barely think or talk. I couldn't even remember what a normal life was like. I had become a scattered bundle of nerves, impulsively following urges, unraveling more and more each moment. With no sense of self, I felt like a spinning top, speeding into oblivion as I whirled around and around.

Suddenly, I said good bye to an old friend, even though I wanted to be near him, and walked away. Impulsively, I went into my room and threw my clothes and books into boxes. Then, I put them into the trunk of my car.

Pressing the accelerator and listening to my motor roar, I visualized my parents' faces, feeling my heart patter with emotions. Soon, I was driving down an endless, monotonous freeway, bordered by shopping malls and parking lots. I had been chasing my family members all my life. Now, they would have to chase me.

"Peter Peter Pumpkin eater had a wife and couldn't keep her. Put her in a pumpkin shell and there he kept her very well," kept running through my mind. Other nonsense thoughts and kaleidoscopic images flashed in fast sequences across my mind.

Well, my new utopia was waiting for me. I would have to be strong and make it work. Like my friend had told me, I needed to know that I could stand on my own two feet. I would stay in the attic of the Krishna house while I looked for a decent place. I would be all right. Like the psychic had told me, I needed to learn faith.

"Consider the lilies of the field," went through my head as I munched on peanut butter, rice cakes, and apples, and chased it all down with Gatorade. Every day, I stopped in a cafe and called Elliott. His kind, supportive voice kept me from going insane.

My legs twitched with sharp sciatica pains and my shoulders both hurt. Every time I stopped for gas, I said hello to the various clerks. A kind clerk would mean the world to me. I'd breathe life into myself with every word from them.

After a day of driving ten hours straight, I would walk like a dead person to the front desk of a hotel.

"You will be a butterfly," the psychic had told me, when she encouraged me to make my move. However, I felt like a burnt out, numb, insane, wretched woman. Did moving really change anyone? And did the New Age movement have anything real to offer me or anyone?

A phone counselor, who I had called in desperation, had told me, "Wherever you go there you are". My chakras had been balanced, my mockups had been made, my grounding chord had been set, my aura had been fluffed, my past lives had been read, my protection rose had been used, my Yoga had stretched me, my meridians had been cleared, my crystals had been charged--however, I felt like I had been diced, sliced, scrambled, scattered and smothered.

Soon, four days of non-stop driving had shaken me to shreds and my body ached. Feeling like I was not all there, as numb as a brick, I arrived back at the Hare Krishna house. Parking my car, I looked forward to seeing the devotees. Climbing out of my car, I stretched my arms and legs.

As I walked around, smelling the fresh air, I imagined my grounding chord going down into the center of the earth. Moving dreamily through the yard to the oak tree, I felt uplifted by the birds who sang sweetly in the trees. Giving the oak tree a hug, I sent all my negative energy down into the ground.

Knocking on Jyoti's door, I hoped she was not sleeping. Suddenly, it opened.

"Surprise!" a group of happy voices shouted.

Bubbling in effervescent joy, I received welcoming embraces from loving devotees.

Jyoti had put a huge poster up saying, "Welcome back!" Anne had baked a cake for me. Surya, Bindu, Madhu and other devotees celebrated with me. Jyoti gave me a long, strong hug and kept telling me how happy she was that I had come back.

It hadn't felt like this in Madison. The psychic must have been right when he said Madison was not my home. I heard his voice in my head again:

"This is likely to be a home for you so why not stay here? You're in a rebirth. I think you know that."

Jyoti was getting weaker and weaker, and I wondered how much longer she would last. Eating my delicious, strawberry birthday cake, I absorbed the love of my devotee family. Anne smiled at me and I hummed happily inside, touched deeply that she had taken her precious time and paltry money to bake it for me. She stayed busy raising her young son, with no help from a husband.

I slept in the Hare Krishna house attic while I looked around for an apartment. When I interviewed at a house two blocks away, I prayed that I would be chosen to live there.

The house was old, with two stories and four bedrooms. The high ceilings, hardwood floors and peeling paint gave it an old fashioned look. The landlord and resident, a writer named Sylvia, rented three rooms. She had an abrupt, scrutinizing manner. Her shelves were lined with books about the abuse of women. Yet, I could tell she had a soft side. After talking with me for just ten minutes, she said she would like to rent to me. I thanked her, overflowing with gratitude.

My shoulders ached as I pulled my stuff out of my car and carried it up to my small room with a mattress on the floor underneath a double window which looked out into a back yard, with an enormous elm tree and yellow flowers. The windows had blinds and a dark blue curtain. A tiny closet was in the corner and I shoved my things out of sight, and then hung up my clothes.

Several days later, Jyoti and Surya came to visit. I watched in shock as she struggled to muster the strength to walk up the stairs. She lost her breath, gave up, and then sat down on the sofa. Her skin was a chalky, grey color and she could barely talk. I chit chatted, trying to sound cheerful. After about five minutes, Jyoti said she felt nauseous.

We walked back to her place, and I watched her lay down on her small bed. It was a mattress she and her husband had found on the side of the road. They had placed it in the tiny area where I used to paint. She looked at me with affection as I told her that I liked my new place. A full moon rose outside and I touched my moon stone earring that she had given me, wondering if it responded to the moon. Holding my breath with emotion, I thanked her silently for being consistently kind and devoted.

As I told her good bye, I wondered if she would still be alive when I saw her next.

Sleeping in my new home, I got some much needed rest. The next morning, I made a mock-up of a new, best friend. Marie was the name of the woman who rented the room next to mine. She had shoulder-length, dark hair, and childlike eyes that shone with wonder. She had studied at the E.S.P.

Academy. I listened in awe as she told me about her amazing experiences there.

"A woman I graduated with brought back the eyesight of a blind person. We used to go out at night and look for UFOs. We saw several. When you reach a point where you have cleaned out all of your past programming, you become able to do what Jesus did." Marie talked happily, her eyes shining with enthusiasm.

"Let's feel the energy around the garage. We can explore the energies that are around and see if we get any messages." With her heart shaped face, large dark eyes and cropped hair, she looked like a pixie, working her magic.

I followed her out the back door, through the yard and into the garage. As I moved my hands through the air, feeling for entities and spirits, I felt silly. People would think I was crazy if they heard me talk about the hoodoo voodoo things I was doing.

"Sylvia stores all of her court cases about abuse of women back here." A wave of horror flashed through me. I did not want to know about the gory details.

I imagined the grief countless women had experienced at the hands of men, as I observed the floor-to-ceiling filing cabinets; they filled the entire garage. Opening a cabinet, I leafed through various cases, reading about unspeakable acts of cruelty. Lightning bolts of fear tore me to pieces inside and I had to stop reading.

"Let's feel the energy." Her wise eyes tuned into the cosmos like extra refined antenna.

I moved my hands through the air. Then, I told Marie I felt the energy of anger, frustration, horror, fear and sadness. Suddenly, I wanted to scream.

Following her out of the garage, up the stairs, and into the house, I continued to move my hands through the air, yet I could not feel any energy. Then, I moved my hands around the front closet. I told Marie that I felt the energy of an old man, feeling certain I had just made it up to have something to say.

She laughed exuberantly, then complimented me on my good work. After feeling the energy a while longer, we took a break.

Sitting at the kitchen table, I watched Marie move her slender, petite body. Her dark, slanted Japanese eyes were pretty and her mouth was like a cupid's. She made me tea, and we had fun laughing about all the silly jokes that were told at the E.S.P. Academy. As our friendship deepened, I felt glad that I had returned to Glendale.

She took me with her to her bird store, where she worked, one day, and I filled out a job application. Cute, yellow finches, white cockatoos, red songbirds, parrots and budgies sang all around me like a celestial orchestra sent from heaven. The birds warbled out their thanks, as she filled their supper dishes with sunflower seeds.

I waved goodbye to her and walked out onto the sunny sidewalk. Intensely bright sun shone down on me as I browsed through fancy shops, admiring colorful clothing, soaps and perfumes, jewelry, furniture, sculpture, crystals and books. An intoxicating aroma of freshly baked goods lured me into a bakery, where I admired the exquisitely designed pastries and cakes. I bought myself a warm macaroon and ate it with delight.

I needed a job badly. I had studied hard at my Early Childhood education classes, but now I wasn't using them. Remembering Connie with fondness, I called her when I got home.

She responded with delight, when I told her I would treat her to lunch the next day, at a burrito place down the street from Marie's bird shop.

"I have been meaning to call you, but I lost your phone number. I bet you thought I had forgotten about you. I hadn't. I've been thinking about you and wondering how you were doing. It's great to see you again." Her big, padded arms swept me into a close hug at the burrito place the next day. The cook hurried to keep up with the many orders. The cashier who rung up our order looked harried. Surveying the crowd with curiosity, I walked to a table. We both sat down.

"I'm working full time at the pre-school down the street. They're paying me all right. The kids can be little monsters, but I thank God every day that I have a job. I've got to get out of debt and get my girls into a private school. How about you? Have you gotten a preschool job?" Her nurturing eyes conveyed concern.

"No. I'm not working. I worked in several preschools, but I'm not sure if it's what I want to do. I drove across the country and visited my family for a couple of months and then drove back here."

"It's not easy. One of the kids bit me the other day. I told him, 'You are not allowed to bite me. If you act like a human being and not an animal, I'll listen to you. Otherwise, you can sit in the corner.' He just kept staring at me and screaming. Then, he bit me again. Sometimes, they pull on my hair and pull it out. I was ready to slap one the other day. But I prayed to God and he helped me keep my cool." Like a mother lion, she bravely did whatever she had to do to protect her cubs.

"I don't know how you do it. I should be doing something with it since I took all those classes, but I don't know if I can handle them. I couldn't get them to take a nap before. They just ignored me when I told them to settle down and be quiet. They kept jumping and running around."

"You have to be really tough with them. I raise my voice and talk very firmly to them. I hate to do it, but I have to or they'll run all over me."

"I'm looking for a job doing elderly care. They're not fun like kids. They depress me when they complain about their aches, but I can handle them. I hope I get hired soon because I need cash."

Connie had to hurry back to work. I filled myself up with her warm hug as she thanked me for lunch and said for me to call her any time. I said I would. I got so busy finding a job that I never got around to it though. I missed her every day.

Driving around and filling out applications tired me and, when Marie gave me a free pass to go wind surfing, I jumped on the chance to have some fun.

The day of my adventure arrived. Radiant sun beamed down on me as I walked to the bus stop. Riding the bus, I watched the colorful, eccentric people walk the streets of Glendale. Beggars begged for spare change, hippies sold incense on colorful blankets and looney tunes ranted mind boggling monologues to any poor sucker who would listen to them. Reading the restaurant signs, I imagined tasting the various cuisines. There was Japanese, Vietnamese, Chinese, Indian, French, Ethiopian, Mexican and Persian.

The aqua ocean sparkled in the distance and I watched sail boats move lazily, their white sails shining. Memories of my father sailing with me on a tiny boat in Cape Cod made me long for the lost magic of childhood.

When I arrived at the Wind Sailing business, a friendly, young woman with dark hair and eyes greeted me with vibrant, happy energy. Handing her my free pass, I bubbled with excitement. Smiling sweetly, she handed me a life preserver and led me over to a boat. A middle aged couple held hands and two girls who looked like teenagers talked effervescently.

The driver of the boat, took my hands and welcomed me aboard. Then, he showed me how to hold onto a rope with handles on it and stand on a platform which he would drag behind the boat. With brave determination, I rose up and stood, holding on for dear life, as the motor roared and the boat began to move. Reveling in a feeling of euphoric freedom, I flew over the sparkling water. Seagulls cried and pelicans swooped down to the water and landed, looking like comical characters with their long beaks with the big bag attached. Sea spray misted my face as the glorious sun warmed me. Aliveness vibrated in every cell of me as I drank in the blue sea, the green trees, the shiny, white sails and the friendly waves from people in the boat.

At the end of my adventure, I got out of the boat, guided by a pretty, young woman who held my hand. She took my life preserver and wished me a good day with a sweet smile.

Riding the bus home, I surveyed the scenery. Stepping down onto the sidewalk, I watched a group of adorable children laughing and running in their school uniforms. I wondered what my neighbors were like as I walked into the house.

The clatter of typewriter keys brought me back to mundane reality as I tiptoed up the stairs. I went into my room, sat down and began to run my energy like the psychics had taught me. Cosmic energy from the galaxies flowed into the crown of my head, filling me with the pure, white, ethereal elixir of the heavens. Earth energy moved up from the core of the earth, through my feet, into my legs, and throughout my body, nurturing and nourishing me. Soon, an hour had passed.

Then, I made mock-ups, like my teacher at the E.S.P. Academy had taught me, putting my desire into a colored balloon and watching it float away. I visualized being an owner of my own place. At the end of the session, I felt relaxed and energized, like I'd been reborn.

Glendale got miserably cold in the summer. However, my ex-land lord, who had said I would never go hungry, was right. Looking at the notice in the paper about a place that would give me free food, I listened to my stomach grumble.

Pulling on my jacket, I walked out of the house and to my car. Sitting down in the front seat, I reviewed the directions a soft spoken, humble woman had given me over the phone. Thinking about my father back home worrying about me, I drove through the busy streets. Pedestrians boldly crossed the street in front of me as I eyed the exotic restaurants, feeling hungry. After I passed through the downtown area, I could drive faster. I followed the street signs smoothly until I arrived.

A tall woman with streaked hair and a strong, sculpted body spoke with me while we waited in line. She told me she liked Glendale more than Europe, where she had moved from. I was surprised by how much food the nice workers gave me. They loaded up two huge boxes of fresh vegetables, nuts, fruits and grains.

When I got home, I unloaded my bountiful supply. I couldn't open the vegetable drawer after pushing everything in.

Sitting on the foot of Marie's bed and listening to her talk with her pet bird, relaxation came over me. She chirped cheerfully in response to her funny and endearing comments.

"My birds keep me sane. They always look on the bright side, and they sing so cheerfully. I love them. My ex-boss was a real slave driver, but now my boss is mellow and easygoing. I did mock-ups for a great boss, and now I have her. It's a great change. You can get anything you want by doing mock-ups, like they teach at the E.S.P. Academy."

"I've been practicing doing them. I need to be more consistent with it though."

"Let's go see a play in Danville tomorrow. There's going to be a dance performance and art show down by Lake Saskatoon. We can walk around the museum and playground that is near there." My body perked up with happy anticipation.

A glorious sun shone high in the sky, and birds sang joyfully as the day of adventure dawned. We packed some snacks and drinks into a bag. I put on my sunglasses and hung my camera around my neck. Marie glowed with vibrant energy as I followed her to her car, enjoying her cheerful chatter.

When we arrived at the parking lot near the lake, Marie pulled her mini trampoline out of her car. Her slender body, dark hair in a pixie cut and innocent face gave her the look of a fairy as she jumped up and down, as though she would fly away any minute. Soon, it was my turn. I jumped up and down, flapping my arms like a bird. Her delighted laughter lifted me into the stratosphere.

We had a great time wandering through the museum. Snakes, iguanas, lizards, frogs, and various creatures were all exhibited in interesting ways.

When a young, friendly man began to talk with Marie, she spoke briefly, then excused herself in a polite way. We walked toward the lake to watch the outdoor performance.

Canvas paintings were hanging from ropes strung between trees. A lady sat at a big table to collect money from painting sales. Everyone sat in serene silence as the performance began. A poet walked toward the lake in an elegant, white, flowing dress that touched the ground. Stopping, she faced us and began reciting poetry. After she finished her poem, she began moving her arms and legs in expressive, dance-like ways. The audience watched her graceful movements in spellbound silence.

When she reached the shore, she stepped into a boat and began rowing it with a long oar. Everyone watched in hypnotized reverence until she arrived at a tiny island and disembarked from her boat. She stood on her island stoically, with a mystical expression.

Marie and I sat side by side, contemplating the meaning of this artistic expression. Then, she suggested that we take a walk through the Botanical Gardens. I observed the passing cars, pedestrians and fancy buildings as we walked around the lake and into the gardens, which were free to the public.

The place was spectacularly beautiful. My mouth dropped open in awe as I looked at bright flowers, bonsais, gurgling, exquisitely designed fountains, and peaceful, stone Buddhas. I contemplated on the perfection of God's creation.

"This place is gorgeous!" I exclaimed, looking at Marie with gratitude.

"Yeah. Isn't nature wonderful? The endless varieties of plants and flowers we're blessed with is amazing."

It looked like every color under the sun burst forth before me in every direction. I feasted my eyes on the splendid, visual banquet. Van Gogh would have loved it.

"You are going to find a job soon. Don't worry," Marie reassured me sweetly.

"Yeah. They seemed to like me at the elderly care place. I think they'll hire me."

"Don't let Sylvia bother you. She is a real nut case and is off in another world a lot of the time. I call her the 'bull dyke' under my breath sometimes. Yesterday, I was in the kitchen and she came in and took over the whole counter I was using. She pushed my things out of the way and looked at me like I was a roach. She's rude and very controlling. I've heard her lose her temper and, believe me, you don't want to get her angry. So take my warning and be careful with her."

"Okay. I don't want to get blasted by her. Her abrupt manner made me nervous the first time I met her and I find it hard to relax with her."

"Everyone does. You have to tiptoe and make sure to not ever break any of her rules. She'll give you hell if you do. I'm glad you moved in. I can feel you running your energy through the wall sometimes. It calms me. It's so nice to have a like-minded friend to talk to. I mentioned God one day to Sylvia and she looked at me like I was crazy. She's an atheist."

We walked in silence for a while. Then, Marie said she was ready to head home.

"Well, we'll protect each other from the control freak." she said laughing and putting her arm around me. We walked to her car and, as she drove, we laughed with wild abandon. Passing drivers looked at us like they wanted to join our party.

Once home, we sat in the kitchen talking. Suddenly, Sylvia walked in. Looking at us critically, she reminded us, sternly, that we both needed to do our chores. It had taken me half a day the last time, and I dreaded it. Rebelling against her authority, I continued to talk with Marie. Thoughts of Jyoti flitted through my mind and, after a few minutes, I told Marie I had to go.

Hanging my head with dread, longing to have my loving, lively best friend back, I walked over to Jyoti's place. Shocked sorrow crushed me, like a weight, as I observed her. Her ribs protruded from her emaciated body, and her skin hung loosely off of her toothpick bones. The cancer had been eating her insides, and it looked like it had just about finished its quest to kill her. Her eyes widened with gratitude for my company.

When I asked her what her doctor was saying, she told me that she wasn't going to see a doctor anymore. Wanting to urge her to go through chemotherapy and fight for her life, I remained silent. As much as I wanted to keep her with me, there was nothing I could do.

I asked her if I could bring her anything from the store. She asked me to buy some paper towels and milk.

Walking to a store, my shoulders rose and my breathing stopped as tough, muscular men passed by. Pining for the days when we walked in carefree reverie and breathed in the intoxicating fragrance of the rose garden, I feared being all alone in the world.

She thanked me when I returned. I held her hand and talked with her. Her words came out slowly and laboriously as she asked me to read a story about Krishna. I began reading the delightful story and, soon, a snoring sound came from her. Surya sat glumly on his mat as I tiptoed out.

That night, I dreamed that my father had fallen down on the pavement. His brother and I picked him up off of the sidewalk. A dreadful fear that he was dying tore through me as I awoke with a start. The urge to drive back across the country to be with him surged through me.

The morning came and I busied myself with organizing, running an errand for Jyoti and cleaning the house.

Later on that evening, Marie and I made spring rolls. We laughed and sang as we chopped vegetables and softened the huge rice circles in boiling water. When they were cool, we spooned vegetables inside and rolled them up into neat little rolls. Marie made peanut sauce, which made them extra delicious. We both agreed that we should open our own restaurant.

As we grew closer, Marie confided in me more.

"I had a nervous breakdown. I had a romance with a guy who I thought was really wonderful. He was smart and handsome, and I was in love with him. Then, I found out that he was a sociopath. He was so kind and clean cut, I never would have thought he was anything but great. I kept getting readings about him. One psychic said he was fine, but four others said he was a sociopath, so I believed them. I left him, and I got myself back on my feet, but it took a long time. When I was going through the clairvoyant program, I kept telling them that I was afraid I was having a nervous breakdown."

"They would tease me and say, 'Yeah, you're having a nervous breakdown.' We would all laugh together, and then I would feel all right. Sometimes I tried living at home but could not cope with it because my parents yelled at me. My E.S.P. group kept me sane."

I told her that I had suffered a nervous breakdown in the past. She was sympathetic. My elderly care company assigned me a job caring for a lady with dementia.

After driving down long, strange roads, I finally found her house one day. I swept and mopped her floors and tidied up stacks of magazines. Doing my best to make friends with her, I chatted about the weather and asked her what sorts of things she liked to do. She had gone sour on life and replied bitterly that she didn't like to do anything anymore.

One day, when I was bringing her some pizza, she erupted in a sudden fit of fury.

"I don't want you here bothering me. I didn't ask for you. I don't need you, and I want you to go home!" Her voice boomed with rage as her face grew red.

"Everything is okay. Just calm down. I want you to feel better. This lunch will make you feel better. You must be hungry. What would you like to drink?"

"I want you to get out of my house. If you don't leave here now, I'm going to break this plate over your head." She grabbed the plate of pizza out of my hand, lifted it with her bony arms, and began to thrust it down toward my head. Freezing with fear, I stared at her crazed, maniacal eyes.

With a burst of adrenalin, I turned toward the front door and ran as fast as I could. With all my might, I pulled it open, then ran on trembling legs to my car. Driving down the road I held my breath, reeling, yet feeling grateful that my head was not bleeding.

Sitting in the kitchen, when I got home, I told Marie about it. She joked about it and, soon, my fear faded. My happiness came back as we laughed and laughed uproariously.

The next morning, I sat at the kitchen table and ate breakfast with Julia, an older woman who rented a room on the first level near the front door. She was about ten years older than me, overweight, and wrinkled. An illness, which I could not pronounce, made her shake. I tried to not stare at her wobbling hand as she brought her fork to her mouth. She styled her brunette hair, put on makeup, and looked attractive. Beauty radiated from her inside and out. Listening, with sincere interest, she gave me a feeling that I was special.

After a pleasant talk, I told her I had to go take care of my responsibilities.

Calling my elderly care agency, I missed the fun nights I had had laughing and watching funny movies with Surya and Jyoti. When a well-spoken woman greeted me, she looked up my file. Then, she assigned me a new job taking care of a woman who was confined to a wheel chair.

Driving through downtown Glendale, two days later, I wondered what she would be like. Putting my blinker on, so I could slow down and look for her apartment number, I searched with laser focus. Finally, I saw her number and recognized the color of the building she had described.

Scanning for parking signs, I parked my car. When I saw a meter, I put in a dollar. Walking to her apartment, through long, bleak corridors and up difficult, concrete stairs, I felt lost in a maze. Dizziness dazzled me as I read the various numbers.

Finally, I found it and I knocked on her door. She opened it and looked at me suspiciously. Her small, brownish green eyes narrowed with judgement as she told me to come in. Her tiny, ugly apartment was cluttered and the colors were depressing browns and blacks. Observing her salt and pepper, short hair and her pinched, unhappy, ugly face, I wondered if she would be as crazy as the last one. With a stern tone, she described my duties to me.

I cleaned her bathtub and kitchen, swept and vacuumed and went grocery shopping for her. Doing my best to do things right, I hoped to please her. Sometimes, I helped her get into her tub and I washed her back. Then, I helped her get out and I towel dried her. Everything went smoothly for the first week.

Then, she asked me to cook pancakes for her. I mixed up some batter and poured it into her cast iron frying pan. When the pancake was done, I lifted it out with a fork and put it onto her plate.

"I told you to not use metal in my frying pan. Use the wooden spatula," she yelled, exuding a fury that might break out and hit me, I feared.

"I'm sorry. I forgot", I stammered, then apologized again and again.

Using the wooden spatula, I cooked her another pancake, then put it on a plate and covered it with butter and syrup. As I handed it to her, she glared at me, which shook me to the bones.

Later on, my shoulders hurt as I helped her get into her bath tub. Longing to be pain free, I poured warm water over her and lathered her up with all natural soap. Drying her off with a towel, I tried my best to be gentle. Then, I helped her dress and lay down on her bed. After asking her if she needed anything, I went into her kitchen and cleaned.

When I got home, I ate dinner with Julia, my older house mate. She told me she lived on a government disability check.

"How long have you lived here?" Her interest touched me as I relaxed into her humble, sensitive energy.

"About two years. I came here from the East coast. It's like a different country here. There are so many psychics everywhere. I've never been in a place like this. I've been interested in ESP since I was a child."

"Yeah. It is really interesting. They say that everyone is born with the ability. Some people just develop it more."

"I took some interesting classes at the E.S.P. Academy. Marie went through their complete clairvoyant program. I've been enjoying talking with her about it. I would go through it, but I don't have the money. I live on a government check."

"Yeah. It's hard to just feed yourself on a government check. My daughter helps me a lot." Her sensitive eyes relaxed me.

When Marie suggested that I do a healing on Julia's sick cat, I made my offer to Julia. She gratefully accepted and watched with interest, as I placed my hands on her cat and sent her energy. I hoped it would work and wondered anxiously all afternoon and night if it had.

Reading a book in my quiet room that night, I learned about the energy body. Thoughts flitted through my mind like fireflies as I tried to fall asleep. Then, still, silent darkness took me away from the world.

Singing birds, sounding like an angelic choir, woke me the next morning and I lay there, yawning and stretching. Meditating and praying silently, I looked forward to talking with my house mates and enjoying a day of freedom from work. Typewriter keys clattered as I passed the room by the stairs. Slowly and carefully, holding onto the rail, I walked down the stairs and into the kitchen.

"Julia's cat ate a whole bowl of food and drank some water. She's been running around with so much energy. You're a powerful healer," Marie told me, in a tone of congratulation.

Suddenly, Julia walked in and, with a look of supreme gratitude, thanked me for healing her cat.

I felt overjoyed. The things I had learned at the E.S.P. Academy had given me a new life. I never would have dreamed that I could be a healer. My confidence rose like mercury in a thermometer. Suddenly, I felt like a contribution instead of a parasite sucking on the government's funds.

Soon, Sunday arrived. I felt complimented when Julia asked me to go to church with her. Friendly ushers greeted us and a big, lively choir sang. Gem like colors glowed in the big, stained glass windows. A soulful speaker gave an inspiring, hopeful sermon.

Julia talked in a friendly, relaxed way with me as I walked with her to her car after the service.

"I've got to go to the instant teller and get some cash. I can check on all my millions and millions of dollars" she laughed, looking at me with a funny face.

Patting her on the shoulder, I laughed along with her, thinking what a blessing it was to know another pauper who understood my situation. Pinching our pennies, afraid to even splurge on a restaurant meal, it was challenging to listen to people talk about purchasing boats and vacation homes and traveling to Europe and elsewhere. Enjoying the humor about it helped.

This was an amazing place I had moved to, with interesting people and beautiful scenery. Healthy looking, smiling pedestrians, wearing unique, colorful clothes, walked by as she drove us home.

The moment Julia and I walked into the kitchen, Sylvia reminded us to do our chores. Then, silently, she poured green, nutritional powder into her blender full of blueberries and whipped up a smoothie. The kitchen was too small for three of us, and we felt relieved when Sylvia left.

Sitting at the small table by the window, Julia and I ate some lunch. She sympathized when I told her that my best friend was dying of cancer.

That afternoon, Jyoti and another Hare Krishna devotee came and sat in the backyard with me. I brought Jyoti a pear from the pear tree. Even though it was hard, tasteless and completely inedible, she thanked me.

"We used to have pears that grew on our trees in Wisconsin. We made jelly out of them." Her face looked hollow and her arms were skinny like twigs.

Soon, she would fly away from this troubled world and live forever on the planet of peace and love. She would enjoy the fruits of all of her dedicated service for Krishna.

I talked with Julia later on at the kitchen table. I confided in her that I was considering going back East.

"Don't you want to stay until after your friend dies?"

"I don't know." Cringing at how selfish I sounded, I couldn't bring myself to tell her that I was terrified of seeing a dead person.

I thought about how feeble my father had looked and how he had brightened so visibly when I'd hugged him. The dream of him falling had been emotional and intense. Maybe it was God telling me to go back home.

I sat on Marie's bed later on and poured out my distress to her.

"A psychic at the E.S.P. Academy told me I should live here but I'm feeling like I should go home. I don't know if I should or not."

"I don't have your answer. I need to call it a night so I can get up early for work." Sheepishly, I told her good night and went to my room.

I needed cash. Luckily, when I called the elderly care agency the next morning, they gave me another job. This time, I was to take care of a woman who needed me to drive her to her doctor and to the hair salon.

I did my work for four hours a day, and then visited with Jyoti. She got weaker every day.

One day, I received a letter from my father. I opened it eagerly and read it, holding my breath with emotion.

"I hope you are okay, and I hope that you will come home soon."

He had written a check for two hundred dollars in his shaky handwriting. Tears welled up in my eyes.

I took the train to Santa Rita and visited with Hansa. She treated me to a delicious meal in a Chinese restaurant.

"You're doing great. You found a place so fast. I don't know anyone who can do that. I know you're worried about your father, but you had a visit with him. I'm going through the same thing. My mother might die soon."

"I'm sorry to hear that."

"Yeah. You just have to take care of yourself because there's only so much you can do for them, and God is taking care of them. It's really better for them if you focus on taking care of yourself."

"I've been doing the healing exercises you gave me. They really help me ground myself in the morning."

"That's great. You have really done a lot since you came here. Aren't you glad you moved back?"

I didn't tell her I was going to hit the freeway again. She would worry about me and I didn't want to disturb her.

"You still have to meet my boyfriend. He's traveling now. He travels and teaches meditation. When he's at home, he works on the book he's writing."

"I can't wait to meet him."

At my next therapy session with Jiang Lee, I told her that my parents and teachers had said I was smart, but I felt stupid because I couldn't decide where to live.

"You aren't. You're a remarkable person. Anyone who could move and find a job and an apartment and make friends like you have is not stupid. And you've also studied at the E.S.P. Academy. You need to give yourself some credit for the great strength you have. All you need is your own studio to really progress. You can get that. I know your father will be very happy to see you and will continue to support you. You've made great progress since I started seeing you."

When I walked home, I observed various characters on the street. A couple of them asked me for spare change, so I began avoiding their eyes and walking as fast as I could. A thick, pungent smell of marijuana came from the drug supply store across the street from my old apartment. Trucks roared by, shaking me like a leaf in the wind.

Finally, I turned into the driveway and walked into my house. Marie looked at me with apprehension and judgement.

"I had to go spend the weekend with my parents. Those Hare Krishnas, which you hang out with, have been coming through your aura and disturbing my space. The man who you visit with is working through you and trying to get me to teach him the psychic knowledge for free. Are they the only friends you have?"

I looked down with shame, feeling scolded, humiliated and hurt. It reminded me of my mother complaining about me.

"Yeah. They are. One of them is my best friend and she is dying of cancer." I hoped she would understand. It wasn't my fault that her energy was getting disturbed.

Grief ravaged me when she started avoiding me. I missed the fun times I had enjoyed with her.

Jyoti was constantly loyal though. She had kept me sane. Pain filled me as I drove her to the Hare Krishna temple and watched her teach children every Sunday night. Her eyes were wide with emotion as she savored every moment, knowing her last breath would soon dissolve everything and everyone. She was shockingly thin and her drawn face looked fearful. Her body had weakened so drastically that she needed someone to lift her up off of the floor after the feast.

As I drove her home, I asked her how she was feeling. She said she felt awful, and that she had been throwing up.

I parked my car, and we climbed out and walked into her shack. I helped her as she struggled to lay down in her bed. She winced with pain as her body, which had been sliced in surgery, hit the uncomfortable, second-hand bed, which she had found on the sidewalk. A draft blew through the cracked window, and I asked her if she wanted more blankets. She replied that she was all right in a weak whisper. I wondered if she would still be alive when morning came.

My voice quivered with sadness as I told her good bye. Fear held me in a tight grip, as though one of the demons, which Krishna conquered, had taken me over. Dark shadows swallowed me as I felt myself being sucked into a black hole of emptiness and isolation.

The next morning, I told Sylvia that I wanted to leave. I could not stand the thought of seeing Jyoti lying lifeless on her bed.

Then, the next day, I told her I had changed my mind. She sighed with irritation and looked firmly at me with eyes that flashed with anger.

"You have to go. Another woman is moving in this afternoon. I told you that you could not change your mind again, remember?"

My decision was made for me. I had nothing to do but pack my car and drive across the country again. Jyoti would soon die and I would be homeless, without enough money to rent another place.

In truth, we both were blessed with the opportunity to get out of hell. Jyoti would fly on wings of love as Krishna lovingly carried her to the Vikuntha planet, where she would live in peace and bliss. I would still have planet Earth to deal with. However, I'd settle back home and get my sanity back.

Walking down the block to see Jyoti, I contemplated that Krishna must have arranged for me to live so close to her. Like an angel, she had taken care of me, without expecting anything in return.

Death hovered in the air, like a sinister demon laughing at my grief, when I stepped inside her hovel and saw her, lying like a corpse on the bed. She said few words as I sat at the foot of her bed searching for something to say. Touching her foot, I looked into her fading eyes and asked her if I could bring her anything. She said she didn't need anything.

After a while, she said she would like to get up and sit in the sun. With great tribulation, she pulled herself out of the bed. Leaning on my arm, she walked through her tiny, roadside camper kitchen and then stepped out the door and into the sun. Bunny looked up at us and then scampered happily through the yard. The ancient oak tree showered us with love and oxygen as we sat down on plastic, fold-up chairs.

"Thank you for being such a good friend. I don't want to leave."

"It will be better for you. I've never felt at home here. Don't worry about me." Her eyes and voice were soft and she looked like an angel as she beamed her powerful love into my heart, cracking me open.

We both gazed into the sun for a while.

Then, I told her goodbye, feeling like a baby being pulled from a womb. Tears filled my eyes as I walked to my car and sat inside.

Again, I headed out toward the expressway. Soon, I was driving down the endless expanse of expressway, which glared like Babylon, with money mongering billboards and loud, smelly, poisonous cars.

I would never see Jyoti again. Her laugh rang though me, and I longed to make sweets for Krishna or trim temple hedges with her. I remembered her gentle, loving face as she sat in the temple room teaching the young, restless children about Krishna. She'd spent her life serving others and had never experienced being equal to others. Yet, in all her wisdom, I think she knew that earthly power didn't mean anything.

CHAPTER SEVEN

"If anyone wants to go to law with you over your tunic, hand him your cloak as well. Should anyone press you into service for one mile, go with him for two miles. Give to the one who asks of you, and do not turn your back on one who wants to borrow." Matthew 5:40-42

Always go beyond what is required.

There's a moon in my body...
There's a moon in my body, but I can't see it!
A moon and a sun.
A drum never touched by hands, beating, and I can't hear it!
The musk is inside the deer but the deer does not look for it;
It wanders around looking for grass.

Kabir, There's a Moon in my Body

Here I was out in the middle of nowhere again. That damned psychic had done nothing but take a huge chunk of my money and turn my life upside-down. I had three thousand miles to drive and my back was aching like hell. Cars roared by as I looked at the shopping malls and parking lots on either side of the road. Trucks shook me to the core as they lumbered by, and I imagined the horrendous accidents that were happening all around the country.

Driving over ten hours a day, I had trouble sleeping in the tomb like Motel 6's. I got lost several times when looking for a hotel after dark. The desk clerks who spoke to me must have thought I was strange, with my staring, vacant eyes, longing for a touch on the shoulder or a pat on the back.

The pain in my lower back, legs and shoulders got worse every day.

When I first arrived back East, I went to my cousin's lakeside house in the country. Sleeping in the comfortable guest bed and talking with my cousin lifted my spirits greatly.

The second day there, I got a call from Bindu saying that Jyoti had died. Grief paralyzed me. All I could do was stare at the wall and listen to her sweet voice in my mind.

Torn between two worlds, I paced back and forth. I wanted to visit my ninety-four-year-old friend, Harry, but I felt that he probably had passed away. Months before I had moved, I had stopped picking him up at his house and going to the health food restaurant. His son had told him that he did not want me coming over anymore because he didn't trust me. He thought I was draining his bank account because he had loaned me two thousand dollars to record my music.

I thought it might be upsetting for my elderly friend if his son started locking him in or yelling at him. So, I just stopped calling him. It must have broken his heart. He had made my musical ambitions possible when my father thwarted them.

He would look at me and then point at the sky and say, "Thou art that!"

Other times, when I left him at his house after a great dinner in the health food restaurant, he said, "I love you with all my heart and my soul. We will always be together."

Sometimes, I told him that my parents had not opened the door when I went over to visit them. His response always lifted my mood.

"I don't understand why they don't welcome you. Don't let them bother you. Just keep that money coming because you need it."

He made me laugh when we went to our favorite health food restaurant. Walking up to peoples' tables, he would cheerfully surprise them.

"Can I have a bite of that?" he would say, taking something off of a stranger's plate. No one could get angry at this sweet man.

"I'm ninety-four years old, and I haven't had one bite of meat, fish, or fowl for sixty-five years. And look at me! No doctor, no medicine." He would hold up his arms and flex his muscles like Charles Atlas on the beach.

I called my friend, Gary, who had often invited me to work out at the Fitness Center. He was great fun, and I had loved being beside him as we ran on the treadmills. We had graduated from the same college.

My spirits always rose when he generously filled my hands with vitamins or complimented me. Nothing but encouragement was in his words, not like my father. My confidence rose when he wrote a wonderful review of my hypnotherapy for my brochure. When he talked, a vast reservoir of knowledge about natural health and world history poured out, renewing my mind like a fresh, spring breeze.

One time, we both took an acting class. Our mutual friend was an eccentric, poverty stricken, yet brilliant woman. She had us act out scenes from several plays that she had written. We had performed a comic sketch about two people shopping together in a health food store.

I had missed him since I moved almost two and a half years ago. I dialed his number. A sinking feeling went through me when he gave me a feeble-sounding greeting.

"I had to go to the emergency room at Grady. It was a horrible experience and I couldn't get anyone to listen to me. I was on a stretcher next to stabbing victims and people with gunshot wounds. It was chaotic with everyone piled into this noisy room together. They treated me with some unusual chemical and it burned my skin off. I'm not going to live much longer. There's nothing that can be done. I'm fried like a French fry."

"Oh, I'm sorry to hear that. I want to come see you."

"I'm not anything to look at. You don't want to see me, really... believe me."

I had become so numb I didn't shed one tear. I wondered what was wrong with me. He was the best man I had ever had. Respectful, kind, generous, encouraging, interesting, reliable--his virtues went on and on.

I wished I had married him when we were both young college students. He remembered that we had been in the same poetry class together, when we attended summer school. Yes, my face had, long ago, been so beautiful that it was unforgettable. Now, it was getting more hideous every day.

One afternoon we had climbed to the top of a big hotel and looked out over the city. We had talked about how we hadn't been prepared for the high tech world with our liberal arts college education. We'd talked about God and the mess the planet was in.

I came back to the present moment. Sitting in my cousin's kitchen, I watched her prepare dinner. I told her that I was worried about not following the psychic's advice. She replied that she was worried about me because I was worrying too much.

She led me upstairs, gave me a fluffy towel and some bath salts and suggested I relax in a hot tub. The hot water, with its massaging jets, sent tingling, pleasurable sensations through me and my muscles became like jelly. My pain dissolved.

Later on, we sat on the sofa. The T.V. buzzed with chatter and, now and then, I looked at a show about women who transformed their appearance by having surgery. In between curious looks, I concentrated as my cousin showed me how to crochet a scarf.

I did not want to leave the next morning but I had to get myself settled. Driving to Madison, I felt strangely disconnected from everything and everyone. I got a hunch to call my younger sister's best friend.

He drove me around to look for a place to rent. I felt grateful when he talked to the landlord and sealed the deal for me, sparing me the task of explaining my income. Being poor was embarrassing. Soon, I had a home down the street from him.

I started pounding the pavements at local malls. Soon, I landed a job taking surveys. I felt guilty for wasting people's time as I asked them irritating questions about what brands of cereal and toothpaste they bought. Every hour, I earned four dollars and hated every minute of it.

After a couple of months I quit.

Luckily, the symphony hired me to ask people to donate to their children's' music programs. When I found out I got free symphony tickets, I hoped my father would attend it with me.

I called my old friend, Margaret, who I used to exchange hypnotherapy sessions with. She had given me wonderful massages. Her mother lit into her sometimes, she had once confided to me sadly. Her caring listening gave me trust in her, as I told her about living out West and how I was happy to be back in the South. Telling her I had missed her, I felt glad when she said she felt the same. There was a hesitation in her voice and I wondered if she was alright.

I invited her to go to a country music concert the symphony sponsored with me. Her voice lifted with happy anticipation as she replied that she would love to go. As I drew the conversation to a close, I mentioned that I hoped her mother was being nice.

A few days later, I picked her up at her house to take her to a country music concert, thanking God that my telemarketing job gave me two free tickets.

"Don't ever say anything like that again. My mother cussed me out."

"Oh, no. I'm sorry."

"The drugs they're giving me are killing me, and they make me wish I was dead. I'm always drowsy, and my mind is foggy. But if I go off of them I'll have panic attacks. You don't want to see me have one. I shake all over and relive the bad car accident I was in."

I listened to Margaret's anxieties as I drove us to the concert. She sadly told me that she had had to give up her healing practice, and that her life had shrunk to nothing. I was the first person to ask her out in ages and her face beamed with gratitude.

The concert was fun and uplifting. The funny, country song lyrics made me laugh. People danced around gaily. Lovers kissed and friends swayed with their arms around one another. They looked happy as they drank wine and ate delicious food out of picnic baskets. When Margaret said she loved the performers, I felt victorious because I had brought some joy into her difficult life.

As I drove home, cars screeched by, blasting loud music. I noticed her looking frightened as we passed through busy intersections, with red, yellow and green lights flashing and carbon monoxide assaulting our nostrils. Sometimes, a bump in the road made her flinch in fear.

Finally, with relief, I pulled into her driveway. Her gentle voice calmed me as she thanked me and wished me the best. Watching her with peaceful nostalgia, I watched her disappear into her mother's house. Emptiness grabbed my guts as I drove home in silence, feeling pins and needles stabbing my buttocks and legs.

The next day, I felt like a contribution, doing the good service of raising money for the children's' music programs. My co-workers were kind and I liked having their company. The boss was friendly and encouraging and I liked the familiar feeling of the place. It was right across the street from where I used to take drawing classes in high school.

"Just keep your eyes on the script and repeat it word for word. After a while, it will be second nature to you," my new boss said.

When I mentioned that I had just moved back from Glendale, he lit up and looked at me with protective eyes.

"I used to live in Glendale. People are very friendly at first, and then you never see them again. It's very expensive. I've had it with Glendale."

I gave all I had to my job, listening to Tony Robbins tapes to get energized and passionate before I started work every day. There was nothing that could compare to the feeling of success I felt when someone said they would like to contribute. I was nurturing the young Mozarts of the world.

Just when I thought I had cleansed Glendale out of my system, Madhu called.

"You are not a ping pong ball! You left all of a sudden. I was shocked when I found out you were gone. I've been worrying about you. What's going on? You have a lot of people out here who love you. You found a nice house, and you were working. Come back here. You can stay with me until you find a place. I miss you. You're more alive here. You're a very sweet girl, and I want you to be happy."

I told Madhu I had to go and hung up the phone.

The West coast could go to hell. Enjoying the familiarity of home, I called my father and invited him to go to the symphony on Friday. The weather was cold and bleak, so I spent the weekend reading, in my bed, buried underneath lots of blankets.

Soon, Friday arrived and I looked forward to having one on one time with him. He lit up like a sunrise when I picked him up. He was standing, waiting expectantly, leaning on his cane. Shocked by his frailty, I watched him struggle to open the passenger door and sit down beside me. His hip must have been hurting but he never complained.

Driving through the lush, green neighborhoods, I felt safe with him by my side. When we arrived at the Symphony Hall, I pulled up to the valet and gave him my keys. Opening the door for my father, I watched him struggle, with his back severely arched over. Leaning all his weight on his cane, he hobbled along as though he might collapse at any moment.

Well-dressed people walked along and conversation buzzed around us. After a long, precarious walk, he slid into a red, plush symphony seat. Sitting beside him, I rooted myself into the earth, listening to the orchestra members tune their instruments. As he helped me pull my arm out of my sweater, I wanted the moment to last forever.

The orchestra began to play. The music carried me away to a simpler time, when I slept in my cozy childhood room without a care. I envisioned us swimming at the country club or sitting on the porch in the summer eating barbeque and drinking sweet, Southern iced tea with mint. Admiring the gorgeous trees, bushes and flowers my mother planted, I had sat with my father and listened to him talk about history and wars and science. He was an encyclopedia of facts, overflowing with interesting, unique wisdom. I would give anything to be a child under his roof again and hear him say, "It's a hard, cruel world out there."

When I was young and naïve, I'd thought he was just a cynic who saw the worst in everyone. Now, I wished I had been less trusting. It would have saved me from a lot of hellish experiences. Basking in the safety of his sheltering protection, I remembered the touching, old T.V. show "Father Knows Best".

The symphony sounded vibrant, like the music of the spheres carrying me into a dimension of peace and love. The beautiful tones of the violins and cellos, oboes and flutes blended together in perfect harmony. Calm energy swirled through my body, refreshing and enlivening me.

I remembered my high school days when we sat in this same enchanted hall and listened to my older sister play her violin with the symphony. She had bullied me through my first three years of high school.

During intermission, we stood up and walked out to the aisle. A dark haired, distinguished-looking man looked at my father and greeted him.

Kundalini Rising

"He's my hero," he said, looking at me and then my father. Feeling glad the evening was bringing sweetness, I watched them shake hands.

"Hi, Dan. This is my daughter," my father said proudly, sending a rush of emotion through me.

Another one of his hospital co-workers was sitting nearby. When he noticed my father, he walked over, beaming with fondness, and shook his hand.

Dad smiled. I studied his thin, aged hands. Time was running out.

The rest of the concert was delightful, as I tingled with goosebumps, thrilling to the exquisite music. When the concert ended, I sat in awed reverence, not wanting to leave my seat. We sat in silence for a few minutes and, then, began walking.

He hobbled along the crimson carpet of the symphony hall, barely mustering the strength to hold himself up on his cane. Slowly and with careful effort, he sat down on the front bench. A friend of his appeared, and they talked with each other for a few minutes. Happiness filled me because I had succeeded in giving him some greatly needed happiness.

Outside, a valet drove my car up near the entrance. Standing up, I took my father's hand and we walked slowly to the car. He struggled to maneuver himself in and groaned in pain when his backside hit the seat.

The motor roared and I turned out of the symphony grounds and merged slowly into the line of traffic. I tried to think of things to say as I drove him home, swallowing my remorse that I had never told him I loved him. I'd never told him much about what was going on in my life, besides the fact that I was always broke. I decided to tell him about a talk I had had with someone about politics the other day.

"I don't keep up with politics enough to express much of an opinion," I started, eager to say something he would approve of.

"So, when this person started talking about their dislike of a politician, I remembered a quote from some famous person who said, 'If you want to have friends, don't ever talk about sex, politics, or religion.' When I repeated it, I felt glad to get out of discussing politics. I can't figure it out."

"Yeah. Mark Twain said that," my father, the walking encyclopedia, replied. He was an interesting conversationalist. I learned something new every time I talked with him.

Longing to spend the night in my old, magically beautiful childhood home, I watched him push, with the little strength he could muster, to open my car door. Shocked by his frailty, I watched him hobble into the house through the side door, leaning for dear life upon his cane. Wailing with sadness, I drove home.

My mother called the next day and angrily told me that my mail was at her house. Longing for her to ask me how I was and tell me she missed me, I stared at the wall, drowning in hurt, as she hung up abruptly. Once, she had loved my company and I missed those times. Now, she thought I was a scoundrel.

Depression tied me into knots as I went through the day. That night, I had a nightmare, in which I drove to the country club to meet my parents and a black vampire attacked me with a large, sharp knife.

The next morning, I dressed for work, feeling foggy. Praying to my angels to give me an answer about where I should live, I walked to my car. I turned my key in the ignition and the motor roared.

"I'm gonna take you on a trip so far from here," played on my radio. It must be a sign from my angels telling me to return to Glendale.

My boss complimented me when I arrived at work, and I felt valuable.

"You've really improved. You're bringing in a lot of money. How do you do it?" His encouraging eyes glowed with caring.

"I really believe in the cause. I love children, and I want them to get the music education they need. I've been listening to Tony Robbins and getting myself to feel passionate. I've been getting really nice people on the phone."

"Well, keep up the good work." He shook my hand in congratulations. A wonderful rush of happiness flowed through me as I enjoyed his approval.

Later on, during a break, he talked about his experience living and working as a waiter in Glendale. He used to wait on celebrities like Dean Martin. Life had gotten too hard for him because of the high expenses, so he had decided to move to the East.

That night, Madhu called me. I was getting sick of being hounded by her. It was nervy of her to try to run my life.

"You've got to come back here. You have people here who love you," Madhu insisted.

"I would have to pay twelve hundred dollars to break my lease and leave here. I'm trapped. I can't save that."

"That's ridiculous. People back there are jerks. They shouldn't expect you to pay that just to move out. No one here would do that. It's all screwy back there. People don't care about you. I'm gonna tell Krishna you need help. Don't worry. He'll get you out of that trap. Oh, my God—twelve hundred dollars. That is highway robbery. They should not be allowed to get away with crap like that. Tell them you don't have twelve hundred dollars! That you've been a good tenant, but now it is time for you to move. If I were there, I would tell them that God is going to strike them dead for putting you through so much worry. They are criminals. You belong here. Everyone misses you."

At work the next day, my boss asked everyone to work on Saturday, promising to cook delicious treats and show his appreciation. On our break, I listened to Mark talk, as we stood outside and watched the traffic pass by the art college. People gunned their motors as they drove by.

"The way people drive here is crazy. A man cut me off and then blew his horn at me the other day. I'm fed up with this place. I'm moving back West. I've had one bad experience after another since I came here. I can't even find a place to play my music here." His long, wavy hair made him look like a bohemian.

It seemed like the angels were giving me a sign to move back there. I decided for a minute that I was going to move back.

Then, I heard the Tarot teacher, psychic's voice: "I don't think you're meant to live here all the time. I think you came here to learn a lesson."

Okay. I didn't have to move back, I decided. That was then and now was now. My dear spiritual sister, Jenny in Australia, had given me a different perspective by saying that, maybe, Madison had not been the place for me, at that particular time. That did not mean it would never be the place for me.

I loved receiving Madhu's attention and love, but I didn't have to do what she told me to do. I'd hang up on her the next time she demanded that I get in my car and drive back. Driving across country was no fun. In fact, it was agonizing, sitting in my car for ten hours a day, feeling the aches and pains in my back, worrying that a gang would strand me on the side of the road and rape me.

The week flew by and Saturday arrived. Driving to work, I looked forward to hearing words of approval from my boss. Luckily, I got several huge donations. Taking a break, I munched on his special food. He was an excellent chef.

As I was leaving at the end of the day, he talked about his experience running a restaurant when he lived out West. I told him I had lived there and wanted to return.

"People are more aware and progressive there." I reminisced about the psychics, staring at the floor.

"There are people like that here. It's too expensive out there. You're better off here. You have family here don't you?"

"Yeah."

"Well, I hope you'll stay here. It will be better for you."

Loneliness came over me when I left work. Sitting on the sofa my cousin gave me, I stared into space, feeling deadened by the silence.

I called Madhu. All week, I had been observing husbands/wives, best friends and parents/children combos that I envied for their warm closeness.

"You need to come on back. You have a lot of friends here. Did you talk with the apartment manager about the lease? It's not fair of them to keep you trapped there. Everyone misses you out here. Bindu has been asking me how you are doing."

"Well, I'm really sad. I've only gotten to take my dad to the symphony a few times. I'm afraid to go over to the house and see my mother. I'm afraid she'll tell me to leave. She won't even take the time to speak to me on the phone."

"Oh, poor dear. You need a mother. I'm your mother. I will always listen to you, and I'll never be cruel to you. You're a very sweet girl, and I love you. You're going to be all right. I think you feel more alive out here than you do back there. Those people are stuck in their ways. You need your friends out here. I worry about you being too isolated back there."

Maybe she was right. Suddenly, I made my decision to get out of my lease, somehow. As though I was under a spell, I called my apartment manager.

Miraculously, she said she would waive the fee because I had been such a good tenant. She sympathized when I told her I was on a fixed income.

When I told my boss I had decided to move, he said he wished I would stay. However, he called the manager of the Santa Rita symphony and gave him an excellent review of my work. He also wrote me a very complimentary letter of recommendation.

Like an obsessive-compulsive zombie, I gave the sofas my cousin had given me and the bed my sister had given me to the Salvation Army. My boss looked disappointed and sad. He got everyone to sign a big card for me. They all wrote kind notes wishing me good luck.

Sadness filled me as I told my sister's friend goodbye. I would miss having him pick me up at my place every Sunday to take me to his church, where the atmosphere was informal, friendly and fun.

My sister said she wished I would stay when I told her goodbye. I felt deeply sad, knowing I would miss her.

The drive across country was grueling as sharp, shooting pains ran from my buttock down my leg. After a few days, I'd driven all the way to Arizona. I turned on the car radio and the song lines "Just keep heading to the East!" blared out.

It seemed to be a message from the angels, so I turned around and started driving back East.

Then, I turned around again and drove west. Nonsense ran through my mind as I drove nervously with my shoulders pushed up around my ears. Like a deluded, raving lunatic, I listened to various voices in my head as I flew to my illusive, deceptive, imaginary utopia. A self-deceiving, isolated traveler, I sped down the road vacantly on a destructive journey to nowhere.

When I arrived at the Hare Krishna compound, I parked my car and walked, as numb as a door knob through the wooden door, securing the iron latch behind me. Longing for Jyoti, like a lost child, I knocked on her door. Her husband was steeped in grief and, as he spoke with me briefly, Jyoti's ghost seemed to hover around, sending me love.

When I stepped out of the cluttered hovel, Bunny came running toward me and bumped against me, rubbing affectionately against me. I patted his sweet head and knocked on Bindu's door. She welcomed with a hug. When I told her I needed a room, she told me I could stay in her extra room until I found a place.

The droning, non-stop sound of a deep-voiced man singing, "Hare Krishna, Hare Krishna," over and over again rubbed my nerves raw. I couldn't sleep on Bindu's uncomfortable, thin futon. I could feel the hard, wooden slats underneath pressing into the inflamed, painful areas of my buttocks, sending spasms of pain through me. Fear of aging dragged me into deep depression as the sharp pain seared my nerve endings. Longing to have my youth back, I thought regretfully about all the things I would have done differently.

I boarded a train to Santa Rita and, when I arrived in the telemarketing office, I worried that I seemed frazzled. The boss introduced himself and spoke a little about the job. All the while, I prayed that he would hire me.

My whole body relaxed when he told me he had faith in me and welcomed me aboard. Luckily, I was hiding my depression well.

Bindu congratulated me when I told her I had a job. She was sweet company and I enjoyed her encouraging words and attention. However, her "Hare Krishna" tape droned on all day, irritating me to the point where I felt I would sell my soul to have some silence. I went into my room and sat staring blankly at the Hare Krishna books.

I called Meryl, a friend I had met at my Saturday morning Al Anon meeting, in Glendale, two years ago. She sounded glad to hear from me and invited me to attend a meeting with her that evening. Happiness surged through me when she said she would pick me up. I gave her directions.

After I hung up, I poured through apartment listings, worrying about the rapidly dwindling numbers in my checkbook. I would need to go to the Social Security Office the next day and update them on my income. After making many calls, I finally set up an interview.

Walking around downtown Glendale, I inquired in various shops, asking if they could use part time help. No one needed me and I got tired of asking.

So, I stepped up into a bus and rode it to the ocean.

The waves gleamed like lightning as the powerful sun shone on them. Seagulls called, soaring effortlessly through the wind tossed air. Fluffy clouds floated against the radiant, blue sky, moving and changing shapes with hypnotic, effortless fluidity. Sea salt smells drifted into my nostrils, stimulating my senses. Wiggling my toes in the wet, soft sand, I watched the white capped waves cresting onto the shore. Watching them rush over my feet, I felt myself sink into the sand, with a flying sensation, as they moved back out to sea.

Walking along, I saw a man flying a bright, yellow kite with his daughter. She laughed playfully and ran and jumped with great energy. She had her whole life ahead of her. I winced in embarrassment over my envy.

Beginning to run, I sucked in the power of the sun, imagining it filling every part of me. The blazing heat seemed to sear my skin and a cool breeze felt marvelous as it touched me mercifully. Watching white sails shine in the sun and huge cargo boats chugging along, I heard the song "I'd rather be a hammer than a nail" play through my mind.

Being out in nature, in the vast expansiveness opened and expanded me. As I rode the bus home, I dreaded feeling cramped in my tiny room.

Laying down on my futon, I read a book until it was time for Meryl to pick me up. I craved her friendliness as I walked out to the curb and waited.

"How are you?" she asked as I got into her car.

"I'm okay. It is difficult living with my Hare Krishna friend though. She keeps a chanting tape playing constantly and yells at her boyfriend on the phone. I need some peace and quiet."

"Oh, that sounds like a challenge. I hope you find a better place soon," Meryl replied with sympathy.

The Al-Anon meeting was in a tall, medical building. People listened to me attentively as I told my story about driving back and forth across the country. I told them my father was the alcoholic, and that I had longed to have a closer relationship with him all my life. Tears welled up in my eyes when I told them that I had moved back there to be close to him and that I had never been good enough for him. He had wanted me to make straight A's, and I never had. Then, I talked about how I had never been good at making money and how my parents had shamed me for it.

A woman with dark, wavy hair, in a pretty, green dress, told me that her father used to rage at her. She listened with compassion as I told her I was living in a difficult situation where I could not get any peace or quiet. After everyone had shared about the challenges they were facing, we mingled and talked with each other.

As my friend drove me home, I remembered seeing her at meetings when I lived in the Glendale hills. She had invited me to her small apartment, one day, and fed me blueberries. When I moved, I had lost her phone number. God must have brought her back to me. Relaxing into her generous energy, I enjoyed her positive voice. Pulling up to the curb at my place, she said she would pick me up in five days for our next meeting.

At the next meeting, I talked about my fears. I shared that I thought I must be in the middle of a midlife crisis. Like a lunatic, I had driven across the country ten times, by myself.

When the meeting was over, a blonde, frail woman gently took me by the hand and looked into my eyes. Her name was Cathy.

"You're going to be all right. God is taking care of you. Here's my phone number. You can call and talk with me."

I gazed into her eyes with gratitude. Cathy, Meryl, and I talked as we rode the elevator down to the ground floor and walked to our cars. Meryl dropped me off at Bindu's place and wished me the best.

The noise and chaos sent me plummeting even deeper into depression. "Hare Krishna. Hare Krishna. Hare Rama. Rama. Rama." her tape player droned non-stop. Lying back on the uncomfortable futon, I longed for a good night's sleep. Pins and needles stabbed sharply into my buttocks and legs. I fell asleep wincing in pain.

When morning came, my mind felt feeble. It had gotten hard to remember things. Fear of aging froze me, especially when I observed how miserable the elderly clients I worked for were. Fumbling into the kitchen, I opened the refrigerator and gobbled down some cold beans. Returning to my room, I sorted through my wrinkled, torn clothes and found a halfway decent looking shirt and pair of pants.

Riding the train to work, I wrote in a journal. Hellos from my co-workers lifted my spirits. My boss congratulated me when I got a donation.

After I got home, I eagerly called Cathy. She listened with empathy as I told her about my unhappiness. When she invited me to visit with her, I felt suddenly special.

The next morning, I rode the train to Cathy's house. She smiled in a motherly way as she sat on the sofa in her sunny living room.

"I'm going to interview at an apartment tomorrow," I told her. "It is not too far away from where I'm staying now. I'll be glad to move. I can't get one second of silence."

"Yeah. I wouldn't like it either."

"I lived in the Glendale Hills when I first moved here. I worked as a substitute in preschools, and I did elderly care. Lately, I've been telemarketing for the symphony. I raised money for the children's programs that the symphony does in schools. I did that when I was back in Madison. I went back there to be near my father but didn't get to be with him as much as I wanted to. I don't think he's going to live much longer. But I came back here because two psychics told me that I belong here."

"Oh. I went to a psychic once. What they told me was right. I was surprised. I moved out here after I graduated from nursing school. Some girlfriends and I formed a caravan and drove out here together. We had fun following each other. The truck drivers used to move over to let us pass by. They would smile and wave at us. It was friendly back then, but that was well over twenty years ago. I wouldn't do it now."

"I remember that my first two years here were difficult. I wondered why I had moved here and didn't think I would last. Luckily, I made friends and things got easier. I married a famous medical doctor and had his two children. We've been divorced for fifteen years now, though. He fell in love with someone else."

When I went on my interview the next day, an elderly lady talked with me and showed me the room I could rent. It was a small, basement apartment in the bottom of her house. She seemed to be well-off, and talked about her experience teaching and her travels around Europe.

"My husband died several years ago," she said sadly.

Frightening headlines about the increase in the cost of utilities had been sending me into black holes of anxiety. Breathing deeply to stay calm, I still tensed up when she told me the rent was five hundred dollars a month. Continuing, she informed me that, in the winter months, she had to turn the heat up high and run it constantly because the house didn't have good insulation. I shuddered with dread, visualizing two hundred dollar utility bills.

"You seem like a nice person. Sometimes I get free food and you are welcome to have a box of it every couple of weeks."

Her aged face was wrinkled and her hair was short, dark brown, thinning and had some grey areas. She asked me what I did for a living and I told her that I lived on a government disability check. Luckily, it did not seem to disturb her and she said she would like me to move in.

With fear, I wrote her a check for two hundred and fifty dollars, for the deposit. She smiled as I handed it to her.

I visited Cathy the next day and told her I had paid a deposit and was planning to move in with a woman who had interviewed me. She handed me a glass of grape juice as I sat down.

"Did she give you a receipt?"

"No. She just said that I could move in after she returned from Europe. She seemed nice, like she wanted to help me. She said that she would give me free food when she got it."

"She hasn't given you anything in writing. It is not a real agreement. You don't have a leg to stand on and your utility bills are going to go sky high. It could go up to three hundred a month now that all the rates have increased. You can't afford them, and she can tell you to leave the minute you don't pay them. I don't think you should move in there. I'm going to ask Joe what he thinks." Joe was her neighbor, who dressed as a clown and went to children's' parties.

"Yeah. I see what you mean. It is a tense situation since I have so little money. I didn't know what else to do but take it."

"You can move in with me. I don't want you to be isolated there, worrying and maybe getting kicked out. You're a good person. I could tell that the minute I met you. You're vulnerable and you need some help. I see you trying hard, but you just can't make it all alone. You need someone to talk to. I'm a trained counselor, and you can talk with me any time. I think you should call that woman, and tell her you're not going to move in and that you want the deposit back."

Receiving such attention felt so unfamiliar that I nervously knocked the glass of grape juice off of the table. I apologized again and again as she cleaned it up.

Like a lost child, I followed Cathy outside to her station wagon. As I sat down in the passenger seat, she asked me to navigate her to the apartment of the woman I had given my deposit to. Driving along the winding streets, Cathy talked to me, reassuring me, giving me a feeling of safety.

We arrived at the house. Cathy parked her car and got out. Determined and firm, I walked forward. Soon, I was near her. She sat on the front porch with her daughter. I told her, in a calm tone, that I had decided I was not going to move in with her.

She said she could not give me back my deposit. Looking over my shoulder, I saw Cathy silently cheering me on, sending me mother lion energy.

Suddenly, electrical jolts of energy crackled in the air as Cathy denounced her bravely. My inner child basked peacefully in her loyal protection. With admiration, I listened to her strong, firm voice.

"I am a Glendale land owner. I know that you have not given her a proper rental agreement. I would not have treated a tenant the way you've treated her. You have given her nothing in writing, and you could tell her to leave at any time, and she would have no ground to stand on. You should give her deposit back."

"I don't agree," the woman said.

"Come on, let's go," Cathy said.

Thinking of the times I wished my real mother had been on my side, I followed her to her car, feeling grateful that she had taken me under her wing.

Surveying the shops and pedestrians, I looked out the window, feeling like a teenager with her Mom, as we rolled down the busy streets.

Soon, we were home and she parked in front of her gorgeous, crimson Camelia bush. Watching her unlock the door, I breathed in safety and security. We sat out on her sunny porch. Feeling grateful for her protection, I relaxed in my chair, enjoying the sound of birds.

"These are the end times. We need to turn everything over to God and be in the company of good, spiritual people. The love of Jesus is there for us if we will let him into our hearts. They teach us at my church that we must love everyone unconditionally. A lot of people are suffering. We must reach out and show them we care."

Hummingbirds flew around her lemon tree. The hill across the way glistened in the sun, its twisting trees casting interesting shadows. The sun felt warm on my face. Cathy looked at me with sensitive caring, like a fairy Godmother.

Back at Bindu's, I felt in the way. My interaction was limited to quickly grabbing my plastic container of beans out of the crowded refrigerator every day. Bindu's son would look through me coldly.

When I moved in with Cathy, a soft sand dune of welcoming love relaxed me. I basked in her openness and generosity. My room had a dresser, chest and a comfortable, queen-sized bed, with a royal blue bedspread.

As I sat on the sofa talking with her, I suddenly felt lovable, after feeling all my life that no one wanted me.

"You're like a feral child." Cathy commented. I drank her love thirstily, wanting this rare eye-contact to last forever.

"You can just pay four hundred a month here, and that includes the utilities. You would have been desperate if you had moved in with that dishonest woman. When the cost of utilities went through the roof, she would have told you to leave. Put your shoulders down. You can relax now."

Cathy told me funny stories and we talked late into the night.

I slept deeply as silence soothed me and my mind became as still as a mirror. There was only the moment. Pure peace and love washed over me, as I connected to Cathy's heart beating in the next room.

"How was it to sleep in a real bed?" she asked the next morning, looking happy to see me.

"It was heaven. I'm so glad to be here and out of that hellhole madhouse. You've saved my life."

"I'm glad that I could. There's some grape and apple juice in the fridge. Help yourself. I'll show you where the farmer's market is. It's just down the street in the mall. They have wonderful produce there, and the prices are low."

We talked most of the day, and then I headed out to make calls for the symphony. My manager greeted me with a smile. I said hello to my co-workers. A guy, with a good sense of humor, told a funny story that made everyone laugh.

After our shift, everyone went out to a restaurant to celebrate. The symphony had reached its financial goal for the year. I listened to conversations buzz around me as I enjoyed belonging to a team. The Italian food was delicious and the sweet desert with coffee pleased everyone.

I observed people as I rode the train to the station and the bus to my neighborhood. When I finally arrived at home, Cathy gave me a long, wonderful hug.

"Let's go to an Al-Anon meeting this Saturday night. I go to a meeting at least once a week. My friend is going to pick me up. You need to be with people who understand what you've been through."

Safe, mellow feelings flowed through me as we sat and talked. Her short, bleached blond hair and curious blue eyes gave her a child-like innocence.

"I had a horrible childhood. My father would get angry and scare everyone. Sometimes, he'd play the piano until three in the morning. He didn't care that no one could sleep. My mother let him get away with anything. She wasn't strong enough to speak up to him and set limits. He was a well-respected doctor so no one ever had the courage to disagree with him. He hit me across the face one time when we were at our summer house. I got so upset, I went to sleep in the car to be away from everyone. No one came to check on me."

"That's sad. My father used to lose his temper and strap me with his belt," I shared. "I never deliberately did anything wrong. My mother would never stand up for me. He treated her like shit too."

Cathy listened intently, her eyes wide and moist with empathy and her brows furrowed. She continued to tell her story.

"One time, my father was drunk, and he was in the bathroom swearing and cussing. My brother got upset and banged the door down. A splinter of wood came out of the door and stuck in my brother's eye and blinded him. He never forgave my father. My other brother left home. They are twins. It was a horrible home environment. My father was such a control freak, he would not let me make phone calls or have friends over. I felt trapped."

"I felt like that too," I said. "I would stay alone in my room to be away from the sound of my parents arguing. Sometimes, my father would get drunk and follow my mother around the house. She would slam doors in his face and yell at him. Once, I intervened trying to protect my mother. Suddenly, he hit me across the face. I went to school with a black eye. When classmates asked what happened, I replied that I had run into a door knob accidentally. I was too embarrassed to tell them what really happened."

"I'm sorry to hear that, sweetie. You've been through a lot. You need to build healthy relationships. No one can cope with life all alone. You need friends to talk to. My father would not let me have any friends or talk with any friends on the phone. I had to get out of my trap at home. When I was in high school, I started training with an Olympics coach. I practiced diving all of the time to stay away from that miserable house. My coach was really wonderful, and I got so good that I competed in the Olympics."

"Wow. That's incredible."

Now, even though she was only fourteen years older than me, she had been through two horrendous surgeries. All they had given her was more pain. Most of the day, she lay on a sofa with a heating pad on her back. It never took the pain away though.

If I was going to achieve anything, I'd have to hurry and do it before my body gave out. I needed to get my act together right away. In only two years, I would be fifty. It scared the hell out of me. I had failed at romance and I had no children, so the only thing left for me was a career.

"You are co-dependent. A lot of children of alcoholics struggle with that. I have it too," Cathy told me.

I wondered if it was true.

"You don't know who you are," she said, looking at me with empathy.

I wanted to reprimand her for criticizing me, yet I knew that she was right. All I knew was how to clean a window, wipe a counter, or mop a floor. I could scoop ice cream, and I could run a cash register, but I did not know who I was beyond that. I wanted more.

I wrote journals and dreamed of being a writer. However, everything I wrote sounded dull--nothing like the spellbinding, riveting writing I read in books when I browsed through bookstores. No one would want to read my self-obsessed, depressing writing.

I loved music but my voice was undeveloped and the tunes I composed were repetitive and lacking in brilliance. I'd never had money for lessons.

"I was trained as a Christian counselor. I will counsel you."

I gave my two CDs to Cathy and told her about the efforts I had made to find out who I was. She walked to her CD player and put them in. My voice filled the room. I didn't like the sound of it.

"That's you," she said, smiling as though she was proud of me.

I looked down in shame.

"You have a beautiful voice. And you wrote all of the songs? I'm really impressed."

"Yeah. I'm too old to do anything with it though."

"No, you aren't. There's a lady I know who got on the radio, and she's over fifty. I will take your tapes to the radio station, and they will play them. Your life is just beginning. It's not all over until the fat lady sings."

Later, we went to a Mexican restaurant where they served huge enchiladas. It was somewhat crowded with cheerful, chatty people.

"You can look into the kitchen and watch them rolling up the burritos," Cathy said, smiling at me with affection.

Purring like a kitten, I enjoyed her mothering energy. She winked at me and said she was treating me. Then, she said I could walk over and watch the Mexican laborers rolling tortillas out on a long table. As I watched, I got hungry. Walking back toward Cathy, I felt light and peaceful. Her caring smile relaxed me as I sat down.

The spicy beans and warm, soft and crunchy, cheesy tortillas were delicious. I ate with gusto and washed it all down with Sprite.

Cathy talked lightly as she drove us home.

Kundalini Rising

The next morning, we sat on her porch by her beautiful lemon tree. The lush, green pine and cypress trees towered above sending us oxygen as frogs ribbeted. I watched the gnarled, twisted trees sway in the wind. Cathy looked at me, eager to sooth my soul.

"We're all the walking wounded. We need someone to listen to us. I'm a Christian. I believe the power of love is the greatest thing there is. I will pray for you. One time, about twenty-five years ago, I saw a huge, flaming cross in the sky. It was amazing. I knew then that God was calling me to minister to people. I stared at it with awe for most of the night. It was incredible. I knew that it was Jesus communicating with me, telling me to develop a close relationship with him and to help other people by giving them his word. You have a beautiful, pure spirit, and Jesus and God are blessing you every day. I'm glad I met you."

We sat on Cathy's sunny porch every day. I didn't have to go to work until 5 p.m., so I enjoyed letting her nurse my broken spirit back to health. Yet, sometimes my rebellious inner child unleashed its angry voice. I squirmed and resisted and even got sarcastic with Cathy.

"You need to process your feelings," she said, when we were sitting on the sunny porch.

"Is that like processed cheese?" I stared down at the ground, not allowing her to penetrate the wall around my heart.

"You're co-dependent and you have A.D.D. I know it must be hard for you when you forget things. It will help if you'll get a big calendar and put it on the wall. Then you can write things down and look at it every day. You can go to a support group for co-dependence. I go to one. I'm co-dependent. It's nothing to be ashamed of, but it's not something to ignore. It can kill you."

I didn't want to listen to her. That stupid label was just another pop psychology fad, I thought doubtfully, in total denial about my issues. The wall around my heart was so solid that I had not let love in for decades. Lying to myself and others, I kept up my independent front, telling people I was fine when I was in despair.

Sometimes, she smoked and I started wheezing. Horrible memories of asthma attacks sent me reeling into a black hole of misery.

"I can't breathe in the smoke," I complained, as we talked on her porch one day. I felt like a dying fish trapped on the land.

"I'm trying to point it away from you."

"Thanks. I don't mean to be difficult. I've been feeling really depressed thinking about how my mother ordered me out of the house. She used to pick up a broom and chase me out. She has this explosive personality, and she has told me I'm a horrible person."

"Your mother is a sicko. She should get counseling, but she shouldn't take her crap out on you. That's using you as her scapegoat."

"Yeah. She attacked me more than the others because I would never fight back."

"Well, you're going to be all right. You've done very well moving here and getting a job, and you're making friends. You'll get better and better if you keep going to Al-Anon. No man is an island, and you can't change all by yourself."

"Yeah. I know I need someone to talk to," I replied, finally allowing myself to be vulnerable. Every day, I felt sucked dry by depression. Not able to move a muscle when I woke in the mornings, I would lay in bed for two or three hours, rehashing the miserable experiences I had had, wasting time.

"I feel depressed and lonely. I would have liked to marry and have children but I'm afraid of men. My parents think I'm a failure because I have had to ask them for money. I get a disability check but it doesn't stretch very far. I don't like being disabled. I want to be successful and have a full life like other people have."

"Well, you have talents and abilities. You will get more in touch with them. You are doing very well and you're a good, kind person."

My pride swelled when I got free tickets to the symphony. For decades, I had never had the extra money for concerts. Inviting Cathy to attend with me, I looked forward to an evening of soul stirring, passionate music.

The magical night arrived and we rode the train to Santa Rita. Then, we enjoyed a Greek salad at a deli near the symphony hall. Some of my coworkers were there. Cathy kept me laughing, telling a hilarious story about incompetent workmen who came to fix her corner streetlight.

"I thought they would never fix that puppy. They came back seven times and never had the right equipment with them or knew what to do. Finally, on the eighth trip, they fixed it. They were total idiots. I couldn't believe it!" She laughed uproariously and I laughed along.

"That's hilarious. I love the neighborhood. It's so quiet. I haven't had this much peace in ages. And I'm sleeping so deeply. That big bed is wonderful."

"Yeah. You were in a real hellhole with them trying to convert you. It's amazing you lasted as long as you did. I would have gone nuts. Pat yourself on the back for surviving. You're a strong person. You have so many gifts. You can do anything you want to do. You can overcome your dysfunctional family. You have so much to give to the world. You're talented, you're smart, and you're courageous. You're going to be cured of your co-dependence and A.D.D. You've got to build a network of friends. I have people who I can call on the phone and talk to. You need to have that too. You can't live in isolation."

We finished our Greek salads and paid a handsome waiter. Then, we walked up the street and into the symphony hall. Walking down the aisle to our seats, I noticed someone I worked with.

Silence came over us as the maestro walked onto the stage. He bowed deeply to the audience. Then, the mystical music began. Feeling as though I was waltzing with angels through the universe, I surrendered to the rapture. Time dissolved as I floated on the glorious music.

It ended too soon. Cathy raved about the exquisite music as we rode the train.

When we arrived home, I fell into bed and a heavenly slumber carried me to another world.

CHAPTER EIGHT

"Stop judging, that you may not be judged. For as you judge, so will you be judged, and the measure with which you measure will be measured out to you." Matthew 7:1-2

How you look at others is a reflection of how you look at yourself.

"Through the use of the Kriya key, persons who cannot bring themselves to believe in the divinity of any man will behold at last the full divinity of their own selves."
Paramahansa Yogananda

Since the soul is immortal and often born, having seen everything that is on earth...there is nothing it has not learnt; so there is no wonder it can remember about virtue and other things, because it knew about these before...for seeking and learning is all remembrance.
Socrates in Plato's Meno

I t had been sickeningly dry since I'd moved to Glendale over three years ago. I missed the torrential rains that had refreshed the air and left a lovely glisten on the greenery in Madison. It seemed like an answer to my prayers when, the next day, it rained heavily for hours.

Climbing like a mountain goat, up the steep hills from the train station after work, my jacket felt cold and wet. Unlocking the door, I looked forward to talking with Cathy. As I walked into the kitchen, my eyes fell on a piece of paper laying on the kitchen counter.

"I would have come to pick you up at the Bart station if I had known it was going to rain. It's not fit for man or beast out there. Make yourself at home, and I'll be back soon."

A pleasant feeling spread throughout me as I peeled off my clothes and dried off with a fresh, fluffy towel. Without the love of my female friends, I would have died of depression. Sitting in the arm chair in the living room, wrapped in a blanket, I read a book about Jesus.

That Sunday, white sailboats glistened on the water as I rode the train to visit Nancy. She had moved, once again, and it took me a while to find her new apartment. After walking up and down in confusion, reading various numbers on buildings and apartments, I finally found it. Ringing the door bell, I reveled in happy memories.

Welcoming me with a hug, she said she was looking forward to singing. Her roommate was studying French at Glendale University. As she introduced me, I filled myself up with her sweet smile. Then I sat down and relaxed, as Nancy served me tomato soup and spinach and cucumber salad.

Our voices flowed like honey, harmonizing with celestial exquisiteness, sounding like they came from heaven.

We sang it in the pub later on, as delighted faces beamed with appreciation. Before the open mic, Nancy played her fiddle with a lively group of musicians, as people danced. There were no music and dance hangouts like this back East in Madison.

I rode the train to Santa Rita to visit with Hansa a few days later. Her big, dark eyes glowed with happiness, as we ate Chinese food in an elegant café.

"Cathy really cares about you and wants to help you. I'm so glad you are in a stable living situation. That is very hard to find here because everyone wants to live here. You've done well working with children, and now you have more regular money with your symphony job. You can start saving money. Just put away a hundred dollars a month and in a year you'll have twelve hundred in savings. I'm proud of you. Things will keep getting better for you. Soon, you'll find a nice boyfriend. You're an attractive woman."

"Thank you. I don't know if I want a boyfriend. I always attract the wrong type."

"You'll start attracting the type you want if you do affirmations and build up your confidence. There are a lot of really nice guys out there. My boyfriend is great. He is so supportive. I did a lot of healing work on myself and, because I felt better about myself, I attracted him to me."

"I'm glad you found him. I'd like to meet him," I said, trying to hide my envy.

"You will some time. He travels a lot teaching people how to meditate. He's writing a book. He's very intelligent."

We walked back to Hansa's apartment. As she gave me a healing, my feet absorbed the magnetic force in the earth, and I felt rooted after years of floating in space. She instructed me to feel the pain sensations and then focus on the parts of my body that felt good. My aches and pains subsided as I followed her.

When the time came for me to leave, I tried to not appear clingy. As I rode the train back to Glendale, I missed my parents and my home town.

Cathy took me to eat at an old fashioned, fifties-type hamburger joint a few days later. She ate a burger, while I ate a plate of French fries. When she asked me if I'd like anything else, I said I'd like a root beer float. Remembering drinking a root beer float at the drug store counter, when I was a teenager, I wished I could grow younger instead of older.

Later, we walked all around the neighborhood. She told me about people she knew who lived in the different houses. Some of them cost a million dollars, even though they were small and plain. I understood why people had warned me that Glendale was expensive.

Later that night, my mind felt scattered and my emotions surged like a tidal wave as I contemplated my past, lamenting that I had lived on the edge for too long. Grey hairs and wrinkles were making me uglier every day. I wondered what would become of me when I was old, and caring people, like Cathy, no longer took me under their wing.

"It's too expensive here. I think I made a big mistake moving here," I said.

"Well, I'm giving you a good deal, and you are working and saving money so what's the big worry?"

"I don't know. It just feels so unfamiliar here. My father didn't want me to move here."

"You're a grown woman, and you have the right to choose where to live. Your father cannot tell you what to do. This is the best place in the country to live. I wouldn't live anywhere else. You know you'll just be the goat if you go back to your family. You've got Al-Anon here, and you've got me and your friends. You've done a great thing moving here all by yourself. You've got to be your own person. Sometimes you have to step out of a dysfunctional family in order to do that."

Her words stung me to the core. She was right. I did not have any sense of identity or confidence. All I knew how to do was struggle to survive, go home to my lonely room and sleep excessively to escape my emotional pain.

"Well, I do my music and my writing, and that gives me some identity."

"You have glimpses of knowing who you are." Her words hit home. I had needed someone to discuss this with me for a long time.

"Yeah. I know what you mean. I appreciate you understanding me." I looked down at the floor in shame, longing to be confident and accomplished. Much to my regret, I was nothing but a timid, invisible telemarketer.

"You can borrow my book about co-dependence. It will help you break out of your old patterns. It's nothing to be ashamed of. I deal with it too. These affirmations I do every day really help me. You can change but you've got to share yourself with others and let them help you. You can't do it in isolation. I am always here for you whenever you want to talk."

Cathy did a hypnosis session on me to help me talk people into donating over the phone. Over the next month, my donations increased so much I won the prize for the best telemarketer.

I went to the farmer's market and bought some gorgeous, fresh vegetables and fruits. They were bigger, juicier, and prettier than any produce I had ever seen.

When I got home, I sat on Cathy's stool, gazing out her window at the mountains, flowers and hummingbirds. Daydreaming, I ate gorgeous, purple grapes. I remembered the stool I had sat on in my mother's kitchen, when I was seven and she had been my world. One day my jealous, older sister had attacked me.

"You would take the best piece of chicken", she had accused, glaring at me with condemnation.

"Why she didn't even look at that piece of chicken", my mother had said, standing up for me. A golden glow had warmed me from the tip of my toes to the top of my head. The happiness that Mom's approval gave me was the best feeling I ever had.

Later on, when I was in High School, she had praised me for being smart and sweet. The gardens of daffodils, irises, daisies, camellias and azaleas had been a fairyland in the spring and summer. I had been energetic and free of pain, without a care in the world.

Time had passed very quickly. Grief trickled through my heart like rain as I worried that the cruelty of my father and siblings had driven my mother insane.

Now, as I approached fifty, I needed Cathy's love more than anything. This sweet, Christian woman who had seen a huge, flaming cross of Jesus in the sky, was bringing me back to life. Her nourishment was making me bloom, like a beautiful flower.

Cathy sat beside me. I offered her some grapes and she declined.

"There's an Al-Anon meeting this Saturday night. You really came out at the last meeting. I was proud of you for speaking up. Everyone there really liked you. You'll keep getting better and better if you keep sharing. You'll be a new person before you know it. Next thing I know, I'll hear that you've been in bars dancing on the tables!" She laughed cheerfully, and I laughed along with her.

After I finished eating, I called my father to see how he was doing. I mentioned that I was having back pain. Cathy listened and watched, with concern. After the terse, brief exchange, I hung up feeling there were many loose ends that I needed to tie together. I wanted more from my parents.

"Well, most parents would say, 'I'm sorry your back's hurting sweetie. I hope you feel better soon.'" Cathy crossed her arms and frowned toward the phone.

"That's just not their way. I have to forgive them," I replied.

"Well, they should have given you the love you needed when you were growing up. They didn't even treat you like a human being. They were selfish, and they did a lot of damage to you. You have every right to be angry. The bad news is that they are not going to change. The good news is that you are a wonderful, intelligent person, and you can form healthy relationships."

I had a helpful session with Jiang Lee, my therapist, the next day. I told her about my longings to drive back across the country and settle down like my father wanted. Then, I told her about my desire to write an angry letter to my parents. She suggested that I write them a letter of appreciation. She laughed when I told her that the psychic had told me I belong on the West Coast.

"What does your inner psychic say?" she asked me.

"I don't know. I feel afraid of my mother."

"She's a little, old lady. You could knock her over. Whenever she says something you don't like, you have the power to say, 'I expect you to speak to me in a calm, kind tone.' You have the power. You are finding your voice with your parents, and you will do fine. I suggest that you not write an angry letter to them. They will feel, 'She is blaming us, and we don't know what to do.'

"Instead, tell them you love them and thank them for their continuing support. They love you, and that is why they continue to help you. They are from a different generation, and they simply can't understand you sometimes. They want to protect you from the corruption in the world."

"I want to go home but it's hard to do because Cathy is so kind and this is such an interesting place. I'm more stable now than I have been since I moved here over three years ago. But her smoking really bothers me. I've been wheezing at night and having trouble sleeping."

"Did you tell her you have asthma?" Her total attention, empathetic eyes and grounded, relaxed presence calmed me.

"No. I just told her I needed to stay away from the smoke. She always points it away from me."

"That's not enough. It can still get to you."

"Yeah. I thought I could tolerate it, but I don't think I can. It frightens me terribly when I wheeze all night and can't sleep."

"You need to tell her that you cannot talk at all while she is smoking. Then, you need to leave the room whenever she smokes."

"It's so hard for me to set boundaries with people. Once she starts talking, I can't stop her. I don't want to be rude."

"The next time she starts talking, tell her that you can talk for ten minutes and then you will have to go work on your writing. Setting boundaries is a muscle you will develop with practice. It will become easier for you the more you do it."

As the session ended, I absorbed the empathy in her eyes. Not wanting to go, I told her goodbye.

Walking to my car, the foreign streets felt threatening. Luckily, my car did not have a ticket on it. As I drove, my sciatica hurt. It made it hard to sleep that night.

In the morning, I started searching for a chiropractor to relieve my pain. Everyone I called refused to see me, on the grounds that they did not take Medicaid. After I had gotten about fifty refusals, I called another.

He sounded so genuine, so willing to listen, that I was surprised. He gave me his address and I went in for an appointment. His kind receptionist seemed like an angel as she greeted me.

As he examined me, he explained that my pelvis continually went out of place. He suggested I purchase a strap-around, Velcro brace.

Cathy gave me sympathy when I showed it to her and told her it was keeping my pelvis in place. My hip pain lessened and I felt grateful, as I walked with more pep in my step.

I was hurrying down the street one day, in downtown Glendale, when I noticed a yellow flyer posted on a telephone pole. It was an ad for a creative writing class. I remembered my psychology professor had liked my college papers and had encouraged me to write. Reading had always been a favorite activity, which allowed me to escape the mundane routine.

My English composition teacher, in prep school, had scared me with his rules of grammar and his criticisms of my papers though. Although I'd enjoyed keeping journals, I felt inferior to the great authors whose words I breathlessly hung onto.

When I called the number on the ad, a man with a resonant, calm voice answered and told me his name was John. As he answered my questions about the class, I felt my trust in him grow. When I asked him if I could pay half up front and the other half the next month, he replied, in a caring, gentle tone, that I could.

The next Tuesday, I drove to his small apartment. When he opened the door, I blushed because of his healthy handsomeness. His wavy, brown hair fell below his shoulders and his brown eyes shone with intelligence. As he spoke, his voice conveyed empathy, making me realize that he was the wise, earth loving hippie I had always wanted to meet and learn from. I sat on his comfortable sofa and looked at the five women who were studying with me. We exchanged names and friendly greetings and a lovely peacefulness vibrated in the room.

John began the class by introducing himself and telling us about his writing background. Then, he let us each talk about our desires regarding our writing. He encouraged us to play and have fun as he led us through various exercises.

In one of them, we randomly arranged a bag full of assorted objects on the floor. Then, we wrote about them for fifteen minutes.

In another exercise, he had us take individual sentences out of something we'd written and write them on index cards. Then, he had us arrange the cards in a different order and rewrite the composition in the new order.

My therapist was proud of me for taking the work shop. The eight weeks passed very quickly.

Then, my teacher told me he was teaching a retreat in a house which looked out over the ocean. I couldn't wait to have more time with him and, when he gave me a discount, I enrolled with great excitement.

He agreed to give me a ride to the retreat, after I courageously told him that I was disabled and afraid to find new places by myself. I savored the views of the hills, the redwoods and the ocean as he drove in peaceful contemplation. Feeling odd, I sat in silence, wishing I had the gift of gab.

The retreat was joyful. We stayed in a house that had one huge, plate glass wall that was directly over the ocean. My mouth dropped open in awe as I watched pelicans and seagulls fly over the dazzling, aqua water. I had a quiet, simple, private room.

We did writing exercises in the cozy house and outside in the rolling hills under gnarled, twisting, ancient trees. John struck a Zen-like gong to end our writing sessions.

It was challenging to keep my pen moving as he instructed. Even when the words were not coming, he said we should write anything, not worrying about punctuation.

"Just keep the pen moving", he repeated over and over as everyone wrote.

When we finished our free writing, we read our work out loud. He never criticized and he instructed others to give feedback in the same way.

I enjoyed getting compliments. One woman described my words like a waterfall of uplifting, exhilarating energy. John told me to etch her words into my memory.

In one exercise, I was blindfolded and led around the room. My mistrust of people reared its ugly head and I had nightmare visions of being led off of the dock and drowning in the ocean. An upsetting memory from my childhood surfaced from its cave of repression.

"You deserve to have a rock tied around your neck and to be thrown into the middle of the ocean", my mother had yelled furiously. I could not remember what I had done that was so evil.

Realizing I needed a therapy session, I did my best to talk with people positively for the remainder of the retreat.

The ride home with my teacher was scenic and serene. His energy was encouraging and sincere and it meant the world to me.

Cathy welcomed me home and listened, with curiosity, as I told her about the retreat. Then, she tuned the T.V. in to Animal Planet. I relaxed and leaned back in my soft, royal blue armchair, watching lions roam around.

After the show, she made me a cup of hot chocolate, in a new, violet mug which she gave me. Soft rain pattered on the windows as we talked and laughed late into the night.

That Saturday night, an elderly friend of Cathy's picked us up and drove us to the Al-Anon meeting. As I observed their old faces, wrinkled like raisins in the sun, I dreaded getting older. I needed to get busy and accomplish my goals before the pain got worse and I stayed sacked out on the sofa with an ice pack. Poor Cathy spent most of her time that way because of the horrendous surgeries she had survived.

I shared a little more about my moves back and forth across the country.

"I often felt like my parents did not love me at all. It means everything to me when I get a letter from my alcoholic father saying he misses me and wants me to come home. I realize I have to forgive him. He was under extreme stress when I was in grammar school, and he beat me with a leather belt. I never did anything intentionally mean, but I was always the one who got into trouble. My older sister used to complain about me to get me in trouble. She's been violent with me and it has hurt me profoundly. We never talk. My older brother lives here and I have tried to get together with him, but he will not return my calls or letters. My mother won't write or call. I haven't spoken with her in over three years now. She wouldn't speak to me, even after I drove three thousand miles to visit. It broke my heart. My younger sister writes back to me, luckily. She and my father are the only family I have now. And now I feel heartbroken because my father is going to be gone soon. He's gotten so frail, and I've rarely gotten to spend quality one on one time with him. It's always been a triangle with him and me and my mother. She always dominated the conversation, and I couldn't get any attention from him. He was so sweet to me when I was back at home, and I drove him to the symphony. It meant so much to me. He couldn't help the fact that he was alcoholic and had a short temper. I see how my mother's nagging and complaining drove him to the end of his rope. I've avoided him and judged him and not forgiven, and it has been eating me alive all my life. I want to move back there and spend time with him before I lose him forever. He's the only person in the world who really loves me. I feel sorry for him. He's tried his best to be a good father, in spite of his alcoholism and diabetes."

"You'll make the right decision when you're ready. Just turn it over to your higher power," a brunette woman with glasses told me, after everyone had finished sharing. As she held my hand, love circulated through all my cells, healing my frayed, ragged nerve endings. The steel bands which tightened my heart loosened and I felt my chest expand with love.

Time flew by. I divided my time between visits with the Hare Krishnas, psychics, singing in my duo with Nancy at the pub, doing Irish dancing there, going to Al-Anon and telemarketing for the Santa Rita Symphony's Children's Program.

It was almost Christmas. Sad nostalgia seeped through my bones as I remembered gathering around the Christmas tree with my parents and siblings and opening presents. Cathy said her children might come to visit her.

When Nancy invited me to go south and spend Christmas at her parents' house, I pounced, like a hungry cat, on the chance to have some fun.

Nancy drove and I enjoyed the scenery, as we bubbled with cheerful talk. Her laugh tickled me, bringing back my ability to laugh. Sooner than I expected, we arrived at the house where her parents lived.

She had two twin beds in her room, like my best friend in grammar school had had many decades ago. Memories of our fun, carefree times when we used to play Kick the Can or throw a ball against a wall came to me. Endless energy had poured from within me as I worked hard in my ballet classes or walked around school, feeling cool in my bell bottom jeans.

Nancy had many assignments to complete for her Ph.D. program. I played the piano or read while she spent most of the day working on her computer. Her statistical biology studies were very demanding and, as I observed her working, I thought that she must be a genius.

Sleeping deeply that night, I dreamed of happy times.

As the sun rose the next morning, I felt young and fresh again. Nancy's mother looked at me with special tenderness as she served me warm waffles with fruit. I listened to her talk with her daughter, realizing that the bond between a mother and daughter was the most special one of all. Lightness and laughter lifted my spirits and I enjoyed their company, until Nancy had to get back to studying for her Ph.D.

I basked in the warmth of the sun, picking tangerines off of a tree in their backyard.

Then, I walked into the house. Nancy asked me if I would play the piano. I made an embarrassing, feeble attempt to play some Chopin, which I hadn't played since I took piano lessons in high school. I laughed nervously and blushed when she complimented me.

"We can go skating tomorrow." Her dark eyes radiated light and love.

"That sounds like fun. I haven't skated since I was in high school," My heart skipped a beat as the joy of childhood filled me like fresh, spring air.

That evening, her parents and the two of us went out to see "The Chronicles of Narnia".

I feasted on the visual miracles and splendor that played on the huge screen. Every time a mystical creature died, I worried that my father was dying and tears rolled down my cheeks.

When the magical movie ended, I walked as though I was dreaming. Her mother patted my shoulder. Pellets of light rain moistened our faces as we searched the packed parking lot for the car. Enjoying the light conversation and laughter, I rode home in the back seat, sitting next to Nancy. Sirens split the silence and red, green and yellow lights flashed against the black night. Resting my back against the sturdy seat, I felt my feet on the floor and sent roots down into the earth. Remembering what the psychics had taught me

Kundalini Rising

in my classes, I dropped my worries down a grounding chord into the center of the earth. My grounding chord looked like a huge redwood tree.

It had been a pleasant trip from the theater and Nancy's father parked the car in front of their house. Following Nancy to the front door and watching him unlock it, I listened to the happy sound of her mother's voice.

The fragrance of pine, cinnamon and peppermint sent a wave of bliss through my senses, when I walked into the living room.

After some light conversation, I retreated into Nancy's bedroom and put on my pajamas. Slumbering like a carefree child, I floated in divine peace throughout the night.

I woke up well-rested the next day. Refreshing, joyful energy surged through me. The sounds of singing birds reverberated outside the sunlit kitchen window as we ate breakfast together. An aroma of baking bread brought good memories to me as I sat at the round table. Her mother smiled and greeted us sweetly, then began searching the cupboards for ingredients. Nancy told me her mother was a fabulous cook, and was going to prepare a feast for Christmas.

After breakfast, Nancy studied and I played the piano. After a while, Nancy suggested that we go skating. As she drove us to the skating rink, we chatted cheerfully.

We arrived at a large building and parked in a full lot. Walking into the expansive entrance, I watched young, well-built people talk, gesturing expressively. Their voices enlivened me. My hands shook with excitement as I put on my skates and tied the laces.

Nancy and I laughed playfully as we walked onto the ice, wobbling precariously. Starting slowly, I pushed one foot in front of the other and held out my arms to keep my balance.

With each successful movement, I got a little more daring, until I was speeding ahead and going around the corners with ease. Feeling like I was flying, I pretended I was going to Never Never Land with Peter Pan and Wendy.

We enjoyed a fabulous Christmas Day at Nancy's aunt's house. I savored the delicious tastes of pound cake dipped in chocolate, strawberries, and other delicious fruits. Talking with friendly people, I munched on turkey with dressing, vegetables, fruits, cakes, pies and cookies galore. Her cousins, brother, sister, aunts, and uncles were beautiful people. All of them were lovely with their shiny, dark hair and huge, soulful eyes. Like nature-loving, island natives, they exuded a peaceful joy that uplifted me.

I got a gorgeous, gold embellished vase from Nancy's mother and some cute, smaller gifts. Nancy, her siblings and parents loved some funny videos I gave them.

Lively conversation hummed through the house. The aromas of food enveloped me, and I enjoyed the visual feast of multi-colored decorations hanging on the fresh-smelling, cedar tree, which reached the ceiling.

Nancy asked me to take on her usual duty of playing Christmas carols on the piano.

I sat down on the piano bench, praying that I would play well. Fear of being a fool unraveled me as I began nervously, sight reading carols from a large book. Soon, my confidence grew and my playing flowed smoothly. Out of the corner of my eye, I saw happy faces that glowed with approval. They sang along, sounding joyful. A magical, electrical vibration charged the air, and I reveled in the glory, feeling like a star.

The whole day glistened with light laughter and holy hospitality. Nancy's father took a picture of us standing side by side. I looked serene in my pink pantsuit from Goodwill, and Nancy had a lively sparkle in her eyes. Her father laughed a lot and made silly comments.

Nancy would respond, "Dad, that's a crazy thing to say!"

Later on, as we fell asleep in her bedroom, Nancy told me that her father used to have a horrible temper but that, in his old age, he had really calmed down. My father had mellowed in a similar way.

The next day, Nancy's cousin took us to a restaurant. She had a rounded, cherubic face and a short, chubby figure. Her dark, innocent eyes exuded vulnerability, and a halo of wavy, black hair framed her face. I listened in peaceful reverie as she and Nancy caught up with each other. Their peals of happy laughter rang through me, bringing me to life as I enjoyed the moment, munching on spinach and artichoke salad with blue cheese dressing.

"This is my treat," Pam chimed in, eager to please, sending pleasurable vibrations through me. Various aromas of foods wafted into my nostrils as I listened to screaming babies, observed stylish, beautiful women, and pined over handsome men, who spoke lovingly to their children. Waitresses hurried back and forth, yet the calm patience of our waitress touched me.

Kundalini Rising

"Let's go shopping for clothes. There's a Ross store near here," Nancy said cheerfully, as we all got close to finishing our meals.

Pam drove us through the endless suburban sprawl of shopping malls and skyscrapers. Cars seemed to be multiplying like rabbits as she drove into a crowded parking lot and searched for a place to park. After circling around and around, she finally found one. We got out and walked toward the store.

My eyes grew wide as I observed the vast sea of clothes hanging on racks inside the store. Though I looked, I didn't see anything that appealed to me. I sighed, feeling frustrated, but I grabbed some things to try on anyways.

Once in the dressing room, I discovered none of them fit. Sighing impatiently, I discarded them onto a chair.

Back on the floor, Nancy and Pam were looking through the endless racks and filling their arms with clothes. I loaded up another armful myself and returned to the dressing room.

This time went better. I pulled on a dress full of pastel colors, made of light, chiffon like material and cut with a fairy like zig zag hem line. Admiring myself in the mirror, I felt pretty. Next, I put on a royal, blue jacket. I looked magnificent.

Leaving the rest, I carried my two treasures out and found Nancy and Pam. They were still looking. After a while, they took armloads back to the dressing room.

Soon, they had gathered what they wanted, and we walked to the cashier. I smiled with delight as I put the total, which was less than ten dollars, onto my debit card. That would leave me five dollars to last until my next disability check came in on the third of the month.

I remembered how my feelings had been hurt when my father yelled at me to write down my expenditures. Now, though, I realized his tough love had made my life easier. I always knew exactly what my balance was.

"I haven't bought new clothes in twenty years!" I exclaimed with excitement.

"Well, you deserve new ones," Nancy said, putting her arm around my shoulder. We laughed happily as we walked out of the store.

Pam dropped us off in front of Nancy's aunt's house. Affectionately gazing at us, she wished us a happy holiday, then handed me a page of writing she had done. As I read it, I was deeply touched by her expressions about the unconditional, transforming love of Jesus.

The next few days at Nancy's house rollicked with good vibrations. In the afternoon, Nancy, her parents and I piled into their car and drove to L.A. to see a wonderful Cezanne exhibit. Later, we sat at an outdoor café under an umbrella table. Her mother encouraged me to get anything I wanted, saying it was her treat.

Soon, New Year's Day arrived. She smiled as she served us an incredible banquet of special dishes, which she had worked an entire day preparing. With great enjoyment, I ate pieces of sushi, seaweed soup, roasted vegetables, chicken, roast beef, tarts, cakes and a huge variety of fruits.

I observed Nancy's handsome brother talking with his girlfriend. She was dreading going back to her teaching job. It made me feel lucky to be a telemarketer.

Nancy's sister was talkative, dramatic and loud. We were the opposite—quiet and shy. We were both middle children, and I remembered reading a book that described middle children that way. The loving harmony and merriment filled me with such peace, I did not want to leave.

However, the day of departure came. Her mother packed us a big bag of food to eat on our trip up the coast. Whenever I took a break from driving, I munched with delight and we had fun, laughing over silly things. Then, Nancy would take the wheel.

When we got back to Glendale, she got busy with her scientific research. I returned to telemarketing and enjoying Cathy's caring company.

After a week flew by, Nancy called and said she looked forward to singing our next duo together. I arrived with excitement at her small, rented room the following Sunday. Wondering how we survived our nomadic lives, I realized that this was the sixth apartment she had had since I met her.

"Let's cook something to eat. Then we can practice for a while." Nancy's bright, dark eyes gleamed with enthusiasm.

I chopped a big bunch of broccoli. We chatted as she put it in a pan and poured a jar of special, spicy Indian sauce over it. The aroma pleased me.

As we sat down to eat, I relished the gorgeous view of the blue bay, in the distance, dotted with white sails.

When our stomachs were pleasantly full, Nancy got out her guitar. She played the chords of our song and, then, looked at me, cueing me to sing. Our soulful voices soared, blending together exquisitely, creating magic.

Later on, at the pub, people listened, mesmerized. They gave us a standing ovation.

Cathy was lying on the sofa, with a heating pad on her hurting back, when I walked in.

"I had a great time singing at the Pub. We got a standing ovation." Beaming with pride, I floated on air, anticipating her encouraging words.

"Her family will adopt you. You're going to keep getting better and better. I was sick the whole time you were gone. It's lucky you were gone, so I didn't give you my bug. I just stayed in bed and talked with my Al-Anon sponsor. Keep spending time with Nancy and your other friend and you'll feel more and more at home here. You have people who care about you here."

"Yeah. It's great to have. I think about the times my mother chased me out of the house with a broom, and I wonder why I want to go back. I think it's just because it's more familiar back there."

"Your mother is a sicko. She should get counseling instead of taking it out on you."

"Yeah. She has a really shocking temper. I never could figure it out. I never yelled back at her. I just tried to forgive her, because I knew she was frustrated and unhappy."

"You didn't get what you needed, with your father drinking and being absorbed totally in his work and your mother using you as the goat. It's very hard to cope with life when you've been through abuse. I know. I've needed Al-Anon to recover. It gives you a support group of people who really care and accept you the way you are. You are worthy, and you deserve love. You can find healthy relationships but you've got to go out and be with people. You can't recover from all you've been through in isolation."

Her small, blue eyes shone with concern. Looking at her deeply wrinkled face, I realized that life was short. My face would be the same in ten years. I had no time to waste and I needed to settle in the right place and get my act together.

"I don't know what I should do," I lamented, wringing my hands with anxiety. "I worry about getting by on my disability income and the violence, which I see in the headlines of the newspaper, keeps me frightened constantly."

"It's very sad that we live in a world where there is such cruelty. This time has been predicted in the Bible. We're in the end times. You're going to be all right, dear. You've been through hell, but you are strong. You have more abilities and strength than you give yourself credit for. The more you surround yourself with good, loving people, the more relaxed you will be. It takes time to build a new life for yourself, and it takes patience. Al-Anon will help you feel stronger. You can get a sponsor. My sponsor helped me immensely. You need to detach from your family and grow up."

"Yeah. I really feel a lot of love in those meetings. I like going." I covered my hurt feelings. I hated it when people told me to grow up. It felt humiliating.

I drifted off into watching a man catch wild snakes on Animal Planet. They wriggled and slid like liquid lightning along the ground. He followed them and scooped them up with a long rod with a hook on the end. With an English accent, he talked about Cleopatra and her asp, who she had gotten to kill her. A snake bite sounded less painful than shooting oneself in the head with a pistol.

I started yawning and told Cathy I needed to go to bed. While walking to my room, there came a sudden, eardrum-bursting sound that made me jump.

"That burglar alarm goes off sometimes. It's a real nuisance. But you can rest assured that you are well protected here."

Cathy walked to a box on the wall across from my room. I watched her press buttons on the alarm until it stopped. We laughed with happy relief. Then, she gave me a hug and wished me a good night. I closed the door behind me.

I tried to sleep but kept wheezing, coughing and clearing my throat, which felt clogged with dust or cat fur or God only knew what. Finally, I fell into a deep sleep. Swaddled in serenity, I floated far away from the troubled world.

"Come home," my father commanded, his voice piercing my heart. I sat up in bed and stared at the wall, stunned and deeply moved. I looked at my clock. It was three o'clock in the morning.

He had been so sweet and appreciative when I drove him to the symphony. I saw him in my mind's eye, limping on his cane with his hunched back. I remembered the comforting feeling of his touch as he helped me remove my sweater at the symphony, and I wanted more than anything to be by his side.

I walked, bleary-eyed, into the kitchen the next morning. Cathy had been up for three hours. She talked with me while I sat next to her on the sofa, drinking one of her small containers of grape juice.

"Would you like to go to church with me?" Her voice lilted with lightness. I said that I would, then went into my room and put on my nicest outfit.

"You'll love my church. The people there are great," she said, cheerfully, letting us out of the front door and locking it.

She wore a conservative, well-made pantsuit. Her bleached, blonde hair was nicely brushed and a trace of makeup brightened her sun-wrinkled face. I reminded myself to start wearing sun screen every day.

We arrived at her church. I played an upright piano while she chatted with a loud, tall, brunette woman.

Then, Cathy led me into her Sunday school class. Three sofas and some chairs held various people of different races and economic statuses. They held their Bibles hopefully. Some of them looked worried. I felt empathy for them as I wondered what demanding jobs they were struggling with.

The minister talked about the many tests that Jesus' disciples went through before they developed full faith. When he finished, an advocate for the poor talked about how important it was to help the less fortunate. He said that he carried Cliff Bars in his car. Whenever he saw some poor soul holding up a sign saying they would work for food, he handed him a few.

My diet of Cliff bars had not been nutritious. I imagined a team of charitable people cooking broccoli, beets, spinach and other healthy things for them at some reliable cafe. The government ought to stop wasting money and, instead, donate it to people who sincerely wanted to help the poor.

Cathy introduced me to everyone, and they breathed youth into me with their friendliness. We stood around and chatted for a while. I watched Cathy interact in her sociable, charming way. She laughed buoyantly and talked effervescently, making direct eye contact with people.

I listened, speaking now and then, and enjoying the friendly vibrations coming from the humble, sweet people, who were genuinely interested in me. It was so different from going to a cocktail party, where people bragged about their latest win.

Later, Cathy praised me.

"Everyone really liked you at church. You're getting better and better. Socializing is just like any muscle. You get good at it by doing it. The more you practice making friends, the better and better you will get at it." We sat watching Animal Planet in her living room.

"Yeah. You're right. I'm enjoying meeting all the new people I've been meeting at Al-Anon, church, and elsewhere. I think maybe it's best if I stay here. People are smarter here, and there are such interesting things to do."

"You're right. I wouldn't live anywhere else. This is the best neighborhood. The neighbors here get together for drum circles, and they have procedures to help each other if there's an earthquake."

"I love it here. I was scared in that neighborhood I lived in before. I couldn't sleep at night because there were drunks and drug addicts and gang members outside my front door, and the door was never locked. There was a house across the street where people went to get marijuana, and I kept having nightmares of some tall, muscular man walking in and raping me. I was losing my mind. And in another neighborhood I lived in, my landlord had gotten shot at. A bullet had flown by, two inches from her head."

"You've gotten better dear. I'm always here for you. You're safe now. Things don't change overnight, so just be patient with yourself. You're doing all the right things: going to Al-Anon, getting together with friends, and talking with your counselor. Give yourself a pat on the back. Not many people have the kind of courage you have. And you're so gifted! You don't even realize how gifted you are. You're really pretty too."

"Thank you. I haven't had a date in twenty years so it's hard to believe it." I felt ugly compared to the slender, light hearted, gorgeous younger woman I saw every day.

"There are a lot of nice men out there. You will find someone who's right for you. You're not ready for that yet though. You need to surround yourself with friends you can trust. Keep on getting together with Nancy and your friend in Santa Rita. They really care about you like I do. You're doing well at your job. You're not the little girl who has to do what her father says. We have everything here: perfect weather and great opportunities. I wouldn't live anywhere else!"

Like a pendulum, my mind and heart swung back and forth between the East and the West as I tried to sleep that night.

The bright sun woke me. I felt like riding the train into downtown because I didn't have to go to work. Pulling on my clothes, I left the house

Kundalini Rising

without a sound. Moving lifted my mood as I walked to the train. Soon, I arrived in Glendale.

As I walked through the streets, I thought about all the places I'd lived the last few years. There was the homeless shelter, the mansion in the hills, the high rise with the ninety-three-year-old man, the apartment with the cold, Asian women, the basement apartment with the doctor who had five dogs, the ghetto house where I had worked as a scullery maid, Jyoti's floor, the dusty, junk-filled attic of the Hare Krishna house, the bleak room with no kitchen or heat in the dangerous, noisy neighborhood near the marijuana store, the tiny room with the rude, lesbian landlord who made me toil hours a day, the noisy, book-cluttered room with the uncomfortable futon in the Krishna house, the basement room in the childhood house of my friend, whose filthy kitchen I had cleaned and now, last but definitely not least, Cathy's house. Her tranquil, wooded sanctuary full of hummingbirds, chipmunks, eagles, frogs, lemon trees, redwoods, pines and mountains was reviving my body, mind and spirit.

I walked past the E.S.P. Academy and looked inside the open door. Realizing that I had not gone there regularly for a long time, I remembered what fun I'd had learning in classes, going to the psychic fairs, doing aura cleansings, laughing at jokes, playing games, singing in the choir and listening to channeled messages about the future earth changes.

I went into the library and waited in line for a computer. Confusion came over me as I clicked the mouse and tried to navigate to a website that listed jobs. All the words, pictures, changing windows and demands from the monster machine overloaded me. My shoulders rose with tension, as I stared, in an overwhelmed stupor, holding my breath.

"You have just performed an illegal operation. Press cancel now."

I felt like a bad toddler being reprimanded. Watching suave, confident people zip through their computer work, as though it was as easy as eating Jell-O, I wondered what was wrong with me. Staring helplessly at the screen, I clicked the mouse repeatedly. Frozen with fear, I watched a befuddling continuum of senseless screens flash before my eyes. After a while, my mind was so frazzled that I gave up.

Walking to the E.S.P. Academy, I felt like the world was moving too fast and I wanted to get off. Lamenting about my little, dysfunctional life, I walked up the stairs, into the sacred sanctuary.

A Hispanic, big eyed woman, who had graduated from the clairvoyant program, asked me if I would like a healing. With a sweet smile and gentle wave of her hand, she directed me to sit down. As she moved her hands around my aura, I floated in relaxing waves, feeling blissful. Smiling with gratitude, I thanked her at the end of the session.

Walking around downtown, I observed people with curiosity. Eccentric characters played guitars and sold things from sidewalk blankets. A heroin addict slouched, standing on a street corner, holding out his hat and asking for change. I remembered how frightened I had been that I would end up begging like him.

I looked out over the landscape as I rode the train back to Cathy's place. It was dotted with thousands of houses. Huge, tall cranes loomed over construction sites that seemed to multiply every day. The world had too many buildings and shops and it needed more trees. I wanted to scream out loud.

When I arrived at the train station, I walked down the long stairs and through the turnstiles, remembering my father say that his happiest times had been when he was swinging his feet under his father's table. I agreed with him, as I cringed over how fast paced and complicated life had become.

Climbing up and down the hills, I looked forward to seeing Cathy. Thinking about the Doctor Seuss book, "Are You My Mother?" I laughed to myself. God had sent her to me, I realized gratefully.

Breathing deeply, feeling tired, I finally arrived. Turning my key in the door, I opened it. Cathy walked up to me and gave me a hug. Contemplating that I must be like a substitute daughter for her, I felt her pain. She was estranged from her own daughter, who she had had to put into an institution. She had mentioned it to me once, saying it was the only thing she could do because her daughter was disturbed.

As my stomach rumbled with hunger, I made a salad out of gorgeous, big, ripe tomatoes, carrots and zucchini I had bought at an outside farmer's market. Sitting on Cathy's tall stool, I looked out the window, observing birds and bumblebees. Tiny hummingbirds sipped nectar from Cathy's feeder. The Seals and Crofts song "Hummingbird" played in my mind.

Later on, Cathy made me a cup of hot chocolate. Then, she put a heating pad on her sore back and reclined on the sofa. Gorillas, zebras and giraffes delighted me as I savored my hot chocolate. The evening passed in cheery coziness, as we talked about this and that, listening to a light rain fall outside. A grey, mysterious fog covered the land like a blanket.

After a while, she wished me sweet dreams and we both went off to bed.

As the sun came into my room the next morning, I stretched and yawned. Cathy greeted me in the kitchen with another one of her wonderful, healing hugs. We went to her church and I enjoyed the friendly people.

Later on, we took a walk around a nearby park on the side of the ocean, where people walked their dogs and threw Frisbees. The fresh air invigorated me.

The next work week began and I enjoyed my friendly co-workers as I raised money for the symphony's children's' music programs.

When I got home, it relaxed me to sit under the lemon tree and talk with Cathy. Sitting far away and breathing shallowly, I didn't wheeze because of her cigarette smoke. It was a great relief.

I managed to sleep through the night without wheezing too. It felt liberating and healing.

Soon, Saturday arrived, and it was time for therapy. Jiang Lee listened intently, the next day, as I told her I was thinking about moving back home again.

"Cathy is saying I should stay here. She is so kind to me, and she loves me so much that, now, I don't want to go. But I keep worrying about my father and feel sad that he is coming to the end of his life. But I'm afraid of both of my parents, and I feel like I can't take it if either of them yells at me again. The psychic said I belong here and Cathy says I belong here," I said in confusion.

"That is Cathy's opinion. What is your opinion? The psychic has his opinion too, but it is not better than your opinion. What does your inner psychic say?"

"It is telling me to go home,"

"Then follow your heart. Your inner spirit is calling you." Her clarity and grounded support washed away my fears.

I walked around Glendale and remembered all of my favorite things: the beautiful marina with the sailboats sailing, people wind surfing on the ocean, seagulls and pelicans flying in the bright, sunny skies, singing and dancing at the Irish Pub, seeing deer, fabulous restaurants, sweet children that I'd taught at preschools, the E.S.P. Academy, the Hare Krishnas and their delicious feasts, the ballroom dancing classes, the weight loss class I'd taught at the Mind Growth Depot, the easy days with Jyoti, our transformational seminar, the kindness of Cathy and the Al Anon group.

I smiled at the woman selling Indian clothes in the train station as I walked toward the train. I missed spending time with the psychics. I hadn't been to a church service with them in a long time.

"This is likely to be a home for you," the psychic's voice echoed through my splintered, confused brain. I had listened to him in amazement years ago when I had first arrived, and was sleeping on Gene's (the ninety three year old man's) sofa.

Worrying that he was right and that I should stay, I walked down the stairs of the train station and followed a crowd onto the train. Averting my eyes away from the murder headline on a newspaper, I sat down. Unsafe feelings overwhelmed me. Thank God for Cathy. She was my life preserver in a raging sea.

Cathy was soothing her hurting back with the heating pad, reclining on the sofa, when I came in. She told me that her stomach was upset and she wished she had some Pepsi Cola because that always helped. I told her I would go to the supermarket and buy some.

Once at the parking lot, I observed two emaciated, ugly, female drug addicts talking to themselves. They wandered aimlessly through the packed parking lot of the huge supermarket. They depressed me. If ever Cathy decided she did not want me as a housemate anymore, I could easily end up wretched and insane like them. The misery, corruption, and violence in this city was staggering. I heard my father's drunken voice and saw him swaying and staggering, in my mind, as he proclaimed: "The world is going to hell in a handbasket."

I walked up and down the long, supermarket aisles reeling with shocked disappointment about how the world had deteriorated. The shelves were loaded with thousands of garish, deceitful packages of cancer-causing foods and drinks. The noise and commotion rattled me as whining children demanded sugary Cocoa Crisps and harried mothers scolded them.

After looking for the drink aisle for quite some time, I asked a clerk to assist. He told me the aisle number and I walked toward it, passing sad eyed men desperately clutching bottles of whiskey. They would go home and drown their sorrows in it, only to wake up with a blinding headache and another day of loneliness and misery to face.

When I arrived at home, I poured Cathy a tall glass of Pepsi and took it to her. Her face lit up with gratitude, and she thanked me sincerely. After talking with her for a while, I told her I wanted to take a walk through the woods.

I had been reading books about how angels guide people. Someone had heard an angel whisper in their ear. Hoping to hear my angels, I walked up the path behind Cathy's house breathing deeply, enjoying the fresh air. Gazing up at the majestic redwood trees, I asked them, in my mind, if I should move back to Madison.

I heard nothing. Still, I kept walking and enjoying the fragrance of the tall, gorgeous pine and eucalyptus trees, and the enchanting melodies of the singing birds. Maybe this angel stuff was just a bunch of hype, I thought cynically.

A cheerful couple greeted me, as I walked toward the preschool at the top of the hill. Peeking through the back door, I observed a long table surrounded by happy children who were enthusiastically coloring with crayons. It made me miss my days of substitute teaching.

It seemed as though nature spirits flitted through the trees as I walked back down the hill to Cathy's. Suddenly, I heard a whisper in my ear.

"Don't go back to Madison."

The voice was barely audible, but, still, I had heard it. Flabbergasted, I walked in a daze and, suddenly, bumped into a lamp post, receiving a painful blow to the top of my head. It throbbed as I walked home.

"You look hurt!" Cathy exclaimed. "Are you all right?"

"I bumped into the lamp post, and my head is hurting. It hit me so hard, I'm afraid I might have a concussion."

Cathy got some ice from the freezer and wrapped it in a paper towel. Then, she held it against my forehead.

"Don't feel stupid. I did the same thing. It's hard to see that post."

The burning cross she had seen in the sky so long ago had definitely filled her with Jesus's teachings about unconditional love. Soon, the swelling and pain had subsided. I thanked her, enjoying her soft eyes as they beamed love to me.

I prepared a salad with the spinach, mushrooms and plump, ripe vine tomatoes I had bought at the farmer's market. I'd never seen such attractive, fresh produce. I poured salad dressing on top and, as I munched away, savoring the taste, I watched a delicate hummingbird flutter its wings a million times a minute and sip nectar from a red-orange flower.

When I went back into the living room, Cathy was doing her homework for her Bible study class. I retreated to my room and called Hansa. She asked me to visit her on Saturday.

A long week of telemarketing passed quickly and Saturday arrived. I rode the train to Santa Rita, observing people of all ages, sizes and nationalities. Most of them sat in silence but one skinny, malnourished, black man held out his hat, asking people for alms.

"I won't spend it on anything but food", he said, plaintively. His sweet eyes grew wide and hollow with desperation as everyone ignored him. Pulling twenty dollars from my wallet and handing it to him, I looked into his exceedingly grateful eyes. His desperation was transformed into childlike trust, as he floated on the gift of human kindness, breathing with precious awe, as though he wanted the moment to last forever. A ragged voice came from his haggard body, thanking me from the depths of his soul. A feeling of fulfillment came over me.

The train stopped and I walked out and up the stairs, surging with energy. Watching people curiously, I began to walk up and down hills lined with humble houses. A Gothic church stood majestically on the corner. I studied it with awe, trying to remember some art history I'd learned in college. Then, I turned left to walk downhill to Hansa's place. I looked forward to her giving me another healing. She never charged me. Instead, she had asked that I give a dollar to a homeless person.

Her affectionate smile took away my fears, as she opened her door and let me in. I sat down on her new, green sofa, and she brought me a glass of pineapple juice. As I talked about living with Cathy and working at the symphony, she listened with respectful attentiveness. I felt important. When I told her I had given twenty dollars to a homeless man, she praised me.

After a while, she began her healing session. My muscles relaxed, and I sunk down into the safety and comfort of her loving presence.

"Feel all the places in your body that feel good", she instructed.

"Now, dip into the areas that feel pain. That's right, just briefly. Once you feel them for a few seconds, switch immediately back to those areas that

Kundalini Rising

feel good. This is like peeling off the layers of an onion. That's right. Very good. Feeling your feet on the floor. Feeling the air on your legs and arms. Feeling all the sensations in your body, grounding on the earth, feeling the floor touching the soles of your feet."

After my healing, I felt light and relaxed, as though the weight of a truck had been lifted off of my shoulders. Smiling with gratitude, I looked into Hansa's gentle eyes.

"What would you like to do about dinner? We can walk to a café near here, or we can eat here."

I liked being in her kitchen, so I told her I'd rather eat at home. Relaxing into her gracious generosity, I watched her pull various types of boxed soup out of her cabinet. She showed them to me.

"I'd like the butternut squash soup," I said, as my mouth watered in hungry anticipation.

Hansa heated the soup in a small pan on her stove. Her motherly energy flowed through my cells. I looked at her computer and marveled over how proficient she was on the maddening machine that kept me conquered. Most jobs would require me to handle a computer well. I worried about my future.

The pleasant aroma filled my nostrils and a carefree, cozy feeling came over me. I wanted to stay with her and never leave. As I ate, I told her that Cathy was counseling me.

"See, she wants to help you. You are a good person, and you deserve it."

I admired her beautiful, heart-shaped face, big, dark eyes and shiny, black hair. She was much more grown up than me, I thought, with her ample money and her loving, committed boyfriend. The aroma of cooking soup wafted into my nostrils.

She pulled a blue and white bowl from a light wooden cabinet and set it down on the beige Formica counter. The sound of pouring soup soothed me, as she filled up the bowl. Setting it in front of me, on the dark wooden, round table, she smiled. Her slender body moved gracefully and she hummed a tune to herself as she put a spoon and napkin down.

The soup nourished my body and soul. Admiring her clutter free apartment, I wondered how she stayed so organized. A tea kettle began whistling shrilly and she asked me what flavor tea I would like. I chose mint, because my grandmother used to put mint in my southern iced tea, when I spent the summers with her. Hypnotized by amber honey swirling down into my tea cup, I enjoyed the moment. The raw honey tasted delicious and I felt as contented as Winnie the Pooh with his honey jar. I was blessed with a sweet friend.

After I ate, she gave me a lesson on her computer. I watched with amazement as she showed me how to send emails. I had to admit that computers could do great things, even though they confused me.

"Just practice and you'll get better. Then, when you get a new computer, it will be easy. It's hard to work on an old computer like you have. They're always breaking down. Her understanding look made me feel less ashamed of my lack of technical skills. We sat in silence for a few minutes as she scrolled through various pages on her computer.

"I have something to give to you. I'll be back."

Watching her walk into her bedroom, curious anticipation titillated my senses. She walked out carrying a big, green bag. As she pulled clothes out of it, my eyes grew wide with delight. The lovely pants and shirts looked brand new. My favorite was a soft, long royal blue jacket, which tied loosely in the front and would show a shirt worn underneath.

"That was sewn by hand", she said, looking pleased that I liked it.

We talked for a while and, then, she looked at her watch and remembered the catching up she needed to do for her bank job. We walked out to her underground parking lot and I slid into the front seat of her clean car. We arrived at the train station and I told her goodbye reluctantly.

Walking down the stairs, I felt an energy of desperation in the air. As I boarded a train, I heard a disoriented, emaciated man jabbering nonsense to himself. When I looked away from him, I noticed a murder headline on the front page of a newspaper, on an empty seat. A woman with unkempt, wiry hair chattered about how aliens were going to take over the planet. A feeble looking man wrung his hands as he worried silently. It seemed like the whole world had gone insane. The mental institutions did not have enough room for the lunatics.

CHAPTER NINE

"You will tire quickly of all material things once you have them...But one thing you will never be tired of, either now or through eternity: the ever new joy realized in God-communion. Joy that is always the same may cause boredom, but joy that is ever new and continuous will entertain you forever. Such joy can be found in deep meditation."
Paramahansa Yogananda

We are what we think.
All that we are arises with our thoughts.
With our thoughts we make the world.
Speak or act with an impure mind
And trouble will follow you
As the wheel follows the ox that draws the cart...
Speak or act with a pure mind
And happiness will follow you
As your shadow, unshakeable

The Dhammapada

Home soothed me like a soft sand dune full of sun, when I got back to Cathy's. She greeted me with a hug and asked me how my visit was. Then, she suggested we go sit in the sun on the porch.

"She sounds like a really nice friend. I can tell it was good for you to be with her. You seem a lot happier. You're not talking in a monotone like you usually do."

I cringed as she lit a cigarette. Another sleepless night of wheezing would drive me over the edge. She held her arm down to keep it away from me, but the poisonous, second-hand smoke traveled through the air to me, even still. Anger and fear raged within me as I remembered asthma attacks from my past.

I went to talk with my therapist the next day.

"Cathy thinks I should stay here. I do like it here a lot. There are so many interesting things to do. Her smoking is really bothering me though."

"Did you tell her you have asthma?"

"Yeah. I finally told her. She holds her cigarettes away from me. I haven't had anyone ever listen to me like she does. The thought of moving away and leaving her makes me sad. I don't have any close friends like her back in Madison and I worry about getting lonely living all alone. Cathy says she worries about me living all alone."

"Well, you've lived alone before, and I think you will be fine. You have a lot of inner strength. People's opinions are just their opinions. You don't have to take them as the gospel truth."

"I feel so worried about my father. He was very frail when I took him to the symphony. He could barely walk, even with his cane. My father said I always have a place there. I'd give anything to hug him now, and I have hopes that my mother will give up her anger toward me."

"I'm sure she will."

"I'm afraid of her."

Jiang Lee laughed.

"She's an old lady. You could knock her over. I think it's funny that you're afraid of her."

"Well, I literally start shaking all over when she yells at me."

"There is nothing she can do to hurt you. She is just blowing off steam when she yells. You can't be hurt by it unless you allow yourself to be hurt."

"I feel so helpless, like I can't stand up for myself."

"I suggest you say in a firm voice, 'I expect you to talk to me in a kind, calm tone.'"

"She'll just keep yelling, and I'll stand there trembling, feeling used."

"You can say, 'It hurts me when you yell at me. If you yell at me again, I will not speak to you.'"

"Okay. I'll try that." I remembered how my mother used to say complimentary, loving things to me.

"You've accomplished so much with your hard work. You're a remarkable person. You moved to a new place, found a job while moving back and forth, and now you've saved up some money. You were penniless when you first came out of the hospital. I want you to congratulate yourself for all that you've done in a short time."

"Okay," I responded.

The session came to an end, and I clung to her kind eyes as I said farewell. As I walked out onto the streets, I wondered how various friends were doing. Passing the Hare Krishna house neighborhood, I missed Jyoti. I reminisced about our carefree afternoons spent pruning plants in the Tulsi house and making sweets for Krishna. Glendale wasn't the same without her.

I looked out over the rapidly multiplying houses and apartment buildings. The beautiful, Glendale landscape was being ruined by concrete. Couldn't they see that we had enough buildings and stores? What we needed was more trees.

Walking up and down the hills after I got off the train, I felt enlivened by the moving and stretching. The sun was so bright, it seemed to blaze through to my inner core, setting my cells on fire. My muscles burned from the fast walking as I arrived at Cathy's and unlocked the front door. Ambling slowly into the kitchen, I saw Cathy leaning against the counter, holding herself up on her elbows.

"You." She looked at me with bloodshot eyes and a dreamy, dazed face. Her body swayed back and forth and her face was flushed.

"Hi, Cathy."

"Hello, dear. I'm so glad to see you," she slurred. She looked into my eyes with deep devotion. Then, she staggered several steps, swaying like a reed in the wind. With fatigue, she leaned all of her weight against the kitchen counter. I smelled alcohol on her breath. She came toward me with tenderness radiating from her face.

"You're so gifted, and you don't even know it. I want you to be happy. You've been put down and held down for so long-- just surviving, not living. You've touched me," she said slowly, swaying back and forth. She spoke very slowly, and it was hard to follow her, yet I clung to every word.

"Cathy, have you been drinking?"

"Yeah. I drink Scotch sometimes. It helps me forget my back pain. I feel bad for you. I'm concerned about you going back East. I don't want you to be the goat again. Your family belittled you and made you wrong and it's held you back." Tears of compassion rolled down her face.

"I'm not going to go. I like it here."

I let her lean on me as I led her to the living room sofa. She reclined back with her heating pad, and I settled down into my comfortable arm chair. Kangaroos and aardvarks, gorillas, zebras and camels marched across the T.V. set.

Soon, Cathy passed out on the sofa. My eyes drooped with drowsiness and I left the room to prepare for bed.

The next day, the city's chaotic energy agitated me as I rode the train to my telemarketing job.

My manager greeted me politely. He always wore the same black outfit. I felt empathy for him, just scraping by in poverty. My depression lifted when he congratulated me for getting a donation.

On my lunch break, I talked with a young, charming man who told me he was struggling with poverty. He wanted to move back to his hometown because he was tired of working like a dog just to make ends meet. He lived in a rooming house and worked in the kitchen there, in addition to telemarketing, to reduce his rent. His face looked drawn with anxiety as he told me that he also did other work---whenever he could get it.

"I've been struggling ever since I moved here from Ohio three years ago. I want to go home." His eyes had bags under them from lack of sleep."

"I know what you mean. It's expensive here."

My concentration began to slip away as I made calls for donations. Worries that my father might suddenly die kept racing through my mind.

When I got home, I relaxed into the comfort of Cathy's arm chair and enjoyed Animal Planet. She reclined on the sofa with her heating pad.

"Are you going to Al-Anon this Saturday night?"

"No. I've started to see my counselor then. She had to change my time." Holding my temper, I counted the times I had already told her.

"That's too bad. We have a great group. The only way you can get over the toxic messages you were given by your family is to talk about it and have other members understand you. You'll learn about what it's like to have healthy relationships. You don't know what it's like because you've never had it."

"Yeah. They are a great group. I'm sorry my therapist had to see me at that time. I get more from one-on-on one counseling. I get shy and quiet in groups. I'm just feeling so down and depressed. I never have any energy. My father forbade me to come here and I'm afraid this city will eat me alive."

"You're not the little girl, remember? If you go home, you better be saying 'baa, baa,' because you're going to become the goat again."

"Yeah. I know old family patterns don't change. I'll think about it."

The next day I ran to my telemarketing job, after I got off of the train. It lifted my depression. A woman with a tall, thin body and shoulder length, bleached, blond hair smiled at me in a friendly way that relaxed me. We talked on our work break. She told me she had been hit by a truck. Her arm had been so badly injured she had had to get an artificial shoulder. Counting my blessings that I had not been through the same, I admired her cheerful, optimistic attitude and her total lack of self-pity. I needed to learn how to be like her.

When she invited me to go to a restaurant with her, I accepted with gratitude. Friends made my life worth living.

A few days later, with a new pep in my step, I told Cathy I was going out with a friend for the evening. After a long walk, I got on the train and rode it to Glendale. Then, I walked through the station to transfer to another train. As I went through the turnstile, I realized I did not have enough money to pay.

A large, black woman who sat in a glass cubicle noticed my distress. She called me into her office, and then called an officer.

After a few minutes, a tall man, dressed in black, with a gleaming, silver badge, walked toward me scowling with disapproval.

"If you ever come through here again without money you will have to pay a fine of two hundred dollars." My mouth dropped open in shock. I wasn't a criminal.

"Did you know that there is a missing person's report out on you?"

"No. I didn't."

"Well, your father filed a missing person's report. Where does he live?"

"Madison."

"Well, I suggest you go back there, because you can't afford to pay the fine you're going to get the next time this happens."

Feeling like a scolded child, I continued on my way. How authoritarian the world had become. It was like George Orwell had predicted: spies watching over people and poor people experiencing severe discrimination. I watched people walk by on the streets and wondered what their daily struggles were, observing their expressions which were weary and worried.

Soon, I arrived at the restaurant where my friend had said she would meet me. Walking in the front door, I looked around the elegantly decorated place and listened to the animated chatter. I breathed deeply, relaxing all over when my friend touched me gently on the shoulder. She introduced me to her friend and a smiling hostess led us to a table. She and her friend caught up on old news in the lively, posh restaurant, as I looked at the menu.

When my friend asked me what I was ordering, embarrassment blazed with a red, hot sizzle on my cheeks. Stammering, I told my friend that I had run out of money.

She said that she was happy to pay for me. I was amazed that a complete stranger could like me that much.

Soon, my delicious vegetable plate arrived, and I enjoyed the variety of flavors. I munched contentedly as I listened to them catch up. My friend said she was struggling with getting money from her trust fund because her brother was in control of it. With a sigh of frustration, she said that she wished her parents had set it up so that it was easier for her. I knew she needed it. We got paid peanuts for our telemarketing.

Lively music and laughter tickled our ears. When she said she had to go, I felt disappointed. I wanted to enjoy the fun atmosphere longer. She was like an angel, kind and caring.

I observed her long, thin body and bleached hair, soaking in her kindness as she walked me to the train station. Thanking her for a wonderful evening,

I hugged her. Her blue eyes lighted the dark corners of my weary, jaded heart. God breathed new life into me as she gave me a hug.

A tall, black man played violin in the subway station. He stood against the graffiti-scrawled walls. An elderly, emaciated woman with stringy, blonde hair and a wrinkled face played an autoharp and sang in a warbling, off pitch voice. There was another gruesome murder story on the front page of the newspaper in the grey box I passed. It sent a jolt of fear plummeting through me, which rattled my bones and shattered my core. Fumbling with my token, I dropped it in the slot and pushed my way through the turnstile, down the long stairway, and onto the loud, screeching, chaotic train platform. Searching the faces of various strangers surrounding me, I pondered that the most traumatized people were the kindest.

Soon, the train arrived. I squeezed my way through the open door. Sitting on the closest seat, I averted my eyes from yet another murder report. Gazing out of the window, I winced at hostile looking graffiti and garish posters. The train started speeding down the tracks and my mind wandered. I never knew how long my new friends would be in my life because people were always moving, changing jobs, or just running out of time to spend with friends.

Some, like Jyoti, weren't even alive anymore.

The train arrived at my departure point. I walked quickly out of the station. Traffic rumbled by and the rap music I hated (which my mother called missionary cooking music) pummeled my eardrums mercilessly. Breathing deeply, I walked up and down the flower-sprinkled hills to Cathy's house.

Cathy greeted me cheerfully and asked how my outing had gone. Settling down into the soft cushion of my arm chair, a secure feeling lulled me into a pleasant sleepiness. After a while, she made some popcorn. Munching on the buttery kernels, I dropped all worries down my grounding chord (as the E.S.P. Academy taught).

My frequent nightmares vanished this blessed night. Deep, contented emotions rocked me, like a baby, through my sleep.

Every morning, Cathy greeted me with love. This morning, she asked me how I slept and how I was feeling. I told her I was going to a therapy appointment.

Kundalini Rising

Riding the train into Glendale, I savored thoughts of Cathy's kind eyes and undivided attention.

Jiang Lee greeted me with a smile and bright, awake eyes when I arrived at her office. Her beautiful, long, black hair was in a ponytail. Sitting down, I began complaining about Cathy.

"I've told her I can't go to Al-Anon Saturday because I see you. She keeps asking me over and over if I'm going. I've told her fifteen times now that I can't go. It feels like she's trying to control me. And she tells me that I'm going to be 'the goat' if I go home, and I better be going, 'Baa, baa,' all the way back to Madison. She's trying to get me to stop being a victim. She's really funny about the way she gets me to look at myself. 'You better load up on a big bale of hay because that's what you'll be eating,' she'll say and get me to laugh about it. 'Sometime, you ought to walk up to your mother and go, 'Baa, baa,' and then say, "No more! When you start standing up for yourself, then the abuse will stop.'...... I know she is right. I've always been too afraid to stand up for myself. My brother used to tell me to fight back when my parents criticized me, and I never could. I'm embarrassed that I'm so weak."

Jiang Lee's peace flowed into me as she looked into my eyes, gluing the shattered pieces of me together.

"Standing up for yourself is a muscle that you will develop with practice. Remember to speak to the person in a calm tone and state what you want. Yelling at someone never accomplishes anything but you can say, 'I expect you to talk to me in a kind, calm tone.' You are finding your voice, so congratulate yourself for what you have accomplished."

I did not want to leave when it came to an end. As I walked to my car, a group of tall, tough men crossed the street in front of me. Trembling with terror, I ran to my car, let myself in, and then pressed the door lock desperately.

Speeding through downtown Glendale, terror gripped my guts as I prayed to make it home without any car troubles. If my car stalled, the gang members would surround me and eat me alive like jackals.

Serene safety swaddled me when I pulled into Cathy's driveway. Unlocking the door, I pulled it open, bursting with love for my home. Cathy appeared and welcomed me with a priceless hug. I didn't even mind inhaling the foul smelling cigarette smoke that her wool sweater had absorbed.

Feeling blessed to have her genuine love, I floated off to bed and crawled under the covers. The soft sheets soothed my soul. Adjusting the pillow under my head, I looked up at the ceiling, longing for sleep. Just as I was about to drift away, a wheezing sound came from my throat. I tried to ignore it but it continued with every breath I took.

I sat up and cleared my throat. Then, laying back, I tried again to fall asleep, but the wheezing defeated me. I couldn't get enough breath. I sat up again and stayed sitting up for the rest of the night, coughing and trying to get a satisfying breath.

Exhaustion conquered me as the sun rose and made patterns on my walls. My hip hurt as I rolled onto my side and curled into a fetal position. I worried as I hugged myself. Then, like a Raggedy Anne doll, I pulled my old, ugly clothes on despondently.

Cathy greeted me, with her usual welcoming exuberance, when I walked into the kitchen the next morning. I sipped from her small cartons of apple and grape juice. We talked most of the lovely, sun-drenched morning.

Later, she took me to Target. I read books as she looked for a rug for her living room. After about ten minutes, I walked over to her. When she asked my opinion about what she should buy, I replied that I liked everything she had chosen. As we browsed through the clothes, she encouraged me to buy something.

"Come on. It will be good for you!"

"No. I don't need anything." I worried about getting an insufficient funds notice and a thirty five dollar fine from the bank. I had gotten enough of those, in the past, to pay for a trip around the world.

Eventually, I changed my mind when I found a beautiful, rose-colored turtleneck which was discounted. Cathy beamed at me, saying it was the perfect color for my complexion.

When we got home, Cathy gave me a book she had gotten at Al-Anon. My heart overflowed with love when I read the message she had written inside.

"For one of the most remarkable people I have had the privilege to know and love".

I went to my room to take a nap. Sinking down into a pit of depression, I felt myself unraveling. If Cathy died or went into the hospital, I would have to sleep on a park bench. People I observed, day after day, enjoyed such confidence and I did not have a shred.

Vague wishes for death flitted through my mind as I drifted off to sleep. Nightmares about escaping from men who were trying to kill me split me apart.

The next day, I didn't want Cathy to hear my plans. Walking into the living room, I sat down, feeling revived by Cathy's greeting. As we talked, her voice calmed me.

For lunch, I ate a healthy salad made of vegetables I bought at the fabulous Farmer's Market. Then, I told Cathy I was going to run some errands.

I drove to a coffee shop and called Hansa. Her voice came on the phone, sending warmth through me. Feeling sad that I would lose her company, I told her I had decided to drive across the country and move back to Madison.

"No. Don't go. This is a very bad time of the year to be driving across the country all alone. You have a nice roommate and a job. There are people here who care about you. You need to settle down. Don't worry. You'll be all right. Everything is going to work out. You're living in a good area now, and you can start saving money. If you just put away a hundred dollars a month, you'll have twelve hundred at the end of the year. You worked so hard to get yourself out here. Have faith in yourself. You're a special person." Her wise, calm voice relaxed me.

I told her I would think about what she said and told her goodbye. Driving my car, I felt like a seesaw going up and down ceaselessly.

Tension tied me in knots as I parked my car, dreading finding yet another ticket on it. I walked restlessly around downtown Glendale and thought about my old psychic friends.

Suddenly, I noticed one of them standing in front of a newspaper box reading the headlines. He shook his head back and forth with disappointment. My angels must be giving me a sign. They must be telling me that I was planning for disappointment if I went back East.

I hurried down the street and up the stairs of the E.S.P. Academy. A kind woman who had given me readings, and told me I was a nun and a healer in past lives, welcomed me.

"I was wondering if I could sit here for a while and run my energy."

"Sure. Would you like to sit in on a group reading in about half an hour? The graduates of the clairvoyant program are doing it and they need a few more people."

"Okay." Breathing in their giggles and light voices, I longed to be like them. I sat in a chair facing the wall of windows and meditated.

After half an hour, I walked over to receive my reading. A slender, blonde woman read me as I sat there in a row of people.

"Your family didn't approve of things you said often. You stopped sharing your ideas because they often got a beer can energy thrown at them, like they were saying, 'That is really stupid' to your idea. You internalized all that disaffirmation."

The group reading illuminated many dark crevices in my subconscious closet. During my childhood, in which my father had repeatedly told me to "shut up", I had become afraid of speaking. The rare times when I did speak, I spoke in a whisper. No wonder I had felt invisible all my life. Remembering times when my parents had said I was stupid, I cringed in pain. Memories of not being able to get a word in at the dinner table, because my brother and father were spouting off scientific knowledge, made me ache with the pain of being not good enough. My father had wanted me to be a boy and, sometimes, I felt like my mother had not wanted me at all.

As I headed home, I longed to be young again, and to be confident and certain of who I was. Crowds jammed onto the trains and the hectic vibrations made me nervous. The nomadic life had drained all the life out of me.

Soon, the train arrived at my stop. I walked down the stairs and through the turnstiles. Grey fog rolled over the massive sprawling skyline, yet the sun warmed my face with its intensity.

Arriving about a block from Cathy's house, I noticed there was a deer staring at me. He was standing as still as a statue. His legs looked as thin as match sticks. With sweet eyes, he looked into my soul. Then, he pranced away into the cover of the trees.

I couldn't get my key to work, so I rang the doorbell. Cathy opened it and greeted me with a long hug. I bloomed like a flower and, then, went into my room and wilted on my bed.

After a short snooze, I walked out to the living area and told Cathy I had made the decision to go. A concerned expression filled her face as she scanned through the T.V. channels. Landing on the Weather Channel, she cried out in horror.

"There are blizzards going on all over the country. Please don't go. I don't want you to get stuck all alone on the freeway in the middle of nowhere."

"My father might be gone any day now. I need to get on back there. It is too competitive here."

"Just settle down and relax. You're working yourself into a frenzy. Your father is okay. He's walking around and your mother is taking care of him. You're doing well in Al-Anon. A lot of people here care about you."

"I know. I will really miss you. It just feels too unfamiliar for me here. It's so big and confusing and expensive. You might decide to have your daughter stay in my room."

"No. That won't happen. She's grown and gone. You'll always be welcome here."

Colors glowed on the T.V. screen, and I stared at it listlessly, knowing I couldn't rev up the energy needed to drive across the country again.

Back at the symphony the next day, the pressure was on. My manager lectured all the telemarketers, saying we would have to start bringing in more donations. I tried my best to put on a happy voice and inspire people to make donations, telling them they would greatly enrich the lives of children if they did. Yet, I was disappointed as, call after call, people refused to donate.

Whenever I listened to my young friend, at work, talk about how he wanted to get out of the city, I remembered myself in my twenties. I had been overwhelmed, broke and lonely back then too. Later that night, I sprawled on my bed and talked with him on the phone.

"I'm thinking about leaving here too. My father wants me to go home," I said.

"I'd be out of here in a second if I could be. I don't have the money to go anywhere though. The cost of living here keeps me down to my last nickel, even though I work like a dog." He sighed with frustration.

I wheezed and worried all night. When the morning sun chased away the darkness, depression weighed me down like a sadistic gargoyle sitting on top of me, staring me down with evil eyes. A desire for death came over me. It would be sweet to be released from this world of broken dreams and constant struggle.

Longing to feel something, anything, I forced myself out of bed every day. Pulling on my clothes, listlessly, I worried about others and about myself.

Finally, one morning, I filled my arms with clothes. Tiptoeing through the hall and to the front door, I pictured my parents wondering and worrying over me. I opened the door slowly, so as not to make a sound and looked back to see if Cathy was coming. Hopefully, she would sleep through it all and I would be far down the freeway before she discovered I was gone. I dropped my old clothes into the back seat and headed back to the house for another load.

Soon, my car was bulging with my worthless stuff. Tiptoeing back to my room for one last check, sadness dripped through me like a leaky faucet, as memories flooded me. The psychics, the Krishnas, the crazies, the therapists, the teachers and friends, close and not close, had all touched me deeply.

I walked into the kitchen to leave Cathy's key on the counter. I jumped nervously when she appeared behind me.

"Good morning. How are you?"

"I'm going to leave today. I just finished packing my car."

"Please, please, I beg you. Don't go!" she pleaded, dropping to her knees and looking up at me with motherly concern.

"I'll be all right. I've driven across the country before."

"Please just forget about it. You can go after spring gets here. It's too dangerous to drive across the country by yourself now. There are blizzards going on all across the country. You'll get stranded in the snow out in the middle of nowhere. Just settle down and relax. Let me make you some apple cider."

I watched her put oranges, cloves, and apple juice into a big pot. Outside the window, a hummingbird sipped nectar from a red flower, teaching me to seek the sweetness in life. Mist floated on top of the mountain outside and pink streaks filled the sky as the shimmering, orange sun rose ever higher.

Steam drifted from the pretty, blue teacup of hot apple cider which Cathy handed to me with love. Cozy contentment came over me as I drank cup after delicious cup, purring like a kitten.

"Your father is all right and you're all right. You have a home and a job and someone who really loves you here. You need to just relax. Please settle down and go easy on yourself. You're a special person, and I want you to be happy. I'm going to call you 'Road Runner'. You're wanting to take off and speed down the road all the time," she chuckled affectionately.

Kundalini Rising

After I'd enjoyed about five cups of cider, I looked toward the front door. The sky was churning with quickly flying dark clouds.

"It's not fit for man or beast out there. Come on, you need to stop worrying. Look at this funny doll I have."

She pressed on the abdomen area of a funny troll with white hair and a loud farting noise came out. She laughed uproariously and, as the doll farted again and again, I began to laugh. My abdomen heaved with uncontrollable surges of hilarity as I laughed the deepest, fullest laugh ever. As I listened to her laugh, I laughed and laughed until tears of joy ran down my face.

Later on, I went to the supermarket to get some Pepsi Cola for Cathy. She said it cured her stomach aches. Her back surgery had caused her such intense pain that she had become addicted to pain pills. It hurt me to hear her cry in intense pain one day, gripping her fingers on the kitchen counter. I felt angry at the medical system that presented surgery like a miracle cure and the pharmaceutical companies that pushed drugs to gullible, desperate people.

The next morning, I tried to leave again. However, I couldn't because Cathy had barricaded the front door with a tall bookshelf on rollers. Sitting with me while I ate breakfast, she said she wanted to keep me safe and that it would be better to wait and go when spring arrived.

"She's trying to keep me trapped," I told my therapist later that afternoon.

"She can't. You can walk out at any time. You don't need to worry about her being worried. She has her opinion but it is not the gospel truth. The same thing applies to the psychic. You have free will, and your intuition is telling you to go home. Trust your inner voice. Your spirit is calling you."

Finally, early one morning, I got up my nerve and I drove and drove until I reached the freeway. This time, I didn't turn back. I pressed the accelerator and kept going until Glendale faded away like a distant dream.

Ten hours later, I pulled off of the highway at a crowded city junction. A traffic jam slowed me down, and I watched cars speed along the high, curving overpass in the distance. After crawling like a snail for eternity, I pulled into the parking lot of a cheap hotel.

I tossed and turned on the lumpy bed. Frightening nightmares fragmented me.

Deep depression weighed me down as I pulled my aching body out of bed the next morning. I dreaded the drive ahead of me. The desk clerk acted cold when I turned in my key. Sitting down at the steering wheel, I gripped it, feeling fear scramble my brains and guts. My cousin had told me I was getting too old for this, and she was right. Painful pins and needles burned in my lower back and down my leg.

"Some people just survive. That's not living," Cathy's voice echoed in my head. I stopped in a car repair facility in Texas and called Cathy. Shaking with indecision, I told her I was thinking about turning around and moving back in with her. "Go west, young man," she quoted. "I'm always here for you."

Her caring voice resonated through me after I hung up. Walking toward a black mechanic who was checking my car, I longed to hear a human voice. I told him I had lived in Glendale and that, now, I had left there.

"I went to Glendale. Everywhere I went, they wanted money. It's very expensive out there."

I smiled inside. It must be my angels telling me I'd made the right decision. Maybe Cathy had seen a burning cross in the sky, but that didn't mean she was my prophet. I could decide for myself.

For the next four days, my life was a blinding blur of asphalt freeways, shopping malls, the foul stench of car exhaust and tomb-like hotel rooms. Pain pounded in my back and the sound of rushing traffic unraveled me.

My back and legs ached as I drove for ten and eleven hours a day, sometimes getting lost in rush hour traffic as I searched for a hotel at the end of each day. The loop shaped ramps on the freeway were daunting. My body stiffened with tension as my mind raced with scenes of crashing and dying.

I burst with joy when I saw the Madison city skyline in the distance. The golden dome of the capital glimmered in the sunlight and my heart opened like a flower as I rejoiced over being home. I loved this city with an all-encompassing passion now. Its vibrations of southern hospitality spread, like healing balm, through my ragged being. My shoulders dropped as I breathed in deeply.

I'd used up all of my savings and would have to wait five days until I got my disability check. I hated to impose on people, but I would have to ask for help. I called my parents and told them I was back. They could let me sleep in a brother or sister's room.

Luckily, my aunt gave me her sofa bed to sleep on.

The next morning, I called Cathy.

"God, they didn't even ask you if you had a place to stay? You'd treat a dog better than that. They could invite you over for some cake and ice cream. I know what you can do to get back at them. You can leave a bowl of dog food by their door and then run away. They should get the message if they're not too dense. Or leave a big bale of hay in their driveway. Tell them you're stocking up on food. God, they just don't know how to treat you like a human being. They just use you as the goat and stay in their own little worlds," Cathy said sympathetically.

"Well, that's just the way they are. I'm going to take them some lunch tomorrow. I want to sit and talk with them."

"Okay. Be careful what you put in that lunch!" We laughed for a while. Then she told me she was praying for me and that she would counsel me over the phone.

I called an old school mate. He said I could stay with him for a couple of nights. We went to church together. The casual, relaxed atmosphere calmed me. I recognized a couple of faces I had seen ten years ago. Telling people I was looking for a place to stay, I hoped they could help. A thin woman, with greying hair, gave me a number of someone who had a room for rent.

Later, I sprawled on my friend's guest bed and wrote down numbers from the newspaper. The days passed quickly and, soon, I had been living with him for ten days. I hated to be a nuisance.

I drove from apartment to apartment the next day, feeling too embarrassed to tell prospective landlords that I depended on the government. Dialing my father's number again and again on the phone, all I got was an answering machine message. I decided to surprise him and my Mom.

Around six in the evening, I drove up their driveway and ambled, like the prodigal son, into my parents' lives once again. My mother's face lit up and she hugged me when I walked in. Tears of joy rolled down her cheeks as she looked at me like I was the most precious person in the world. My father hugged me, looking overjoyed to see me. Absence does make the heart grow fonder.

Soon, my younger sister arrived to take them to a musical at the college she worked at. We all had a great time listening to the uplifting, entertaining singing.

Later, I stretched out in the guest bedroom of my sister's friend. Calling a woman I knew at the church, I felt hopeful when she gave me the number of a man who was renting a room.

The next morning, I drove to a neighborhood I had never seen. A tall, thin man with scraggly, dark hair told me my duties would include cleaning, sweeping and mopping the upstairs hall and taking the garbage out to the street every Monday and Thursday.

His stern voice intimidated me. However, I wrote him a check for five hundred dollars and asked him to please hold it until the third of the month. I didn't have much to spend on groceries. Maybe I could make soup and freeze it.

My sister's friend sighed with relief as I packed my bags and told him goodbye. Memories ran through my mind as I drove down the familiar streets of my hometown.

I stopped by my parents' house and banged on the door but there was no answer.

My new landlord let me in, with a distant, disgruntled manner when I arrived. As I moved my two small bags and several boxes of books and toiletries, loneliness crept through me like ice. I sat on the bed twiddling my thumbs, feeling restless. Worries ravaged me as I tried to sleep that night.

In the morning, I walked down the stairs and out of the house. Sitting had taken a toll on me and it felt good to move. Walking as fast as I could, I observed the houses in the modest neighborhood. Longing to have someone listen to me, I imagined the things I would tell them about my cross country odyssey.

Soon, I finished my long, fast walk. Grabbing my shoulder bag, I went to my car and drove to the Farmer's Market. The anemic fruits and vegetables disappointed me as the passing strangers looked through me.

When I got home, I put my food in the crammed refrigerator and went upstairs to my room. Faces of my Glendale friends drifted through my mind as I wrote stream of consciousness feelings in my journal. I called my parents' house and got their answering machine. With a shy voice, I told them I loved them.

Then, I drove to the Madison Symphony to interview for my old job. My old boss wasn't there anymore and I missed the approval he used to give me. Luckily, the new boss hired me.

Driving home, I enjoyed the familiar streets and reminisced about old friends. Later on, I called Cathy. When her voice came on the phone, my loneliness subsided. She counseled me for about an hour, building my confidence and appreciating my good qualities. I loved the way she always asked me how I was feeling and then listened.

My first day back at telemarketing went well and I got a couple of donations. I looked forward to telling my parents about my success when I saw them next.

I read the local new age newspaper the next morning, while sitting at the kitchen table. Happiness bubbled within me as I read the announcement that John of God was coming to do a program in Madison. Jumping up with excitement, I called the phone number and registered.

The weekend full of healing sessions was incredible. I sat in a room with about forty people to absorb the divine current of all the entities (healing spirits). A giant movie screen showed movies of John of God performing surgeries with no instruments. The entities worked through him, cutting incisions and removing tumors—all with not a drop of blood and not one shriek of pain. As I watched, I felt dumbfounded.

Eating lunch with two women from Florida, I listened to them talk about what they wanted for themselves and others. We celebrated the fact that the world was going through a spiritual revolution.

At the end of the day, I turned in photographs of my family members with a request for John of God to send them healings.

The entire John of God seminar was incredible. An ethereal energy of sublime, powerful love filled me all three days as the loving spirits showered me with healing. Kind volunteers, all dressed in white, oversaw the day to day activities. One of them gave me a bottle of blessed water to take home.

The day after the seminar, I went to my favorite restaurant. Sitting and writing in my journal, munching on pumpkin seeds, I thought about the amazing miracles I had seen and heard about.

A petite, Indian woman with a sweet face looked at me and we began to talk. I told her that I used to live in Glendale. She told me her name was Chandra.

"Oh, I miss Glendale. I used to live there and I want to move there."

"You will get back to Glendale. Here is the phone number of a Hare Krishna devotee who will rent a room to you. She's a friend of mine", I responded. I found my notebook in my shoulder bag and wrote down Bindu's number. Then, I handed it to her.

We began talking five days a week, when I went to the health food place to buy lunch for my parents, on my break from telemarketing.

I couldn't wait to get to work every day and hear the friendly hellos from my co-workers. Working double shifts telemarketing from ten to two and then from five to nine, I saved every dime. Power surged through me as I grew more confident with my speaking voice.

One day, I took Chandra a little bottle of John of God holy water. She lit up with happiness as she told me she was going to buy a plane ticket and fly to Glendale. Her humbleness, sweetness, compassion and generosity touched me deeply.

She gave me a DNA reading for free. She had paid a huge amount of money to study this method but was willing to give it to me for nothing. The results of my DNA reading said that I needed to trust myself and set limits with others.

She was always glad to see me and it felt wonderful to be so loved. When she told me, with happiness, that she had lined up a room to rent in Glendale with Bindu, I felt like a good person. Remembering times when my mother had told me I was not good, I realized that she had told me lies.

Clinging to every moment, I visited with my parents. My mother talked about various things as my father sat in grim silence, or groaned in pain when he moved his hip. Every time I left, I wondered how much longer they would last.

Back in my rented room, anxiety swallowed me as I sunk into a dark pit of isolation. Superficial acquaintances at work were my only contact with humanity. There was no one I could call on the phone just to talk about myself. The countless times when I had been a sounding board for someone, who was having a difficult time, ran through my mind.

The man, who rented to me, knocked on my door one morning. With disdain, he complained that I was not consistent with my chores. Then, he told me I was evicted.

Feeling helpless and terrified, I worried about getting raped and murdered as I slept in my car. I felt myself shrinking into oblivion. In silence, I stuffed my worthless clothes and books into the trunk of my car.

I called Cathy, out in Glendale, since my own mother had never let me cry on her shoulder.

"God! How do you find these people? You never should have moved in there."

My body trembled as I dialed the number of a man I knew. He was a close friend of the woman at church, who had told me about my current landlord. Every time I had talked with him, in the past, he had been kind and gentle. He was interested in metaphysics.

"I'm frightened. I've been kicked out of my place, and I'm going to have to sleep in my car."

"Don't worry. You can come stay with me. I live near some woods and they are fun to hike in. You'll like it."

Once again, my guardian angel had delivered me from a miserable, downward spiral. Sleeping in my car would have tipped my balance scales so drastically that I would have plunged into permanent insanity.

Now that a roof over my head had been supplied, I wanted to focus on my priority--pleasing my rapidly fading parents. For far too many years, I had not seen them often enough. I wanted to make up for lost time.

Quickly packing some art supplies and a peanut butter and jelly sandwich, I headed to my car. Reminiscing about my teenage years, I drove past my old high school. My art teacher had awarded me the prestige of attending the Art Honors Program.

Parking my car, I sauntered through the forest, remembering serene walks I had taken through this old, favorite park. Trees embraced me with outstretched, loving arms as I walked down the asphalt drive. Lovers sat together on the beautiful rolling hills, surrounded by gigantic magnolia and oak trees.

Dabbing paint onto a canvas, I remembered how my mother had encouraged me. Long, long ago, I had walked through this park, with a handsome man. I grieved that he had not pursued me after the third date. How lovely it would be to live with him and our children in a big house.

Soon, my two paintings for my parents looked half way decent and I wiped off my brushes and put everything into my canvas bag. Magnificent trees soothed me, blessing me with fresh oxygen as I walked to my car. Driving through the familiar, lush streets, I got lost in memories of high school and college.

Pulling into my parents' driveway, I felt my heart expand. My father looked feeble and overwhelmed as he sat alone in his office, which was cluttered with piles of magazines and newspapers and other things. Hugging him, I remembered the way he used to squeeze my hand. Showing him the paintings, I let him know he could have the one he liked the most.

"I like the sky in this one. Mom can have the other one."

We sat on the porch. My mother did most of the talking while my father sat in silence. They talked about their friends dying and trips to the doctor. Mom brought me a glass of orange juice. Stories about my siblings, the grandchildren and aunts and uncles brought good memories to me. Holding onto their words, I wished we could grow younger together. Finally, I told them goodbye, not wanting to leave.

It was a long drive to my friend's apartment. He partially cleared a cluttered room and set up a massage table for me to sleep on. It was uncomfortable, but I was grateful to have a roof over my head.

My birthday was approaching. My mother called and asked me to have lunch with her and my father at the Country Club to celebrate it.

He had driven all the way to North Carolina to visit my sister. I admired his fiery, Aries determination but worried that he was straining his frail body. He looked frail and tired as I sat down at the cloth covered table underneath the sparkling chandelier. Birthday flowers, a box of expensive oil pastels and my parents' devotion made me smile. The salad, asparagus, squash, zucchini and sweet potato was delicious. Mom lit a small cake and they sang Happy Birthday to me. Settling into the precious, wonderful moment, I recovered my balance.

My raggle taggle nomad days had worn me down. Gentle times like these gave me warm, fuzzy, stable, grounded feelings. Balance, stability, grounding and building a life appealed greatly to me.

Crying inside, I told them good bye and drove for an hour to my new home. My friend/landlord was interested in natural health, like me, and we had good conversations. When I wasn't telemarketing, I hiked with him through the woods. He taught me some Martial Arts moves that I could use to defend myself with a person who had ripped my shirt in half and thrown me down on the ground. That was after she'd dragged me down her staircase. Her muscles were much stronger than mine.

After months of working double shifts and taking my parents lunch, I

Kundalini Rising

decided that I had made a mistake. I called Cathy and told her I was planning to drive back across the country and move in with her. She told me she was looking forward to me coming back.

As the time for my departure came nearer and nearer, I felt my heart breaking. I kept calling my parents, telling them I wanted to bring them some watermelon.

"Well, why don't you just eat it yourself?" my father would reply. I didn't really care about the watermelon. I cared about them.

I wanted to scream, "This might be the last time I ever see you!"

CHAPTER TEN

"Do to others whatever you would have them do to you."
Matthew 7:12

"If you forgive others their transgressions, your heavenly Father will forgive you. But if you do not forgive others, neither will your Father forgive your transgressions." Matthew 6:14-15

"Then Peter approaching asked him, 'Lord, if my brother sins against me, how often must I forgive him? As many as seven times? Jesus answered, 'I say to you, not seven times but seventy-seven times.'" Matthew 18:21-22

Let my life now merge in the all-pervading Life
Ashes are my body's end.
Om. O mind, remember the Reality
O mind, remember thy past deeds.
Remember the Reality
Remember thy past deeds.

Isha Upanishad

"**W**ell, it's about time for you to get in your wagon train and head back here," Cathy said the next time I talked with her. "Yeah. Things are going well with my parents, but my father is so frail that our days together are numbered. I'm not sleeping very well. It's not comfortable sleeping on my friend's massage table. I miss being with you and sleeping in your comfortable bed."

"It's beautiful out here! Seventy degrees and sunny. I saw a deer yesterday. Last week, I went to the ocean with a friend. You're welcome here, always. Just let me know when you get on the road. I'm praying for you, and I'm here for you whenever you want to talk."

I enjoyed the serenity of sitting on my parents' sunny porch the next day. They were very glad to see me. I asked them what they had been doing.

"Well, we've been making the funeral arrangements." Sadness rolled through me and I wanted to stretch the day so that it would never end.

Suddenly, I looked at my watch. It ticked rapidly toward the time of my second telemarketing shift.

Reluctantly telling my parents good bye, I headed out to my car. Traffic was awful, as I drove to work, and I wished I could go back in time to when there was less traffic.

The next time I called Cathy, she complained that I had ruined the knob on her stove. She said she had to pay someone to fix it. She was also upset that I had not cleaned the bedroom before I left.

"My daughter couldn't even stay in there. You used to slam the microwave door and now it is not working. And something has gone wrong with the tub. It is leaking constantly. I think you should pay me to cover the repair bill I got."

"Well, you can sue me," I retorted angrily.

Maybe it was not a good idea to return to her. I hated being criticized and accused of damaging things. I decided to stay in the East.

Then, I changed my mind and called Bindu. She said that, if I sent her five hundred dollars, she would hold a room for me. Obsessive-compulsive urges flooded me.

I resigned from my telemarketing job. When I got home, I told my landlord/friend good bye. It didn't take long to put my worthless stuff into my car.

Congested traffic made me nervous. After navigating through the city chaos for a while, I merged onto the expressway. Turning the radio up loud, I listened to David Bowie sing "Changes", thinking about what a fascinating place Glendale was, with its explorations into the psychic and spiritual frontiers, and its advanced ideas about health and clean energy. Shops and parking lots sprawled endlessly on either side of me. Trapped people worked at their low paying jobs and went home to eat TV dinners in front of the boob tube in little cement cubicles.

After my ten hour drive every day, I pulled into a hotel and showered. Then, I did Tarot readings over and over, asking the cards if I should live in Madison or in Glendale. My mind thought and analyzed and weighed the pros and cons until I was completely exhausted.

Three days of non-stop driving passed in a flash. Soon, I was flying past a vast dessert covered with cactuses. The expressway stretched before me, long and endless. Like an astronaut floating in the black void of outer space, I flew along in my capsule. My lower back was still hurting and I was returning to square one: my hellhole with the Hare Krishnas. I was the hopeless case my father called me, I thought in self-disgust.

When I needed sleep, I would dream of driving along winding, treacherous ramps on the expressway, which looped like endless roller coasters. I was getting older fast, and my life was flashing by. Every morning, I felt lost in a nebulous fog of uncertainty. It was as though I was floating in space disconnected from everyone. The hellos and goodbyes of hotel clerks lit my heart like a brief candle. Then, the fear and alienation would overcome me again.

Feeling foggy about who I was, I would pull on my clothes and walk to my car in the dark at four or five in the morning. As I pushed the accelerator to the floor, I heard the psychic's voice echo in my mind.

"You will be a butterfly," she had promised.

Yet, I felt like a pathetic, destitute madwoman--not pretty at all.

Treating myself to a break from driving, I took a tour of the Grand Canyon. A friendly man picked me up in a van at my hotel one sunny morning. Tourists greeted me, as I stepped up. Sitting in a window seat,

I enjoyed the spectacular scenery. After a half hour drive, we got out and walked around.

Stretching my legs and jumping with joy, I relished the freedom of moving my body around. Then, I gazed into the immense, deep canyon with its gorgeous, glorious ripples of pink, red, blue, purple, brown and its energy of eternity. In contrast, my little life was a blink of an eye.

A knowledgeable speaker explained how the canyon had been formed by water, and the various stages it had been through. Then, she explained how the earth formed various types of rock. Awed fascination filled me.

Laughing with the kind strangers, as we sat at a picnic table eating lunch, revitalized me. A glorious feeling of peace pervaded me.

Cathy greeted me when I arrived at her cozy home nestled in the redwoods. I followed her out to the porch and we sat and talked. Fearing that I was not welcome, I didn't mention my desire to rent her room again. However, when she asked me to help her, I jumped at a chance to get back into her good graces.

Surveying the huge piles of new clothes she had bought, I realized that she was as crazy as I was. One by one, I called out the price of each garment and then neatly stacked it in a pile. She checked the prices I called on a long receipt. When that was finished, she asked me to help her clear out her closets.

Watching her in disbelief, I felt like I was in Macy's. Pulling endless outfits on, she asked me how they looked, then tossed them on the floor. Immaculate pants, blouses, skirts, and dresses were hung neatly, tightly packed in numerous closets. She never even looked at them. For hours, I filled huge garbage bags with them.

Then, I drove them all to the Salvation Army and left them in a big, outdoor bin. When I got back to her house, she thanked me over and over, telling me she felt free with them gone.

I drove to the Hare Krishna house and talked with Bindu. She told me that she had rented the room to someone else because she was afraid that I would change my mind. However, she would let me stay for a couple of nights in her extra bedroom. The futon on the floor was uncomfortable. Burning, sharp pains shot down my leg from my sciatic nerve.

Early the next morning, I applied for a job in a preschool, where a kind woman was happy to meet me and eager to hire me. Traffic frazzled me as I drove around town, looking for a place that would take my fingerprints so my background could be checked.

When I got home, Bindu was yelling at her boyfriend on the phone. I called Cathy.

Luckily, she said that I was welcome to move back in with her, I felt like a child who had gotten back into the good graces of her mama.

We talked in the mornings, like we used to do, and I relaxed into the safe, simple security. She effervescently talked about the fun she had had with her neighbor when she went with him to a children's birthday party. He had dressed as a clown and entertained the children. As I talked about walking through the Grand Canyon, she listened with interest. Being listened to was heavenly. It was an experience I had rarely had.

We fell into silence after a while and I gave myself an angel card reading with a deck of Tarot cards I had bought. The psychic who had said I should move had created them. Now and then, I looked up at Cathy who was seriously studying her Bible.

"Oh, Archangel Michael is protecting me!" I exclaimed with joy. Delighted, I showed her the card I had pulled.

"Michael is a fallen angel. Michael is in league with the devil." She squinted her eyes and looked at me with disapproval. A tense feeling and an urge to run came over me. She thought I was in league with the devil because I was reading Tarot cards.

"If it doesn't involve the Holy Trinity, it just doesn't have any substance." Her eyes were filled with righteous certainty and the judgement in her voice tightened every fiber of my being.

I fumbled with my cards nervously. She might accuse me of "spreading the devil dust" like my mother used to do when I was in high school. Her Christian narrowness was closing in on me like a trash compactor. Disappointment ran through me. Her love used to feel so wonderful.

I thought back to my mother. She had cried with joy when I walked into the house with a container of chili from the health food store. All I had been seeking during my years of racing across the country had been given to me in that priceless moment. Feeling my heart burst open, I remembered the days when she was my world.

She used to love me. I heard her voice saying the things she had said in my youth: *I can't be happy as long as you're not happy. The only thing you look forward to is eating. You're an all-American girl. You're my shadow. I want you to step up and take your rightful place. You're the sweetest and smartest. It's hard for you, being the middle child. The first child gets the most attention. Always remember you're special because you're an artist.*

"I'm going to go out for a while," I told Cathy. "I'll buy us lunch at a Mexican restaurant I found, and then we can bag up your clothes."

"Okay."

I looked at the familiar sights as I drove through the neighborhood. The parking lot was crowded, but I was lucky enough to find a space in front of a Mexican restaurant. The waiters sweetly and humbly served me, their dark eyes and skin glowing softly.

When I got back to Cathy's house, we settled down in the living room and ate. She looked at me with gratitude.

"I'm glad to have you back, sweetie. Thanks for all of your help. I'm so happy to be getting rid of all these excess clothes. I've got enough to clothe a whole town in this house. I picked up the habit of hoarding from my mother."

I slipped out of the house later on and drove around Glendale, looking with love at the E.S.P. Academy, the Hare Krishna temple, the pub where I had danced and sang duets with Nancy, and the marina with its screeching seagulls and funny pelicans.

Then, I went to see Bindu. When I told her I had a nice place to stay she was happy for me. She returned my money and told me my friend, Chandra, was renting her room.

Walking up the stairs, I came alive, anticipating her kindness. Knocking on her door, I felt my emotions heal. When she opened the door, her voice rose with happiness as she greeted me with surprised delight.

Sitting on a spare bed, which was across from her bed, I admired a Japanese screen with a beautiful painting of a heron on it. She heated a cup of jasmine tea on a little hot plate and handed it to me with a smile. Then, she gently placed a jar of honey and a spoon on the small table near me. Her sweet nature filled me with comfort and the day became soft and whimsical, with nothing to do and nowhere to go.

"I love it here. I walk to the Krishna Temple every day and do service. There are so many interesting things to do here. I took a class about Astral travel in downtown Glendale. People drank tea and had cookies and they were all so friendly."

Her eyes sparkled with a new vibrancy. I felt happy for her, knowing she was overjoyed because she had escaped her boring routine of cashiering in stagnant Madison.

The next day, I met her at a recreation center and we played ping pong. Laughing like children, we batted the ball back and forth playfully. Her friendship did wonders for me.

She had great compassion for me when I told her I wasn't sure if I wanted to stay in Glendale. We rode to the pier together, in my car.

As pelicans and seagulls flew above the shining bay, she taught me muscle testing. Holding my hand, she patiently showed me how to put my fingers together and ask myself a question. If the answer was "yes" my fingers would stay strong and together when I pulled my connected thumb and first finger through them. If it was "no" the fingers would separate. After asking many questions, I still felt confused, and unsure about where I should live. Looking out at the lovely, blue water and sky billowing with clouds, I sighed. The sound of waves lapping on the pier calmed me.

As I drove us back to the Hare Krishna compound, I enjoyed listening to her cheerful chatter about her experiences doing service for Krishna. Suggesting we browse through the shopping area, I drove to a popular street. I parked the car and we walked past the unique pedestrians, awed by all of the activity. Hare Krishnas walked along in their saffron robes, chanting and banging drums. We went into a shop which overflowed with gorgeous jewelry and clothes. Chandra bought me a lovely, silky, blue and green scarf.

She looked at me with affection as I drove through the traffic, back to the Hare Krishna house. As I parked the car, I hoped I would see Bunny, who Bindu raved about, because he gave her so much love.

It had been almost two years since Jyoti's spirit had flown to the Vikuntha dimension of peace, love and joy--finally liberated from earth hell. I knocked on the door and Surya answered. He seemed very depressed.

Walking up to Chandra's room, I towered over her, feeling very tall. Her petite, slender body was small but strong from her vegetarian diet. Her Eastern Indian heritage had given her much knowledge about spiritual laws and she lived with wisdom. She had studied herbal medicine extensively and sometimes made suggestions to me, if I mentioned I wanted to sleep better or have more energy. She told me that her father had been very loving and had encouraged her to learn.

Unfortunately, her marriage was full of turmoil. She generously gave to me, never behaving in a needy way, though no one gave love to her.

Her devotion to Krishna was moving. Making offerings to Krishna on her altar every day, she focused on all that was good, pure and loving in life. Like an innocent child, she accepted and loved everyone and trusted in Krishna to bless her.

Not wanting to leave her, I told her good bye. When I got home, I told Cathy I was thinking about going back to Madison.

"That's not a good idea. You need to rest. It's dangerous."

I talked to my therapist the next day. Her kind eyes and totally attentive listening calmed me as I told her about my experiences in Madison, and how I had worked for the symphony's telemarketing department. She told me I was a remarkable person to have handled all of that. Then, she congratulated me for improving my bond with my parents.

I told her that Cathy had taken me back, though she hadn't wanted to at first. I wrung my hands as I confessed I still couldn't decide whether I should stay or go.

"What does your inner psychic say?"

"I don't know. I like it here, and Cathy really loves me. My mother was really glad to see me though, and that meant a lot to me. I've applied for a job here as a preschool substitute."

"Can you afford to get your own studio here?"

"No. I'll have to stay with Cathy."

"And you'll have to deal with her smoking and drinking. And she can be controlling."

"I was really glad to be with my parents. My father isn't going to last much longer. He had weakened a lot. I just can't decide. I'm afraid of going against the psychic's advice. He told me that this is definitely the place for me."

She laughed. "That is merely the psychic's opinion. What is *your* opinion?"

"I think I want to go home."

"Your spirit is calling you, so listen. You will be happier in Madison. My intuition is telling me. Are you going to pack sandwiches for your trip?"

"Yeah. I'll take sandwiches, and trail mix, and a bottle of water."

"Everything will work out for you in Madison. Your parents will be glad to see you and you can live in your own studio and concentrate on your writing. You've made a great choice. You will continue to grow spiritually. There is no spiritual growth without money. Your parents will continue to help you. You've made a great decision. Trust yourself. You have the desire to go home for a reason."

I tried to slip out the next morning but, once again, Cathy had barricaded the door. She slumbered in her large bed and I was afraid she would hear me if I moved the big, plywood board away from the door.

A weariness came over me, and I went back to my room and collapsed on the bed. Falling into a deep sleep, I dozed for hours.

When I woke, I felt disoriented. Trembling with fragile emotions, I dressed myself and brushed my hair. Cathy was sitting on the sofa when I walked in. She looked at me with concern.

"Are you all right? You've been sleeping a long time. It's because you're exhausted from racing down the freeway. I've got to keep my eye on you. You're my little road runner." Her affectionate look meant the world to me.

"Yeah. I'm fine. I just got intensely drowsy all of a sudden."

"Well, it makes sense. You've been wearing yourself out, driving back and forth across the country."

After talking with Cathy for a while, I walked to the train station and rode the train to downtown. Then, I visited the E.S.P. Academy and got a healing.

Afterwards, I walked through the streets, passing people sitting on blankets selling incense, playing guitars and talking. I longed to talk to Priya.

Arriving at the Krishna Temple, I pushed the red door open. Then, I talked with a kind devotee for a while.

Searching for Priya, I found her in her room. Telling her about my visit with my parents and my plan to move back East, I relaxed, feeling a strong current of love radiating from her heart into mine.

We walked into the main room, where the devotees were serving Prasadam. As I ate lunch, my heart swelled with waves of love for Priya. She sat with me, gazing at me as though I was an innocent, precious child.

"Krishna is the Master Psychic. He told me you will be happier in Georgia."

She had loved me as though I was a member of her family. Swallowing tears, I looked into her compassionate, blue eyes.

Later on, I sat with Cathy on her porch, enjoying the perfect weather and the aroma of the lemon tree. She glowed with happiness that I had returned. As I ate fresh vegetables from the Farmer's Market, I watched the hummingbird flutter his wings as he sipped nectar.

The next morning, I rode the train to Santa Rita and visited Hansa. She was wonderful as always, and she fed me soup and salad. Wanting to stay with her forever, I absorbed her kind, calm and competent energy.

On my tenth day at Cathy's, I got up at five in the morning, tiptoed out with an armful of clothes, got into my car and drove until I reached the expressway. I sped like a bullet for about ten hours and, when I finally stopped, I called Cathy on my cell phone. Her concern reached through the phone to me, pouring strength into me, like Popeye's can of spinach did when he faced a challenge. Love had kept me alive throughout my epic cross country odyssey.

I drove ten and eleven hours a day until my back throbbed with pain. When I arrived in Madison, my sister's friend took me in again. Soon, I began to feel like a smelly fish, which stunk to high heaven.

The nights of non-stop thinking and waking up with soaking sheets had been going on for a long time. Presuming that I was having hot flashes, I realized that it was normal for my age. Yet, I longed to feel sane again, as my emotions wavered up and down, like a roller coaster.

I called my parents and offered to bring them some pineapple. When my father said he did not want any, and why didn't I just eat it myself, I fell apart inside. The urgency to heal our relationship before they were dead and gone consumed me. Emotions raged through me, tossing me like the waves of a tsunami. Desperate, anguished thoughts of being left all alone in the world with no one who loved me rattled my bones and I could barely concentrate on anything. I worried that people thought I was odd.

Appearing at their door one day, I handed them a salad from my favorite health food store. They looked frail and I wanted to hold them like little children, to sooth away their tears. I attended church with my neighbor and enjoyed seeing a few people I knew.

Then, suddenly, one early morning, I began to drive back out West. I couldn't trust my decision to stay in Madison. My mind was a battleground of conflicting thoughts and obsessive urges. Unseen and unheard, I drove like an insane person-- like Sisyphus rolling the boulder up the hill only to watch it roll back down. I worried about becoming too overwhelmed to drive, racking up a huge hotel bill and dying of starvation after I spent my last bit of savings.

If my car suddenly died in the middle of the desert, I wouldn't have enough money to pay for repairs. I would die of starvation and dehydration all alone. I had gotten rid of my cell phone. I couldn't even send an S.O.S. bottle or carrier pigeon to deliver a note. My life could be extinguished completely and my remains might not be found for months.

I imagined my parents getting a call from the police that the dead body of their daughter had been found. The police might not ever find their address or phone number, and I may remain a mystery disappearance in the lives of everyone who knew me.

Numbness pervaded me as I drove and drove down the endless, black asphalt freeway. I felt hypnotized by the two yellow lines dividing the lanes. Gripping the steering wheel, I prayed for all of the forces of mercy and goodness to protect me.

Soon, I arrived in Glendale. Cathy welcomed me and I resumed my job, helping her sort through massive amounts of clothes, bagging them up and taking them to the Salvation Army.

I went to visit Chandra and we walked through downtown Glendale to a health food store called the Elephant Pharmacy. Constantly encouraging and supporting me, she was a total joy to be around.

We rode the bus to the Marina and walked out on a pier. With endless patience, she listened to me as I swung back and forth like a pendulum, weighing the pros and cons of staying in Glendale or going back to Madison. Seagulls cried as they flew overhead and the sound of lapping waves relaxed me. Big ships chugged along and tiny sailboats sailed. The powerful, bright sun warmed me from head to toe.

Spending the afternoon with Chandra, I felt my emotional wounds being healed. Her friendship was gluing together the shattered pieces of my psyche. Feeling happy for her, I listened to her talk about the loving Krishna community and the uplifting talks she was going to, which were given by a spiritual master. A kind devotee was driving her to them. The love the spiritual master gave her was oceanic, she said, bubbling with new vitality and love for life. Overjoyed that she had escaped the negative

Kundalini Rising

vibrations of Madison, she greeted each day with ecstatic gratitude and humble willingness to serve Krishna.

Not wanting to leave, I told her good bye.

I tossed and turned that night, and called Jiang Lee for an emergency session the next morning.

When I arrived at her office, I told her I was back because I had doubted myself again.

"Trust yourself. Your inner psychic knows what is best for you. You will do well in Madison and your parents will continue their support." Her dark, sweet eyes glowed with wisdom.

She would be an eternal flame in my heart, warming me through any future hail storms. Tears filled my eyes as I thanked her for saving me from depression. Wanting to keep her with me forever, I reluctantly told her goodbye.

My sciatica hurt as I drove to the expressway. Missing the sweetness of Chandra, I merged onto the expressway. Then, I sped like an astronaut, all alone in outer space, for four long, grueling days.

After driving around the city applying for apartments, I realized I did not have enough money to move into any of them. I found a telemarketing job in Madison and moved into an apartment down the street from the one I had lived in the year before. It took my entire disability check to cover rent so, night after night, I called people and asked them to donate to the Shakespeare Festival. At least I made enough money to buy some groceries.

It lifted my spirits when my younger sister drove me and my parents to a performance at the symphony hall. Tensely, I sat next to them, hoping that there would not be any conflict between us. As the singers sang, with their child like exuberance, I was lifted into a shimmering, magical world of rainbows, lollipops, leprechauns and playful laughter.

I began greeting my co-worker with extra friendliness. She responded with kindness and, after a few weeks of getting to know each other at work, we went to a coffee shop together.

One day, my school friend—the one I'd stayed with—said he wanted to take me somewhere. He drove me to my younger sister's apartment complex. Then, he parked in front of a building and led me up a long staircase.

I walked into a quiet studio apartment. A small kitchen was concealed by mirrored French doors. There was a walk-in closet in the back.

"Do you like it? If you like it your father will buy it."

I breathed in the safe, secure silence. I breathed out all of my anxieties, feeling grateful for the numerous, gorgeous trees in the complex, and the way it was situated far away from a street. I had manifested what I wanted! My harried days of scrambling for shelter were over.

My wonderful sister took care of having it painted and repaired.

Around Christmas time, the Shakespeare Company stopped its telemarketing campaign. Luckily, the new manager of the symphony telemarketing department hired me. Secure serenity flowed through me as I sat in my familiar cubicle and called people to ask them to donate to the symphony. People were friendly and the familiar faces made me secure.

My sister finished my new home in February and I moved in.

The days flew by and July rolled around. The telemarketing office moved across the street. A couple of weeks later, the boss called me into his office and told me he couldn't use me anymore.

I began walking around applying in stores. Taking a break in a coffee shop, a colorful advertisement, in the New Age magazine, kept calling to me as I flipped through the pages. It listed various healing methods, which I had never heard of.

Brimming over with curiosity, I called the number listed.

A man with a cheerful voice answered the phone. He listened patiently as I told him about my studies at the E.S.P. Academy. I told him they had taught me to invite an invisible healing master to plug into my hand chakras. When I asked if the healings he advertised used the same method, he replied that the masters work in many, mysterious ways.

I felt suspicious. None of the spiritual methods I had tried had made me happy. This was probably just one more dead end.

"I would like to meet you. Can you come into the center and talk with me on Friday?"

"Okay," I replied hesitantly.

Friday arrived in no time. Driving through the streets, I got lost in memories connected with various businesses I passed. Seeing the donut shop, I reminisced about care free times, with siblings and friends, watching the donuts drop, from a conveyor belt, into hot oil.

Then, as I drove by a restaurant, I remembered nights there, when waitresses called me dear me and asked me if I wanted anything, in soothing southern accents--more butter, more cornbread or iced tea?

I passed by the old, historic theater where I had seen lively shows and looked up at a starry ceiling. With careful concentration, I parked my car.

Then, I walked toward the brick building he had described to me. When I reached it, I walked through a small parking area, through the door and up a long stairway. Curiosity filled me as I rang the doorbell.

An attractive man with brown hair and sparkly, brown eyes greeted me with a wide, vibrant smile and gentle hand shake. His name was Raja. We sat down and talked. I was touched deeply by how intently he listened, radiating genuine caring so I felt at home.

After our light talk, he invited me to attend Satsang, which he gave every Wednesday night. He explained to me that Satsang meant "in the company of the truth" in Eastern Indian language. I didn't know if it was a Hindu or a Sanskrit word. Knowing nothing about either, I felt my curiosity grow.

I started attending Satsangs. The atmosphere was cheerful and light and everyone who attended was friendly. A blonde woman, who was about my age, gave me long hugs that soothed my worried mind and nurtured my empty emotions. As I listened to the teacher talk about spirituality, I felt amazed.

Things continued to get better and better as I worked and met my parents for lunch every Sunday. Hanging onto their words, I enjoyed feeling lovable.

"We used to wake up every morning and say 'Where is she?' We thought you might be stranded in the middle of the road somewhere. We didn't want you way out there with nothing familiar and no one to help you. We were very worried," my mother said, as I sat munching on vegetables and looking out the window at the rolling green hills, dotted with white golf carts.

A couple of months passed and the leaves began turning gold, yellow, orange and red. Being with my spiritual family and listening to Raja brought new life to me. He planned a Halloween party. I dressed as a black cat and my fellow seekers dressed zanily. One was a mad scientist, another was a mermaid. Raja dressed as a vampire. He gave Tarot readings to everyone. When he read me, he mentioned that I was worrying about getting fired and encouraged me to not worry. Laughter and lightness lifted me and everyone had fun.

As the days got colder, I began to see life from a different perspective. People glowed with angelic sweetness everywhere I went. My fears dissolved as I noticed, with astonishment, that no one spoke to me with annoyance. Everyone appreciated me and spoke kind words.

One Sunday, the streets were slick with snow and ice. My mother called and said the country club was closed. She invited me to have lunch with her and my father at their house. Warm, fuzzy feelings flowed through me as I drove.

My mother greeted me, looking overjoyed to see me. I sat in the living room on the sofa with them and we talked for a while. I asked my father about his experiences in the ski troops in Italy. He said that it was quite an experience performing surgery on soldiers and skiing down large slopes to deliver medical supplies. He looked so tired and frail it hurt me. I knew his broken hip must hurt intensely, and I wished I could stop the pain.

My mother talked cheerfully and told me she was glad to have me home. She brought out a pot of spaghetti and a pot of oatmeal and put them on the table.

"You can eat some oatmeal, and then you can have some spaghetti," she said, looking at me with tenderness.

Eager to help, I watched my father walk over to the table and positioned a chair behind him. He let go of his walker and plunked down feebly, groaning with pain.

"Are you talking with anyone out there?" He raised his voice and narrowed his eyes in anger.

"No," I replied, with tense timidity.

Nevertheless, I enjoyed the rest of my visit. It had been ages since I'd sat with them in my old, childhood home. I was home again, and I was welcome. They had forgiven me, and they loved me more than I had ever realized.

Christmas was rapidly approaching. My boss told me she had no complaints about how I was running the cash register and preparing plates for banquets.

Raja gave me healing hugs every time I arrived in the ashram. A magical energy floated through the air, as he taught Satsang. He explained that the masters were working toward building a new age of enlightenment. Often, they came into the room to bless us. One day, he gave me an assignment. He instructed me to meditate, while looking at their pictures, and write messages from them afterwards. All I needed to do was tune into their energy to receive their guidance. If I did this consistently, I would become able to know when they were in the room.

Another day, he gave me the assignment of mirror gazing. Gazing into my eyes, for five minutes a day, would allow me to get to know my soul and my past life experiences.

As I gazed at myself, I felt experiences and varied emotions and personality traits. There was unlimited depth in my soul. Realizing that I was eternal energy that was never born and that never died, I began spending much of my time in silent contemplation.

I remembered how my mother had chided me for following the "guru" when I went to India. Now, I had a real guru, something I had only read about. He seemed too good to be true. He called me frequently, just to tell me I was "on his heart". It felt so much better than the common "on my mind". He did not want anyone bowing down to him and, one day, he surprised me with what he said.

"Everyone is a guru." I had never looked at life that way.

At Satsang, he said that people, in this day and age, were in their minds too much and that they related in a competitive way, from their third chakra. As they evolved spiritually, they would move into their hearts. Some day, enlightened humanity would remember this time as the time without love.

Raja said that doing selfless service, Seva, was an important part of moving toward enlightenment. So, I began coming early to every Satsang, putting out the chairs, lighting the candles, putting the flyers on the chairs, and setting up the tea table. Working in the ashram felt like floating in a magical bubble. I could feel the masters blessing and healing me as I worked.

I began to start each day with an hour long silent meditation in front of an altar with candles and incense. This calmed me to the depths of my soul. When I told Raja I was enjoying my meditations, he looked at me with love and told me I was going into deep Samadhi, which is a merging with God.

Raja did extraordinary shamanic healings in which he beat a drum. This called forth non-physical beings, or spirits. During group healings, as I lay on the ashram floor, I could feel loving spirits hovering around, pouring blessings onto me. At other times, he did a spoken word meditation which put me into a sublimely peaceful altered state.

When the Dalai Lama came to town, I overflowed with joyful

anticipation. I rode to the event, on a bus, with Peggy, a kind woman in my ashram group. She was blond, beautiful and charming. Such warmth radiated from her that I glowed in a pearly bubble of love. Speaking about growing up in the Mid-West, she said she could not wait to graduate from high school so she could move far away.

With excitement, she told me she was taking a Master Blueprint class. All seekers were given a list of classes to take. Flying to a foreign city, she was learning how to coach people. I told her that I wanted to become a good writer. Hope filled me as she encouraged me.

A large crowd waited in a field, outside of the building where the Dalai Lama was to appear. After a while, we began to walk into the building. Monks from the Himalayas played musical instruments and chanted, looking elegant in their orange robes. An ethereal, meditative vibration charged the air with electricity. After moving like snails in the crowd, we finally sat down.

The Dali Lama sat on stage, looking through the crowd with a sweet, humble smile. A large screen, where scientists showed their researched facts about meditation, glowed behind him. He was dressed in a crimson wrap around garment. As he answered questions from the scientists, he radiated love throughout the room. Humility, relaxation, humor and compassion came from him like sweet perfume, raising the vibrations.

It seemed like I was walking on air, as I walked with Peggy to the bus. We had a wonderful time talking and laughing. She gave me a love filled hug as I told her good bye.

Soon Sunday arrived and I looked forward to being with my parents. Raja had said that one could tell how far they had evolved spiritually if they spent time with their biological family. If they found that their buttons were not getting pushed, the way they used to be, they could be sure that they had evolved.

Driving to the Country Club, a lush panorama of trees surrounded me. The various shades of green soothed me.

Soon, I arrived. A uniformed man, in a stone tower, opened his window. When I mentioned my parents' name, he raised the long plank to let me in. Driving slowly, I enjoyed the trees. Parking my car, I looked up toward the pool, remembering diving off of the diving board when I was a teenager. The beautiful, white columned main house looked magnificent and stately.

Kundalini Rising

Walking up the stairs and into the restaurant, a fragrance of perfume and warm roast beef and potatoes wafted into my nose, and I observed the well-dressed people.

Looking overjoyed to see me, my mother welcomed me. My father was quiet but his appreciation of my company shone through. My mother told a funny story about the long, winding ramp that she had to drive up when she took my father to his doctor appointments several times a week. Her Leo vibrancy shone when she talked, and she looked much younger than women her age.

When I was a child, she had looked like a movie star. Whenever we traveled to the United States to visit our grandmother she got her picture in the newspaper. She had been selected as the May Queen, when she was in High School, and had ridden in a parade through town, smiling and waving at people.

She used to criticize my looks and I had built up resentment towards her. Rehashing the other ways she had belittled me, I felt sorry for myself. It was hard to live with no confidence, and I envied people who had it. However, I knew that I had to release the past and forgive and forget.

As my parents said they needed to go home, I clung to them. Hugging them goodbye, I thanked them for lunch and wished them a good day.

I listened to Raja talk at the next Satsang. His vibrations always calmed me.

"I've always gotten along with everyone. Except for one person. There was a person in my office who I used to get into heated arguments with. I would say black and she would say white--I could never do or say anything that she approved of. Then, I just decided to send her love and, now, we're friends. Instead of seeing her as a scary Bengal tiger I started seeing her as a sweet, vulnerable kitten. We started chatting by the water fountain and eventually we went out to lunch together and became good friends. All it took was that decision in me to send her love and to see her inner light. Everyone is God, and there is not one square inch in the universe where God is not. Whenever we meet someone new, it's a good practice to say to ourselves, 'Thank you for coming in this form.' It only takes one person to have a successful relationship."

Joy flowed through me as I relished my time in this peaceful sanctuary.

This was the home I had been searching for. Everyone hugged one another at the end of Satsang and it felt like an episode of The Walton's.

My spiritual family and my biological family breathed joy into me. As I began tuning into my higher self, life began to make sense.

Though my parents had been abusive, I contemplated that my eternal self, or soul, had chosen them to further its evolution. I may not have been given the foundation necessary for worldly success. However, they had blessed me in many ways. Without a doubt, I had learned the lessons of humility and compassion. I had also learned about being a totally lost soul and rebuilding myself after that. When my ego started to rant and rave because other people were more successful, I detached myself from it and listened to my Higher Self.

Counting my many blessings, I sat at the Country Club the next time. When my mother asked me if I'd bring her some soup, I went to the salad bar with delight. As I handed it to her, she looked at me with such wide eyed gratitude, like a vulnerable child, that all my resentment melted. No longer did I view her as a ferocious, humiliating lion about to attack. Instead, I saw her as a vulnerable kitty cat, longing for love.

They had gotten so old. My father could barely hold himself up with his cane and had to move very slowly. Sometimes, he used a walker which he pushed with great effort and trepidation. He looked depressed and he rarely talked.

Thoughts about the psychic in the New Age newspaper obsessed me as I sat alone in my condo. Suddenly, a compulsive urge to move again overcame me. She had seemed so wise and knowing, far more connected with the divine spirit than I was.

I was getting disenchanted with the meditation group. They did wonderful programs but they were expensive to attend, and I simply did not have the money after I spent my government check on essentials.

I went to the bank to see if I had a hundred dollars for a session with the psychic. Then, I called her secretary and set up an appointment with her.

Driving through traffic to my appointment, I got overwhelmed. Immense relief came over me when I finally found her office in a confusing office park maze. Leaning back on the sofa, I remembered feeling a tightening in my gut when I had my first appointment with her.

Soon, she opened her office door and welcomed me in. Her lustrous, long, blonde hair shone with health and her gold earrings glittered, complimenting her red lipstick. A well-made blue pantsuit flattered her tall, slender body. Sitting down at her desk, she looked seriously into my eyes.

"It's a mistake to stay in Madison. You belong out West. When you go back, the lady that you rented from will give you a room, and you will have a nice boyfriend. Your parents will not be here forever. It is time for you to be in a good place for you and to start living. You will transform like a butterfly. You are not happy here right? Your parents will sell the condo. Don't be around them too much because they will drive you crazy. They talk about you like, 'Oh, that girl. What is she up to now?' They don't want you asking for money. It is just this. Your father has plenty of money, and it is no big deal for him to help you. He didn't have to be so harsh with you. And your mother says she'll help you and then, the next day, she changes her mind. It's crazy-making behavior."

"Is it okay for me to have lunch with them?"

"Yeah. Have lunch with them but don't mention anything about going West because they will go crazy."

I was the one who was truly crazy because I began sending money to Bindu, the Hare Krishna, to save one of her rooms for me.

Feeling like I was in the middle of a hurricane, I looked forward to the peace I experienced in Satsang. Happy anticipation filled me as I drove there the following Wednesday evening, looking forward to loving hugs from all the angelic seekers.

Raja announced that a student in the Lineage was going to travel from New York to teach Yogin Christ Reiki.

"This is the energy healing which Jesus Himself performed, after studying it with the Essenes. Jesus is one of the Ascended Masters who is guiding us to create a new world. He gifted us with the real deal."

A kind, brunette, woman from the Philippines arrived. Wonder and peace filled me as she taught me and attuned me to the energy. She had an effervescent laugh, which made me feel lighthearted and free. Fantasies of giving sight to the blind and curing lepers flashed through my mind.

As I gave and received Reiki with the five other people, a magnificent contentment came over me.

On Sunday afternoons, I began going to the ashram to trade sessions with others who had been attuned to do Reiki. My fear subsided as I received Reiki and I experienced deep, profound peace.

I did a show of about twenty lousy paintings that I'd created from old photographs my sister had given me. My father could not climb the long, treacherous stairs of the stone church to see my show and I missed his presence.

Raja, a few people from the ashram, my mother, my sister, and my parents' came. My sister brought me a plate of fruit for guests. My mother walked up to me, looking like she was worried about me. With a tense coolness, I introduced her to one of my peers from the ashram. I longed to give her a love filled bear hug like Raja always gave to me. Feeling like an angry, bitter old woman, I did not see how I could ever become spiritual.

Later, she called me and said she would like to buy a few of my paintings. Elated to have her approval, which I had craved all my life, I displayed my best paintings, leaning them against the wall.

She came to my condo to pick them up. When she said she couldn't stay long, I asked her if she couldn't stay and have something to eat. She said she couldn't.

Feeling not good enough, I felt that I didn't deserve her love. If only I was a warm, engaging daughter, I could have had a close, loving relationship with her. If I had practiced my art through the years, I could have shared it with her and given her the joy of seeing me succeed with it.

Like a mindless zombie, I fell hopelessly back under the psychic's spell. She had power I did not have, so she must be right about where I ought to live. I ran an ad in the paper to sell my car.

When nobody responded, I took it to a dealership to see what I could get. Just when I was about to sign the forms to hand my car over to them, I heard the lyrics to a song playing on the radio.

"It never rains in California but oh, let me warn you. It pours. Man it pours."

That was my sign from God. I knew it. I walked to the desk and told the worker I had changed my mind and was not going to sell my car.

The peaceful atmosphere at the next Satsang brought my sanity back. Raja did a Yoga Nidra session for everyone. Like a big, happy family, everyone relaxed on their backs on the carpeted floor.

Afterwards, he told everyone that his mentor was coming to teach a two-day workshop.

"She is a remarkable person. Often I repeat her sayings to myself. One of them is, 'If you have to be right, you're dead right.' Another one is 'Drop it'. The past is dead and gone, and the future is but a thought hurled into space. She stresses the importance of being in the moment. Time is an illusion of this physical world. In truth, there is only the eternal NOW, NOW, NOW, NOW. We must drop each moment, and the next and the next, and always be in the present. That is where our power is. Another saying she has is, 'Love is the great transformer.' She radiates immense love. When you experience one of her hugs, you'll know what I mean. They are extraordinary."

I worried that it would be expensive. Then, I impulsively decided to ignore the sign that God had sent me at the car dealership. In a mistrustful voice, I told my mentor good bye as I left the ashram. Then, I told him that I wouldn't be able to attend because I was moving out West.

Suddenly, he burst into tears. I watched his pain-filled face, in awe that someone could feel such love for me. I explained that a famous psychic had told me Madison was not the place for me. With a tender voice, he asked me why I had taken the psychic's advice so seriously.

"I want you to write down the day, time and place of your birth. Call this place and get them to do your Astro Cartography chart. Then, get them to mail it to my spiritual mentor, Purnima. Here is her address. She will give blessings and energy to it, and then mail it to me. Then, I'll sit down and discuss it with you."

I was flabbergasted. No one had ever cried over me moving, which was what I had wanted all along. Now, this city was starting to feel like home.

The time passed and the two-day workshop arrived. We did chanting of sacred names, Karttikeyan Yogic sessions, which cleared the chakras, silent meditations, and Shamanic healing sessions with drumming. As I listened to them talk about spiritual evolution, I was impressed by how loving, respectful, gentle and patient Raja and his spiritual mentor, Purnima, were.

One of the training days fell on the celebration my sister had planned for my mother's eightieth birthday. She had invited my Mom's grammar school friends and everyone who knew her. I thought about going to the birthday and leaving after twenty minutes but exhaustion had overcome me, and I did not feel I had the energy. I should have called my mother, explained why I wasn't there and told her I loved her.

For months afterwards she looked at me with hurt eyes. "You didn't go to my birthday."

Then, I remembered that the most important teaching in the ashram was "Do not hurt the human heart for that is where God dwells." I was just a spiritual mud puddle.

A couple of weeks later, I went to the ashram for my appointment with Raja.

"Are you a masochist?" he asked. A memory of my mother telling me I was a masochist when I was in high school came to me.

"Yeah, I guess I've always done things the hard way."

"The West Coast is hell for you. Read this," he said, pointing to the description of the place I was planning to move to.

"The most undesirable place to live. Violence, poverty, loneliness, hardship. Basic training goes on forever."

I was awestruck. The document explained that my Mars and Saturn conjuncted directly over the West Coast. That explained the struggle with homelessness, mental illness and poverty I had experienced. I was fascinated. I'd never believed in astrology but nothing had ever described so precisely those experiences which I'd shoved deep down and far away, to be hidden from everyone except an occasional therapist.

There was some truth to astrology after all. My curiosity bubbled over. My Astro Cartography chart said that my Venus and my Sun conjuncted above Madison, which made it one of the four best places in the world for me. My Venus gave me life-long friendships and the ability to become a famous artist, and my Sun gave me great energy, drive, good health, and the ability to be my own boss. Venus and the Sun hovered above me, bringing me love, mercy, honors, and happy, Disneyland endings.

I laughed and laughed at myself for taking the psychic so seriously. Like Chicken Little, I had been racing back and forth, clucking and worrying as though the sky would fall any minute. Totally deluded, I had given my power away to a stranger who barely knew me. Feeling released from my self made prison, as free and light as a feather floating on air, I watched my conflict dissolve, and savored the peace as my mind rested for the first time in almost five years.

Raja said I had missed a session in the last Karttikeyan healing training.

He told me to make myself comfortable on my yoga mat. Then, he held out a pack of cards and asked me to pick one.

"You are in the right place," it said. I stared at it in overjoyed wonder.

"That's what you've been going through," Raja said, with love sparkling in his eyes.

"This is one of the four best places in the world for you. If you place the card underneath your root chakra, you will absorb the teaching."

I spread out a yoga mat and laid down flat on my back, then placed the card under my tail bone. Raja's love filled, gentle voice took me to a place of profound peace, for the next forty five minutes, as he did a Karttikeyan healing session.

CHAPTER ELEVEN

"Whosoever will not receive or listen to your words--go outside that house or town and shake the dust from your feet." Matthew 10:14

"Jesus came to his native place and taught the people in their synagogue. They were astonished and said, 'Where did this man get such wisdom and mighty deeds? Is he not the carpenter's son? Is not his mother Mary and his brothers James, Joseph, Simon and Judas? Are not his sisters all with us? Where did this man get all this? And they took offense at him. But Jesus said to them, 'A prophet is not without honor except in his native place and in his own house.' And he did not work many mighty deeds there because of their lack of faith. Matthew 13:54-58

You cannot please everyone. Move on. Spend your best efforts on those who believe in you.

When through the practice of yoga the mind ceases its restless movements and becomes still, one realizes the highest Reality... Then he knows the infinite happiness that can be realized by the purified heart. He stands firm in this resolution...Yoga is the breaking of contact with pain.

Bhagavad-Gita

Sunday arrived quickly. Sitting at my parents' reserved table at the country club, I was safe, protected, and loved. Looking around at the well-dressed, prosperous people, I contemplated on how fortunate I was to live in the richest country in the world.

"Sophia was so funny. She loved the Gila monster and wanted to touch him. She cried, 'I want to touch the Gila monster!' No one else wanted to touch that creepy looking creature."

"Another time she started stretching her mouth. She would stretch it really wide and we would say, 'You're going to stretch it permanently if you keep doing that.' So then she would pat around her mouth, like she was pushing it back into place." My beautiful mother looked at me with great affection and love.

"The circus was in town and you were imitating the clowns with their down turned lips. I said, 'That's what you're going to look like if you keep doing that,' and you never did it again," my father said, coming out of his silence.

The waiter came over and asked if we needed anything. He was from Mexico. His dark eyes twinkled when he smiled. Cheerfully, he carried platters loaded down with ten full plates, as though they were as light as a feather. Wondering what kind of poverty he had struggled through in Mexico, I felt touched by his humble, kind service. His face moved expressively as he told a funny story, hamming it up like an actor. Soon, we were all laughing.

I enjoyed the view of the rolling, green hills of the golf course. Golf carts moved along and players swung their sticks, hoping to score a hole in one. Biting into a juicy artichoke, I listened to my mother talk, in her charming, southern belle style. She had aged drastically and was thinner than ever. Now and then, she coughed.

Lunch ended and I walked with my parents to their car. Hugging them, I told them I loved them. My mother asked me to ride with them to my car. I replied that I would walk to it because I needed the exercise.

One day, I got a call from my cousin. My mother's brother had died suddenly. Confusion overcame me as I tried to get someone on the phone and get the address of the church. No one answered and, after a while, I gave up.

My mother talked about it, with deep sadness, at lunch the next Sunday. "We were very close. He used to ride by my house with his group of cyclers, and I would hear him tell my name as he flew by. He stayed so healthy riding his bike every day. He was the last person I thought was going to die."

I looked at her grief-stricken face as I ate my salad. Not knowing how to help, I asked her if I could bring her anything. She said she'd like some chicken salad. I walked to the salad bar and put some on a plate for her. Her face lit up with great gratitude as I handed it to her.

It proved to me one of the principles Raja had taught me----"When you change the way you look at things, the things you look at change."

Instead of looking at her as though she was a fierce lion, I realized that she was a fragile kitty cat longing for love. Wanting to spend more time with her, I wished she would invite me into her house. However, she preferred to see me at the Country Club.

Every wonderful Wednesday night I felt blissful, as I sat in the magical ashram listening to Raja talk about spiritual truths. Some evenings, he did shamanic healings and other evenings he did meditations that put the seekers into an altered state. He talked about the masters who were sending blessings to us. I could feel their presence--- loving energy swirling lightly around me.

Raja said, "The power of gratitude is immense. Mahavatar Babaji teaches that gratitude is the key to having more of what we want in life. Too often, people see contrast in their lives between the way things are and the way they could be. They concentrate on what they lack and that brings more lack into their lives. My spiritual mentor often says, 'What is is and what isn't isn't.'"

"As Westerners, we are encouraged to do and to achieve but, too often, we do and do in order to experience a state of being. We can love ourselves and others better if, instead, we put more focus on being. Being in deep peace in meditation heals and balances us. Then, we can go into the world and do with more power, presence and love."

As I reviewed all the spiritual paths I had tried, I realized that I had finally found the one that would elevate me. Journeying in my mind to the past, I remembered trying Buddhism. Driving long distances, I used to attend meetings and chant, with other members of a Buddhist World Wide organization, in front of a scroll filled with Calligraphy. They would encourage me to chant for what I wanted, urging me to make myself happy. Sometimes people would give testimonials about how they had gotten what they chanted for---new houses, better paying jobs, and cars.

In my search for understanding, I had gone to Christian "Born again" meetings in high school. Later, in college, I had attended some Bahia and Sufi meetings. The people always seemed much more peaceful and satisfied with life than I was. In desperation, I had even taken some Scientology classes. Nothing had worked for me however. Even the meditation group I had traveled to India with felt lacking to me. I was not peaceful and happy like its other members were.

With hopeful curiosity, I anticipated the next Satsang evening. The evening finally arrived and I told my cat good bye. Driving through the city, I marveled over the incredible things I was learning. Watching people and listening to the honks and screeches of cars, I imagined living in the new, heavenly world that the spiritual masters were working on creating.

Parking my car a few blocks away from the ashram, I then walked along the sidewalk, feeling as light as a feather. Climbing the stairway of the small, brick building near a stone church, I felt a new aliveness circulate through me.

My spiritual brothers and sisters greeted me with smiles and hugs and I sat down in a blue back jack, feeling totally at home. Raja blew me a kiss. I could see the church through the windows. The sun made patterns on the freshly painted walls with a mural of OM on one side. The beige carpet was freshly vacuumed. Crystals and framed pictures of ascended spiritual masters glowed on a beautiful, dark wooden chest.

Raja began to speak. Wonder filled me as he told us how Mahavatar Babaji had disguised himself as a beggar to test him once. He had been sitting in the ashram alone one day when, suddenly, he had heard a knock on the door. When he opened it, a scraggly dressed man asked him for some money. Even though there was a rule that they were not supposed to give money, he had given the beggar money, out of compassion.

Then, the beggar had disappeared suddenly. Gazing down the staircase, he knew that there had not been enough time for him to walk out of the building. He knew that Mahavatar Babaji had materialized and then dematerialized.

Another time, Mahavatar Babaji had taken him to his cave in the

Himalayas. Awe and wonder filled me as I listened. Mahavatar Babaji is one of the ascended masters who is working day and night to awaken humans out of their slumber of ignorance and evolve them spiritually so that they love one another. He overshadowed and blessed Jesus when he was dying on the cross, Raja explained.

I wanted to be in his sacred sanctuary and listen to his wondrous stories every day. It was down the street from the theater which had brought me many happy evenings in my youth, including my first Cat Stevens rock concert. It was around the corner from Appletree Street. There were so many things I loved about this city—the sweetness of people, the southern sun, the easygoing pace, and the diversity of cultural programs.

He explained that Siddhis, or powers like dematerializing and being in two places at the same time, had surfaced in Mahavatar Babaji because of his intense Sadhana or meditation. Sometimes, these powers end up being the booby prize though. They are not the essential purpose of evolving spiritually.

Asking seven students to line up in a row, he laughed playfully. Then, he began to explain the seven bodies.

"The first body is our physical body", he laughed as his student made a cute courtesy, putting one leg over the other and bending his knees.

"The next body is the Etheric body, which is an energy egg surrounding the physical body", he explained, touching the shoulders of the tall, blond man standing in line smiling.

"The next body is the astral body. This is made of the mental and emotional bodies. We call them The Terrible Twins, because of the commotion they cause. That is why we learn how to be in control of our thoughts, instead of letting them control us. When we think a thought, that causes an emotion, then that emotion causes another thought and it continues in a vicious cycle until we learn to master it. Thoughts and emotions hang out in the aura and they can be seen, by some people, as colors and shapes. When negative thoughts and emotions stay in the energy surrounding the body, after a while they move into the physical and create illnesses. That is why people do energy healing and clean the aura."

"The next body is the Causal body. This is the body which carries our karma from lifetime to lifetime. It is also called the Bliss Body." Laughing playfully, he pointed to a smiling African American veterinarian.

"The next body is the Temporary Personality. It is the being who we are in this life, who is totally unique." The sweet, blonde woman bowed.

"The next body is the Higher Self, which is also the Christ consciousness, the Buddha consciousness, the Krishna consciousness. This is the observer or witness side of us which is able to transcend the ego and look at life from the broad perspective of what the soul is learning. Instead of reacting from ego and fighting with others, the Higher Self releases the reactions and calmly observes, knowing that one is evolving ones soul by learning the lesson the challenge is teaching. With practice, we learn to respond rather than react. This is earth school and it is not always easy. However, if we listen to our Higher Self, instead of our ego, it makes our lives more peaceful."

"The next body is the part of us which is connected with God", he said, laughing gleefully as a smiling student posed like Charles Atlas, pretending to be God.

He explained for a while longer and, then, finished up his talk by saying, "Remember to listen to the voice of your Higher Self and not your ego."

Then, he talked us through a deeply relaxing Yoga Nidra session. Relaxing muscle after muscle, I became loose and limp as my mind became like a still, clear lake. His soothing voice massaged my entire being until I melted. Floating in great bliss afterwards, I hugged my sweet fellow seekers good night.

The next day, I heard honking outside my condo. It was my mother. I walked down the stairs and held my breath as I studied her anguished face.

"Daddy fell. He's at the hospital. He was in the emergency room for five days. He had a horrible time there. Let's stick together."

A lightning bolt struck me. I had been dreading this day for years and now it was here.

"He told me to write a check for your condo fee," she said, writing with a trembling hand, then handing it to me.

As she drove down the road to the hospital, red and yellow leaves brought back memories of a lovely hike in the mountains I had had with my parents over twenty years ago. I wished I had gone to the mountains with them more.

"I tried to lift him off the ground and couldn't. He scraped his back dragging himself to the porch. He suffered a long time until someone came and took him to the emergency room. They kept jabbing him with needles and pricking his finger to draw blood."

The hospital was just down the street and, soon, my mother pulled into the parking lot and parked the car, nervously. We walked into the hospital and down a corridor. Arriving on his unit, I followed Mom to his room.

The IV machine dripped fluid from its hanging bag and the needles sticking into my father's arm made my own skin ache. He had such a distant look in his eyes that I knew the energetic, hero Dad I had once known was gone forever. I touched his arm and told him I was sorry he'd been through such a hard time.

"Hi, Daddy. Are you all right?" My mother looked vulnerable and hurt.

"Yeah, Mama. I'm all right." I touched his arm, disappointed to see his frailty when I had always depended on his strength. Sitting down, I felt guilty about my lack of gratitude.

"How are you, sweetie?" I loved it when he called me that endearing name.

"I'm okay. I'm sorry you've been through so much. I would have come sooner if I had known."

"Well, thanks for coming. It's nice to see you."

My mother looked overwhelmed as she talked about all they had been through and how their doctor had abandoned them.

After a while, my mother said she had to go home. She said goodbye to Dad, touching his hand since she couldn't hug him. Then she blew me a kiss and left quickly.

"I remember when I found you out there," he said, referring to the time when he had rescued me from the homeless shelter.

"You saved my life," I said, brimming over with gratitude for the opportunity to express my appreciation. I had so rarely done it.

He played with the drinking straw on his lunch tray, seeming exhausted by the ordeal he had endured.

"How long were you on the ground after you fell?"

"Seven hours."

An ambulance should have picked him up within fifteen minutes. Touching his arm, I beamed energy to him, like I had learned at the ashram.

After a while, I told him goodbye and drove up the road to my apartment. Staring at the wall, I could not sleep as I imagined the pain he had gone through.

The next day, I went to the hospital. After a while, my mother arrived and sat next to his bed, looking lost as he said delusional things.

"Move those boxes over there." His eyes had a vacant look, as though he was lost in another world.

My mother and I looked at each other with bemused dismay, then went through the motions of moving the imaginary boxes for him.

"Who is that?" he said, pointing behind me. I glanced over my shoulder. There was nothing and no one there.

"What do you mean?"

"That lady behind you. She looks like someone I've seen before."

He had lost his mind. Searching for him, I wished his eyes weren't so far away.

At other times, his old, smug doctor behavior surfaced.

"You don't know how to treat diabetes," he told the nurse when she told him he needed to take some insulin. His arrogance was childlike and funny. He deserved to gloat. After all, he had worked hard to earn his credentials as an internationally recognized expert in his field.

She would insist that he needed some insulin and he would argue that he didn't, sometimes raising his voice in intense anger.

"I don't want that yappy little Indian doctor telling me what to do. You have been giving me too much insulin. I'm sick and tired of it, and I'm not going to take it anymore!"

"Okay, Dr. Moon. I know that you are the expert. You don't have to take it this time."

My mother told me that he had tried to wheel himself out of the hospital. An orderly had had to grab him and wheel him back in, as he flailed his arms and yelled. Another time, he had gotten so angry that he had thrown the IV machine against the wall.

His favorite nurse smiled at him with affection and let him refuse his insulin sometimes. I gave him Reiki energy for about an hour, hoping it was easing his suffering.

When a different nurse came in and told him he needed an enema, he looked at her suspiciously.

"No. I'm not going to let you. You're trying to kill me!" he yelled, with a river of rage rushing in his voice.

"Come on, Dad. You'll feel much better after you have an enema."

"No! They're trying to kill me!"

"She wants to help you, Dad. It will be easier than you think. Come on and let her help you, Dad. It will be over before you know it."

"No! I'm not letting her do it!"

I sat and looked at him for a while, considering what to do.

"I'm going to go home and give myself an enema. I know it's going to make me feel much better," I said, telling a white lie, hoping it would make him want an enema.

I told him good bye, walked through the maze like corridors and found my car in the parking lot. As I drove home, I prayed for him to get better.

Walking up the stairs to my door, I missed Raja. I unlocked the door and headed straight to my phone to call him. He listened with sympathy as I told him I was afraid I was losing my father.

"He's spending a lot of time on the astral realm, and he's seeing people he knows. He's disconnecting from his body and realizing that there is something beyond the physical plane. He's not crazy. He's feeling controlled, so he's rebelling. I'm sending him healing energy and he is receiving it."

Raja's voice calmed me and I melted in gratitude for his extraordinary love. Out of millions of people who were going through the same challenge, I was the only one who could receive support from someone who could see beyond the physical.

The next morning, my father looked more cheerful. I felt grateful that Raja's healings were bringing him some peace. Indian summer sun poured gloriously through his tiny hospital window. He looked bored as he folded a little napkin over and over, lost in thought. I touched his arm and sent Reiki energy to him.

After a while, he became charming and chatty. He talked about seeing Obama walking down the hospital halls. The I.V. needles sticking into his arm were surrounded with red and blue tissue, and I winced in pain as I imagined the struggle he had endured.

A nurse placed a lunch tray in front of him and he looked at it with disinterest. When I encouraged him to eat, he lifted a forkful of black-eyed peas to his mouth, his hand trembling. He chewed it slowly, looking childlike and vulnerable. Opening a can of coke for him, I wondered how he could stand sitting all day. Handing it to him, I patted the crown of his head.

"Oh the joys of Coke! The joys of Coke. It's nutritious, it's delicious!" he sang cheerfully. The poet in him came out when he felt loved and relaxed. He had worked hard all his life, so it was good to hear him play—something he had only been able to do after a few glasses of wine in the past.

I asked the nurse for a handkerchief so I could blow my nose.

"Something has been making me sneeze." I sneezed, and then blew my nose.

"Yeah. You were snorting and cavorting," he said, with a childlike lightness. I laughed at his humorous poetry. Then, there was a long silence as I hung on to memories of his strong days.

"Lord, I don't know how we make it through," my father said seriously, after a long pause.

"I know what you mean. This old world is unpredictable."

"I remember Husky when he got lost. We looked all around the neighborhood for him. He decided he didn't like it here and went back up to Toronto." My father's face was reflective and sweet.

"Yeah. He was a wonderful dog." I remembered cuddling up close to him as he lay against the front door, on freezing, snow-covered days in Canada, when I was in grammar school.

"We had three Samoyeds. One in Columbus and one in Toronto and one when we came down here."

"They were all great. They used to be so gentle, and they loved children."

He was absolutely charming and so much fun to be with, that I didn't want to share him when his younger brother came to visit him. All he could do was sit there and look at my father. His wife did most of the talking.

"Well, can I bring you a Big Mac?" his younger brother asked him, looking at him with love.

My father didn't answer, so he broke the tension by telling a funny story about how he used to shine my father's shoes for him, before he went out on a date. He had been a great uncle to me, pulling me in his boat, teaching me how to water ski. His funny stories and imitations of Donald Duck had brought me fun days of laughter.

My mother walked in later on, looking overwhelmed and worried. She sat down in a chair and I longed to hug her but worried that it would be awkward. So, I tried my best to contribute by listening. She told me she had talked with Dad's nurse.

"Daddy, you need to eat something. You didn't eat any breakfast or lunch."

"No. I don't want to."

"Daddy, eat!" She raised her voice in anger.

He shrunk back, looking shaken. I watched him attempt to lift a forkful, struggling to muster the energy. Finally, he swallowed a small amount.

I listened to my parents talk for about an hour.

"Daddy, I'm tired. I'm going to go home now." My mother looked exhausted.

I wanted to offer to walk her to her car, but she blew me a kiss and left so quickly I didn't get the chance. I touched my father's hand and told him I hoped he would feel better soon. I suspected that he wouldn't and that his days were numbered.

We watched the presidential election news on the T.V. until late, and then I drove to my home five minutes away.

The next morning, he looked brittle and sad. He told me he couldn't wait to get out of that place. Touching his arm, I gave him energy. He didn't ask what I was doing and I felt relieved that I didn't have to explain it to him. Most people would think I was crazy if I told them about the energy I was radiating from the cosmos.

When his sister came to visit him, later, he lit up and became more talkative. She greeted me in her wonderful, warm way.

"Obama Bin Laden," Dad said in a comical way, as election news hummed in the background. My aunt and I looked at each other and laughed.

"Barack Obama," his younger sister corrected him, glowing with happiness that Obama was winning the race.

"You've always been so smart. You know how to pronounce all the words because you've read so much." Dad looked with love at his little sister.

He was the first born; the responsible leader who had worked, carrying pails of milk and delivering newspapers when he was a child. His efforts had put food on the table, through the depression, for his sister, brothers and parents.

After my aunt left, Dad's medical partner, who had worked with him at the hospital, came to see him. I listened to them talk and felt grateful to him when my father began speaking with more liveliness. With a sensitive, caring expression, he gave a shot of vitamin C to my father.

At times, my father rambled like a madman about how he had seen Bill Clinton and Bush walking down the halls of the hospital. Another time, he asked me to look at my list of phone numbers and call people. I called his sister's son.

My father looked hopeful as I handed the phone to him.

"Hi, John. I was wondering if you would come and get me out of here."

I heard the silence on the other end of the phone and observed my disappointed father, as he hung up, after getting a refusal. He looked like a child who wanted to go outside and play. His innocent face exuded loneliness and I wished I could take him out and run through the woods with him, holding hands and laughing. He had worked hard all his life, traveling, lecturing, writing books and seeing diabetic patients. He hadn't had time to have fun.

My mother came to visit. She felt anxious.

"This is awful. They don't know what they're doing. This is what socialized medicine has done to the country. It is awful the way they treat people, just like they're disposable. They don't ever have any time to talk to patients. They just drug them up and leave them all alone. They kept pricking poor Daddy's finger again and again in the emergency room to draw blood. Finally, he got so angry that he raised his hand and gave the nurse a karate chop. He shouldn't have been in the emergency room for so long. If our regular doctor had come to help, Daddy wouldn't have had to go through that, but he didn't even bother to return our phone call. He's just abandoned us."

Dad looked frail as he sat in his hospital bed listening to us talk. Being with my mother brought memories of happy times, when we were all younger, into my mind. Love for me shone in my mother's eyes.

I thought about advice I had learned in a book about spirituality. It advised--"Never take anything personally". I wished I had been wise and never taken any of my mothers' temper explosions personally. Tender feelings filled me as I soaked in her love, remembering when I was a baby and had had her undivided devotion.

When she said she had to go, I felt emptiness overcome me. Asking if I could help at the house, I hoped to extend my time with her. However, she said she didn't need me and left.

I got to the hospital early the next morning. I sprayed my father with some charged healing water that I had gotten at a health fair. His feet were red and his toes were chapped and frayed from complications with his diabetes. I imagined them soft and soothed and pain-free as I misted my magic water on him.

"That feels good," he said looking at me with gratitude.

The nurse came to give him his insulin.

"It's time to give you some insulin. You need fifteen units. It's been a while, and your glucose level is way up high."

"No! I do not need any insulin. You've been giving me too much. You gave me fifteen units the last time and it was too much." His voice boomed with fury.

"Well, Dr. Moon, I know you're an expert, so I'll let you decide. I won't give you any now. I'll leave you alone and not bug you for a while. Does that sound good?"

"Yes. You're a good nurse. I like you better than that other one who comes in the morning."

"Well, I want you to feel comfortable and relaxed. Is there something I can bring to you or do for you to make you feel better? I'm on your side."

He looked so frail and weak. I remembered sitting with him and watching birds from the kitchen table through his binoculars. He told me that medicine had been ruined long ago, and that many of the doctors he had trained were only in it for the money.

I knew what he meant as I observed the suffering patients who were being overloaded with drugs and deprived of human warmth. Their doctors talked with them for five minutes, just enough time to write out a prescription.

"Old age is not for sissies," Dad said, looking sweetly into my eyes.

My mother came into the room. She glanced at me and then turned her attention to my father. They'd traveled the world together, and he had never invited just me to travel with him. Jealousy boiled inside me as I imagined the exotic places I had missed visiting.

"Oh, poor Daddy. Can I bring you something from home? Are they treating you all right? I'm so sorry you've been through so much. You're handling it with your usual bravery and cheerful spirit. Bob misses you," she said. Bob was the family cat.

She looked so sad, I wanted to cry. I must have broken her heart many times with my aloof behavior. She looked so much younger than her friends that I hadn't realized she was old. I'd been too selfish to walk in her moccasins. She suffered pains, tiredness, frustration, and the humiliation of being old and unimportant. I'd never put my arms around her and told her I loved her or helped her with her emotional distress in dealing with my volatile, aloof family members. She must have believed I didn't love her. My heart pounded with regret.

My father sat propped up against his pillow. He rarely said anything because he had no energy.

"Tell Bob, the cat, I said hello. I want to come home and see him," he said, finally.

"Oh, we'll get you home Daddy. You're going to get well," my mother replied.

"I saw President Clinton and President Bush walking through the hall earlier. I wonder who is going to get elected."

I kept silent to hide my ignorance about politics. My father looked like a vulnerable child as he looked at my mother in gratitude.

"It's good to see you, Mama."

"It's good to see you, Daddy. I'm glad we got you out of that emergency room. I can't understand how Dr. Brown could neglect you like he did. I'm sorry you went through that horrible experience."

A nurse brought a tray of dinner in for him and left after a few words with him. My father looked at it with disinterest. Then, he stared into the corner of the room like a madman.

"Who is that person over there? He stared at a person who no one else could see.

"Oh, poor Daddy. You're imagining things." My mother looked very sad.

.After a while, my mother got tired of sitting on the hard chair.

"My back is hurting, Daddy. I'm going to go home. I'll see you tomorrow." My Mom blew me a kiss, and left. I felt the urge to run after her and put my arm around her shoulder but I held back.

My father rested in his hospital bed sadly, longing for my mother, breathing shallowly, and staring listlessly at the tray of food in front of him. I touched his arm and sent healing energy to him.

"Someday, when you're older, you'll understand," both of my parents had told me.

I was just starting to understand. It was difficult coping with aging minds and bodies. Embarrassment warmed my cheeks as I realized my selfishness---only looking at them as people to fulfill my needs or to blame when I did not succeed.

My mother had harshly told me, "I'm an old lady!" once, many years ago. I had felt attacked, but now I understood that it had been a call for love.

At the ashram, we were discussing how to see every behavior, no matter how unpleasant, as a call for love. Love was the great transformer, my spiritual studies were teaching me. I had waited too long to start expressing love to them. Tears filled my eyes.

"If you walk out of here, you're walking out on your best friend," my father had said, once, when I had left in anger twenty-five years ago. He was right. As I languished in memories of the past, an overpowering sleepiness came over me, and I told him I needed to go home.

The next morning, a young, handsome man I had met at a health fair called. His words flew rapidly, in high frequencies of urgency, as he pushed me to sell his health product. My irritation grew by the second until I wanted to scream at him. Being with my father was more important than selling anything. Finally, I told him I felt pressured and ended the call.

My poor father looked lost and lonely as I arrived in his hospital room. Cupping my hands over his arm, I sent him Reiki energy, wincing at the ghastly bruises and swollen places where the IV needle sent fluid into his weakened body.

A nurse brought breakfast and put it down in front of him. I encouraged him to eat something, but he said he didn't want anything.

My aunt dropped by later on. My father felt energetic enough to get out of bed and sit in a chair to talk with her. He talked about "Obama Bin Laden" and Bill Clinton walking through the halls of the hospital. They had waved at him, he said. We laughed.

"Barack Obama," my aunt corrected my father, looking at him with amusement. He had been a tough brother to deal with but sisterly love shone through her eyes when she spoke to him. Their Southern accents lulled me into a peaceful mood as I listened to them talk for an hour or so.

After her visit was over, she signaled for me to join her. As I walked to her car, she told me that my mother had attacked her saying, "You know I don't want you here."

I said that my mother had these explosions sometimes and it was best to just not take it personally. A spiritual book I had been reading emphasized the importance of this. Raja often told his students to respond, rather than react. Listening to the Higher Self made it much easier to do this.

My aunt had sometimes sympathized with me over the fact that my father had not paid any attention to me. When she told me that he had humiliated her in public, when they were growing up together, I realized that his bad behavior had nothing to do with me.

Back in the hospital room, I talked with my father. He said few words but seemed very grateful that I was there. I was losing him. He had gone on as long as he could, dragging himself on his walker and cane so he could have lunch with me every Sunday. He had made me a homeowner and cherished his time with me. The autumn days were getting colder and the rainy, bleak winter would follow. Hanging onto every word he said, I gave him energy, resting my hand on his arm.

Later in the evening, I went home.

My father was cheerful the next time I arrived at his bedside. I told him I had brought him the telephone numbers he'd requested. I dialed his brother, and they spoke briefly. Then, I tried his other brother, and then his sister but there was no answer. Finally, I got my mother on the phone and his face lit up.

"Mama, when are you coming to see me?" he asked, like a child. I gave him energy and listened.

After a while, she arrived. She sat down in a chair and started complaining about the horrible service the nurses were giving and how they didn't have any manners. I listened with sympathy. When she said she didn't know where Daddy was going to go, after they let him out of the hospital, I told her I hoped she found a solution

They both cheered up when my father's partner came to visit. Like vulnerable children, they looked at him with gratitude as he gave them both a shot of vitamin C.

The weeks passed very quickly, and my mother decided to transfer my father to an Alzheimer's treatment facility owned by a sweet, little, old lady who went to their Sunday school class. He would receive the medical attention he needed there.

Walking through the hall to my father's room in the back, feeling shocked. I did my best to ignore the crazy people who shuffled by and babbled nonsense to themselves, dressed in mismatched clothes and staring vacantly into space. He did not ever want to leave his room, and he had nothing to do but stare at the wall or eat the awful food they served.

Day after day, I sat at his bedside and gave him energy. The physical therapist tried to get him to walk around. However, he seemed afraid of all the crazy people and wanted to stay in his room.

My mother called him to tell him she had pneumonia and, though she wanted to visit, she was too sick to get out of bed. He said he missed her and the cat and that he wanted to come home. The desperation in his voice made me want to put him in my car and steal him away, but there was nothing I could do. I wished I had not lost the last four and a half years with him, when I was racing back and forth across the country.

One day, I watched him refuse to put on his clothes and do exercises with the physical therapist. She forced him into his clothes. Following him, encouraging and praising him as he walked through the halls, leaning on his walker, I watched his weak body hunch over as he shuffled along tentatively.

The month of November dragged on in its bleak, rainy haze. Going to Satsang and receiving Raja's extraordinary hugs and healings brought light to the darkness.

When Thanksgiving arrived, my older sister arrived, with her husband and son. She called me an angel, much to my surprise, and thanked me for staying beside my father's bed. She had considered me a troublemaker when we were children. I remembered her crying to other children on the sidewalk that I was "torturing" her, as we walked to grammar school down the freezing, snow-bordered sidewalks in Canada.

Her husband told my father to take his insulin, saying that he'd never get home if he didn't take it. I watched him give my father a shot, admiring his handsome intelligence. My father respected him because he was a doctor too.

He bought a big chart and posted it on the wall. There, the nurse could record what he ate, the time, and the number of units of insulin he had taken.

Most of the time, my father refused to take any but, once in a while, he'd let the nurse give him some. I would write it down with renewed hope, praying that he would get better enough to go home.

David, the music director at my father's church came to visit him every day. He had a wonderful, self-deprecating humor and he played, composed and sang folk songs. His auburn hair and blue eyes gave him a Scotch Irish look. My father's face lit up when he prayed for him out loud.

He was healing the fragile heart of my father--it must have been shattered by his son's refusal to forgive him for his alcoholic, explosive behaviors. Although my father had tried, again and again, to show his love, my brother would not let him in. Wishing I could tell my brother that my father had been taken over by a demon, when he knocked him to the floor, sat on his knees and pummeled him, I wondered if he would believe me.

My father's former diabetes clinic partner continued to visit, too. He said that my father would do better at home with an in-home care service, when he observed how the babbling Alzheimer's patients upset him.

I suggested a service I had heard about, but my mother found another one.

After a few weeks of doing nothing all day but lying in bed, my father roused enough energy to walk down the hall and get a haircut. An orderly walked with him, as he shuffled along, leaning on his walker.

I watched the barber shampoo his hair and dry it with a towel.

"That feels good," he said. I empathized, considering how deprived of touch he was.

The barber talked in a cheerful tone as she snipped his hair. I wanted to tell him I loved him, to tell him some jokes, to sing a song, dance a jig, and thank him for all he had done for me. He seemed so far away, and I longed to feel his strong hand holding mine.

His physical therapist helped him walk back to his room after his haircut. He fell back on his bed. I yawned with a drowsy sadness and then asked him if he would like to experience a meditation I learned at my ashram. He said he would, and I opened my manual to begin.

The method was called Karttikeyan Yogic Method and it had been created by Raja's spiritual mentor. Mahavatar Babaji, the ascended Master who was evolving the consciousness of humanity, had channeled it through her.

I read the words slowly, hoping it was beneficial. It seemed to be relaxing him, at least. Pouring my heart into the healing words, I loved him like God loved him.

I was surprised when the session was over. Forty minutes had gone by in a flash.

"Thank you. That was really relaxing, sweetie." A warm river of emotion flowed through me as he looked into my eyes, and I wanted to make the moment last forever.

His nurse brought his lunch in on a tray. It looked unappetizing, and he looked at it with annoyance. The nurse told him he needed to eat, and he said that he would.

After she left the room, he asked me to eat it. It was like mush and it smelled and tasted awful.

"If I get out of here alive, I'll have a real story to tell," he said forlornly.

"You will, Dad. Hang in there." Looking at him, cupping his thin arm, I told him that my mother had said he could leave on December seventh.

Day after day, all he would consume was milk. I worried that he was starving to death. Then, I realized that he was getting ready to leave his body. Eating, going to the bathroom, and getting cleaned up were all just holding him back from shedding his dark cocoon so he could fly like a butterfly into God's arms.

December the seventh arrived in the blink of an eye. Arriving at his room, I began to pack his suitcase. Suddenly, David arrived.

"Ready to go home, dear one?" My father's face lit up with happiness, as he touched him on the shoulder, then helped him stand up. Pulling on his shirt and pants by himself, he beamed with fresh, new pride. Steadying himself slowly on his walker, he began putting one foot in front of the other. His body trembled and I could tell he was straining to hold himself up. A burning desire and love drove my father forward, past the babbling, spaced out Alzheimer's patients. He stared straight ahead, his face shining with hope, moving, with determination, through the noise and confusion.

Then, the front door whooshed open, and he got his first breath of fresh air in months. We shoved his luggage into the back of the car. He fumbled his way into the front seat on his weak legs.

The city noises blared through my ears as they began to move down the road. I followed them. Soon, I parked my car in the driveway behind them.

My father stepped carefully out of the car and got a precarious grip on his walker. Shuffling and wobbling, he moved down the path to the front door.

David held him as he stepped up and crossed the threshold, then moved slowly through the hall, and down the step into the living room. Then, he assisted him as he put on something comfortable and reclined back in his hospital bed.

"I'm so glad to be home. Where is Bob?' he asked my mother, who sat on the sofa looking at him like he was a sick little boy.

"He's upstairs, I think," my mother replied.

After a while, Bob came strutting down the stairs, stretching his long, black legs and tinkling the red bell against his snow white chest.

"Look, Bob is coming to see you. He's glad you're home," my mother said.

I held Bob up, and my father patted him on the head. Bob said a cute meow, and it made my father happy.

"Oh, I'm glad to be home! There's no place like home," he sang cheerfully.

He asked me to bring him a Coke and, as I handed it to him, he sang, "Oh the joys of Coke! The joys of Coke! It's nutritious, it's delicious."

My mother looked overwhelmed. She shuffled listlessly out of the room and escaped to the quiet of her bedroom. Her pneumonia had brought her to a state of compete exhaustion.

I touched my father's arm and sent healing energy through him. Looking out through the French doors, I contemplated about how Mom had made it look like Monet's Giverny. She'd planned for hours like a professional landscape architect, then planted all the bulbs, seeds, bushes and trees herself, laboring like a field hand for days on end. She deserved an award for all of her work. I regretted that I had not praised her for it more.

"I am painting on the landscape", she used to say as she worked. Every spring, I was transported to fairy land as I enjoyed daffodils, camellias, irises, azaleas, roses, dogwoods, tiger lilies, wisteria, petunias, tulips and Bradford pear trees.

I loved both of them so much, but I let fear get in my way of expressing it. I wished I had looked behind the fierce fronts and seen the scared, hurting children my parents were inside. If I had looked into their eyes and told them I loved them more, they would have felt loved and given me love in return. I hadn't learned anything in my life. I was just a spiritual mud puddle.

An array of caretakers came to help my father. They changed his diapers, chatted with him, and gave him insulin. He got so aggravated when they told him to eat that he yelled at the top of his lungs

"That is force feeding! I'm going to call and report you!" he roared, like a lion tearing into a fresh kill. His entire body tensed as he raised his hand in anger.

Finally, a female caretaker said she could not work for him anymore and left.

I sat at his side and gave him energy and did spoken word meditations. After a few days, a male attendant started staying with him.

My mother looked anxious and worried, and I felt shocked by how skinny she had become.

I wanted to stay around the clock but errands and cat care and various things kept me driving here and there.

Sadness sat in my heart when my friend at the temple, who gave me wonderful hugs, decided to move back to her home town. She asked me to help her.

I worked an entire day scrubbing her shower, bathtub, floors, windows, oven, walls, and folding and boxing clothes. In return, she paid me a hundred dollars which I really needed. If I hadn't needed it, I would have spent the day with Dad.

We had dinner down the hall with a kind man who regularly attended the ashram. He had a train set up in front of a magnificent, twinkling Christmas tree. It reminded me of my childhood neighbor who ran a train around some tracks on his floor one wintry, freezing evening. We laughed and talked and enjoyed his excellent cooking.

When the time to leave came, I clung to the togetherness, wanting to hold it forever. My friend, who was going to move, gave me a genuine, love filled hug.

As I drove home, I thought about all the great hugs she had given me and how I would miss her. All of my life I had lived in fear and mistrust, and I did not have any close friends. Except for the people in the ashram, who I saw regularly, no one else knew me at all.

Pulling in front of my apartment and parking, I felt grateful for my home. Loneliness fell upon me like a dark cloud as I brushed my teeth and put on my pajamas. It would feel more like home if I had a husband and child. Feeling angst over the emptiness of my life, I considered making an appointment with a therapist.

The next morning, I woke up feeling foggy. When I walked out of my front door, I saw my neighbor. He looked somber.

Kundalini Rising

"Your father died this morning."

A lightning bolt of anger and grief struck me. *"Sweetie"* My father's voice vibrated through my mind and bones, and opened my heart, massaging it like fluttering butterflies. He had been released from his suffering and I tried to be happy for him. Raja had told me that the Sufis refer to death as the great wedding day because the spirit goes to be embraced by God.

As I drove to my childhood home, I wished I had been with him through his last night. His David was sitting on the bench near the front door, when I arrived. He told me that my father was dead. Tears poured down my face. He handed me a cloth handkerchief.

Wanting to hear his voice and feel him squeeze my hand with affection, I walked to his hospital bed with dread. He was frozen still, looking up with his eyes open, with an unforgettably innocent look on his face. His mouth was open, and I looked and looked, not believing that he was gone. I touched his arm with desperate longing to have him back.

"He's dead!" my mother cried, with a look of sorrow.

Hoping she would accept my hug, I reached my arms out. Feeling relieved when she did, I hugged her, feeling guilty for all the times I had been cold.

Just then, the minister and associate minister from the church walked in. They talked with my mother while her special friend, David, began writing an obituary for the newspaper.

In shocked denial, I sat next to her, trying to think of some comforting words. The sunny porch was cluttered and needed a good dusting. Wishing I had done something to make the housekeeping of the big house easier for her, I looked at her bony body and anguished face, thinking how difficult it must be to be eighty.

She looked forlorn when she arrived at the church for the funeral. I wanted to give her a long hug, but someone told me to line up with my cousins, aunts, uncles, and sisters. A myriad voices rattled my nerves as I followed them into the sanctuary, vibrating with the powerful waves of the organ music.

Raja and a sweet friend from the ashram came to the funeral. When I sat down next to my younger sister, she handed me a handkerchief. The coffin was covered with an American flag. David, the music director, gave a moving speech, telling the story of his friendship with my father.

We rode in hearses to the cemetery. David sang a moving song as they lowered my father into the ground. My mother looked overwhelmed with grief.

"Oh, Daddy. We love you, Daddy." She picked up some dirt to throw onto his grave and then hesitated.

"Is that too Meryl Streep?" she asked, not wanting to behave too dramatically.

My cousin and her husband stood next to her and put comforting arms on her shoulder. They said it was fine. She threw a handful of dirt onto the casket. Her face was gaunt and her eyes were big with sorrow.

Everyone went to a nearby pizza restaurant afterwards. I sat across from my first cousin and his wife and didn't say a word. Looking at cousins and aunts and uncles, I tried to think of things to say.

Suddenly, I realized my mother had disappeared. I told my relatives goodbye and drove a couple of blocks to my old childhood home. My father's brother came to deliver some fig preserves and a fruitcake he had made.

"Tell them I'm not seeing anyone," she called to me from her room. I thanked him, took the bag and put it in the refrigerator.

Wanting to comfort my mother, I decided it would be better to give her her space. Tears ran down my cheeks as I drove home, feeling the pain of being an orphan.

Christmas Day came and my younger sister drove my mother to our aunt's house. Neglecting my mother in her grief, I went to celebrate with my friend from the ashram. Feeling obsessed by the need to make some friends, I tried to be talkative, but I was surrounded by strangers and it was hard.

My mother welcomed me when I came over later, hiding her hurt feelings. My cousin was there. She had helped my mother organize and clean the house. We all sat down at the kitchen island. Vegetables, macaroni and cheese, fruitcake and turkey pleased me with its tantalizing aroma. My mother told me to help myself. The delicious flavor satisfied me as the comfort and safety, which only a mother can bring, washed away my fears.

"I love you, Mom, and I'm sorry you've been through so much," I said.

I had learned in the ashram that love was the great transformer. If only I had believed in it and expressed it more, my life would have been better.

"Well, we're just so glad our baby is back. We didn't want you way out there alone. We used to wake up every morning and say, 'Where is she?'

"We're glad you're back too," my cousin said.

My cousin talked sweetly about how she had met her husband.

"Oh, how romantic," my mother replied. I listened to them talk, absorbing the comfort of home and admiring my mother for her warm, cheerful personality.

I went back to my regular routine of meeting her at the country club for lunch every Sunday. Her sweetness soothed me and I enjoyed talking with her two Sunday school friends who joined her. One of them taught grammar school children and the other one did genealogy. They were both fun, loving and interesting, in spite of their old age.

I offered to drive her to the beach because I wanted to spend some one on one time with her there. However, she told me that my father's brother was going to take her. She needed to get some repairs done on the condo that had been her art studio. She had blossomed beautifully as an artist while she lived there, thirty years ago. Waving good bye to her, I watched her depart for the beach with my father's younger brother.

Staying in my childhood home, I looked through old books and scrap books and relived my years. Eating peanut butter crackers became an obsession because that was what my father used to eat. Looking through my mother's art books and admiring her paintings, I treasured the sounds of my parents' voices playing through my mind.

One dark, lonely night, I heard a knock on the door. It was my mother. My father's brother wished her the best and said a brief hello to me. She looked surprised and happy to see me and gave me a hug.

"I brought some shrimp and crab. Would you like to have some?" she asked.

"No, thanks. I just ate something."

"The beach was beautiful, and we got a lot of work done on the condo. Joe installed a new stove and cleaned up a lot. It looks much better."

That place had been her painting sanctuary; her refuge from my boorish father, the bad memories of family fights and the work of running her huge house, putting the needs of others before her own. She had done her best with a difficult marriage, and I sympathized with her over the fact that she had been blamed by my siblings for staying with him. She was just an imperfect human being like the rest of us.

She looked tired and so sad that I longed to see the spark in her eyes she used to get when she talked about painting. I sat with her a little while but couldn't think of anything to say. I wanted to apologize for not expressing love to her more, but I froze in fear.

Finally, I gave up and told her I was tired. I walked upstairs and went to sleep in my sister's room.

I left her house early the next morning, not stopping to think about how neglected she would feel. She lay sleeping on the living room sofa, covered with a blanket.

At Sunday lunch, she told me she had not been able to go into the bedroom. It hurt her too much to see my father's clothes and things. Mario, the Mexican waiter cheered her by telling a funny story and soon, she and her two friends were laughing.

She said she had gone to hear her favorite theological speaker, who had grown up down the street from me. Soon after my family moved south from Canada, I had swum in her swimming pool. My mother talked, with fondness, about how she had written her a letter of appreciation for putting on a party for the neighborhood—the best party she had ever attended, she said. My mother was an expert at preparing and spreading an incredible banquet and at decorating.

This speaker also wrote books and my mother had read several of them. She praised them, saying that her writing was unique and special. Her friends chimed in, saying they had been to hear her speak.

The people, we had bought a poodle from when I was in high school, came over and gave their usual, friendly greeting to my mother. The three boys and girls all loved my mother and called her "Aunty". I felt guilty for focusing on her temper so much and ignoring her loving, soft side.

Their father, a man I remembered who had once been full of life, and who used to read our palms at family gatherings, sat next to my mother and put his arm around her.

"You look great Dede."

"Oh, I'm all skin and bones."

She had once been gorgeous, like a movie star. I looked at her thin, drawn face in shocked denial. She squeezed her friend's hand and looked at him with vulnerable gratitude. All of her life, she had been deprived of tender touches because my father lived in his scientific head and only, very rarely, expressed from his heart.

Her friend was losing his eyesight and, after he returned to his table, she talked sadly about how he was going blind. Then she talked about how friends from her Sunday school class were dying, one after another. Even the teacher of the class was falling to pieces.

"Charles is failing. He's been sick for a long time, and I don't think he's going to make it much longer. He is a wonderful teacher and always so loving and kind. We've lost so many people from our class these last few years." Her eyes exuded sadness. Bones protruded from her skin and I wondered if she was eating. She coughed several times.

"We sure have. It's been really hard. I miss them," her friend said. Her other friend agreed.

I enjoyed the beautiful view of the rolling hills and the sound of my mother talking with her friends. There must be something I could do or say, but I didn't know what, so I just listened. Some part of me was still in denial that my father was dead.

Suddenly, tears started streaming down my face and my mother looked at me with concern.

"Sorry. It's really hard losing a parent." Holding back sobs, I looked into the eyes of my emaciated mother.

"I know," my mother responded, her eyes glowing with love as she looked into my soul.

Her friends looked at me with sympathy too. They were sweet ladies who had been friends since first grade. My mother was just getting to know them, and she did very well telling funny stories and making herself fun company. I wished I was that good at being sociable.

Sunday was my favorite day because it was my mother's favorite day. She said it was the highlight of her week to hear beautiful music at church, see her friends, and then see her children at lunch.

CHAPTER TWELVE

"Just so, every good tree bears good fruit, and a rotten tree bears bad fruit. A good tree cannot bear bad fruit, nor can a rotten tree bear good fruit. Every tree that does not bear good fruit will be cut down and thrown into the fire. So by their fruits you will know them." Matthew 7:17-20

Prove your worth through your work, not your words.

"Why should you think he is not? The ether is filled with music that is caught by the radio--music that otherwise you would not know about. And so it is with God. He is with you every minute of your existence, yet the only way to realize this is to meditate."
Paramahansa Yogananda

There never has been a time when you and I... have not existed, nor will there be a time when we will cease to exist. As the same person inhabits the body through childhood, youth and old age, so too, at the time of death he attains another body. The wise are not deluded by these changes.
Bhagavad-Gita

As the winter chill gave way to spring flowers, my mother felt more and more unable to live in the house alone. As I sat in the living room with her one day, she told me about an elderly assisted living community which was nearby. When she asked me if I thought she should buy an apartment there, I said it sounded like a good idea.

She said she would live at my childhood house and then, after a couple of years, move into the apartment there.

I rode with her to see her apartment in the elderly community, one day.

We arrived. My mother fumbled in her shoulder bag for the keys, then opened her apartment. The big glass wall in front looked out onto a lake. Canadian geese walked right up to it and munched on the grass.

"See how nice this is? It's a perfect place to paint with all this sunlight. I'm going to start painting again."

Looking around, I thought it was a nice place, even though it was tiny compared to the house she was used to. I could feel how much she had missed her painting while being a full time caretaker for my father.

"I'm tired. I didn't get my nap today." She reclined on the floor.

"I have to go", I said after just a few minutes.

She stood up and drove me home. Looking sad, she told me good bye.

Running various errands, I felt shocked that the day passed so quickly.

As I began to fall asleep that night, I regretted having been in such a hurry. I hoped I hadn't hurt her feelings.

She called me the next day. I took three days to call her back.

Sunday arrived and I had lunch with her and her friends at the country club. Sadness came from her as she mentioned, briefly, that she had received a double whammy---losing both her husband and her brother. The rest of the time, she talked in a cheerful way with her friends.

After her friends headed home, I walked part of the way with her to her car.

"I could die in that house all alone. You call me back when I call you the next time."

Guilt froze me in my tracks and I longed to do something that would renew her faith in me. Mustering a weak apology, I longed for the strong bond we had once enjoyed. I wondered why she was talking about dying.

As though I was frozen emotionally, I stood there, unable to think of the right thing to say. With awkward fear, I gave her a half hug. Purnima's voice echoed inside me.

"If you hug someone, give them a real hug."

Thanksgiving arrived in a flash. She must have felt so hurt by my refusal last Thanksgiving that she didn't invite me this year. Instead, she drove herself over to my aunt's house to have Thanksgiving.

I was working on having some friends of my own, so I forced myself to go to the gathering a striking, blonde woman who attended the ashram had. I felt too depressed to socialize.

I left a package of tea in my mother's mailbox with a note wishing her a happy holiday. Later on I called her.

"I had Thanksgiving with Uncle Fred and Aunt Dianne. They didn't miss you. They think you're just neglecting me. I knew naturally how to love my mother."

I reacted like a firecracker, exploding with decades of suppressed anger.

"You ordered me out of the house again and again, and you never once apologized!" I yelled.

She yelled louder and louder, and threw accusations at me until I began to tremble, like I had when my father threatened me.

"I'm not going to take this crap!" I yelled and hung up.

Two days later, I got a call from my older sister. Outside of brief hellos at reunions and Christmas gatherings, we hadn't had a relationship for thirty years. She asked me to meet her at a local pizza restaurant, and I reluctantly agreed. I remembered how devastated I had been by her violent attack on me seventeen years before.

Admiring the beautiful fountain which people threw coins into, I walked into the restaurant and saw my sister waiting for me at a table. A slender, brunette waitress led me over and I sat down. She was still beautiful though decades had passed as she raised her three children. Her heart shaped, clear complexioned face with its almond shaped hazel eyes, dark, perfect brows and delicate, rose bud mouth far outshone any other face in the place. She looked at me with a sense of urgency.

"Mom is in the hospital. She couldn't breathe all of a sudden. Dr. Clements drove there. She's been having problems with damage in her lungs for a couple of years, and she hadn't told anyone. She's going to die."

"I knew she was making plans to move into the elderly community, but she said she was going to wait a couple of years to do that."

"Well, she doesn't have a couple of years left. Her lung damage is severe. I was on my way from North Carolina when I got a call that she'd been rushed to the hospital. I was going to take her to stay with me for a while. She was isolated and depressed in that big house, and I thought it would be good for her to sit in the sun and be with me."

"She didn't tell me she had something wrong with her lungs."

"She didn't want anyone to know."

My heart dropped through the floor as I recalled how I had hung up on her and wondered if it had triggered her inability to breathe. Guilt surged through me as I remembered her sweet face lighting up every time I joined her for lunch.

To lose my mother was unspeakable. It couldn't be true. I couldn't let it happen, not to her. Not to the mother who had loved me, driven me to drawing classes, encouraged, and praised me. I had been feeing closer and closer to her and was overjoyed that we were beginning to have a relationship again. She had forgiven me. After years of ice between us, she was now my best friend and the person I looked forward to being with more than anyone. No. She couldn't go now.

I hit the table with my fist. I'd been looking forward to another lovely Sunday talking with my mother and her friends. I loved the stories she told of how cute I was as a baby. It filled me with comfort and joy. Her affection was healing me, and I couldn't wait to have another Sunday lunch with her.

"She's in the hospital. I'll be over there in a while. I just need to do some errands. Her room number is 747," my sister told me.

A feeling of doom came over me as I walked down the street to the hospital. I hurried up the stone stairs and through the elegant entry room, which was opulent with beautiful paintings and upholstered chairs. My heart galloped as I rode the elevator to the third floor. I walked briskly until I made my way to her room.

"You look like a mirage," she said as I walked in. I overflowed with love and gratitude for her company.

"I'm sorry I was short with you," she said.

Her words were so sincere, they opened my hard heart. She had been desperate for love, sick and frightened, dying of loneliness, and having trouble breathing. I must have seemed cold and aloof as I went about my activities. When I thought about it, I had noticed that she'd been coughing more over the last year or so. I even recalled telling her I hoped it would get better. Still, I never would have thought she had damaged lungs.

She smiled at me as though I was the most precious child in the world, though I felt like the opposite. I wanted to rock her in my arms like a forlorn infant, but she was confined behind a large table that held a tray full of plastic bowls and plates filled with food.

Suddenly, my older sister walked in.

"I heard you've been just drinking Coca Cola at home and not eating anything. You need some nutrition. You're not taking care of yourself. Sit down and eat this lunch the nurse brought you", she ordered in a voice that shook the room.

My mother looked at the food with distaste and started to try to stand up.

"I want to lie down," she said.

"Sit down," my sister ordered in a bossy, humiliating tone.

My mother tried to stand up, but my sister hovered over her and blocked her.

A nurse came in and gently helped her, walking her to the bed and then lifting her onto it. I felt grateful for her and watched my mother calm down.

The nurse left. My mother and sister began to argue bitterly.

"Sit down," my mother rebelled, imitating my sister's harshness. "Your name is ARMADA. You want to knock me over."

"You used to hurt my feelings, but now you don't."

"You're full of criticism and boorishness."

"Oh, yeah? You've ruined the lives of all your children," my sister fired back.

I coiled into a ball of tension as the arguing got nastier and nastier.

"No. I love my children. You just go on now," my mother said.

"Well, they have a different opinion."

"Oh, yeah. You are full of hatred. All you ever think about is yourself."

"No. That's not true. I've done everything I can to help you, and you have never appreciated it because you're too selfish to think of anyone's feelings but your own."

"No. That is a lie. You just go on now. I want you to leave me in peace," my mother said.

"No. I'm staying here. I'm not going to let you manipulate me into leaving after I drove all the way here. You're trying to make me look bad and trying to control everything, as usual," my sister said.

"Oh, I can't stand this anymore. Just go and leave me in peace!" My mother's voice cracked with anguish.

"Just ignore her," I said, rubbing her feverish forehead, feeling guilty because there must have been times my mother had needed me to defend her against my older sister. Sad that I had not been there for her, I looked into her fragile face.

Turning on the T.V., I found an animation with cheerful fairies flying around and helping people.

"Oh, that looks good", she said, relaxing and smiling at me. It was good to see her emotional stress subside.

Soon, my younger sister arrived. After a brief stay, she rushed off with my older sister to a lawyer's office to manage my father's estate.

The nurse came in and asked if my mother was all right. She said she needed to go to the bathroom. She crawled out of bed and sat on the bed pan. As she released the contents from her bowels, she clutched her hospital gown around her chest.

Then she climbed back into bed feebly, as though it was taking every ounce of energy in her. I held her hand and it calmed her. A short, stocky Spanish maid with short, dark hair came in and Mom talked cheerfully with her. She cleaned and tied the garbage bags. Looking at me with love, she asked me to take good care of my Mama.

After she left, Mom told one of her adorable stories about how the maid called her "Mama" and said, "Don't worry Mama". In spite of everything, she was still my charming, theatrical, Leo lion Mom.

I had bought a Scalar Wave Laser at a health symposium. People around the world had experienced miracles by using it. It had a setting for Pulmonary Fibrosis and, at my next visit, I beamed the light from it onto her, feeling hopeful that it would cure her.

All the love she had given me vibrated through me like an echoing, celestial song as I sat and talked with her. With great love, she expressed her gratitude for me.

Later in the day, our love filled peace was shattered.

"I can't breathe," she said in a voice that tore my heart. She punched the button on her bed.

Luckily, a nurse arrived in only a few minutes, rolling in a big machine. She put a plastic cup over my mother's mouth and I watched the numbers climb higher as my mother breathed in oxygen with all of her strength.

"Very good. You're doing well. Your oxygen level is back to normal now. Just call me whenever you need me," the nurse said.

"Just getting out of bed exhausts me," my mother said. "It's boring sitting in bed all day, but that's all I have the energy for. Every time I need to move my bowels, this is what happens."

"Can I bring you anything? Something from the house or maybe some Hagen Dazs?"

"Some Hagen Dazs sounds good."

I put on my coat and prepared to head out to the store.

"Will you check on Bob and make sure he has plenty of food and water?"

"Okay," I promised.

I went to the house. A blanket and pillow were on the living room sofa where she had slept. Reading her prescription bottles suspiciously, I wondered if one of the drugs had caused her decline. Bob ran up and rubbed against my leg. He followed me to the kitchen, and I filled up his food and water bowl. His black fur was shiny and he looked healthy.

I walked back into the living room and noticed a cute, light blue Easter Bunny. When I pressed a button on his paw, he began singing.

"You're nobody 'til somebody loves you. You're nobody 'til somebody cares. You're nobody 'til somebody loves you, so find yourself somebody to love!" A playful piano tune played along as he sang. I put him in a plastic bag along with her face and hand cream, books by her favorite minister, her photo album, a book of Van Gogh paintings and various other things.

Driving back to the hospital, I wondered where I could park. Luckily, I realized I could park in the nearby church for free. Walking rapidly down the street toward the hospital, I floated on the wings of love.

A worshipful, adoring look came over Mom's face when I walked into her room and showed her the bunny.

"Oh, I got that for Daddy when I went to Cedar Mountain with Ms. Rudy. Thank you so much for bringing it." She looked through the bag I handed her. "Oh, and my dry skin cream and my pictures. You are so sweet. Thank you."

"You're welcome. Bob is fine. He jumped up in my lap and rubbed up against my leg. He's always happy to see me. I left him plenty of food and water."

The nurse brought my mother dinner on a tray.

"I don't feel like eating anything. Why don't you eat that for me? I don't think you eat enough. You light up like a Christmas tree every time you see some food. What have you been eating?"

"Oh, believe me, I eat plenty, Mom. I've been eating a big pot of onion and garlic soup that I made."

"Why don't you go down to Evans and get a vegetable plate? You need something nutritious. You can't live on a pot of garlic soup for God's sake. Your breath smells awful."

"Okay, Mom. Don't worry about me. I get plenty to eat."

"No. You look hungry. Go ahead and eat my dinner. You need it more than I do."

I sat and ate spinach, carrots, fish, and mashed potatoes. I was impressed that it tasted so good, considering it was hospital food.

"It's good to see you eating. I don't want you ever going hungry."

"Thank you, Mom. They have good cooks here. But I'm worried about you going hungry."

"No. I don't want anything. If I eat, then I'll have to get up and go to the bathroom. Every time I get up, it exhausts me, and then they have to put me on the breathing machine."

We watched T.V. and I sat by her bed. She said I could run my Laser on her if I would not poke her. As the Laser ran, she became more and more relaxed. I hoped it would cure her so we could go to the beach together.

Sleeping in the chair near her bed, I appreciated the good in her, more than ever.

The next morning, her doctor came in to talk with her. He was a young, handsome, brunette man. He greeted me kindly and spoke in a clear voice.

"You're always so kind. I'm glad you're my doctor." My mother looked up at him with grateful eyes.

"Thank you, ma'am. The news I have is not good. Your lung damage has gotten much worse over the past two years. There is nothing that can be done. You might live another five weeks or you might live another two months."

Her eyes grew wide with emotion as her face turned white. Pain moved through me as I hoped that he was wrong.

"Well, let me know what I can do. I want you to be comfortable," he said. I followed him out to the hall.

"What is wrong with her, and why isn't she getting better?"

"She has interstitial pulmonary fibrosis. She has had it for a few years, and over the last two years it has gotten much, much worse. There is nothing that can be done to cure it. All we can do is give her oxygen and give her steroids to reduce the pain. She might live another few months, or she might die in a few weeks. There is no way of knowing."

My eyes filled with tears. Sadness and regret over the unsaid words of love, the undone visits, the cards I had not sent--- all of it weighed on me heavily now. I wiped the tears from my face and walked back into the room. I sat at my mother's side and gave her healing energy. She looked at me gratefully with her eyes wide and childlike, vulnerable and sweet. Struggling with her difficult relationship with my father and the heavy weight of blame from her children had exhausted her. It must be hard for her to trust me I thought. I hoped that she could tell I loved her.

Nurses came in and out and I looked out the window to the clinic where I had gotten my first job in high school. I longed for those simple days when I lived in my mother's big, beautiful house-- safely and simply. She was my biggest fan, pointing out abilities and powers in me that others never noticed. Memories of our carefree summers at the beach when she pampered and complimented me, and the peaceful afternoons we'd spent on the porch looking at her flower gardens nourished me. I wanted to travel back to that time.

The next day, my mother perked up and started talking cheerfully about the funny maid who cleaned her room.

"She always says, 'Hi, Mama. How are you doing today?' She's so sweet to me. It always makes me feel better. She works really hard keeping this place clean. She's from the Philippines."

A few minutes later, she walked in.

"How are you?" my mother asked.

"Oh, my hip is hurting but I'm doing well," the maid said. She said that she had injured it twenty years ago and had had the pain ever since. She had bright, dark eyes and a round, chubby face framed by short, dark hair. Her chubby but strong body looked tired as she leaned over to empty the trash can.

"Take good care of your sweet mama. Bye-bye, Mama. I'll see you tomorrow," she said. She left carrying a large plastic bag full of trash. My mother wished her a good day.

The nurse carried in a lunch tray and my mother looked at it and groaned.

"Oh, I don't want to eat anything. It makes me have to get out of bed and sit on the pot, and then I get out of breath. Why don't you eat it?" She looked at me with love.

"I don't want to eat your food. You need nutrition."

"No. I don't want it. Really. You've been eating nothing but a big pot of garlic soup. You need more than that. Go ahead and eat it. You're looking too skinny." I remembered the cheese soufflés, salmon croquettes, fried chicken, roast beef and vegetables she had lovingly cooked for me when I was a growing girl.

She looked skinny and breakable as she lay there in the small bed with the railing raised to protect her from falling. The T.V. flashed with ads and various things I was not interested in. The fish, broccoli, peas, and carrots tasted alright, but they were bland compared to her home cooked food. I ate a piece of chocolate pie for desert, even though I knew I wasn't supposed to have sugar.

My mother's sweetness made me feel like a care free child again and I floated happily on feathery, soft clouds of her love. Memories of security and peace calmed and nurtured me. Her voice from the past whispered in my ears, calling me her "shadow" because I loved being at her side, watching or helping with whatever she was doing. When I was a painfully shy ninth grader, she praised me for being the "All-American Girl"; the sweetest and the smartest of her children and the best artist. She complimented me for my independence and my fertile mind.

She recited lines from my poetry with admiration, something my father had never done. He was a sick man battling with a disease and a difficult career who simply didn't have much to give to me.

However, my mother saw the artist in me, and she encouraged and nourished her, giving her a voice. With love, she did her best to undo the damage my father had done to my ego. He had reduced me to a catatonic teenager with his threats of violence against me. She lovingly sewed me together at the broken places and gave me a feeling of importance when I felt worthless.

Dusk began to fall outside and the darkness of winter crept in. It was my mother's most abhorred season, and I could feel the dread rising in her body. Depression filled her face, though she covered it with sweet words of appreciation.

"It is so wonderful to have you here."

I slept on the big armchair. The night clattered with the sounds of machines and stretchers rolling down the halls.

In the morning, the sunlight that brightened the dark room brought emotional pain with it. My mother was awake and staring at the wall with an overwhelmed, yet resigned look. The room grew gradually lighter as daylight filtered through the window.

After a while, an attendant wheeled in a tray with breakfast. I stood at her bedside and encouraged her to eat, but she said she didn't want any.

With the nurse's help, she got out of bed and sat on the port-a-pot. She looked so helpless. I turned my back to her to give her some privacy.

The nurse cleaned her body, and then helped her back onto the bed.

"I can't breathe!" she wailed in despair.

"Okay. We'll give you some oxygen," the nurse replied.

A machine was wheeled into the room, and a nurse put a plastic cup over my mother's mouth and nose. A hissing sound came from the machine as my mother desperately pulled oxygen into her scarred, damaged lungs.

She had focused intently on breathing when she studied singing. I remembered covering my ears when I sat listening to her class with the music professor at the conservatory, when I was three years old. Her powerful, operatic voice would soar through the neighborhood as I played outside, roller skating, skipping or playing hide and seek.

"Okay. Your oxygen level is back to normal," the nurse said. Then, she took the tube from my mother's nose and wheeled the machine out.

"Whew. I'm glad that's over," she said, looking at me with love.

"Sorry you're having such a hard time."

"Oh, you're so sweet. Why don't you eat my breakfast? I don't want it."

"Okay." I ate toast and jelly and oatmeal, lapping up her love. It could sustain me more than any food ever would. It had been silly of me to ever doubt it. It had always been there.

Raja had taught me that God is love and that everyone is God. I wished I had changed the way I looked at her long ago.

"Do you want to turn on the T.V. and see what's on?" she asked.

"Sure." I flipped it on and surfed through the channels, feeling bored by all of them.

Suddenly, the song my mother used to sing to me played through my mind. It went, "You've got to walk that lonesome highway. You've got to walk it by yourself."

I had often acted as though I didn't need my parents. Yet, through the arguments, the explosive, angry blowouts, a deep, abiding love had remained. It was a special, priceless love, a kind unique to us that I would never have again.

I thanked God for my energy machine, my Scalar Wave Laser. I used it to beam healing frequencies into my mother as often as I could. Sometimes, she complained that I poked her. However, most of the time she would allow me to put it on her chest or abdomen.

A social worker came to talk with my mother. She impatiently raised her voice when my mother got confused. My mother told me she didn't like her after she left the room.

Telling her that I sympathized seemed to relax her. Commenting that the doctors and nurses had many fancy machines and "miracle" drugs but very little kindness or time to share, I watched her frightened eyes widen with gratitude.

"That's the system," she said, looking into my eyes.

"Yeah. They just run rules over people, and they're stuck in their rigid ways."

"That's why we're artists!" she said. We enjoyed one another's' company in silence for a while.

"Do you think James will come and see me if I give him the beach house?" she asked. Her hurt longing shook me. My three siblings and I all sat on a dynamite shack full of rage and resentment. We were all dysfunctional and wanted to blame our parents. It was very sad. All of the therapy sessions we had been through had not transformed us.

I wanted to crawl into the bed and hold her, let her know that she was loved. Hanging on to each precious moment with her, I slept in the chair.

The next morning, I had my mother all to myself again. I felt lucky. I asked her if I could bring her something, and she said she'd like some coffee. Her hair was messy and dirty, and her hospital gown hung low on her shoulders, exposing her bony chest. She had gotten so alarmingly thin in the last year that I wondered why I hadn't suspected she was seriously ill. Sweet, grateful love lifted me like perfume as she thanked me sincerely for bringing her coffee. I wanted to hold onto the moment forever as I looked into her receptive, innocent eyes and gently touched her shoulder. Raising the blinds, letting some sunlight in, I looked down at the traffic and pedestrians.

Mom sipped her coffee and looked as though she had resigned herself to the struggles the day held for her. The intense strain, stress, and struggle that the simple act of breathing caused unraveled her. Placing my hand on her side, I sent energy to her.

Suddenly, she said she needed to move her bowels.

"Call a nurse," she said.

I punched the button and a nurse arrived shortly.

"I can't breathe!"

"Okay, I'm getting the oxygen," the nurse replied. She called for the respiratory therapist.

The therapist appeared in a few minutes, and she rolled the big machine into the room. My mother looked desperate as she placed the cup over her nose and mouth. Like a fish floundering on sand, she breathed in, struggling to get oxygen into her lungs. With a face as white as a ghost, she tried but she couldn't get enough oxygen. Time stood still.

"Okay," the nurse said. "We've gotten some results now. Your oxygen level is rising."

My chest expanded as I breathed in with relief. I watched the nurse remove the cup from my mother's mouth and roll the machine away.

"Every time I have to use the potty, this happens to me. I can't stand another day of this. I'm going to jump out of the window if this continues," my mother lamented.

An attendant brought breakfast in.

"I want you to eat that," she said.

"Some vitamins would be good for you, Mom," I replied.

"No. I don't want it. It will make me have to get up to eliminate again, and I'll have to go through that ordeal. I can't stand it anymore. This is just misery. I don't want to live like this."

I ate some oatmeal and toast and jelly, watching her stare somberly at the wall. She used to be alive and inspired and she would stay up all night painting lovely pictures. Now, she didn't have a drop of energy. She couldn't pour her heart into her creativity like she used to. I wanted my old, enthusiastic mama back.

Beaming my Scalar Wave Laser on her, I prayed that it was healing her lungs. After about twenty minutes, she drifted off into a peaceful snooze. Sitting and meditating, I thought about all of the love I had received from Raja and Purnima. Now, I was blessed with an opportunity to give love. It was the great transformer.

When she woke, she looked as sweet and innocent as a child. She smiled at me and said, "Hi, baby. I'm so glad you're here. Let's see what's on T.V."

I turned it on and flipped through the channels. I wasn't interested in people trying to sell me things or robotic-looking, cartoon animations.

"Is it okay if I turn the noise off and just leave the picture on?"

"Yeah."

A silent fifties movie played on the screen, and I stared as grief overwhelmed me. Mom was my only friend to have lunch with. I had been hopeful that we were going to take a trip to the beach together. Our summers there had been the most wonderful times in my life. She had praised her three daughters and made sure they got the attention, which was impossible to get from our father.

Doctors and nurses, my two sisters, and a social worker came in and out of the room. My heart broke open as I felt her fading away from me. I hung onto each moment as the day droned on in a cacophony of voices, the clang of food trays, squeaky wheels, discussions, vitals checks, oxygen treatments and bad T.V. shows.

Christmas day arrived. My mother radiated deep, eternal love to my sisters and me as we sat near her.

"The best present I could ever have is being with my three wonderful daughters."

My older sister talked about the beautiful music she had heard at the church the night before. I had begun attending that gorgeous, classically designed church when I was eleven years old. A genius played the organ there and the music vibrated electrically through the place, bouncing off of the high ceilings, making peoples' arm hairs stand up.

"Why don't you go to those wonderful programs?" my mother asked me.

Her eyes conveyed love and adoration, the kind she had felt for me when I would climb in bed with her when I was a toddler. All her agonies over having an abusive husband had been bravely concealed from me, as she did her best to love and encourage me. I had taken her for granted. Skipping out of the house to be with my friends, I had left her alone with her pain.

Then, I had returned at the end of the day expecting her to grant my wishes and heal all my scrapes. Cooking cheese soufflé, salmon croquettes, fried chicken, pot roast and vegetables and cleaning up afterwards was a full time job and she couldn't give me everything I wanted.

Now that she was fading away from me, I clung to her sweetness, appreciating it for the first time.

Late in the afternoon, I brought her some Hagen Dazs. The look of joy on her face made me wish I had brought her some every day of my life. Gratitude poured from her, warming my heart and giving me the deepest happiness I'd felt in ages.

The day after Christmas, a social worker came to talk with her about where she was going to go next. My sister had set up her apartment in the elderly assisted living community, but the social worker felt that hospice would provide more of her needs. My mother couldn't make up her mind, and she looked at the social worker with a dismayed, helpless look.

"I'll let you decide," she said, turning her head to look at me.

"I think hospice sounds the best, Mom," I said.

"Okay."

She might collapse on the floor in her apartment and not be able to breathe and there would be no one there to help her.

The next day, two women came into her room and lifted her onto a stretcher. An ambulance drove her to hospice and I followed in my car. It was not far from my apartment.

I put a Frosty the Snowman on her window. It shimmered colorfully when the sunlight came through it. Outside was a charming courtyard with a fountain. Birds flew around and perched on top of it, singing in unison.

My sister and I put our mother's plants around. Up high on a shelf, where she could look at them, my sister put a big photo of Mom's mother, surrounded by smaller photos of family members. Then, she bought her a CD player so she could listen to classical music.

When I gave her light with my Scalar Wave Laser, she drifted off into a peaceful sleep. Taking a walk around the grounds, I prayed and meditated. When I returned, I talked with a nurse briefly. Walking down the hall to my mother's room, I admired the paintings on the walls.

"Now I feel like I want to live. This place is so much better than the hospital. They take good care of me and everyone is so sweet," she said, when I sat down beside her.

There was a comfortable fold-out bed. Some nights I slept there and other nights my older sister had already claimed it.

One morning, I woke to the sun streaming in the window.

"Hi, baby," my mother said in a voice that melted my heart.

"Good morning. Are you all right?"

"Yeah. I feel fine. It was so nice to look over and see you there."

"Well, I'm so glad to be with you," I replied, smiling.

I brought her some coffee. She looked at me with adoration. Her mother, my grandmother smiled down on me from the T.V. stand. Her voice echoed through my mind. "You've always been my favorite."

"You're the sweetest and the smartest. I love you. I love all of my children with all my heart," my mother said. I relaxed with a satisfied sigh, feeling like a happy child.

"That sun coming through the window is glorious. Let's let more in," she said.

I pulled the curtain open and golden rays washed over us, bathing us in eternal, spiritual love. It felt cozy, safe, and warm being her baby.

Soon, a friendly nurse walked in full of kind morning greetings. Then, she brought my mother some breakfast.

Later on, various peers from her Sunday school class came by to visit with her. She talked in a sweet, cheerful way, and told funny stories that made everyone laugh.

After a while, her friends left. She asked me if I would bring her some coffee and I felt overjoyed to have the chance to serve her.

A nurse smiled at me as I walked to the kitchen. The coffee was ready and warm, in an electric pot. I poured some into a cup. Then, I opened the refrigerator and got some half and half. After pouring that into her cup, I mixed in some sugar.

"I aim to please," I told her as I handed it to her.

"Well, you do."

Suddenly, another church friend walked in. Moving to a small desk, I worked on a drawing of a Native American Indian, copying it from a book.

"I'm not going to die today", my mother said, looking at her church friend with wide, vulnerable eyes.

I showed my mother my drawings later. She asked me to spread them out at the foot of the bed.

"Oh, those are beautiful. They look just like a real Inian. That's just how you used to say it---Inian. You were so funny. You used to make us laugh. You were a wonderful child. People would say, 'The other two are great but, that Sophia, she is special.'"

As I gave her some Reiki and ran my Scalar Wave Laser on her, I asked her how she was feeling.

"The worst thing is to think the children don't love us." The sadness in her voice moved me and I sat in silence, unable to think of a response.

Noticing the VCR machine for playing movies, I remembered I had seen a stack of them in her bedroom. Telling her I would return soon, I left. Driving to her house, I relived all the sweet moments we had shared and the compliments she had given me.

Rummaging through piles of things in her bedroom, I found many movies.

Returning to her, I placed them on the stand which held the VCR player. Then, we began watching, enjoying one another's company in the peaceful atmosphere. Reclining on a fold out bed, with a pillow and a blanket, I basked in her love.

We watched "My Fair Lady", "Carousel", "Oliver", "Willy Wonka and the Chocolate Factory", "The Girl with a Pearl Earring", "Out of Africa", and "The Sound Of Music".

With each new day, she looked younger. Sometimes, a pleasant physical therapist came in and talked her through exercises. Her face strained with effort and she groaned as she did leg raises.

As I gave energy to her, wondering how I could I could cheer her up, I spoke a little.

"What do you want to watch, Mom?"

"Anything you want. Just not that Willy Wonka that has children talking mean to their parents."

I put in "Out of Africa". A tender look filled her face as she watched. It must have reminded her of her romance with my father. It was her favorite movie, and she watched it over and over again.

Soon, New Year's Eve arrived. When I told her I was driving to the ashram, near the Running Bear Theater, for New Year's Eve chanting, she didn't want me to go.

"The Running Bear Theater?" she asked in shock. "That's a long way. It's going to be awful traffic. You just love danger, don't you?"

She was trying to protect me, but I reacted from my animal mind with anger.

"Just leave me alone and let me go." I raised my voice in anger, turned my back to her abruptly and left. Then, I realized that I was reacting out of ego and not listening to my Higher Self.

Driving through the streets, I remembered New Year's Eve parties full of drunk, rowdy people which had stressed me out. When I drank alcohol, it had given me a headache.

Now, I had Raja. He had commented that drinking alcohol did not contribute to a person evolving spiritually. Like a mother, he made my life safer.

Arriving on the street of the ashram, I parked my car a couple of blocks away. Happiness bubbled within me as I sprinted down the street and up the stairs. Loving spiritual seekers greeted me with hugs and love filled eyes. Serenity washed through me, cleansing away my negativity.

"Invite your family members in", Raja said before we began the chant. We are going to chant the Sri Gayatri Mantra.

The Sanskrit words were written on a piece of paper on my back jack. The fragrance of incense, the softly glowing candles and the serene vibrations sent me into a state of bliss. High vibrations revitalized me as I chanted. The voices blended into one and the feeling of being an energy being who manifested as many yet remained one unlimited consciousness filled me.

Om bhurbuvassuvaha tatsa virturvarenyam Bhargo devasya dheemahi Dhiyoyonaha prachodayat.

We repeated this over and over for eight hours. It was as though the source was moving our mouths and making the sounds. Divine Shakti or God Power filled every square inch of the room with a high frequency.

Raja cooked breakfast for everyone. We ate in silence, still floating in divine ecstasy.

As I drove to hospice to see my mother, I felt full. Raja often told us to take time to do things that benefited us. Then, we would be giving from a full cup instead of an empty one. The hectic traffic did not bother me like it usually did and I arrived quickly and parked my car.

She looked like a peaceful, cheerful child as I walked into the room. Unsure about what I could do for her, I felt grateful for my Reiki. Sitting down in the chair beside her bed, I began beaming Reiki to her. Those moments were full of magic as love flowed like nectar between us. I looked at her in her bed, and then looked up at the photo of her mother—my grandmother—looking down on us. Her voice echoed through me.

"You've always been my favorite."

They had both loved me profoundly, even when I did not know it. I recalled the times they had called me "special" with great fondness.

My sister came the next night, feeling glad to have a break from talking to lawyers and getting lost on the freeway. As she read Mom a book, I mentioned I wished I could write like that.

"Well, you can. You're a wonderful writer," my mother replied.

I wanted to have her for myself and wished my sister would leave. Then, suddenly, I felt like I should give my sister time with her. I left without a word.

The next morning, I received a call from my older sister. She said my mother had passed away. An empty chill blew through the depths of my soul as tears rolled down my face. Wishing I had stayed through the night with my dear mother, I drove to hospice.

She lay on the bed, cold and motionless. Her spirit had flown beyond the lifeless flesh. A deep, dark sadness came from the partially closed eyes. I hugged her again and again, resting my face on her chest while her sweet words of endearment resonated through my heart.

It had been paradise being close to her, spending the night and watching musicals, hearing her words of love for me. No one else had carried me for nine months and watched me grow. She had understood me when the psychiatric experts said I would need medication for the rest of my life.

"I'd take them all on at the Barkley Forum," she would say, when I was in the mental institution I was committed to when I was seventeen.

The funeral chapel was esthetically pleasing with its classical architecture. The coffin was covered with flowers. Beautiful music played and an operatically trained singer sang a lovely classical piece. My mother's church friends comforted me. A friend I had made at the ashram sat next to me and held my hand.

CHAPTER THIRTEEN

"Enter through the narrow gate; for the gate is wide and the road broad that leads to destruction and those who enter through it are many. How narrow the gate and constricted the road that leads to life. And those who find it are few."
Matthew 7: 13-14

Take the road less traveled.

> *It is not for the sake of the husband that the husband is dear, but for the sake of the Self. It is not for the sake of the wife that the wife is dear, but for the sake of the Self. It is not for the sake of the children that the children are dear, but for the sake of the Self... It is not for the sake of all beings that all beings are dear, but for the sake of the Self... It is the Self that should be realized, heard of, reflected on and meditated upon. By the realization of the Self, all is known.*
>
> Brihadaranyaka Upanishad

Raja said that he would channel my mother for me so I could talk with her. She had died on January twenty-fifth, and he set the date for the channeling for February the fourteenth. I couldn't wait to talk with her.

I rummaged through her bedroom, sorting through old books and papers. Reading letters she had saved, I felt the longings for love that had never been satisfied within her. As I read her diary, I cried over the deep betrayal and loneliness she felt because of the cold behaviors of my siblings, my father, and I. One page had been written when I was around eight years old. She had been in Europe with my father and he had been drunk and sloppily dressed. When she told him that the restaurant, they had reservations at, would not admit him dressed like that he had twisted her arm. My heart pounded with empathy and guilt that I had been unaware of her pain. I read another page. She commented that she thought I must be writing a book about her which was like "Mommie Dearest".

"When you get home, put your arms around your mother and give her a hug", my high school biology teacher had advised, when I told her my mother criticized me, thirty six years ago. Steeping in resentment, I had ignored her good advice.

It was too late now. She was gone.

I walked around the house I grew up in, looking around like a deer staring into bright headlights. Reading newspaper articles and letters my mother had saved, I imagined what she had been feeling. Wishing that I had comforted her when she was sorrowful, I experienced her deep and frustrated emotions.

I read things she had written about me and wanted to defend myself. A memory I had buried came back to me, as I read something she'd written about how I had come to the house demanding money. I had not had enough money to pay my car insurance, and a cop had stopped me and given me a ticket for driving with expired insurance.

My father had yelled at me cruelly and told me I was grounded. I did not recall ever demanding money.

The evening for the channeling arrived. Raja welcomed me when I arrived at the center.

"She really wants to talk. I can smell her," he said.

Soon, everyone had arrived and we sat around in a circle. Raja gave us the instructions to focus on someone we loved with all our heart. Then, he had each person state the mental images or feelings they were receiving. Someone saw a black coat. Someone else said my mother was communicating to me to keep singing, and someone said she was sorry that I had suffered in the West. Someone else said she was sending me love and thanking me for spending time with her. I wondered what was wrong with me that I couldn't pick up messages from my own mother that others were picking up. Raja told me to say "yes" or "no" to each thing that was said if it applied to my mother.

Soon, he said we had made contact with her. His face became blank, and he became completely absorbed in channeling my mother.

Suddenly, great sobs came from him. "I'm so sorry, I'm so sorry, I'm so sorry for judging you, for not believing in you. Please forgive me."

"Well, you had a lot of struggles," I replied to my mother on the other side, longing with every fiber of my being to hold her close and comfort her. Grief moved in tidal waves through me as I denied the fact that she was really gone.

"It was very difficult with your father."

"I wanted things to be easier for you. Please forgive me for not expressing love more."

"You're forgiven," she replied.

A golden, warm glow nourished me to the core.

"Thank you for all that you taught me. I lost control of my temper too much," she continued.

"That's okay. You had reason to. I was proud of having a feisty mother," I replied.

"Is there anything you want to say to her?" Raja asked.

"I enjoyed watching 'The Girl with a Pearl Earring' with you. Thank you for giving me a wonderful life. I love you," I said, longing to see her face light up with happiness. No one could ever replace her. I clung to her presence, wanting to keep her with me forever.

"Are you ready to ascend her?" Raja asked.

I said, "Yes," hesitantly, my heart pounding with longing to hug her once again.

"Okay. Repeat after me: I forgive, and I am forgiven,'" Raja said. I repeated those words.

Then, everyone concentrated together, and we ascended her to the source.

Purnima told me that she would be held in the arms of Jesus for ninety days to receive healing. Then, after that, she would return to God. I asked him if there was really a heaven. He replied that it does exist, and that it is a beautiful place.

My neighbor passed me on the stairway, and I told him what had happened. He sympathized with sincere, compassion. I was deeply touched.

The next day, I visited with him. Guiltily, I told him I had been cold to my mother. He said that he was sure my mother knew I loved her.

A huge, gaping wound sat within me, as though part of my inner self and my identity had been obliterated. No one would ever praise my paintings and poetry like she had or light up with happiness when I walked into a room. I wanted to crawl under my covers and sleep forever. No one would ever send me money or stay up late worrying about me again. No one would tell funny stories about how cute I was. Thinking back to the summers at the beach, when she had savored every moment with her three "beautiful" daughters, I knew I would never mean that much to anyone.

My father had wanted to me to be a boy and I knew, growing up, that I didn't have any value in his eyes. I was just a silly, pea brained woman who he could not talk to about medicine, physics or world history. However, my mother had saved me.

I couldn't wait until the next Satsang. I walked into the room and a wave of peace and love massaged my grieving heart. People were sitting down in the navy blue back jacks arranged in rows on the floor. Raja sat very still. His spine was perfectly straight and his eyes were closed in meditation. I did the same. After about five minutes, he softly told everyone they could open their eyes.

"Some of our teaching in this lineage is done by telling stories," he said in a kind, gentle voice. Then he proceeded to tell one such story.

There was a certain man named Danish who had a pomegranate tree. One year, his pomegranate tree bore exceptional fruit. He selected three of the best and took them to the palace as a gift for the Emir. He was generously rewarded for his thoughtfulness.

Some months later, Danish's turnip crop proved unusually fine, so he filled a basket with the best turnips and set out for the palace. Just then a neighbor, who knew where Danish was going called out, "How can you give the gift of turnips to an Emir? Shame on you! Take him something grander and sweet. Take him some figs!"

Danish thought about it and decided that his neighbor was right. He arrived at the palace with a basket of figs. It just so happened that the Emir was in an angry mood so, instead of rewarding Danish, he ordered his courtiers to throw the figs back at Danish and chase him out.

Every time a fig hit him Danish cried out, "May God reward you with his blessing, dear neighbor!" and "God grant you abundant riches, dear neighbor!"

The Emir was curious about Danish's statements and finally ordered his courtiers to stop throwing the figs so he could ask Danish why he was praising his neighbor.

"Your Majesty", said Danish. "I was bringing you a basket of the largest and fattest turnips you have ever seen, white and as sweet as apples, but my neighbor told me that figs would be a better gift. Should I not thank the man who has saved my life? For had this basket been full of the large turnips, surely every bone in my body would be broken by now."

The Emir laughed and, regaining his good humor, sent Danish home with a purse of gold!

Everyone laughed gleefully. I listened to Raja laugh with abandon and wished I could laugh fully like that. He was innocent, happy and alive. Being in his presence lifted my vibrations and made everything look shiny and new.

Hopefulness lifted me, as I went through my days, observing the God within people. I couldn't wait until the next Satsang. Luckily, it arrived soon.

Raja blew me a kiss and said, "Welcome sweetheart." He expressed love so freely, with such generosity and humble selflessness. Asking everyone to set their intention, he listened with total attention to each person. Then, one of his seekers sang our mantra Om Namah Shivaya, while waving a bowl of incense, frankincense and myrrh. This was called Arati and it was meant to honor the light of God which resides in everyone's heart. After a ten minute, silent meditation, Raja began a story called, "A Wishing Tree".

There is a parable about a poor man walking through the woods reflecting upon his many troubles. He stopped to rest against a tree, a magical tree that would instantly grant the wishes of anyone who came in contact with it. He realized he was thirsty and wished for a drink. Instantly, a cup of cool water was in his hand. Shocked, he looked at the water, then decided it was safe and drank it. He then realized he was hungry and wished he had something to eat. A meal appeared before him.

"My wishes are being granted!" he thought in disbelief. "Well, then! I wish for a beautiful home of my own," he said. The home appeared in the meadow before him. A huge smile crossed his face. He next wished for servants to take care of the house. When they appeared, he realized he had somehow been blessed with an incredible power, and he wished for a beautiful, loving, intelligent woman with whom he could share his good fortune.

"Wait a minute. This is ridiculous," said the man to the woman after she'd appeared. "I'm not this lucky. This can't happen to me." As he spoke, everything disappeared. He shook his head and said, "I knew it," then walked away thinking about his many troubles.

Raja talked about how we create our reality with our thoughts day after day. He stressed the importance of thinking about what we want. He explained that what we focus on expands. If we focus on what is not working, then we create more of what is not working for us. If we send a request for what we want out into the universe, the universe sends us what we ask for.

"Think of something you want to create in your life. Make a symbol for it in your mind. Feel this symbol filled with your powerful intention. Watch it light up with your desire and positive expectation."

"Now, watch it fill the room. Now, watch it fill the entire block, now the whole city, now the state, now the U.S.A., now the world. Now, watch it moving into space, enveloping the galaxy."

"Now, see it moving through space, the sky, the clouds, the trees, coming back to you to fulfill your desires. Now, it is coming down through the roof and into your crown, filling your body. Feel roots growing down into the earth, grounding your desire into manifestation. Feel it filling every cell, atom and molecule of your body and mind so that you are at one with it. Know that God always listens to our needs and grants us our desires. Never limit the universe. Let it give you more than you asked for. Be willing to accept its great generosity and know that you deserve to have what you want.

You are a child of God and you are made in His image, so live your life like God in your own universe. You are meant to be powerful. As you raise your frequency, you raise the frequency of others."

"The goal of this ashram is global evolution through personal evolution. When you overcome a limit or issue, you allow other people to do the same. Your consciousness affects the consciousness of others. There is a story about monkeys learning to wash potatoes by imitating other monkeys. When the hundredth monkey began to wash his potatoes, then a wave of change went through the monkey population, and they all started washing their potatoes. So, by making yourself happy and overcoming your sorrows and difficulties, you are sending a wave of high frequency through human consciousness, which is allowing others to raise their frequency."

Floating with happiness, I skipped to my car. My heart felt new, like a soft rose opening in summer.

A supernatural exhilaration began to fill me when I was alone in my efficiency apartment. Sitting down at my keyboard, I would play music for hours, making it up. It felt as though God was playing through me.

When I was at the grocery store or the gas station, I would look at people with new appreciation, seeing God glowing innocently within them.

At the next Satsang, Raja told another story. The name of the story was, "Beginner's Mind".

Once, a professor went to a Zen master. He asked him to explain the meaning of Zen. The master quietly poured a cup of tea. The cup was full, but he continued to pour.

The professor could not stand this any longer, so he questioned the master. "Why do you keep pouring when the cup is full?"

"I want to point out to you," the master said, "that you are similarly attempting to understand Zen while your mind is full. First, empty your mind of preconceptions before you attempt to understand Zen. If your mind is empty, it is always ready for anything; it is open to everything. In the beginner's mind, there are many possibilities. In the expert's mind, there are few."

Raja let us consider the lesson in silence and then, he continued to talk.

"My teacher taught me the importance of having a beginner's mind. Here in the West, we are taught to be independent and to not be subordinate or bow down to anyone. It is very different in the East, where there is a tradition of a disciple honoring their guru. They start from the premise that they are ignorant and know nothing."

"Here in the West, we are raised to be confident, and so no one is willing to admit that he is ignorant. My spiritual mentor, Purnima, says, 'If you have to be right, you're dead right.' I've come to understand this. In considering ourselves right and not opening up to learning, we lose the precious opportunity to really know ourselves. When Jesus' disciples asked him what they should do, He replied 'Know yourself.' They asked Him, 'What should we do after that?' He replied, 'Know yourself some more.'"

"On the spiritual path, I learned that part of evolving was learning how to chip away all that was not me. It was like peeling layers off an onion, until I came to know the real me, the essence of me, which is eternal. We are full of voices, beliefs, and ideas that have accumulated since we were children. Most of the time, the voices are not even our own. We call it the 'Monkey Mind' when the mind or ego starts telling us stories about how we are not good enough, how we don't deserve good things, and on, and on. When we meditate, we still the mind and distance ourselves from the chatter which disturbs us. Soon, the chatter becomes like the words you see flash by at the bottom of a news report. We can watch them float by and not be affected by them."

"Now, let's do a silent meditation. If your mind starts wandering, bring your attention to your breath. If it wanders again, which it will do (that's the nature of the mind), bring it back to the breath. Keep your spine straight, because the Kundalini energy travels up the spine to evolve you spiritually. Do whatever you need to do to make yourself comfortable. Keep your shoulders down and relax."

Blissful, peaceful feelings filled me as I meditated. When Satsang ended, peaceful contentment relaxed me as I fell gratefully into one hug after another. Happy laughter filled the room as people drank the tea and ate the cookies I had set out on the table.

Going through my weekly routine, I noticed a new energy in the air. People everywhere smiled and spoke to me with an angelic kindness I had never seen before. All of my life I had been afraid of people, expecting them to be angry or annoyed by my presence. Now, everyone seemed to love me. I felt like an Oscar Mayer wiener--like everyone was in love with me.

I loved the story at the next Satsang. It reminded me of the psychic who had told me that, if I moved West, I would be a butterfly.

"The great Taoist master, Chuang Tzu, once dreamt that he was a butterfly fluttering here and there. In the dream, he had no awareness of his individuality as a person. He was only a butterfly. Suddenly, he awoke and found himself laying there, a person once again. But then he thought to himself, 'Was I before a man who dreamt about being a butterfly, or am I now a butterfly who dreams about being a man?'"

"We have a saying in our teachings that illusion and reality are one and the same. We create our personal realities with the thoughts we think, the words we use, and the actions we take. We create our experiences mainly from our subconscious minds which hold the beliefs we have accepted since childhood. Maybe a teacher told us we learned slowly, so we find ourselves learning things more slowly than we would like. Our unconscious mind likes to be right, so if we hold a certain belief, we will create experiences in our life that prove it is right. For example, if we believe 'I always get blamed', we will create situations in which people blame us so we can say, 'See, I told you. I'm right.'"

"We have the power to change our subconscious beliefs and heal our issues. All we have to do is replace the old programs we're running with new programs, like installing new computer software. My teacher, Purnima, has sent me to seminars and they have allowed me to update my software. The process I went through was like what Michelangelo said he did when he created the statue of David. He said he just chipped away anything that was not the David."

I was amazed by how lovingly and joyfully Raja interacted with his students. His jubilant laugh rang through the room like chimes, lifting and purifying the vibrations. He announced that he was going to teach a class on mastering the elements. Excited curiosity rose in me as I wondered what it would be like.

The day of the class arrived and my fellow seekers and I gave one another friendly hugs. Raja and Purnima both gave the most loving hugs in the world.

As I looked into Purnima's eyes, I felt that I transcended to a different dimension. She told me that we had been best friends in seven life times.

Raja began by greeting everyone with a radiant smile and welcoming words. Then, he explained the purpose of mastering the elements. I read the bullet points on a handout he had given me.

1. Maintain a personal sense of balance and feelings of wellbeing.
2. Assist others around us in maintaining a sense of balance and feelings of wellbeing.
3. Assist healing in therapeutic setting.
4. Purify and align each of the chakras.
5. Raise the Kundalini energy.
6. Experience enlightenment.

Enlightenment must be special I thought. I wondered what a person was like once they became enlightened. I had such a dark side, filled with hatred, fear, selfishness, regret and envy. Would all those negative qualities be somehow magically dissolved? When I observed myself and my life, I realized that I did not really love anyone. Living a fearful, animal like existence, I merely survived, joylessly, on my meager income. I had only one close friend and did not add anything to anyone's life.

Raja said we are made of the elements earth, air, water, fire, and ether.

He began talking about the earth element. He said it is situated in the root chakra, or Muladhara chakra, which contains our fear and anger. This element keeps us grounded and practical. We build our lives and earn our incomes from this energy. It can have both evolved and unevolved aspects. The evolved aspects are grounded and practical. The unevolved aspects are rigidity, stubbornness, and lethargy.

The water element is located in the second chakra, also called the spleen chakra. The Indian name for it is the Swadhistana chakra. One is open-hearted when expressing its evolved aspect and wishy-washy when expressing its unevolved aspect.

The fire element is located in our achiever chakra, the third chakra. It is called the Manipura chakra. Evolved (spiritually developed) fire causes one to be energetic and powerful. Unevolved fire causes one to be overbearing and insensitive

The air element is based in the heart chakra, or Ajna chakra. Its evolved aspects are carefree and relaxed while its unevolved aspects include being an airhead and being selfish.

The ether element is located in the throat, or fifth chakra, also known as Vishudda chakra. It is our center of creativity and communication. When evolved, creativity flows easily. When unevolved, there can be problems with speaking one's truth and being creative.

We learned to tune into our own chakras and observe what was out of balance. Raja reminded us, often, that the only person we can change is ourselves. By concentrating on overcoming our own imbalances and transforming ourselves, we would allow others to do the same, he said.

Purnima began to talk, exuding otherworldly love to everyone. She discussed her favorite sayings with us. "DROP IT" was one of them. She explained to us that the past was but a mirage and that we must let go of all the beliefs we had formed as a result of our experiences.

Her next favorite saying was, "If you have to be right, you're dead right." Observing the love shining in her eyes, I marveled over its beauty and purity. Of course, all the religious wars in history had been fought because people had to be right. I wondered when people would drop their petty egos.

Another wonderful saying was, "What is is. What isn't isn't." Contemplating my tendency to always wish things were better, I realized how much I needed to learn about acceptance.

Next, she talked about her often quoted saying, "Love is the great transformer."

It was true. Her love felt wider than the universe and I could feel it transforming me.

The day was light and easy, full of laughter and joy. I could feel the hardness in my heart chakra melting as I received the love of my fellow seekers and mentors.

My depression must feel dense and heavy to others I worried. Shame filled me. What could I contribute to the world? Not much it seemed. My lack of money irritated others and I had to depend on the government for my disability check every month. Even the government wanted to get rid of me.

Two years flew by in a whirl of interesting classes taught by Raja and Purnima. Sometimes she flew down from New York. I learned about numerology, sacred geometry, shamanic healing, the chakra system, Kundalini energy, and other sacred mysteries. Raja told his seekers that these things were only taught in the ancient sacred mystery schools. They used to require superhuman feats like swimming through a tunnel filled with crocodiles, in order for a student to be granted admission.

And here I was sitting in the comfort of the peaceful, love-filled ashram learning with ease and enjoyment. I was multi-million times fortunate.

Sometimes, we sat on the floor eating chocolate, watching funny movies and laughing to raise our vibrational frequencies.

In the fall, a sacred dinner was planned. It was to be an initiation for the students at the ashram.

All my sweet, spiritual brothers and sisters sat around a long table. We ate delicious filet mignon and lobster. The divine food was filled with a magical energy that surged through every atom in my body. It charged my cells with a profound love that revitalized me and opened the petals of my heart like a flower in the sun. Peaceful smiles lifted me to heaven. Happy laughter surrounded me like ringing bells on a day of celebration. Electricity vibrated in the air as my brothers, sisters and I joined together in the sacred mission to become more God-like. Faces glowed radiantly as the divine vibrations permeated them. I did not understand the mechanics about how the food was charged with transforming energy, but I was enthralled with the delightful mystery of it all.

Soon, it was time for the "Dark Night of the Soul" retreat. Raja's spiritual mentor, Purnima, came on a plane from New York and about fifteen students participated.

The magical day arrived. Raja and Purnima greeted me with immense love.

We learned how to acknowledge and empower one another with love and appreciation. One person would sit on the throne and, then, one after another, students would state the good qualities they possessed. Another exercise was to gaze into the eyes of a partner to see their soul. At other times, we chanted sacred mantras. Some of the time, we exchanged Karttikeyan sessions, which cleared and opened our chakras, allowing us to evolve spiritually.

A woman from New York sang songs for us. She was a trained opera singer. Her smooth, resonant voice enlivened me as she sang songs from "Camelot" and my other favorite musicals. I didn't take her singing workshop because I was afraid to spend the money. However, I gave her one of my CDs. I was encouraged and uplifted when she told me she liked my voice and lyrics.

I sat next to her on our lunch break and she talked with regret about how she had not appreciated her mother more. A pang of guilt went through me as I thought about the times I had taken weeks to return my mother's phone calls or forgotten Mother's Day. I remembered times she had reached out to comfort me, when she sensed my unhappiness. Instead of accepting and appreciating her concern and love, I had been cold.

"There's no love like a mother's love," she said in a contemplative way. I basked in her gentle energy, feeling fortunate that I had been delivered by God from my isolation.

At the next Satsang, I sat sadly. I regretted the conflict that had existed between my mother and me. She had once criticized me, saying that I went through life spewing venom. Shame moved through me as I realized that I was, in fact, a bitter, resentful, selfish woman, spewing venom in subtle ways.

Raja greeted everyone warmly and led a silent meditation. After about ten minutes, everyone opened their eyes. With benevolence and childlike humor, he asked each person to state their intention for the evening. Then, he told a story I loved.

"There was once a snake who had so much venom that the whole village was terrified to encounter it. The snake would go on a rampage, at times living up to its reputation of being a legendary killer. One day, a holy man passed by the town. The villagers rushed to him, gave offerings, and requested the holy man's assistance in ridding the town of the menacing snake. The holy man found the snake and gave it spiritual initiation. After its initiation, the snake took a vow of non-violence. It became kind, humble, loving, docile, and accepting."

"At first, the villagers were very grateful and commended it for having changed its ways. As the years went by, little by little, the villagers began abusing and throwing stones at the snake, until one day the snake came looking for the holy man in another town. The snake had blood dripping from cuts and wounds from sharp objects and stones thrown at it by children and villagers."

"When the holy man saw the snake and found out what happened, he looked at the snake, smiled and said, "Well, you could have hissed, at least."

My venomous envy hissed with resentment that I could not laugh fully, as I listened to everyone else laugh with abandon.

Raja assigned me a Master Blueprint, which was a list of classes which would accelerate my spiritual development.

Kundalini Rising

Soon, I was boarding a plane to fly to Massachusetts and take a personal growth seminar at the Option Institute. I read Will Durant's "History of the World" as I sat on the plane and in the airport.

When I arrived in Connecticut, I walked to the front of the airport and looked for a cab. I began to feel panicked as I wandered, as I did not see a person holding a sign for the Institute. Finally, I saw a kind man holding the sign for me. I breathed deeply and let out a sigh of relief.

After a peaceful ride in a cab for about an hour and a half, I watched in wonder as the driver pulled into an estate. The long driveway wound its way through thick woods full of tall, beautiful trees. Finally, it arrived at a cluster of buildings attractively decorated with natural stone sculptures. The driver let me off at the back of the dining building, and I walked into a bubble of cheerful, warm vibrations. Smiling people greeted me, and someone handed me my room assignment. The building and room number were printed on the card in bold letters. Then, they invited me to eat something. Moving my eyes over the delicious looking food, I told them I would return after I left my bag in my room.

The driver drove me down the hill and carried my bag to my room. I watched him drive away. Then, I hiked up the hill, soaring on the oxygen coming from the trees and the dazzling, bright stars.

Friendly people were sitting at tables in the huge room decorated with flags from every country. Massive windows let in the ever changing sky and the natural, wood beams gave me an earthy, grounded gravity. Already, I loved this place and, as I sat eating delicious food with people from around the world, I loved it more each minute.

The name of the seminar I was taking was called, "Revitalize Your Spirit" and the teachers were a husband and wife team.

Gentle people surrounded me each day. We sat in a circle and processed our various issues. One man struggled with an addiction to watching pornography. Another woman struggled with depression. Her boyfriend had tried to kill her with poison. Another struggled with her urge to be promiscuous. Another woman struggled with being taken advantage of by her husband and children and felt depressed. A woman, who was much younger than me, had wanted to commit suicide when her boyfriend broke up with her.

Clyde, our teacher, had a soft-spoken, kind manner. He welcomed us with excitement, love, and humor every day. When I shared that I had a problem with worrying that I was weird, he gave the depressed woman, with a husband and two children, the assignment of listening to me and supporting me whenever I felt weird.

"You are normal. There is nothing weird about you," she reassured me in a calm voice. Her short, auburn hair and blue eyes made me imagine that she was a beauty when she was young. The lines on her face and her depressed sighs showed that pleasing her husband and children had taken a toll on her.

Grateful for her loving support, I sat eating lunch with her. Feeling her pain, I listened to her talk about her desire to say goodbye to her family and go live on a tropical island. I imagined I was listening to my mother and remembered how she had escaped to the beach to paint. For the first time ever, I began to feel that being single was a blessing.

Each day, we explored our beliefs about life, ourselves, and people, and began to dismantle the ones that did not serve us, by doing the "Option Dialogue" with one another. We learned that we can choose to be happy no matter what happens to us. If someone throws a book at us, we can choose to remain neutral and not react with anger. We don't have to hang out with them, but we can have empathy and realize that their action is a misguided call for love. "Forgive them for they know not what they do," as Jesus had said.

The founder of the Institute talked to us, communicating sensitively, with great compassion. Hope for happiness rose within me as I listened to him.

"We can learn to detach from events and stop making up stories about them. It is not the stimulus or event that upsets us. The thing that causes suffering is the story we make up about what happens to us and the beliefs that we form."

Before each class, everyone lined up at some cushioned benches and drummed on them to welcome in the teacher. This was a fun time with people jumping, jogging in place, shouting with glee and dancing. The air crackled with vibrant, electrical energy.

I did a private dialogue with our female teacher. I told her how I had brought suffering to myself by getting involved with the wrong men. At the end of the dialogue, I felt confident that I would not make a bad choice again.

My roommate had auburn hair. She said she had been teased about the redness of it when she was young and had always felt weird.

"You talked in your sleep last night," she told me one morning.

"What did I say?" I asked.

"You said, 'Why do you mock me?' You said it in a really whimpering voice."

"My grandmother used to stay in my room, and she told me I would talk in my sleep," I said.

We walked up the hill and talked over a delicious breakfast. Sun streamed through the glass walls. My friend smiled sweetly, and I relaxed into her presence. Her cheerful talk about her life in Arizona and her work with children uplifted me.

All around me were happy, friendly people. I observed the behaviors of talkative people who connected well with others. Wishing I could be like them, I tensed my shoulders and wracked my brain for something to say. The entire breakfast passed, and I did not utter a word.

As I walked back to my room to get my notebook and pen, I felt like a social failure.

The next day, I told the teacher and students that I wanted to be more talkative. My peers responded compassionately, telling me that they liked me the way I was. They encouraged me to accept myself the way I was.

Safe, secure, happy feelings filled me as I ate delicious food, walked through the woods, laughed and processed issues with my gentle friends. No one judged. There was unconditional love and acceptance in this lovely, childlike, magical place. With each new day, my defensive armor softened and my heart opened to the hearts of my classmates.

I went back there many times, and each time I began to feel more alive and happy.

The next training on my Master Blueprint was Non-Violent Communication with Marshall Rosenberg in Albuquerque, New Mexico. The exotic landscape of New Mexico intrigued me. Once, I saw a porcupine sitting in a tree.

Our building was on a large plot of ground beside a Catholic school. In the afternoons, I watched cute children in crisp, clean uniforms getting onto the school bus. My twin bed was comfortable and I slept deeply. My roommate talked about her struggles with her son who was addicted to heroin.

Marshall Rosenberg was a funny, charming man. He played his guitar and sang songs before we started each day, and he radiated love and kindness. Everyone sat in a circle around the huge room, around 8 a.m. when the day began. He asked if anyone wanted to share feelings, needs, or requests. In an orderly way, people shared their needs and feelings. After someone shared, they listened to expressions of empathy from around the room.

Hearing about how he had brought peace to ghettos, to gangs, to prisons, and to warring people in Israel and around the world amazed me. He could have lived a comfortable life as a psychologist in private practice, and he chose to give that up to devote his energy to world peace.

One day, the husband and wife team had us go through an exercise together. We spread big sheets of paper on the floor and wrote out each step of resolving conflict using non-violent communication. Two people acted out a conflict, and we listened to both sides. There was empathy for both. The person who was attempting to fulfill their needs was rebuffed and harshly refused again and again. Yet, with respectful, controlled patience, they continued to ask for what they wanted.

Finally, the other side felt so respected and understood, that they gave in and a peaceful agreement was reached between them. I beheld the process with awe, thinking what a wonderful world it would be if everyone felt respected and heard. I regretted the times I had judged the people who got angry at me. I had labeled them incorrectly, and thought of them as monsters. They were just humans, like me, attempting to have their needs met.

Marshall often talked about jackals that we have inside ourselves. They criticize, destroy, judge, label, and attack our inner self and other people. When we hear the voice of the jackal, it is important to balance it with a voice of empathy.

"Yes. I understand that you have a need. Yes, I empathize with your problem. I hear your pain, and I care."

"Listening with compassion is the most powerful way in existence to vanquish anger," Marshall said.

Eating lunch in the cafeteria was great fun. One day, when I was walking to lunch, I saw a road runner darting down the side path. Another time, I saw a sloth hanging in a tree. While I was eating a vegetable plate, an Oriental woman encouraged me to make a treasure map. She told me she had cut pictures from magazines of things she desired and glued them to a

Kundalini Rising

piece of paper. Then, she had looked at it every day and affirmed that she would manifest them. Her eyes sparkled as she exclaimed that every desire had been granted to her by the universe. It sounded like a fairy tale or like Aladdin's lamp. I doubted that it would work for me.

Every day I basked in a contented feeling of belonging as I talked with various souls from around the world. To begin each day, we sat in a big circle and shared needs, requests, and feelings. I imagined I was a Native American living peacefully in a tribe. Americans were too isolated, without community support. That was the reason for the rampant anger in society, I reflected. People were expected to pull themselves up by their bootstraps and handle all their difficulties by themselves.

Faces became softer and voices more loving as each new day brought exchanges full of laughter, hope, tears, learning, and empathy. I could ask for empathy, and I did. My guardedness dissolved as I expressed myself to the group of fifty or more and received understanding. I immersed myself in the joy of belonging to a family.

I met a kind man who suffered from arthritis. His fingers were swollen, and he said it was extremely painful. Yet, he spoke with such loving gentleness that I was impressed. I wanted to be like him, cleansed of the bitterness and anger, which seethed under the surface of my easy-going nature.

I also met a woman named Rhonda, who was my age and worked for the federal government in Washington, D.C. She had thick, dark, shoulder-length hair and big, brown eyes. Like me, she was unmarried. I sensed a loneliness in her that I identified with.

The corruption that government officials engaged in disturbed her. She wanted to retire early. Her father was a medical doctor like mine had been. I empathized with her when she said he refused to listen to her positive experiences with alternative medicine. The humiliating way he responded to her made her feel stupid. She mirrored exactly my frustration over not having a voice with my father.

Another woman was afflicted with muscular dystrophy. One day, when everyone was sitting in the big circle, she said that her father beat her often when she was growing up. Her siblings treated her like a nuisance and wouldn't help her, even though they were rich. Deep hurt poured out in her sobs.

I enjoyed helping her arrange things in her room one afternoon. Watching her maneuver her way, day after day, in her wheelchair, I admired her determination. Whenever she talked, she made people laugh. It was a great quality that I wanted to imbibe.

I didn't want to leave after the program was over. I became so enthralled with talking to the people surrounding me that I completely forgot the day and time of my departure flight. Suddenly, I gasped with horror when I realized my plane would be taking off in fifteen minutes.

My kind teacher, who assisted Marshall, took me under his wing, compassionately, when I told him I was disabled. He talked with a beautiful woman with sweet, brown eyes and wavy, dark hair.

She took me to the airport and talked with the reservations clerk. After speaking up on my behalf and even explaining that I was disabled for quite some time, she could not get me onto another flight. So, with great generosity, she paid three hundred and fifty dollars for me to fly back home.

"All I ask is that you be compassionate toward others."

Her kindness rolled through me like a cleansing wave. I drank in the sweetness in her voice as she handed me my ticket and wished me the best of everything. Her radiant smile comforted me. I relaxed into her merciful hug and then turned and walked toward my gate. Throughout my flight, I contemplated about the love I had been given.

A few days after I got home, I headed to the airport again to take another personal growth seminar at the Institute in Connecticut. Memories of the fun I'd had the first time flitted through my mind as the cab driver drove me through the dark.

When I arrived at the magical place in the woods, I softened and relaxed like I was walking into my own home. The driver carried my bag to my room and then dropped me off at the dining hall.

Friendly people greeted me, and I recognized some of them from my first class. I listened to them talk with excitement about incredible improvements they had made in their lives. A woman who worked in real estate glowed with vibrancy as she talked about how happy she was as a result of taking these classes. A skeptical part of me resisted, feeling cynical and doubtful. I realized that was the jackal part of me Marshall Rosenberg had talked about. Another name for it was "ego", I realized. It wanted to keep me fearful and limited.

In my years of solitude, I had forgotten how great it was to be with people. Everyone I talked to had a wealth of experience and many valuable life learnings to share with me. I listened to an interesting man, from the Bahamas, talk about his field trips digging for ancient treasures. He taught anthropology at a university in his town.

A beautiful woman with shoulder-length brown hair, a heart-shaped face, and innocent dark eyes told me about the incredible improvements her autistic child had made since she began the autism program.

The Institute had been founded by the parents of an autistic child. They had made attempts to connect with their child who would not make eye contact or speak. He spent his time lost in a trance, spinning plates on the floor repeatedly or staring off into space. The experts had said he would need to go into an institution.

His mother had sat with him for hours, day after day, entering his world by joining in his activities, using her intuition. When he spun a plate, she spun a plate. When he flapped his arms, she flapped her arms.

Finally, one day he made eye contact with her and called her "Mommy". She was so overjoyed that her method had brought him out of his isolated world, she decided to share it with other parents who had autistic children.

One evening, I went to sit in a comfortable room, eat popcorn, and watch a movie about the founders and their experience with their child. Tears ran down my face as they went from institution to institution, getting grim predictions of their child's future.

Laughing with my friends in class the next day, I wrote a list of things I wanted to erase from my life and things that I wanted to have. We shared with one another about our experiences of each other. The anthropologist told me that I seemed so afraid all of the time that it made him want to not talk to me. Self-consciousness came over me. Everyone must be repelled by my energy.

My teachers told me that I could choose to be happy. I did not believe them at first. Then, I went through the dialogue process with a partner a few times. I realized that I could free myself of negative reactions by upgrading my beliefs to ones that served me.

One night after dinner, I went to a big room with a classmate and danced to lively music. As I leaped and twirled and spun around like a ballerina, I imagined I was a child again. A new optimism and love for life burned within me as my trust in people grew. A new life had begun for me, and I could feel it in my bones.

I had the opportunity to get to know the autistic child of the Institute's founders. He was a delight, as lovable as a big teddy bear. With humor and humility, he taught a class for singles called "Never Settle". In a personal growth exercise, he had us create signs with magic markers that stated our attraction caption. We each were given a list of the various attraction captions. It included "Little Girl", "Vamp", and "Femme Fatale" etc. Laughter filled the air as the intrigued students looked into their past to discover the behaviors we had used in the past to attract boyfriends or girlfriends. People wore signs like "Little Girl", "Femme Fatale", "Vamp", and so on and mingled around the room.

I seemed to have entered an enchanted forest. It reminded me of a Disney movie my grandmother had taken me to see called the Gnome Mobile. In the movie, fairies that looked like flowers danced and played in the forest. As I walked back to my clean, comfortable room, I listened to the gurgling stream, imagining it was the voices of my dead parents. Talking to their spirits, I thanked them for the money they had given me.

The days were full of love, laughter, tears, hugs and encouraging words. Riding bikes, exploring the nearby town, eating good food, and doing dialogues with people from around the world filled me with happiness. Getting to know myself and my subconscious beliefs gave me a new feeling of stability.

The day came when I had to leave. Tears filled my eyes as I told my encouraging friends good bye. Reading Will Durant's history of the world, I cringed with shame over how little history I had learned in college.

When I got home, gratitude for my choir poured through me. I made an effort to say hello to everyone and to sing to the best of my ability. The rehearsals were full of lightness and ecstatic music. My father's David, directed us with humor and passion and he felt like a brother to me. His funny jokes and stories sent the singers into gales of laughter. The soloists seemed so confident. I wanted to be like them.

Purnima came and taught a Karttikeyan yogic method workshop at the ashram. When I told her I had lost both of my parents, she said that she would send them healing energy and give them great bliss in the spiritual world. Her extraordinary hug sent peace through all my cells.

Sometimes on Sunday mornings, when I sang in the choir, tears began streaming down my face. I looked at the pews where my parents used to sit

Kundalini Rising

feeling utterly alone in the world. No one asked me if I was alright, handed me a handkerchief or anything. One of the soprano soloists looked at me as though I was strange. Though I needed a friend, I could not get a word in when the choir members started talking. They had known one another for a long time. I meant nothing to them. Every time I was with them, I felt invisible.

I went back to the Institute for a third time. As I did more and more dialogues, I uncovered beliefs which I had carried since childhood. They were limiting me, and I made the decision to drop them.

The next class on my Master Blueprint was a two month long training in Hatha Yoga. It was in the Catskills Mountains up above the Hudson River. We wore white pants and yellow shirts and attended classes in yoga postures, breathing, anatomy, Bhagavad Gita, chanting and philosophy.

At six in the morning, we started the day with pranayama and yoga stretches. Then we went to a thirty minute, silent meditation. After that, we chanted for half an hour. People rang bells and shook tambourines and rattles. Someone played a harmonium. The atmosphere was happy and light as the sunshine streamed in golden beams of healing energy through the windows.

The teachers were excellent at their practice of yoga. The pretzel shapes they twisted themselves into amazed me. Their strength was remarkable and I stared in awe as they stood on their hands and heads.

My body resisted, with weakness and stiffness, as I struggled to move my limbs into the various Yoga poses. With painstaking, overwhelming effort, I held long poses. Attempting to stay in balance while doing a tree pose I blushed, wavering and wiggling like a limp noodle.

Yet, my hopes rose as, each new day, I felt my body growing stronger and more flexible. Waking at five a.m., we did yoga for an hour, then meditated and chanted for an hour, then went to classes, then did karma yoga--washing pots and pans or cleaning bathrooms.

Tiredness would overcome me in the afternoon. It was a pleasant tired though. My body, mind, and heart vibrated with fresh new energy. The sweet people who surrounded me filled me with the sensation that all was well.

Sometimes, I sat in a sauna with my classmates. The warm, moist steam seeped through me and, like a hothouse orchid, I felt myself opening to the purity and peace of God, absorbing it into my inner being. A kind guy from Montreal talked about his experiences at the yoga center there. He said he had improved his life greatly by regularly practicing yoga.

One day, I treated myself to a relaxing session in which warm sesame oil was poured over my body. My muscles felt as though they were melting as I went into the most profound relaxation I had ever known. For the rest of the day I floated in bliss, as light and fluffy as a cloud.

At mealtime, I did not talk much with my classmates. I greatly enjoyed listening to them though. One evening, a man gave a sitar concert of classical Indian music. The angelic, dreamy notes vibrated in the air like messages from God. People sat in peaceful trances, eyes closed, breathing deeply, and reveling in the spiritual sound.

On the weekends, we took nature walks. Someone would pull a long rope and ring a huge, red bell which was up high in a stone tower. When everyone had gathered, we would begin our five mile walk. Listening to singing birds, watching scampering squirrels and chipmunks, I marched, like a peaceful warrior, with brothers and sisters from all around the world, enjoying the peaceful harmony.

A pretty blonde woman from Italy gave me attention when I struggled with learning the Sun Salutation. At the end of her stay, she asked someone to take care of me.

One of my roommates was from Montana. She had a boyfriend, and she said she couldn't wait to have babies. The other one was Spanish and was from New York City. She also had a boyfriend. They both complimented me and said they loved rooming with me.

I wanted their approval. When they told me the Indian doctor next door bothered them by talking too loudly too late in the evening, I went and knocked on his door. I politely asked him to be quiet. They praised me for my bravery and thanked me with great sincerity. I loved the feeling that I was a contribution to them. I had often felt like a mere nuisance in other people's lives, and it meant the world to me to feel useful.

We had a great time laughing while studying for our anatomy finals. One beautiful afternoon, my studying partner started singing, "Oh, the thigh bone's connected to the knee bone." I started singing with her and soon we were rolling on the floor, laughing uproariously. Our vibrations rose, like helium balloons, elevating us to ecstatic heights above the physical world.

Kundalini Rising

We shed our shells and became one--floating, flying, celebrating, and at one with our source.

When I wasn't in yoga class or anatomy class or in the kitchen washing pots and pans, I would work in the garden. I enjoyed pulling weeds with a woman who had lost her mother a year ago. She was grieving, she told me. Hoping to say the right words, I told her that I was sorry.

The people I was with day after day felt more and more like family and, at the end of my two-month stay, I did not want to leave them. A kind woman who was my age and worked as a nurse, drove me to the airport. Watching her drive, I felt soothed by her gentle voice. She went into the airport with me and sat with me while I ate a granola bar. After she was sure that I knew my way to the gate, she told me goodbye.

People sat at the gate with their suitcases, talking on their cell phones. Looking forward to seeing my spiritual family, I watched flashes of the people I had met go through my mind's eye. The Joni Mitchell song "Both sides now" played in my mind as the plane flew above the clouds.

CHAPTER FOURTEEN

"When Jesus heard of John's execution, he withdrew in a boat to a deserted place by himself." Matthew 14:12

"After the feeding of the multitude and dismissing the crowd, he went up on the mountain by himself to pray. When it was evening he was there alone." Matthew 14:23

Spend time alone.

*Worn-out garments are shed by the body;
worn out bodies are shed by the dweller
within the body. New bodies are donned by
the dweller, like garments.*

Bhagavad-Gita

Kundalini Rising

Once I had arrived back home, I counted the days with excitement, looking forward to going to Satsang. The magickal evening arrived. My wonderful family members were in the room meditating when I entered. Billows of incense curled through a shaft of sunlight that fell in front of me. I sat down on a cushion and settled in. I felt massaged by molecules of love and peace swirling around and through me. Soon, all the jabbering of my monkey mind stopped. Raja's words fell over me like a cleansing waterfall.

"See the platinum light of the source up above. Now, your crown is opening to the size of a dinner plate, and the light of the Source is entering like a rushing waterfall. The light of the source is filling every atom, molecule and cell of your body. Whatever energies that no longer serve you are being released through your hands and your feet."

He went on to do a fascinating talk about the science of the enlightenment process. He explained Shiva and Shakti.

"They are static and dynamic, like the poles of a magnet. They maintain the equilibrium in the universe. The Shiva energy, or God energy, is in our crown chakra, also called Sahasrara. The Shakti energy is in our Muladhara, root chakra. It is electric and fiery. Because of the spiral-like movement it makes up the spine, it is called "Serpent Power". It can be awakened by doing hatha yoga, meditating, doing pranayama--also known as "breath work"-- or by doing Seva, selfless service for others."

"When it wakes up it makes a hissing sound and breaks open a sack it is contained in. Then, it begins moving up the Sushumna, which goes from the second vertebra of the coccyx to the Brahmarandra, or opening of the skull. It is red like fire."

"If a chakra is blocked, it will not be able to move any further. This is why we clean the chakras by doing Karttikeyan sessions and other practices. There are seventy-two thousand nadis, or astral tubes, which must be purified. The mental and emotional bodies make up the astral body. The chakras and the Sushumna are in the astral body. We must observe and master our thoughts because they create negative emotions which form tears in our auric field. The auric field can be thought of as an egg of energy that halos our bodies. If we don't clear these mental and emotional stressors, they eventually become physical illnesses. This is why the mental and emotional bodies are called the "Terrible Twins"."

"Prana is life force energy which flows through us. It usually flows through the Ida and Pingala. However, when one awakens, it moves into the Sushumna (the central channel.) This is why the Middle Way is often talked about in various religions. The Kundalini rises through all the chakras and eventually unites with Lord Shiva, God, or the Source in the crown."

"The Kundalini is awakened at various speeds depending on the degree of purity, the stage of evolution, and the amount of debris remaining in the nadis. One can assist oneself in evolving spiritually by doing selfless service because this dissolves the ego. Also, having a pure diet, avoiding processed foods, and eating less speeds the process. Regular, consistent meditation is necessary, as well as the practice of watching one's thoughts. Doing asanas--or "hatha yoga"--and pranayama also moves the Kundalini energy along. Sometimes it crawls and sometimes it jumps."

I was fascinated. There was such a divine, wonderful order in the universe. God had it planned beautifully, I thought in awe. He'd planned it to every last detail. I was a microcosm of the macrocosm, so I contained all the energy of the planets and stars. It was all a marvelous, mysterious paradox. Raja had once said, "Every truth is but a half truth." Another time he said, at the beginning of Satsang, "This is not the truth. The truth cannot be taught by any teacher because it is unfathomable."

Everyone drank tea and ate cookies after Satsang(which means 'in the company of the truth'). Happy laughter rang through the room as people conversed. All was well in my world.

Our beloved Raja decided to teach a course called, "Keys to the Kingdom." At every class, the temple vibrated with energy, and love and joy rippled through the peaceful air. My brothers and sisters smiled and their faces glowed as we learned the principles of the universe.

"When you change the way you look at things, the things you look at change." This was one of the important principles we learned. I realized that I must start looking at my life in a different way in order to break out of negative patterns of thinking.

We also learned that for every action, there was an equal reaction. "As you sow, so shall you reap", Jesus had taught.

Learning that I was a microcosm of the macrocosm, I felt fascinated.

Astrology had seemed like silly superstition to me. However, I learned that Uranus and Saturn are in our root chakras. Jupiter and Neptune are in our second chakra, our emotional body. Mars and Pluto are in our third chakra, our mental body and achiever. Venus is in our heart chakra. Mercury is in our throat chakra. The sun is in our third eye chakra and the moon is in our Medulla Oblongata. Feeling like I was on a psychedelic acid trip, I pondered the miracles of the cosmos.

One weekend, Raja taught a course in shamanism. I had great fun clearing my partner's aura with a feather. We were taught how to open portals to the Lower World and Upper World. Our teacher told us we could choose to go to either place. I chose to go to the Lower World. As I moved through my Lower World, I saw hundreds of tortoises. They were all sticking their necks out.

Later that evening, I sat in the dark silence of my bathroom, connecting with the tortoises and contemplating that I must start sticking my neck out and coming out of my shell.

I couldn't wait for the next Satsang. When I arrived, Raja greeted me with a bright smile, a holy kiss, and a warm hug. Incense burned, so it smelled like a flower garden. I watched candles burn beautifully on an altar which was full of beautiful photos of Krishna, Mahavatar Babaji, Lord Elmorya, Jesus, Buddha and other Ascended Masters of the Great White Brotherhood. They were working day and night to elevate the consciousness of their lost children who struggled on earth. The love of God or "the source" as my teacher called him washed through me, calming and comforting me. My divine brothers and sisters sat in back jacks on the floor meditating. I sat down, soaking in the peace.

After ten minutes of meditation, Raja asked everyone to state their intention. I listened to everyone's intention, enjoying their peaceful voices. Then, I stated that my intention was to be peaceful and happy. Raja said he would like to tell a story and he began.

"There was once a time when all human beings were Gods but they so abused their divinity that Brahma, the chief God, decided to take it away from them and hide it where it could never be found."

"Where to hide their divinity was the question. So Brahma called a council of the Gods to help him decide. "Let's bury it deep in the earth", said the Gods. But Brahma answered, "No that will not do because humans will dig into the earth and find it." Then the Gods said, "Let's sink it in the deepest ocean." But Brahma said, "No, not there for they will learn to dive into the ocean and will find it." Then the Gods said, "Let's take it to the top of the highest mountain and hide it there." But once again Brahma replied, "No, that will not do either, because they will eventually climb every mountain and, once again, take up their divinity." Then the Gods gave up and said, "We do not know where to hide it, because it seems that there is no place on earth or in the sea that human beings will not eventually reach."

"Brahma thought for a long time and then said, "Here is what we will do. We will hide their divinity deep in the center of their own being, for humans will never think to look for it there."

"All the Gods agreed that this was the perfect hiding place and the deed was done. And since that time humans have been digging, diving, climbing and exploring--searching for something already within themselves."

Realization rang through me like a deep, sonorous bell, as I analyzed my crazed, obsessive compulsive fixation on moving to Glendale. My fellow seekers and I shared our thoughts about the story. Tears rolled down some faces as they talked about how the story had moved them.

The magickal energy of the ashram filled me with bliss and I wanted to be there all the time. Raja spelled magical with a k because the k represented knowledge which gives one a new life.

"Contrary to popular belief, ignorance is not bliss", Raja often said.

Once a week, in the early morning, I cleaned the ashram. As I vacuumed, dusted and cleaned the bathroom, a profound peace came over me.

Raja's business partner, Helen, taught Yoga, which greatly benefited me. As my strength and flexibility grew, my body came alive. She was full of vitality and funny stories. I wanted to be like her: confident, fearless, communicative, and successful.

Sometimes, people in the community did three hour Yoga intensives, which she led masterfully. I liked the way she went into detail about each pose. She explained the little things, like how to keep the feet together and the abdomen sucked in.

The weekly Satsangs continued to be magnificently serene and full of love.

I exchanged services with Helen's teaching partner, Purnima. She gave me polarity sessions and I gave her foot reflexology sessions. She was a

Kundalini Rising

beautiful red head with a twinkle in her eyes and a gentle, sweet manner. The polarity sessions were profoundly relaxing.

A wonderful woman who had moved from Tucson, Arizona joined the group. She was beautiful and fascinating. I did a session with her in which she balanced my chakras, by playing her crystal singing bowls which cleared each chakra.

When she told me that I had been burnt as a witch in a past life, I held my breath in horror. It was hard to believe that people could be so cruel.

We went to see the Hugging Saint together. This incredible saint from India devoted all her time and energy to alleviating the suffering of humanity. When she hugged me, I felt like a newborn baby in a soft blanket, being rocked on a wave of unlimited, unconditional love.

Later on, I went to my friend's house. I soaked in her hot tub and enjoyed her cheerful, optimistic and loving energy. She had been born with gifts of spirit and had seen ghosts since she was a young child. As she talked about her visions, I imagined being in her shoes.

"That would drive me crazy," I said as she told me about seeing deceased people standing near her, looking like alive people.

Another spiritual sister told great stories at Satsang. Growing up black in the South had been challenging for her. She had called on her inner strength and intelligence and earned her a doctorate in veterinary medicine. She healed sick animals with great love. Being in her kind company was healing and uplifting for me. I enjoyed her wonderful laugh and the way she talked about her own Master Blueprint classes. She studied with a Sufi master and the way she talked about Sufism brought a soft feeling into my heart.

Raja, the founder of the ashram, invited a group of Sufis to come and teach Sufi dances. Another time, one of the top Sufis came and gave a talk. He had written a book about his discoveries on the path of Sufism. His kind, loving eyes and gentle voice touched me deeply.

Raja had a unique way of healing people and assisting them to evolve spiritually. It was called the "Karttikeyan Yogic Method". We participated in an annual retreat in which I exchanged these sessions with my brothers and sisters.

After each session, I felt expanded and extremely peaceful. Everyone had a grand time, giggling like children and eating chocolate. We were instructed to eat it because it grounded us. With each session, I felt more in touch with my energy body. No longer did I identify with the bag of bones called "me". I experienced that I was limitless, eternal consciousness.

"Ye are Gods," one of the sessions said. It was very hard for me to grasp at the beginning, but with each new Karttikeyan session, it seemed more plausible to me that, indeed, I am God.

There was a ten-day program in South Carolina that Raja, Purnima and two other spiritual masters taught. Seekers attended in order to be in an atmosphere in which they could evolve spiritually. After driving four hours, I stayed in the home of a fellow seeker and went to the seminar from ten a.m. until ten p.m. Loving hugs were exchanged and the peaceful atmosphere filled me with bliss.

Raja explained to the group of fifteen that humanity was going to take a huge leap forward in consciousness, and that a new era of peace and love would dawn around 2160. Mahavatar Babaji had revealed this to Raja's spiritual mentor, Purnima, when she met him on the subtle planes when she was thirteen years old. Then, he had channeled the Karttikeyan Yogic Method through her and asked her to teach it so that humanity could use it to evolve.

I reveled in my good fortune as I received love and beneficial attention from the exceptional people. They were teachers, engineers, martial artists, lawyers, holistic healers, and shamans. A kind man read my energy intuitively and recommended some Bach flower essences to me.

Another woman, who was a martial artist, taught me about sacred geometry and light language. She had an effervescent laugh and told hilarious jokes. I wanted to be upbeat and uninhibited like her. One evening, she hosted "Energy Night" in her dojo, where she taught martial arts.

I rode in a car with my sweet sister from New York, who was staying in a kind fellow seeker's house with me and others. She had a warm, relaxed energy which put me at ease. I wanted to learn how to speak to people lovingly like she did. The air buzzed with electrical, transformative energy as people exchanged Reiki and intuitive readings.

After the program, she had me lay on a massage table, and she cleared away all energies which did not serve me.

At the ten day retreat, I felt awed and grateful to be guided by spiritually advanced souls. I wanted to evolve and be a part of ushering in the new earth. At times, my dark side--my ego--with its envy, fear, and anger disturbed my peace.

Luckily, at other times, a feeling of ecstasy came over me and I seemed to be floating in a cloud of peace and love. Forgiving myself for my selfish behaviors with people I loved, I worked on accepting my flaws and human weaknesses.

The ten day retreat ended and no one wanted to leave because they were flying high on love, laughter and joy. Driving back to Madison, I contemplated about all the magickal knowledge and the love I had received.

At the next Satsang, Raja talked about santosh, which is the Sanskrit word for contentment. One of the qualities of an enlightened person is this experience of santosh, even in the midst of difficulties. He talked about the process and science of enlightenment again, and I listened closely.

"A person becomes enlightened by moving the Kundalini energy from the base of the spine to the space between the eyebrows, otherwise known as the "third eye"."

"The first chakra deals with survival. The second chakra deals with emotions. The third chakra is about achievement. The fourth chakra is love and compassion. The fifth chakra is communication. The sixth chakra deals with psychic abilities, and the medulla oblongata provides mystical clairvoyance. The seventh chakra is our connection with the Source, or God." I had many issues and knew that my chakras needed much cleaning.

Raja and Purnima taught workshops that I loved. As I observed them interacting, I was deeply touched by the love between them and their earnestness about creating a new, better world. As they smiled, with the sweetness of angels, their eyes shone with love. My inner being became light and joyful and I floated on a cloud of peace when they hugged me.

One workshop was called, "The Enlightenment Intensive". People paired off and did dyads with one another. "Tell me who you are," one partner would say. Then, the other would respond with whatever came into their mind. This continued for ten hours.

Luckily, we had an hour lunch break midway through the process. It was a wonderful experience of loosening my grip on the labels I identified with. By the end, I was saying, "I am light. I am consciousness."

I continued going to Satsang once a week. The other spiritual seekers greeted me with warm hugs every time. My everyday life became lighter and easier. My thoughts changed from regrets to relaxed acceptance of all of my life's experiences. Purnima often said, "What is is. What isn't isn't." My fear of people melted away and my confidence increased.

One lovely day, she taught about lucid dreaming and numerology. It was not only interesting but also practical. Lucid dreaming could assist me to achieve goals and numerology gave me greater understanding of myself and my needs.

After the class, I drove her to the hair salon. When she reached out and took my hand, I felt healing energy uplift me.

She had students around the world. One of them, Karttikeya, traveled from Glendale to do breathing sessions with us. This breathing method was given to him by Mahavatar Babaji. It allows a person to release old emotions and patterns. As they do this, they evolve.

Karttikeya was charming, kind, and friendly. Everyone lay in a circle on the ashram floor and breathed deeply for an hour. We were to focus specifically on exhaling. He spoke words that soothed me to the depths. As I breathed I felt lighter and lighter.

"You are the wave. You are the dolphin riding on the wave. Each breath you take is a hug from God. Just let it flow. You are love, and you are loved. You are light. You are energy."

At the end of an hour of breathing, my whole essence seemed to be made of light. I felt open and ethereal as space, totally free from my body, mind, and senses. My consciousness flew far above human cravings like a sweet, innocent bird. Detached from greed, envy, anger, and fear, it darted faster than light through a mesh of atoms, molecules, electrons, and protons that appeared and disappeared like magick; beyond real, beyond solid, beyond limitation.

Everyone retired to the sitting area to have lunch. I got lost in a book of photographs of galaxies and star clusters. They were beautiful beyond description. In silent awe, I wondered how the creator created such an unlimited cosmos.

At the next Satsang, Raja talked about how we allow others to overcome their issues when we overcome ours. Like the Hundredth Monkey effect, as we raised our personal vibrations, other people would respond by raising theirs. We were being led into a new age of enlightenment by the Great White Brotherhood. Mahavatar Babaji, Krishna, Jesus, the Laughing Buddha, and others were sending energy to planet Earth to help with the transition.

Kundalini Rising

My next Master Blueprint class was called Sadhana Intensive. The organization that had taught me Hatha Yoga in New York had a teaching center in the Bahamas.

Excitement flashed like lightning inside me as I boarded my plane. In no time, I arrived at the Bahamas airport. A kind taxi driver drove me to the place where I waited for a motor boat. A smiling man held out his arm to assist me, and I sat down in the boat as another man put my suitcase in the back. The sun warmed me as I admired the blue ocean and the seagulls flying below the fluffy, angel-shaped clouds. A light feeling of santosh (contentment) overcame me.

Friendly people greeted me as I arrived at the yoga camp. Walking under tall palm trees, admiring brightly colored flowers sparkling like the Garden of Eden, I felt young and innocent again.

I shared a cute, little room with a quiet, African-American woman. Our room squeezed us together, like two sardines in a can and we each had a narrow, twin bed. However, my sleep went as deep as the ocean.

In the morning, I walked to pranayama class, observing the little cabins on each side of the path, feeling as light as a feather and happy to live in this safe, Mister Rogers neighborhood. I sat in a line of about six students and our instructor showed us how to breathe through alternate nostrils. Sometimes, when I retained a breath, a rush of energy flooded into my head and caused a dizzy sensation. I would have to take in a deep, long breath. Then, I would be out of sequence with the exercise, and I would watch the others performing it well, wondering what was wrong with me.

After breathing for an hour, I went to another area to do my Hatha Yoga poses. As I did shoulder stands, warrior poses, and spinal twists, I grew strong, flexible and more alive.

I enjoyed talking with my friendly classmates at meal times and I felt myself growing healthier every day, as I enjoyed the all-vegetarian, delicious dishes. The long tables seated many people and I overheard interesting conversations.

My alarm would go off at ten minutes until five every morning. Everyone would sit in a large tent and meditate together at five a.m. The still quietness was so profound, we would have heard a pin drop. Sitting up straight, I would go into deep Samadhi, communion with God.

In my spare time, I walked along the beach. I liked listening to the waves roll to shore beneath the screeching seagulls. Raja's voice ran through my head as I gazed at the intensely bright sun.

"Now feel the light of ten thousand suns shining, without blinding, entering into your feet," he would say when giving his students a Karttikeyan session.

I would indeed feel the light of ten thousand suns shining, without blinding, moving through my feet, up my legs, into my abdomen and chest and into my third eye. Knowing that it was cleansing and clearing my chakras gave me a feeling that all was well. I called upon the elements of nature: fire, earth, air, and water. I requested their assistance as I sought to be peaceful, loving, and successful like Raja.

"Do not follow in the footsteps of the masters. Seek what they sought," Raja said.

I pondered his advice and remembered how my mother had made fun of me saying, "Are you just going to follow the guru for the rest of your life?"

Often, Raja quoted Jesus.

"When the disciples asked Jesus what they should do he replied, 'Know Thyself'."

"Then what should we do?"

"Know yourself some more", Jesus had replied.

I realized that she had been trying to get me to come into myself, to know myself. She had told me that I must work at my art to profit from it. Noticing me ignoring my art, looking outside of myself for answers, she had been concerned for me. I forgave her, wishing I had appreciated her love and created a closer relationship between us.

One day, I played with a little boy on the beach. We built a sand castle together. He was free and jubilant, jumping and running. I listened to him chatter with excitement. As the waves approached our sand castle, we tried to keep them away but, soon, the castle was washed away.

It reminded me of the story Raja had told me, called "The Salt Doll".

"The salt doll sat on the sand looking at the sea. She had a deep longing to merge with the reality of who she somehow knew she was. However, she was afraid that she would disappear and no longer exist. After all, she was a beautiful doll, and she liked her salt doll life. It was familiar, and she had grown accustomed to the salt doll way. Still, her longing to know the reality in oneness was becoming so great she could no longer ignore it."

"So she stood up and walked into the sea."

"Ahhhh, now I know I am the same as the sea, and I still exist."

I had been frightened of losing my identity, which was fragile and shaky already, when Raja said that evolving spiritually meant merging with the source of all that is. That would mean disappearing, the last thing I wanted when I already felt invisible, I thought fearfully. If I had strong self-confidence and a clear, grounded knowledge of who I was--besides a cashier or telemarketer--it would be easier, it seemed. However, I felt like I was giving away an identity I had never had by merging with Spirit. I didn't want to be a drop in an ocean. I wanted to be unique and to be recognized by others.

My pranayama instructor gave me the assignment of finding a peaceful place to practice my breathing exercises. I sat in a wooded area where I could see the ocean. Raising my right hand, I closed my nostril. As I did alternate nostril breathing, I went deeper and deeper into stillness.

After about five minutes, I changed my breathing method to the "ocean breath" method. Contracting the opening of my throat, I listened for the hissing sound of air. Deep tranquility slid seamlessly through me, deeply imbibing every nerve and sinew inside me, as I listened to the soft, hypnotic rolling of the waves in the distance. It lulled me deeper and deeper into peaceful bliss. My body started swaying subtly from side to side. Wondering what was happening, I felt awed and, at the same time, loved by a divine force. It felt like God was rocking me in my cradle.

CHAPTER FIFTEEN

"*Suppose one of you has a friend to whom he goes at midnight and says, 'Friend lend me three loaves of bread, for a friend of mine has arrived at my house from a journey and I have nothing to offer him, and he says in reply from within, 'Do not bother me; the door has already been locked and my children and I are already in bed. I cannot get up to give you anything.' I tell you if he does not get up to give him the loaves because of their friendship, he will get up to give him whatever he needs because of his persistence.*" Luke 11:5-8

Be persistent.

> *To those who know Reality, there are two kinds of knowledge, the higher and the lower. The lower is knowledge of learned books and scriptures and fields like phonetics, ritual, grammar, etymology, meter and astrology. The higher is knowledge by which Reality is known directly, changeless and eternal. With this knowledge, the wise perceive things beyond what is known by the senses. This Reality is uncaused, indefinable, without eyes or ears, hands or feet. It is all-pervading, subtler than the subtle---the everlasting Source of all.*
>
> The Mundaka Upanishad

Kundalini Rising

When I got home, I described my experience to Raja. He replied that the swaying had been the dancing of Shiva and Shakti in my third eye (ajna chakra), where enlightenment takes place. I wondered how much longer it would take for me to become enlightened. I contemplated about things he had said in Satsang. I remembered him saying that Shiva was the God energy and Shakti was the Earth energy, or Kundalini energy, that lay coiled at the base of the spine.

I established a routine of doing yoga every day at 5:30 p.m., and it did wonders for me. I also became committed to going to bed every night at nine p.m. My alarm went off at five a.m. each morning and I meditated for an hour. Going into deep Samadhi, a profound, indescribable relaxation and peace lifted me and I floated. A love too limitless for words pervaded me as I experienced being intimate with my creator, God. My worth was more than all the diamonds on earth. My worth was infinite. Now I understood the saying that God could count every hair on my head. If I would just let him in, he was always available to assist me.

I counted the days until the next Satsang. Pondering the wonderful things I was learning, I felt grateful that I was starting to understand the Yogi and the Christ dimensions of the teachings. However, I knew nothing about Taoism.

Love poured from the friendly spiritual seekers when I arrived for Satsang. Raja asked everyone to state their intention for the evening. Then, he told a story about Taoism. It was called The Tao Rainmaker.

"There was a great drought where the missionary Richard Wilhelm lived in China. There had not been a drop of rain and the situation became catastrophic. The Catholics made processions, the Protestants made prayers, and the Chinese burned joss sticks and shot off guns to frighten away the demons of the drought, but with no result. Finally, the Chinese said: We will fetch the rain maker. And from another province, a very small old man appeared. The only thing he asked for was a quiet little house somewhere, and there he locked himself in for three days. On the fourth day clouds gathered and there was a great rainstorm at the time of the year when no rain was expected, an unusual amount, and the town was so full of rumors about the wonderful rain maker that Wilhelm went to ask the man how he did it."

"In true European fashion he said: 'They call you the rain maker, will you tell me how you made the rain?' And the old man said: 'I did not make the rain, I am not responsible.'

'But what have you done these three days?'

'Oh, I can explain that. I come from another country where things are in order. Here they are out of order, they are not as they should be by the ordinance of heaven. Therefore, the whole country is not in Tao, and I am also not in the natural order of things because I am in a disordered country. So I had to wait three days until I was back in Tao, and then, naturally, the rain came.'"

Breathing deeply, I pondered, feeling grateful that I now had a chance to come back into order myself. Lightness lifted me as I heard my mentor's joyful laugh and absorbed the love in his eyes. Next, he performed a shamanic healing for everyone.

After the healing, everyone talked and drank tea. Raja told me my next Master Blueprint seminar was to take place in Salt Springs, Florida.

Later in the month, Raja's spiritual mentor, Purnima, asked me to pick up three of my Northern spiritual sisters there.

Munching on rice cakes with peanut butter and chugging down Gatorade, I drove down to Florida. I arrived at the airport five minutes before my sisters walked off of their plane.

Just a half a minute after I arrived at their gate, they walked toward me, beaming with happiness. Kindness radiated from their faces, and my heart blossomed as they put their arms around me in a grateful embrace.

We walked toward my car and jammed their suitcases into my trunk. As I drove us to the Yogi Amrit Desai Institute of Amrit Yoga Nidra, their light laughter and conversation uplifted me greatly.

When I got to my room at the Institute, I put my clothes into my drawers and made up my bed, feeling like I was in college again. My spiritual sisters reclined on their beds and I commented that they were probably not used to the hot weather we had down south.

I walked down to the pier and looked over the pretty salt marsh with its brown cat tails, dragonflies flying, and fish jumping. A low crooning came from some bullfrogs, and a bird sang from a Cyprus tree. The aroma of sand, salt, and algae mingled with the scent of honeysuckle. A warm, contented drowsiness came over me.

Kundalini Rising

Classes would not start until the next day. My stomach grumbled with hunger as I walked up the path to my room. My roommates were lounging on their beds, laughing and talking. I flopped down on mine and drifted off to sleep.

A sweet voice woke me and asked me if I'd like to get something to eat. I was hungry and I replied, cheerfully, that I would. Following my three friendly seekers up the hill toward the dining hall, I admired the elegant grounds. They were artistically created, with flowers and sculptures.

People sat and conversed in the dining hall. The aroma of vegetarian food brought back memories of coming home to delicious pots of vegetable soup my mother had lovingly cooked. I served myself from the banquet table and sat down with my friends.

When classes began the next day, I listened to the daughter of Yogi Amrit Desai. Yogi Amrit Desai was in his eighties so, even though he was the founder, his daughter taught the classes.

She was strikingly beautiful, with dark hair and eyes, and had a commanding, yet gentle, speaking voice. Her style of teaching was very conducive to learning. I enjoyed reading our assignments. Her soothing voice lulled me into a comfortable, secure state when I lay back on my mat to begin a *Yoga Nidra* session.

"Lie down on your back and assume a comfortable position," she said. "Close your eyes and make any adjustments to make your physical body comfortable. Allow your feet to be slightly apart. Allow your arms to be slightly away from your body in Shavasana, the corpse pose. Once you adjust your body and get comfortable, it's very important for you to remain perfectly still for the duration of the session. This session is about completely letting go of all doing and embracing *being*. So simply command your body in the silence of your heart, 'Be still and know that I am God. Be still and know that I am God.'"

"Yoda Nidra literally means "yogic sleep." Unlike ordinary sleep, while you are in Yoga Nidra, the goal is to remain completely conscious. Yoga Nidra is like the gentle setting of the sun. The sun represents our ordinary conscious awareness. Yoga Nidra is simultaneously like the gentle rising of the moon. The moon represents the deepest level at which we are all connected in oneness. Yoga Nidra is a gentle transition from the radiant light of the sun to the reflective light of the moon. Yoga Nidra gives us the opportunity to reflect, to integrate, and to heal."

"So just relax," the master said. "As you relax, stay connected to your body through your breath and through the medium of your bodily sensations. Set the intention that while you are in Yoga Nidra no external disturbances or internal disturbances will touch you. And remain deeply connected to your intention to go as deep into Yoga Nidra as possible while still remaining conscious."

"During this Yoga Nidra session, follow the guided imagery and direction you are given, not from your mind but energetically, without doing. Know this process is Spirit speaking to Soul, so allow my words to touch the non-physical part of you without any effort on your part. Throughout this entire session, let go of all doing—let go the desire to do, to accomplish, to achieve, and to understand. There is nothing to do; there is only to be. Allow my words to touch your being, bypassing your doing and achieving mechanism and bypassing your mind, which is part of that doing and achieving mechanism. Simply feel what I am saying, and let it create a direct impact on you, easily and effortlessly."

"So in a few minutes, when I tell you to, I'd like you to take a deep breath in, breathing all the way down into your lower abdomen, and chant the mantra, 'OM'. When you chant, use the chant to release any remaining tension in your body. Now inhale deeply and chant with me: OM. Again. OM. OM. OM. OM. OM."

"Let go and just relax. Throughout the session, when I say to relax, do not do anything to relax, just relax. You sense the omnipresent field of gravity of Mother Earth, and you surrender your weight and anything you are holding to Mother Earth. Let any tension, anything you are holding and all your worries and cares fall down to Mother Earth to be turned into healing energy which will return to you. *Just let go."*

"Pay attention to your body without effort, through detached attention and awareness and become aware of any areas where you are holding tension, and simply let go, without doing."

"So just stay relaxed, and do not move. Simply stay aware and remain conscious. Do not fall asleep. At the same time, enter deeper into a relaxed state. Yoga Nidra is a process of coming down from your thinking and doing to a deep state of being."

"Begin taking in several deep breaths, breathing in through the nose and out through the nose. When you breathe in, breathe into the chest first like you are filling a balloon and feel your belly gently expand, and then exhale naturally, feeling the balloon contract. Breathe in freely, and exhale with long, steady breaths, breathing out in ujjayi pranayama--the Ocean Breath--allowing your exhale to be long, steady, deep, and uniform, and then inhale naturally. And let go of any desire to 'get it right'--there is perfection in your imperfection. You can't make any mistakes. Hesitation and doubt will simply create disturbance in your mind. Simply do the best you can without effort. So allow yourself to breathe, breathing in freely, and filling your lungs like a balloon, breathing in through the chest and feeling your belly gently expand, and then extending your exhale, exhaling in ujjayi pranayama, and on each exhalation, release the tension in your body, and the thoughts from your mind."

"When you breathe in, breathe all the way down into the root, and then exhale slowly, breathing from the root all the way up to your third eye. Feel the connection between the root and the third eye. Continue to inhale, breathing all the way into the root, and have the intention on the exhale to feel the connection between the root and the third eye. Exhale in ujjayi pranayama, allowing the breath to be slow, steady, deep and uniform without straining yourself. Do the best you can without strain or effort. Let go of the need to 'get it right'. That will only create distraction."

As the forty five minute session ended, bliss pulsated through my veins and muscles. I continued lying on my mat, savoring the profound peace.

After about fifteen minutes, I stood up, feeling as graceful and light as a butterfly. Bliss bubbled within me for the rest of the day. I felt as if I hung in midair, like a hummingbird feasting on nectar.

Giving Yoga Nidra sessions to others was also blissful. The ability to assist others in letting go of the energies which did not serve them gave me a feeling of purpose. Hearing their heartfelt thanks filled me with happiness.

In the evenings, Yogi Amrit Desai led Satsangs. Everyone meditated and chanted sacred sounds. When he read poetry full of love by Krishna, I burst into tears. Krishna was my own Higher Self. Many times I had whined, complaining that I did not have what I needed when I had had what I needed all along.

I drove my friends around the town feeling proud to be of service. I hoped they felt comfortable with me driving, remembering various people who had called me a space case.

One day, the Yoga Nidra teacher talked about post-traumatic stress disorder and how it affected the brain. I suspected that I had this but did not know for sure. As she explained the symptoms, I realized, without a shadow of a doubt, that I had it.

A new compassion for myself came over me. I realized that I had fumbled through life doing the best I could. From now on, I would stop blaming myself for being a failure. There was much peaceful, blissful, relaxing, joyful energy for ten days, and I reveled in it.

Our teacher decided to turn us into energizer bunnies the last day. She played "Superstition" by Stevie Wonder very loudly and instructed everyone to get up and dance. Pounding our feet on the ground, twirling and spinning, we jumped and kicked with glee.

My heart sank into sadness as I left my friends at the airport and began the long drive home. Their acceptance had made me feel so human. Now, as I contemplated living alone again, rarely seeing a friend, an awful dread came over me. I wished I had taken my mother's advice in high school and done something about my social life.

Through the fall and winter, Raja did relaxing Yoga Nidra and Karttikeyan sessions for everyone at the ashram.

Chandra began having trouble with the high prices out West. She had had to move out of the wonderful area near the Hare Krishna Temple, where she could walk to activities with other people. With no car, she had become isolated and depressed. So, she had moved back to Madison.

I enjoyed going to the farmer's market with her. After we shopped, she always fed me something delicious she had cooked.

Sometimes, we looked at the flowers she had planted in her garden. Other times, I gave her foot reflexology sessions. She gave me a gorgeous, green shawl with sparkles on it. She also gave me a little booklet about color healing. She told me about a miracle tonic she bought at the store we had both worked at. With excitement, she told me that it cured anything, then gave me some to take home, telling me to take a teaspoon every day.

One day, she rode with me to an office park to learn about light therapy. Sometimes, I gave her light with the machine I had bought.

She hated winter and so did I. Sitting with her and talking brought me delight however. Her face lit up whenever she saw me and every word she said was loving and peaceful.

When spring finally came, we traveled to a beautiful place, with a beach and gardens, that my mother had taken me to when I was a child. We stayed in a nice hotel and walked among azaleas, daffodils, camellias, and dogwoods during the day. Sometimes, she wanted to stay alone in the hotel room and worship her deities and give food and drink to Krishna. I gave her as much time and space as she needed.

She expressed deep appreciation over and over, saying I was the only person she knew who didn't think she was crazy for worshipping little, two-inch tall, cloth covered dolls. She offered them food and water at regular intervals, and often expressed deep gratitude to her beloved Krishna. Being needed and appreciated lifted my spirits.

One night, some musicians performed chanting of holy mantras at the ashram. It was wonderful.

Two of my dear spiritual sisters became enlightened after Raja finished teaching his

"Keys to the Kingdom" course.

Peggy, the sweet, beautiful, generous daughter of a minister started teaching Yoga Nidra. Lying on the comfortable, carpeted floor of the ashram, I listened to her mesmerizing voice and went into an altered state.

My homework was to write an original Yoga Nidra session and record it. I could not make the recorder work. She passed me nevertheless, and I greatly enjoyed each moment of her teaching.

Sometimes, Raja taught that everyone is equal to the self. He encouraged us to observe when we were looking down on someone and when we were looking up to someone. Another teaching which his teacher had taught him was, "If you have to be right, you're dead right."

In my Master Blueprint course, the teacher taught us to not place importance on being right or looking good. I realized that I was attached to both.

Raja taught me to watch my thoughts. As I did this, I faced my dark side. I cringed with embarrassment as I observed my prejudice, fear, anger, judgement, envy, cruel, cold behavior, snobbishness and self-centeredness.

He also taught me to get to know myself by gazing into a mirror. I began mirror-gazing for five minutes a day. Sometimes, it felt as though a cry of anguish and desperate longing was coming from my soul. I didn't like seeing my wrinkles and puffy eyes and longed for the days in youth when I had loved admiring my prettiness.

Mira, who was a veterinarian, taught a class about Goddess energy. We had fun and did exercises designed to allow us to listen to our Higher Selves, instead of our egos. I expressed my inability to accept that I had entered the crone stage. I wanted to be a young, beautiful maiden again. As I listened to people around the room express their feelings, I experienced that we were all one energy, one consciousness, expressing ourselves through different bodies.

Raja talked about the Mula Purusha at the next Satsang.

"It is a smokeless, windless flame the size of the end of the thumb. It is within the heart of everyone. It is the original being, God, also called the Source, from whom we were all created. Like wooden Russian dolls that you can open again and again and find a smaller doll inside. In the same way, we evolve by moving from the outer layers of our being to our true, core essence. Moving toward enlightenment is a process like peeling away the layers of an onion. When you start seeing God in other people, then you start seeing God in yourself."

As I went through the week, people looked like glowing angels to me, and I was deeply touched by their sensitivity and compassion. More and more, I dropped my defenses and began to appreciate how much people had to give.

My spiritual brother, Karttikeya, traveled from Glendale and taught us the Munay Ki Rites. The process was a lovely shamanic ritual. We practiced on one another.

"It has great power to heal the earth," he said. He was relaxed and open-hearted. I watched how he moved as though he had not a care in the world and was at one with God.

Another day, everyone lay in a circle, and he talked us through the deep breathing technique that Mahavatar Babaji had requested him to facilitate. After breathing with my wonderful family for an hour, I felt as light as a feather, like a pure parcel of energy, dancing and swimming through multitudes of molecules of eternity.

Smiling faces and open hearts surrounded me as I moved around. I ate a handful of chocolate. Raja gave me a hug and affectionately called me his "little snake".

Every day I became more aware of the divinity inside me, and was more able to accept my human side. I forgave myself for not being perfect.

At the next Satsang, Raja welcomed all and, then, requested that each person state their intention for the evening. People spoke about their intentions with positive, optimistic attitudes. An energy of support and encouragement vibrated among everyone. After everyone had spoken, he gave an inspiring talk. Then, he read a story.

"Once there was a time, according to legend, when Ireland was ruled by a king who had no son. The king sent out his couriers to post notices in all the towns of his realm. The notices advised that every qualified young man should apply for an interview with the king as a possible successor to the throne. However, all such candidates must have these two qualifications: They must 1. Love God, and 2. Love their fellow human beings."

"The young man, about whom this legend centers, saw a notice and reflected that he loved God and, also, his neighbors. One thing stopped him. He was so poor that he had no clothes that would be presentable in the sight of the king. Nor did he have the funds to buy provisions for the long journey to the castle. So the young man begged here and borrowed there, finally managing to scrounge enough money for the appropriate clothes and the necessary supplies."

"Properly attired and well-suited, the young man set out on his quest, and had almost completed the journey when he came upon a poor beggar by the side of the road. The beggar sat trembling, clad only in tattered rags. His extended arms pleaded for help. His weak voice croaked, "I'm hungry and cold. Please help me...please.""

"The young man was so moved by this beggar's need that he immediately stripped off his new clothes and put on the tattered threads of the beggar. Without a second thought, he gave the beggar all his provisions as well. Then, somewhat hesitantly, he continued his journey to the castle dressed in the rags of the beggar, lacking provisions for his return trek home. Upon his arrival at the castle, a king's attendant showed him in to the great hall. After a brief respite to clean off the journey's grime, he was finally admitted to the throne room of the king."

"The young man bowed low before his majesty. When he raised his eyes, he gaped in astonishment. "You...it's you! You're the beggar by the side of the road."

"Yes," the king replied with a twinkle. "I was that beggar."

"But...bu...bu...you are not really a beggar. You are the king! Well, then, why did you do this to me?" the young man stammered after gaining more of his composure.

"Because I had to find out if you genuinely love God and your fellow human beings," said the king. "I knew that if I came to you as king, you would have been impressed by my gem-encrusted golden crown and my royal robes. You would have done anything I asked of you because of my regal character. But that way I would never have known what is truly in your heart. So I used a ruse. I came to you as a beggar with no claims on you except for the love in your heart. And I discovered that you sincerely do love God and your fellow human beings. You will be my successor," promised the king. "You will inherit my kingdom."

Everyone sat in awed silence, absorbing the sacred teaching. After a while Raja began to talk.

"This story reminds us to see everyone as equal to self. As you go through your day, notice when you are looking down on someone or looking up to someone. It is human to make judgements and we all do it. However, as we practice seeing the spark of God in everyone we meet, we will realize more and more that everyone is equal to self. In fact, every person I interact with is myself, because we are all made of the consciousness of the Source, or God. Evolving spiritually requires that you decide to listen to your Higher Self and not your ego. Tonight, I'm going to do a session which is designed to get you in communication with your Higher Self."

He proceeded with a Karttikeyan session, which took me into profound relaxation.

"Close your eyes. When your eyes are closed, you will notice that it is very easy to relax."

"Now, I invite you to take a deep breath through your nose. Hold it to the count of seven, exhale through the mouth, releasing, relaxing. As you exhale, feel your body's content releasing, relaxing, letting go. Inhale through the nose, hold it to the count of seven, exhale through the mouth, releasing, relaxing. One last time, inhale through the nose, hold it to the count of seven, and exhale through the mouth. You have now released and are relaxed. Now, I would like you to breathe normally, watching your every inhalation and exhalation."

When the session ended, I did not move a muscle as I enjoyed the deep trance, feeling like a jelly fish floating in warm, tranquil water, beyond the aches of my body and worries of my mind. As though I was in another dimension, I floated, in astonishingly deep peace.

Soft waves of bliss rolled through me as I drove home. I slept in profound peace and woke up feeling full of passion and gratitude for the day ahead.

I couldn't wait until my next Satsang evening. Every day, I felt lighter and more positive about life. In the past, I had felt different from everyone. Yet, now I saw part of myself in everyone.

For too long, it had seemed that I was the only insecure person I knew. Yet, I realized that everyone had doubts about their abilities and weaknesses to overcome. As I experienced compassion for the frailties of others, I developed compassion for myself.

Surrounding myself with people was more and more rewarding. Much to my surprise, I began to feel like a contribution to the lives of others.

At the next Satsang, Raja told a great story.

"A newly married couple was walking along the beach when the husband noticed a thorn in the sand. He picked up his beloved to carry her past it. Five years later, that same couple was walking the same stretch of beach. When the husband noticed the thorn, he took his wife's arm and gently walked her around it. Five years later, upon seeing the thorn, the man told his wife, "Watch out. There's a thorn over there." Five years later, the man yelled at his wife, "We've been walking this stretch of beach for years. Don't you know that there's a thorn there?! Can't you remember anything?!"

Everyone laughed. Then, my teacher explained that the familiar mind is opposite of the Zen mind. In Zen mind, a person remains totally calm and patient. They do not react to the words or actions of others. A Zen mind is empty of all judgements of self and others. It is totally absorbed in the moment and sees perfection in everything, even when circumstances are difficult. A Zen mind does not react or attempt to control. It simply stays still, not thinking, just being. It is the ultimate in simplicity, not analyzing or trying to understand, just being at one, in acceptance with every moment.

Everyone practiced a Zen meditation together. After a while, my thoughts stopped. The stillness and peace was heavenly.

After Satsang, I enjoyed talking with my spiritual family so much that I had to force myself to leave.

My Master Blueprint classes continued in Madison. I enjoyed not traveling. Exploring and learning with fun, kind people, I shared myself and my ways of being that limited me. My loneliness faded as I bonded with people who got to know me on a personal level. The leader praised me when I finished my book. She also praised my artwork when I brought it in.

When she declared that she was committed to me having a great life, I felt touched. Every session I attended was full of laughs, group sharing, welcoming hugs, and words of encouragement. I began to laugh more and worry less as the kind company of others washed away my defensiveness.

All my life, I had been afraid of people. Now, I looked at the innocence on their faces and knew that they were God. I was God and everyone else was God, and life had become a celebration.

One of the leaders gave extra attention to me. She complimented me on my creativity. At a holiday celebration, I gave everyone a CD of me singing my original songs. At an event a month later, she warmly congratulated me on my singing and told me people were saying that I sounded like Joan Baez. I had always wanted to sound like her.

I had had to stop playing my guitar and performing because I had injured my shoulder lifting the heavy coffee urns at my bakery job long ago. I had stacks of CDs sitting on my shelf at home. Even though I hadn't been paid for them, I felt glad that people had at least heard my creation.

In one of my courses, I worked on a project to assist homeless people. Whenever I saw someone standing by the side of the road asking for help, I gave them money. A couple of times, I bought food for people begging outside of Sam's Club. Also, I sold some fine art prints, which my mother had created, at the Wednesday night supper at my church. The money went to their charity program for the poor.

As I concerned myself with the needs of others, my useless, petty worries faded into nothingness. Talking with a few other people in my program who were working on the homeless problem, I felt a wonderful feeling of belonging. We were united; one body working with enthusiasm to transform the suffering in the world into joy.

Raja encouraged me when I talked about my classes. He said that, when I overcame my own issues, I inspired and allowed others to overcome theirs. He said that happiness was not something that we could acquire from something in the outside world, but that it was a moment to moment choice. All the challenges we experience have a lesson or a gift in them. We can choose to learn the lesson and release the negative emotions.

The next Satsang filled me with peace and love. Raja's loving face dissolved my defenses and his sensitive voice relaxed me.

"If we listen to our Higher Self, we will experience peace and wisdom. If we listen to the ego, we will feel fear, envy, anger, regret, and other emotions that keep us stuck. It is absolutely essential that we meditate every day to give our minds respite from the constant bombardment it receives in the hurried, hectic, multi-tasking world."

Every time I listened to him, I was amazed by how clear his thoughts and words were and how he overflowed with gentle love. The love stayed with me, giving me new energy and confidence as I went through my days.

I liked the story that Raja told at the next Satsang.

"A young and successful executive was traveling down a neighborhood street, going a bit too fast in his new Jaguar. He was watching for kids darting out from between parked cars and slowed down when he thought he saw something. As his car passed, no children appeared. Instead, a brick smashed into the Jag's side door. He slammed on the brakes and drove the Jag back to the spot where the brick had been thrown."

"The executive was angry now, and he jumped out of the car, grabbed the nearest kid, and pushed him up against a parked car. He shouted, "What was that all about, and who are you? Just what the heck are you doing? That's a new car, and that brick you threw is going to cost a lot of money. Why did you do it?"

The young boy was apologetic. "Please, mister...please. I'm sorry...I didn't know what else to do," he pleaded. "I threw the brick because no one else would stop." The youth pointed to a spot just around a parked car with tears dripping down his face.

"It's my brother," he said. "He rolled off the curb and fell out of his wheelchair. I can't lift him up."

"Now sobbing, the boy asked the stunned executive, "Would you please help me get him back into his wheelchair? He's hurt, and he's too heavy for me."

"Moved beyond words, the driver tried to swallow the rapidly swelling lump in his throat. He hurriedly lifted the handicapped boy back into the wheelchair, then took out his fancy handkerchief and dabbed at the fresh scrapes and cuts. A quick look told him everything was going to be okay."

"Thank you, and may God bless you," the grateful child told the stranger.

"Too shook up for words, the man simply watched the little boy push his wheelchair-bound brother down the sidewalk toward their home. It was a long, slow walk back to the Jaguar. The damage was very noticeable, but the driver never bothered to repair the dented side door. He kept the dent there to remind him of this message:"

Don't go through life so fast that someone has to throw a brick at you to get your attention!

God whispers in our souls and speaks to our hearts. Sometimes when we don't have time to listen, God has to throw a brick at us.

It's our choice: listen to the whisper or wait for the brick. Listen to the Higher Self or listen to the ego.

This story reminded me of all of the times I had drowned in a whirlpool of negative emotions because I was listening to my ego. In my frantic, hurried attempt to gain happiness by achieving something, moving or meeting someone special, I had stopped listening to my Higher Self. I decided to turn over a new leaf and learn the lessons that my life was teaching me.

Raja explained that the soul's journey here on Earth happens in spirals. "If we don't learn a lesson, it spirals around again so we can master it. It will keep presenting itself to us in the form of challenges until we learn the lesson. Once we master the lesson by listening to and following our Higher Self, we evolve. Then our soul begins to learn another lesson. We don't have to abuse ourselves in order to evolve, like some religious orders have dictated. Our first responsibility is to love ourselves and be gentle with ourselves. Row, row, row your boat gently down the stream. Be sure to pause and notice when you are swimming upstream. Then, make adjustments in your life so that you go with the flow."

People asked questions and I listened with wonder to Raja's healing voice.

He went over the seven bodies with us again. Then he explained that our chakras are spinning cone shaped centers of energy, moving from the tail bone up to the crown of our 'heads. They get clogged with debris from our terrible twins (our mental and emotional bodies). They must be cleaned

Kundalini Rising

so that the Kundalini energy can move up the spine to the place where enlightenment happens, in the center of the head, our third eye. This was the purpose behind us doing Master Blueprint classes.

"Some spiritual paths stomp on the ego and call it bad. However, we love the ego. We treat it gently, like it is an out of control child. We talk to it and say, 'I hear you. It's okay ego. I love you. Everything is alright.'" Raja radiated love to everyone.

"When we begin to listen to our higher self, the ego knows its days are numbered and it will talk louder, out of fear of being dissolved. So, we must meditate consistently every day. It is best to do it at the same time every day. Jesus reminded us of this when he told a parable of a man, whose perfectly clean house, left neglected, became cluttered again with negative energies."

"Romans, in the Bible, has a verse that says, 'Be not conformed to this world: but be ye transformed by the renewing of your mind.' In these few words, Paul states the entire ministry of Jesus Christ. He taught us to shed limitation and duality and reclaim our true identity as a spirit and to join with our source (our father). When the Kundalini rises up the spine and reaches the third eye, we experience our God consciousness, our Self with a capital S. Claircognizance, Clairsentience and all other gifts then become available to us."

At the end of Satsang, I enjoyed talking with the sensitive souls. When I got tired of talking, I looked through a book of photographs of galaxies, stars and red dwarfs. The creator of this vast universe was a phenomenal magick worker. And I was one and the same with this being.

As I went through the week, I reminded myself to slow down, be in the moment, be grounded and available to others and to see the God in everyone. My mistrust of people transformed into awe over their innocence and unlimited love. They shone like superhuman angels as they blessed my life with their presence. Even when they behaved in ways that used to irritate me, I would see God shining within them.

At the next Satsang, Raja read "The Selfish Giant" by Oscar Wilde. Silent reverence filled the room as everyone listened, enraptured by the words.

"Every afternoon, as they were coming home from school, the children used to go and play in the Giant's garden."

"It was a lovely garden, with soft, green grass. Here and there over the grass stood beautiful flowers like stars, and there were twelve peach trees that in the spring time broke out into delicate blossoms of pink and pearl, and in the autumn bore rich fruit. The birds sat on the trees and sang so sweetly that the children used to stop their games in order to listen."

"How happy we are here," they cried to each other.

"One day the giant came back. He had been to visit his friend the Cornish ogre, and had stayed with him for over seven years. After the seven years were over he had said all he had to say, for his conversation was limited, and he determined to return to his own castle. When he arrived he saw the children playing in the garden."

"What are you doing there?" he cried in a very gruff voice, and the children ran away. "My garden is my own garden," said the Giant. "Anyone can understand that, and I will allow nobody to play in it but myself." So he built a high wall around it, and put up a notice-board. TRESSPASSERS WILL BE PROSECUTED."

"He was a very selfish Giant."

"The poor children now had nowhere to play. They tried to play on the road, but the road was dusty and full of hard stones and they did not like it. They used to wander round the high wall when their lessons were over, and talk about the beautiful garden inside. "How happy we were there," they said to each other.

"Then spring came, and all over the country there were blossoms and little birds. Only in the garden of the Selfish Giant it was still winter. The birds did not care to sing in it and there were no children, and the trees forgot to blossom. Once a flower put its head out from the grass, but when it saw the notice-board it was so sorry for the children that it slipped back into the ground again, and went off to sleep. The only people who were pleased were the Snow and the Frost. "Spring has forgotten this garden," they cried. "So we will live here year round." The snow covered up the grass with her great, white cloak, and the Frost painted all the trees silver. Then they invited the North Wind to stay with them, and he came. He was wrapped in fur, and he roared all day about the garden, and blew the chimney pots down. "This is a delightful spot," he said, "We must ask the hail to visit." So the Hail came. Every day for three hours he rattled on the roof of the castle until he broke most of the slates, and then he ran around and around the garden as fast as he could go. He was dressed in grey and his breath was like ice."

"I cannot understand why Spring is so late in coming," said the Selfish Giant, as he sat at the window and looked out at his cold white garden. "I hope there will be a change in the weather."

"But Spring never came, nor Summer. Autumn gave golden fruit to every garden, but to the Giant's garden she gave none. "He is too selfish," she said. So it was always winter there, and the North Wind, and the Hail, and the Frost and the Snow danced about through the trees."

"One morning, the Giant was lying awake in bed when he heard some lovely music. It sounded so sweet to his ears that he thought it must be the King's musicians passing by. It was really only a little linnet singing outside his window, but it was so long since he had heard a bird sing in his garden that it seemed to him to be the most beautiful music in the world. Then the Hall stopped dancing over his head, and the North Wind ceased roaring, and a delicious perfume came through the open casement. "I believe the Spring has come at last," said the Giant, and he jumped out of bed and looked out."

"What did he see?"

"He saw a most wonderful sight. Through a little hole in the wall the children had crept in, and they were sitting in the branches of the trees. In every tree that he could see there was a little child. And the trees were so glad to have the children back again that they covered themselves with blossoms, and were waving their arms gently above the children's heads. The birds were flying about and twittering with delight, and flowers were looking up through the green grass and laughing. It was a lovely scene, only in one corner it was still winter. It was the farthest corner of the garden, and in it was standing a little boy. He was so small that he could not reach up to the branches of the tree, and he was wandering all around it, crying bitterly. The poor tree was still covered with frost and snow, and the North Wind was roaring and blowing above it. "Climb up little boy," said the tree, and it bent its branches down as low as it could, but the boy was too tiny."

"And the Giant's heart melted as he looked out. "How selfish I have been!" he said. "Now I know why spring would not come here. I will put that poor little boy on top of the tree, and then I will knock down the wall, and my garden shall be the children's playground forever and ever." He was really very sorry for what he had done."

"So he crept downstairs and opened the front door quite softly, and went out into the garden. But when the children saw him they were so frightened that they all ran away, and the garden became winter again. Only the little boy did not run, for his eyes were so full of tears that he could not see the Giant coming."

"And the Giant stole up behind him and took him gently in his hand, and put him up into the tree...And the tree broke at once into blossom, and the birds came back and sang on it, and the little boy stretched out his arms and flung them round the Giant's neck, and kissed him. And the other children, when they saw that the GIANT WAS NOT WICKED ANY LONGER, CAME RUNNING BACK, AND WITH THEM CAME THE Spring. "It is your garden now, little children, said the Giant, and he took a great axe and knocked down the wall. And when the people were going to market at twelve o'clock they found the giant playing with the children in the most beautiful garden they had ever seen."

"All day long they played, and in the evening they came to the Giant and bid him good-bye."

"But where is your little companion?" he said; the boy I put into the tree." The Giant loved him best because he had kissed him."

"We don't know," answered the children; "He has gone away."

"You must tell him to be sure to come here tomorrow," said the Giant. But the children said they did not know where he lived, and had never seen him before and the Giant felt very sad."

"Every afternoon, when school was over, the children came and played with the Giant. But the little boy whom the Giant loved was never seen again. The Giant was very kind to all the children, yet he longed for his first little friend, and often spoke of him. "How I would like to see him!" he used to say.

"Years went over, and the Giant grew very old and feeble. He could not play about any more, so he sat in a huge arm chair, and watched the children at their games, and admired his garden. "I have many beautiful flowers,' he said; but the children are the most beautiful flowers of all."

"One winter morning he looked out of his window as he was dressing. He did not hate the winter now, for he knew that it was merely Spring asleep, and that the flowers were resting."

"Suddenly he rubbed his eyes in wonder, and looked and looked. It certainly was a marvelous sight. In the farthest corner of the garden was a tree covered with lovely white blossoms. Its branches were all golden, and silver fruit hung from them, and underneath it stood the little boy he loved."

"Downstairs ran the Giant in great joy, and out into the garden. He hastened across the grass, and came near to the child. And when he came quite close his face grew red with anger, and he said, "Who hath dared to wound thee?"

"For on the palms of the child's hands were the prints of two nails, and the print of two nails were on his feet."

"Who hath dared to wound thee?" cried the Giant. "Tell me, that I may take my sword and slay him."

"Nay," answered the child. "But these are the wounds of love."

"Who art thou?" said the Giant, and a strange awe fell on him, and he knelt before the child.

"And the child smiled on the Giant, and said to him, "You let me play once in your garden. Today you shall come with me to my garden, which is Paradise."

"And when the children ran in that afternoon, they found the Giant lying dead under the tree, all covered with white blossoms."

Raja cried when he finished. His deep empathy for all of God's creation opened my heart. A tear rolled down my face as I pondered the miracle of love.

"There is not one square inch of the universe where God is not", he said. People asked questions and we had a discussion. As Satsang came to an end, Raja said that there was going to be an initiation the next week. He instructed everyone to dress all in white.

Initiations were magickal happenings. Raja gave spiritual teachings to us through his gaze. He anointed our feet with sacred, blessed oil and spoke to us in appreciative, empowering words that glorified our souls and our human personalities. Great celebration vibrated in the air as the initiate received congratulations from the other seekers. Joy filled me as I sat eating blessed Prasad, chocolate which has been offered to God.

Soon, five years of receiving teachings from Raja and Purnima had passed. There had been fun and laughter. My thoughts and emotions were more under my control and I felt more spiritual.

The end of the Mayan calendar was approaching and sensational movies were being made about the end of the world. When I listened to the news on the radio, the violence and chaos disturbed me. Sometimes I thought that the vanquishing of all life on Earth might be the only hope we had.

Raja gave a talk which explained the meaning of the end of the Mayan calendar. Then, divine Shakti filled the room as we meditated for an hour.

As everyone came back to normal awareness, I read the handout Raja had prepared.

From Thomas Razzeto's fascinating article on the very special astronomical alignment occurring THIS FRIDAY at the end of the Mayan processional calendar, a 25,630 year cycle, and the end of the Age of Pisces, a 5,120 year cycle.

As we move into the Age of Aquarius and the new Great Cycle this is how it will unfold on Friday, December 21, 2012 to create the Mayan Sacred Tree in the skies above us.

Eastern Time--Venus will rise at 5:45 am.

At 6:11 am the Winter Solstice will arrive and the sun will be reborn with the days becoming longer.

Mercury will rise at 6:23 am. and will be the second object on the sacred tree.

Both will be visible until the Sun rises in a blaze of color at 7:29 am. to become the central object on the sacred tree.

Pluto will rise at 8:30 am.

Mars will rise at 9:24 am.

The Sun will be centered between Venus & Mercury and Pluto & Mars in a line creating a branch of light against a trunk of darkness, the dark rift in the center of the Milky Way Galaxy.

At 11:05 am, the center of the Sun will be exactly lined up with the plane of the Galactic Equator.

At high noon, the Sun and four planets will be virtually horizontal to the plane of the Galactic Equator.

At 5:30 pm the Sun will be virtually exactly in the middle of the dark rift in the center of the Galactic Equator, the sacred Mayan birth canal.

At 6:44 pm the Sun will set.

At 8:37 pm Mars will be visible against the night sky as it sinks below the horizon.

Though we won't be able to see most of this magnificent journey because we are in daylight perhaps you can bring your awareness to the heavenly movement and align yourself fully in your place among the stars and planets as we shift into the New Age.

A feeling of wonder vibrated inside me the entire day. Spirit spoke to us through the movement of the stars and planets. I heard Raja's voice saying we are microcosms of the macrocosm as I experienced that everyone was a part of me.

Some teachers in my lineage were masters, and I wanted to catch up with them. One of them, named Karttikeya, traveled from the west coast to do a group breathing process with us. Another master, Ambika, traveled from South Carolina to teach a class. I heard that they did sessions, as partners, to assist people in evolving spiritually. I was eager to progress so I booked a session with them.

The day of my session arrived. Karttikeya and Ambika greeted me. Wonderful memories of the fun we had had together at the Karttikeyan Yogic Method retreat flooded me. They instructed me to lay on my back on a massage table. I got comfortable, and they covered me with a soft blanket.

I looked into the large, blue eyes of Master Ambika, listening to her talk about her method of healing. It was called "Body Talk". After a brief explanation, she began. She asked my body and mind questions as she pressed on my extended arm, seeing when the muscles went weak and when they stayed strong. Strong muscles meant that she was speaking the truth and weak muscles meant that she was saying an untruth.

She said funny things and laughed cheerfully.

"I see that you are having disbelief. No, it isn't really disbelief, it's more like doubt."

Karttikeya, the handsome, kind master, from the West, sent spiritual energy to me and encouraged me to breathe deeply. His loving eyes and relaxing, peaceful voice soothed me to the depths of my soul as he tapped on my third eye.

A wave of tranquility rolled through me as I reveled in the wonderful vibration of healing support, knowing my spiritual brother and sister wanted the best for me. I breathed deeply, relaxing more with each breath and, then, drifted into an altered state. Becoming a molecule of light, I danced in celebration throughout the cosmos, far from the troubled world and completely detached from my body-mind-senses complex. Their voices dissolved as I melted blissfully into indescribable peace, as though I had entered a dimension beyond. Now and then, they tapped my forehead as I swirled and spiraled in a vortex of light, love, and freedom. Faintly, I heard a door open.

"Sweetheart, you are enlightened," Raja said. A rush of euphoria swept through me.

"Let yourself lie here and absorb the energy as long as you want to."

I heard the three of them leave the room. I floated in super sensuous bliss, feeling like pure energy, scintillating, pulsing; a pool of liquid light, detached, free, void of thoughts and emotions, divine and holy. Everything that was not me had been chipped away and I reveled in the sublime peace of my real, eternal self--the Mula Purusha. I was home at last, in the Kingdom of Heaven Jesus had spoken about.

Missing my spiritual companions, I pushed myself up off of the massage table and walked out into the hall. Raja looked at me with love and led me over to a painting on the wall of Krishna steering the chariot.

"See how his face is blue? That's the Mula Purusha. Now, imagine that every single cell in your body is a miniature Mula Purusha."

Love radiated from Raja's eyes and I absorbed it like a sponge.

Wishing him a good day, I left. As I drove home, I visualized the Mula Purusha turning every cell in my body blue.

Parking my car in front of my home, I floated. Walking up the stairs and into my room, I felt as light as air, like pure energy. Leaning my face on my hands, on the kitchen counter, I pulsated with peace, feeling stunned.

CHAPTER SIXTEEN

"He takes away every branch in me that does not bear fruit, and everyone that does, he prunes so that it bears more fruit."
John 15:2

Let go of habits and things that do not make you grow.

It is written: He who has realized eternal Truth does not see death, nor illness, nor pain; he sees everything as the Self, and obtains all. The Self is one, and it has become all things. When the senses are purified, the heart is purified; when the heart is purified, there is constant and unceasing remembrance of the Self; when there is constant and unceasing remembrance of the Self, all bonds are loosed and freedom is attained.

Chandogya Upanishad

A couple of years passed, and the time to go to my next Master Blueprint class arrived. With great excitement, I flew to Oregon to take a class in Alchemical Hypnotherapy. I rented a room from a kind, seventy-five-year-old woman who had gone to Catholic school and been a nun.

I enjoyed the long walk each morning. When the friendly teacher and students greeted me, cheeriness filled me. We started off each day by singing and praying for rain.

Then, we took out our class manuals and began listening to the teacher and taking notes. After learning some basics, we divided into groups and began practicing doing hypnotic inductions. A lovely hypnotist, who had been born in Switzerland, assisted me. We all encouraged one another and laughter and lightness fell through me like a waterfall.

I didn't want to pay the large cost of a private session with the teacher, so I volunteered to have him demonstrate on me.

As he regressed me back to a past life, skepticism gnawed at me. With doubt, I watched vague flashes in my mind. I felt like I was making them up. I saw a dark-haired man named Eugene who was a composer of music for a local church. Anger and frustration had consumed me and I had lost my spirit when my boss fired me for composing songs too slowly. He had found a more prolific, speedy composer to replace me.

"Well, if you want the McDonald's of composing then go ahead. All that cheap, fast food is sure to give the listeners indigestion," my teacher said, in a disgruntled, loud voice, speaking for me. It brought my anger up and out, assisting me to feel the feelings, speak them out, and let them go.

I stated my case. "The congregation loves my music."

I felt satisfied to speak my truth from that past life, and I was grateful to be assisted by the compassionate, insightful statements of my teacher.

Witnessing my fellow students go through past life regressions was fascinating. They talked about what they were seeing and hearing in their past lives very fluidly, as my teacher talked them through it.

When the teacher offered another demonstration a few weeks later, I volunteered again. I decided to work on my inner child issues. An experience with my mother when I was five years old had deeply hurt me. I had cooked scrambled eggs in a flurry of excitement, anticipating the happiness it would bring my mother.

Walking into her bedroom carrying the plate, along with a small vase with a flower, I remembered how cruelly my father had talked to her the day before. Setting the tray down on her lap, my heart brimmed over with love.

"Just what I love: soupy eggs!" she had yelled.

Cowering in humiliation, I hurried fearfully out of the room. As I attempted to clean up the kitchen, my shattered emotions made it hard to concentrate. I dropped a plate onto the floor.

The pounding of angry footsteps froze me. My mother came in and towered over my quivering body, glaring.

"You broke one of our best plates. Daddy won them in the National Diabetes awards."

From that day forward, I felt that I could not do anything right. Stunned that my mother could be so upset with me, I decided that I must be a trouble maker everywhere I went. Feeling worthless, I retreated into a world of silence.

"Your father was a number one asshole," my teacher said. He told the class that emotional release work was an important part of hypnotherapy.

"Yes. My father was very cruel to my mother, and I wanted to cheer her up. She had great anger and it came out onto me," I said.

"I think it's inappropriate to be cooking breakfast at the age of five. Let's do some emotional release work."

He instructed me to imagine that I was breaking the plate into pieces with a baseball bat. My mother had a baseball bat too and she joined me in the anger release session. He had beaten me so he deserved it.

My therapist spoke the words for me since I was too afraid and guilty to say them myself.

"There's your award plate!" I repeated after him, yelling and feeling my rage each time I hit the plate. I watched it splinter into pieces on the kitchen floor. In my imagination, my mother beat the plate and yelled with me, and I felt united with her in a common cause: to free ourselves of my father, the cruel tyrant.

I felt lighter after the session. I had peeled off another onion layer that kept God's light from entering me completely.

One day, a very friendly woman named Betty asked me if I would like

Kundalini Rising

to go with her to lunch. Too embarrassed to admit that I could not afford to eat in restaurants, I told her that I brought my lunch every day because I was on a special diet. Much to my delight, she told me that she was going to start following my example and bring her lunch. When she invited me to be her walking partner, I breathed in gratitude. My prayer for one on one connection had been answered. The talkativeness surrounding me when I socialized in groups intimidated me, causing me to shrink into myself.

The next day, after a morning of fascinating talks and demonstrations, we ate our light, vegetarian lunches. Then, we left the center and crossed the street. Vitality surged through me as we walked past some tennis courts, observing slender, good-looking people hitting a ball back and forth. We walked up a winding, curvy hill and under gorgeous Eucalyptus trees whose branches stretched like welcoming mothers. Lovely wildflowers waved their green leaves in friendly greetings as I listened to Betty talk with enthusiasm about her intention to lose weight.

We trekked up a beautiful path, admiring flowering bushes, moss-covered boulders and magnificent, ancient trees. To the left and below us was a lake. It twinkled in the sun and mesmerized me with its beauty. I stopped for a minute to watch a seagull fly above a group of swans, then ran to catch up with Betty. I marveled at her energy and endurance.

As she talked about her daughter's swing dancing, I remembered how much I had enjoyed learning to dance. Her caring attention seeped into the cold, dark ice cavern that losing my parents had left in me. With genuine, compassion, she let me know that I mattered. She said that she had spoken with our teacher about me, and he thought I had post-traumatic stress disorder.

We partnered up to exchange sessions that afternoon. I slowly hypnotized her, tingling with eagerness to improve her relationship with her husband. After my session on her, she hypnotized me to have more self-confidence. Her voice was soothing.

When everyone reported the results of their exchanges the next day, Betty glowed with happiness, saying that her interaction with her husband had improved. They had held hands and had a wonderful, long talk, which they had not done in ages.

"Well, I had hoped to do couples counseling with you, but it looks like my student did the job," my teacher said. A surge of confidence rolled through me.

Betty expressed her gratitude to me as we walked on our lunch break. When I told her I was going to drive into Santa Rita to visit my brother, she said I could borrow her GPS. She listened compassionately as I told her about my troubled relationship with my brother.

I shared a meal with her and her husband at their home one evening. Their lovely daughter joined us. Friendship was healing me, opening my heart like a flower, and bringing me out of the isolation I had suffered for years.

Every day of my seminar was full of mystery, discovery and intrigue. My teacher talked about curing people of cancer by talking with their subconscious minds. He talked about past life regressions that had solved present life problems. People learned how to heal their ailments by conversing with their inner healer. I was completely captivated.

Asking for help had always been impossible for me. Each evening, I walked home quite a long way. I felt grateful when my Swiss teacher, who assisted my main teacher, asked a guy in my class to give me a ride home. He was a wonderful person with a charming, British accent.

One afternoon, our teacher led him through a detailed and dramatic past life regression. I was enthralled the entire time, and amazed by my teacher's insights and brilliant ways of releasing the emotions and resolving the problems that had carried forward into the present life. I'd never known a person would talk while hypnotized, and it was fascinating to witness him remembering and expressing his past life struggles.

Every day when I got home, I went into my room and studied. One evening, when my landlord invited me to watch a movie with her, I happily tossed my books away and sat down in her comfortable arm chair in her living room. The movie was touching and sweet and we had fun laughing.

Every day became fuller of passion as I explored the depths of the subconscious mind and the vastness of experience each person carried in their subconscious mind. See-sawing between profundity and laughter, we celebrated life and togetherness. I saw myself in everyone as I enjoyed the feeling of belonging. My mind and body relaxed as my heart softened.

When the course ended, I did not want to leave. My sweet landlord drove me to the bus station at 4 a.m., and a huge bus took me to the airport.

My next adventure was coming up and excitement rushed through me like electricity. I was going to Brazil to stay in the healing Casa of John of God. A kind woman, who was to be my guide, had talked me through the steps of registering and purchasing my plane ticket. After only a day at home, I headed out to the airport again.

South America had always pulled me magnetically, and my imagination ran wild with scenes of tropical jungles, filled with colorful birds and wild animals. The flight kept me in the sky overnight. Watching a movie kept me entertained. When I got off of the plane it was a bright, new day.

My guide, Donna, had big, blue eyes and long, blonde hair. She greeted me at the airport in Brazil. Her grounded manner put me instantly at ease. With excitement, I followed her to a van and I rode in silence to the Casa of John of God. He had healed thousands of people of cancer and other serious diseases.

We arrived at a simple but charming hotel a few blocks from the Casa. I was shown to my room. It had a double bed, a shower stall, sink, and toilet, and no T.V. Gratitude flowed through me because the money grubbing advertisers could not bother me. Sex and violence could not disturb me. Velvety smooth silence wrapped itself around me like angel wings as I fell into a peaceful slumber on the soft, double bed.

At six a.m., the woman who stayed next door knocked on my door. Her friendly voice uplifted me. With her dark hair, soft dark eyes and short dark hair, she looked like an elf. Flowers lined the path we walked on and her lighthearted laugh calmed me. Soon, we arrived in the dining hall.

A colorful, large bouquet of flowers shone vibrantly against the muted hues of the walls. We got into the line, and my mouth watered as I inhaled the aromas of fresh vegetables and a variety of dishes. It was arranged in a colorful, festive way. I carried my full plate to a table, I glanced at people around the room and wondered what they were seeking healing for.

A kind Indian woman sat next to me and greeted me. The woman I had walked to dinner with was studying to be a minister with the same person my guide had received her minister degree from. They had met each other at one of his seminars. I listened to them talk lightly as I enjoyed the delicious food.

The next day, I met John of God. He sat peacefully and meditatively in a room filled with huge, sparkling crystals which emitted magical energy.

With love, his dark eyes looked into my soul. He touched my shoulder. Then, he signaled to his assistant that I needed an intervention.

A woman led me gently into the next room. I sat on a wooden pew and watched the angelic people dressed in white who kept things flowing smoothly. The good spirits were going to do surgery on me and my imagination danced. A vibration of pure love oscillated in magickal waves around me. The photograph, my guide had showed me, of orbs of light floating in the air appeared in my mind. I felt these loving, light beings invisibly working their miracles, filling me with a love beyond any human love. Like summer rain, their pure, unconditional, fathomless love moistened the hardened areas in my heart. Tender, new leaves of love grew in me as my armor cracked open and fell away.

"You've had surgery so you need to stay in bed for the next twenty-four hours," my dear guide, Donna said as I filed out of the room with the other people.

She motioned to a taxi driver. He stopped, got out and opened the back door for us. Donna slid into the back seat with me and, soon, we were back at the hotel. I put on my silky, cool nightgown and reclined in the bed. After day-dreaming about spirits and their lives on the other side for a while, I drifted off into a deep slumber.

My own snoring woke me hours later, just before someone knocked on my door. I told them to come in. A smiling African-American woman from Florida greeted me and set a tray of food down on my bed. The fresh vegetables, fruits, and fish tasted delicious.

The spirit beings, that John of God channeled, worked their healing miracles inside me while I rested. Their high frequencies raised my vibrations. I vowed to leave my selfishness behind and said prayers of gratitude to God and the good spirits. Then I fell into a deep, serene sleep.

When my twenty-four hour rest was over, Donna encouraged me to sit in the current. Surveying the packed room, I squeezed onto the wooden pew an angelic, white clothed guide motioned me to. I put a cushion underneath myself and prepared my body for the four-hour sitting. Loosening my jaws and relaxing my shoulders, I felt an energy swirl around me, like a rainbow of loving vibrations filling every cell, atom, and molecule in my body.

After the four hours, I felt like I could fly. Donna walked with me back to my room, holding my hand and assisting me to ground myself.

Kundalini Rising

Later on, I listened to my dinner companions talk about their own experiences with John of God. I marveled over the miracles.

Every time there was an opportunity to sit in the current, I took it. Donna said that I was receiving more healing than the others who did not sit in the current as much.

The days passed in love and laughter, hobnobbing through quiet crystal shops and drinking smoothies in brightly decorated cafes. Relishing the simple kindness and happy laughter of my friends, I wanted to stay forever.

The Brazilian people were very helpful on my return trip to Madison. Donna said I would need to go in a wheelchair because I had had surgery. A beautiful Brazilian woman pushed me to my gate. Memories of being pushed by my nanny, when I was a toddler, came back to me. Farewells from my friends lifted me and, soon, I was rising up to the clouds.

My plane landed and I rode the train home. Then, I snuggled up with my cat. He purred with santosh as I gave him Reiki.

The next day, I went to see my chiropractor. She told me that my scoliosis had been healed. Walking around in awe, I marveled over the abilities of the spirits who had worked as surgeons in past lives and were using their expertise from the other side. They were God like Masters, and they were sending humanity an ocean of love.

I meditated with eager anticipation of the next Satsang. Raja had given me exercises to do that would allow me to recognize individual spirits who came into the room. I had not been disciplined in doing my exercises, so I felt sure I was missing the loving spirits when they were near me. Jesus, Krishna, the Laughing Buddha, Mahavatar Babaji, Saint Theresa, Mahavatar Babaji's sister, Shiva--they were all working on the consciousness of humanity so that planet Earth could usher in a new era of peace. I sang to myself, "Let there be peace on Earth and let it begin with me," as I pondered how I was going to contribute to the transformation of the world.

I remembered Raja talking about "The Hundredth Monkey Effect" and how, by overcoming my own issues, I helped others overcome theirs. I had so many issues--love life, career, money, self-esteem.

My habit of worrying came back as I set about planning my strategy for finding clients. Taking classes in interesting, fun places for five years had been wonderful. Yet, as I thought about presenting myself as a professional to prospective buyers, I felt like a total fool. Who would take me seriously?

The evening for Satsang arrived and my cup ran over with grateful anticipation. My loving spiritual brothers and sisters welcomed me. Raja called me "sweetheart" and gave me a holy kiss on the mouth and a long hug.

Everyone settled down and meditated for ten minutes. Deep peace pervaded the air as Raja asked everyone to state their intention. Love vibrated palpably as each seeker spoke. Then, Raja read a story called "Dad's Blessings".

"A young man was getting ready to graduate from college. For many months, he had admired a beautiful sports car in a dealer's showroom, and knowing his father could afford it, he told him that was all he wanted."

"As graduation day approached, the young man awaited signs that his father had purchased the car. Finally, on the morning of his graduation, his father called him into his private study. His father told him how proud he was to have such a fine son, and told him how much he loved him. He handed his son a beautifully wrapped gift box. Curious, but somewhat disappointed, the young man opened the box and found a lovely, leather-bound Bible, with the young man's name embossed in gold. Angry, he raised his voice to his father and said "With all your money, you give me a Bible?" and stormed out of the house. He left the Bible behind."

"Many years passed, and the young man was very successful in business. He had a beautiful home and wonderful family, but realized his father was very old, and thought perhaps he should go to him. He had not seen him since that graduation day. Before he could make arrangements, he received a telegram telling him his father had passed away, and willed all of his possessions to his son. He needed to come home immediately and take care of things."

"When he arrived at his father's house, sudden sadness and regret filled his heart. He began to search through his father's important papers and saw the still-new Bible, just as he had left it years ago. With tears, he opened the Bible and began to turn the pages. And as he did, a car key dropped from the back of the Bible. It had a tag with the dealer's name, the same dealer who had the sports car he had desired. On the tag was the date of his graduation, and the words PAID IN FULL."

How many times do we miss Spirit's blessings and answers to our prayers because they do not arrive exactly as we have expected?

Tears rolled down my cheeks. I thought about my father, my one support.

I missed his cheerful, "Hi, sweetie," when I walked into the house, and the lovely times sitting on the screened porch watching squirrels leap in the old oak tree. I would give anything to sit with him now. If not for him, I would not be a homeowner or be able to travel to wonderful places. I wished I had told him I loved him.

It had been almost seven years since I lost him. Life as an orphan was very different, and I felt invisible, as close friends chatted about things they had done together in my choir. I watched other members go home to their families. When I looked out on the church congregation, I would imagine seeing my parents there and tears would run down my face. No one ever handed me a handkerchief or comforted me.

It had been so different in Brazil. When I had cried there, a woman had handed me a handkerchief, with a loving smile.

At the end of Satsang, Raja read a poem by Rumi called, "Behind All Things".

> Behind all the things and people we love is the indwelling
> Spirit. Unless we
> connect with That, we remain forever restless in love.
> A woman is God shining through subtle veils...
> loving her you love spirit not a corpse
> spirit is for lovers...
> Heart's ease, laughter, meaningfulness, love...
> Friend! you desire formless things
> You are seeking the Beloved and don't even know.

I looked at the sweet, attentive faces sitting in the circle and saw God glowing behind their eyes. "The journey is the destination," Raja said.

"There is never any final endpoint on the path of evolution because we can always spiral higher. The important thing is to stay fully present, available, grounded, and in the moment. There is no such thing as linear time. There is only the eternal *now*. Walking on this path is called the 'razor's edge' because it takes great concentration and dedication. The Taoist tradition teaches us balance of the inner male and inner female, the Yogi tradition teaches us to awaken our Kundalini, and the Christ tradition teaches us to love ourselves and others, to have humility and to serve others.

Always remember your great fortune. Remember to listen to your Higher Self instead of your ego. Enjoy every moment. If you take one step toward God, he takes a thousand steps toward you. He always listens to you and grants your desires."

Satsang continued to be the highlight of my life. However, changes happened. As Raja sometimes said, change is the only thing we can rely on.

My wonderful companion, Peggy, the minister's daughter, evolved greatly. During one of our spiritual retreats, in which several people became enlightened and self-actualized, she reached one of the highest levels of spiritual development ever reached in the Taoist Yogi Christ lineage.

Her lovely face was radiant and her deep, soothing voice always spoke with great love. I glowed with contentment when she showered me with love and appreciation. She taught with clarity, love, humor and creativity.

Raja began teaching only once a month and I missed him. A different spiritual seeker would teach on each of the other three days of the month. Each one shared a unique, special quality in their teaching.

Continuing with my local self-growth classes, I peeled layer after layer of limiting beliefs from my psyche. A fellow student, who was young enough to be my son, gave me special attention, which brought me out of my shell.

One of my Master Blueprint classes was Reflexology. Studying it was fun and fascinating. Learning how different areas of the feet corresponded with various areas of the body, I felt curious and inspired. My nine classmates and I massaged one another's feet. Learning and laughing with them, I came out of my sadness. The months flew by and I felt proud, when I received my certificate.

Raja planned a spiritual retreat and, while there, I did some Reflexology sessions. The compliments I received increased my feeling of self-worth. He reminded us to stay in the eternal NOW. Yet, I found it hard to control my thoughts, as I drifted in and out of the past and future, spinning in a whirlpool of negative thoughts and emotions.

Going to him for guidance, I longed for peace. As always, his love washed away my worries.

"What happens when you pour clean water into a cup of mud? All the muck rises to the top", he replied.

"I have negative thoughts all of the time. I just don't pay any attention to them", he continued.

From then on, I would not pay attention to my negative thoughts I decided, with determination. It was easier said than done. Soon, I felt my terrible twins, my mental and emotional bodies, wrestling with one another again. They were tackling me and I felt exhausted.

Raja assigned me a new Master Blueprint class. I overflowed with excitement as I read about the spiritual center, where I was going to spend two months. A sweet woman, with an Indian accent, registered me for the course over the phone.

Soon, I was on a plane flying to Pennsylvania. I'd always loved flying.

The plane landed and I wandered around the airport feeling confused. After telling several people that I was looking for a driver to take me to a spiritual center, I met the man with the answer. He directed me to the correct place to stand, outside. In a few minutes, an Eastern Indian man waved at me from his vehicle.

Stepping out and smiling at me, he lifted my suitcase into the trunk. I climbed into the passenger seat.

He was delightful company on the ride and during my stay at the center. With reliable promptness and compassion, he drove me to the Emergency room and pharmacy, when I got shingles. For two months, my body itched like crazy. However, the joy of doing Yoga, meditating, chanting and eating delicious, vegetarian food with loving people made me forget the discomfort.

The building, where I attended early morning classes, looked like an Indian Temple, with exquisite designs and carvings. Every day, I rose at five a.m., quickly pulled on some loose clothes, and walked under the gorgeous cypress trees absorbing soft, feminine moonlight. Inside the temple, two Hindu priests, dressed in wrap around cloths, lovingly gave their care to a beautifully sculpted statue which represented God--also known as Ishwara in Hindi. Sitting in the velvety smooth silence, I would watch them pour milk and water over the statue, while people chanted ancient Sanskrit words of love and devotion to God. The fragrance of incense deepened my meditative state.

Doing my best to pronounce the Sanskrit and follow the correct rhythm, I kept glancing from the book to the lovely ritual. Sometimes, I stopped chanting and simply gazed, mesmerized, as the two priests rang bells, chanted, washed the statue with milk and water, patted it dry with towels, dressed it and decorated it with flowers.

The energy of love for God and God's love for all circulated through the air. The sweet voices of God's beloved vibrated with a frequency which was so high, it seemed like the whole building could levitate and fly on the wings of God's love.

After the chanting, a Swami, in an orange robe, lead a thirty minute guided meditation. Then, he taught Vedanta, which is based on the ancient Indian scriptures which were revealed to the Rishis when they merged with God in meditation. Since there were no pencils or paper thousands of years ago, they were passed verbally, from generation to generation.

Riveting emotions passed through me as he talked about how humans are in a trap, swinging back and forth between fear and craving. I thought of myself searching for pleasures when he told a story about a frog who was being swallowed by a snake. The frog extended his tongue, out of the snake's throat, overcome with desire for one last, juicy fly to eat. Feeling foolish, I thought of the traps I had gotten myself into, in my search for happiness in things, achievements, places, love affairs, friendships, food, drugs and other diversions. Also, I reflected on how much I had missed because of my fears. I listened to his wisdom, feeling it was my last chance to salvage my wrecked life.

When his deep teachings ended, I walked in silent contemplation to the Yoga studio. A delightful Indian woman led us through stretches, twists and lunges with articulate clarity, encouraging and inspiring us cheerfully. Several times, during the hour long class, we did breathing exercises (Pranayama).

As I breathed through alternate nostrils, I became centered and balanced. I realized that I was balancing the Yin and Yang, the male and female parts of me that Raja had taught me about.

After class, I walked to the main building that contained the meditation hall and the dining hall. Everyone spoke with loving kindness and I realized that many people in the world were nicer than I was. My ego swung back and forth--from self-loathing and shame to spiritual arrogance. Sometimes, I felt smug because I was enlightened and people around me might not be. Raja's voice came into my mind.

"Everyone is equal to self. Watch your thoughts and notice when you are looking down on someone and when you are looking up at someone."

Helping myself to the breakfast buffet, I overheard conversations and smelled the aroma of food.

Sitting down at a table with some Indian men, I listened to them talk.

"None of this is real", a sweet Indian man said, as I sat across the table from him eating oatmeal with raisins.

It was as though I had stepped into another dimension as I listened to the mystical talk. I never heard a negative word. The soft, sweet eyes and generous words of my fellow seekers shone light into my heart, causing it to grow and open.

On the weekends, our Swami taught a class on the Bhagavad Gita. I liked the way he simplified the teachings. In life, he said, we have repeated opportunities to choose the pleasant or the good. If we choose the pleasant, we can be swept away in a raging torrent of lust, eating or other sensual pleasures. If we choose the good, we can enjoy the satisfaction of being a contribution and living with righteousness.

One day, a woman looked at me with compassion and pointed to a comfortable chair that I could sit on. Enjoying talking with her, I felt myself relaxing all over.

The next day, she gave me a nice tote bag with a design and the name of the ashram on the front.

On weekends, I had fun with my friends walking through the flea market. I felt thrilled when I bought some dirt cheap walking shoes and bedsheets.

A woman who was my age befriended me, inviting me to her room. Laying back on her extra bed, I watched a Bhagavad Gita class with her. She gave me a banana and some water.

Every time I saw her, she asked me how I was feeling and listened with great compassion. She told me that her grandmother had grown up in India and had given birth to thirteen children.

When I had free time, I went into the bookstore to read. Guilt over how spoiled I had been moved through me, as I read about people in India who had the job of picking up piles of human feces with their hands. So many of my days had been wasted in self-pity, when I had lived like a queen compared to them.

When the course was over, I did not want to leave my wonderful friends.

As I rode to the airport, I reminisced about all the sweet things people had said to me.

Happiness bubbled within me when the night for Satsang arrived. Raja sat there in peaceful tranquility. His deeply peaceful vibrations calmed me as I walked in and sat down.

After silent meditation, he asked everyone to share their intentions. The voices of my spiritual family filled me with bliss, as I listened.

Raja said that there was going to be an initiation that evening. Then, he looked at me and asked me to come forward.

Sitting in front of him, I looked into his eyes which exuded an ocean of love and wisdom. Putting his hands on the crown of my head, he sent teachings to me through his steady gaze for several minutes. Then, he pulled me close and embraced me.

In a celebratory voice he proclaimed that I was now a spiritual master. I had spread the God essence, the Mula Purusha throughout my body.

My spiritual brothers and sisters raised their voices in congratulations, lifting their arms in glee.

It had been a wondrous and mysterious journey. And I would continue to evolve. The journey was the destination and I was enjoying the journey more with each new day.

Alcohol, sugar, movies, parties and pleasures no longer pulled me. Serving the elderly and children brought me joy. Giving Reflexology sessions gave me joy. The advertisers could not grab me anymore.

Soon, I was teaching Yoga and giving Karttikeyan sessions. Serving others filled my cup more than anything. I bought some home study courses. As I studied Kriya Yoga, Astrology and the Bhagavad Gita at home, I thanked Source for his/her divine plan. My body and mind became best friends to me as I realized how multi million times fortunate I was. The planets became friends to me, instead of foreign objects. Getting to know their unique energies and gifts, I appreciated them for the opportunities for growth and success they gave me.